SIMPLY
BEING

One Year with Spirit

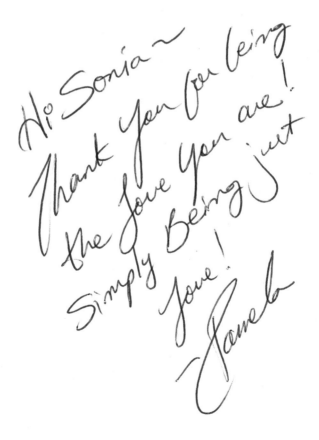

Hi Sonia ~
Thank You for being
the love You are!
Simply Being just
love!
~ Pamela

First published by O Books, 2008
O Books is an imprint of John Hunt Publishing
Ltd., The Bothy, Deershot Lodge, Park Lane,
Ropley, Hants, SO24 0BE, UK
office1@o-books.net
www.o-books.net

Distribution in:

UK and Europe
Orca Book Services
orders@orcabookservices.co.uk
Tel: 01202 665432 Fax: 01202 666219 Int. code
(44)

USA and Canada
NBN
custserv@nbnbooks.com
Tel: 1 800 462 6420 Fax: 1 800 338 4550

Australia and New Zealand
Brumby Books
sales@brumbybooks.com.au
Tel: 61 3 9761 5535 Fax: 61 3 9761 7095

Far East (offices in Singapore, Thailand, Hong
Kong, Taiwan)
Pansing Distribution Pte Ltd
kemal@pansing.com
Tel: 65 6319 9939 Fax: 65 6462 5761

South Africa
Alternative Books
altbook@peterhyde.co.za
Tel: 021 555 4027 Fax: 021 447 1430

Text copyright Pamela Silberman 2008

Design: Stuart Davies

ISBN: 978 1 84694 126 9

A CIP catalogue record for this book is available
from the British Library.

Printed in the US by Maple Vail

O Books operates a distinctive and ethical publishing philosophy in
all areas of its business, from its global network of authors to
production and worldwide distribution.
No trees were cut down to print this particular book. The paper is
100% recycled, with 50% of that being post-consumer. It's processed
chlorine-free, and has no fibre from ancient or endangered forests.
This production method on this print run saved approximately
thirteen trees, 4,000 gallons of water, 600 pounds of solid waste,
990 pounds of greenhouse gases and 8 million BTU of energy. On its
publication a donation for planting a tree was sent to The
Woodland Trust

SIMPLY BEING

One Year with Spirit

Pamela Silberman

BOOKS

Winchester, UK
Washington, USA

Contents

The experience of human living is resplendent with occasions of pain, stress, anger, guilt, self-deprivation, abandonment and loneliness.

Can you love yourself anyway?

Preface: Open Your Heart

A Message from Pamela:

Why Here, Now?

Psychologists James Prochaska, Ph.D and Carlo DiClemente, Ph.D identified five processes that most human beings experience while transitioning through a major life change. These stages of change include: Pre-contemplation, Contemplation, Preparation, Action, and Maintenance. In general, psychiatric counselors and therapists refer to this Transtheoretical Model for Change when a client embarks on the path to recovery from drug or alcohol addiction. Although I never had this specific issue, I surely am familiar with addiction.

Throughout my life, I have been addicted to my self-limiting beliefs. In this addiction, I have excessively judged my experiences, the world and myself. Often, I allowed myself to play the role of victim, finding reason to blame the past, others, or circumstances of the world for my own feelings of loss and limitation. Addicts often do the same, until they realize that no matter what their justifications for blame or hurt, they, deeply within, still feel trapped by their patterns of thinking and reacting. Likewise, there came a time in my life when I genuinely felt sick and tired of equating myself with thoughts of loss and limitation. Actions or accomplishments within the world alone, I recognized, would not bring peace to a mind that felt isolated. All I truly yearned for was a deep connection to peace, happiness, and love. The wish to recover was obvious. I needed to take action in answer to this inner yearning. However, seeking peace from self-loathing, would require a major change and I was unsure if I truly was ready.

Changing would not involve a quick cosmetic dusting. I would require a complete overhaul of my thought system. If I really wanted this self-transformation to work, I would need to give up my victim stories. I would have to force myself to bring to light all the ways I suppressed feelings of loneliness, unhappiness and hopelessness. To succeed, it appeared that I would need nothing short of a miracle. Coincidentally, I found one – or shall I say a miracle found me.

Ask and Receive

Soon after declaring my desire for change to the universe, a book titled *A Course in Miracles* found me. Now, when I say found me, I mean it. Spending a beautiful summer day wandering in one of my favorite local antique villages, I felt drawn to one of its old bookstores to poke around. Unexpectedly, as I pulled on several books in the overstuffed shelves above me, a thick, soft-cover blue book fell to the ground, grazing my head. Picking up this book, I was immediately engrossed in the title, *A Course in Miracles*. It was not published by a person, but by some group called the "Foundation for Inner Peace." I remember finding that bizarre, but my intrigue as to how the book had selected me, led me to buy it anyway.

Fast-forward now, maybe three years, and I've intermittently been reading *A Course in Miracles*. I found the writing equally convoluted and profound. Conceptually, it made points that I was longing to accept, but when it came to practicing with the diligence and discipline for which it asked, I often came up short. I joke now that when someone decides to invest in *The Course*, they should purchase two copies, one to read and one to throw around when the frustration of reading it becomes too much. However, inspiration within motivated me to chug on even when I felt confused or disheartened. *The Course*, I realized in time, bestowed a magnanimous gift. This gift was the discovery of peace I had fervently craved and told God I was willing to do anything to find. Finally, despite all the clouds the world presented, as I set my mind to practicing *The Course*, the sun began to shine brilliantly within.

Listen

Prior to finding and practicing *A Course in Miracles*, I had another hobby that helped me cope with life's uncertainties: journal writing. Since the age of twelve, I had kept a journal, which had always been my favorite avenue to venting. Entitled "my letters to God," I filled each page with all the judgments, fears, and suppressed emotions that I could never express verbally. In these early writings, occasionally another voice appeared from within. First, I related to this voice as my Guardian Angel or Spirit Guide. There was no audible speech;

however, a presence, more male than female, made itself known. His wisdom always contained the peace for which I longed. Rarely did I seriously consider what I was receiving.

To me, He always was a loving and gentle best friend, encouraging me when I felt most confused. One aspect of His answers which did feel challenging was the style. Whereas I tended to speak informally and plainly, Spirit's responses frequently required me to deliberately slow down my reading pace, research His vocabulary and focus. It was after noticing this style, throughout most of the writings, that I became convinced that there was no way this Voice was wholly coming from me.

Some people wonder about the mysteries involving channeled or scribed material. Where does this material come from? What does it mean? Is the ability to scribe real or a fraud? Is it a psychic gift? Why do certain people hear and not others? To be honest, these questions were never a concern for me. I simply trusted and was having fun. These conversations became a surrogate therapist rather than a key to transcendental or mystical inquiry. Fact was, since my outside ventures were not working, I was desperate and willing to listen to someone, ANYONE, who could possibly point me in the direction of inner peace. In time and continued practice, I came to accept the presence of Holy Spirit through these words of wisdom. To me, Holy Spirit is the unified Voice of Truth and Love. He has no particular body identity and does not restrict His existence to any exclusive religious ideology. Holy Spirit represents the pure wisdom, knowing and love existing far beyond human comprehension. Indeed we all have access to His words and each relays God's Own Remembrance of our True Self. Accepting His Presence, I kept on writing.

All Is Coming Together

As you can see, my journey with Holy Spirit's guidance all began rather simply. Essentially, in order for the guidance to flow, I had to step out of my own way and acknowledge that listening beyond resistance was my truest desire. In retrospect, I can now see how the Voice within had been gently prodding me continually toward change. The awareness that my life was not working as I wanted was the *Pre-contemplation* stage in the Transtheoretical Model for Change. *Contemplation* occurred as I hoped and prayed for another way of seeing. *Preparation* arrived through my dedication to writing as a way to grow closer to the Voice within and continued through my later discovery of *A Course in Miracles*. Next, all I needed were the final stages of *Action and Maintenance* and these continue to unfold everyday. In willingness, trust, and surrender, deeper lessons emerge. Overall, the Voice within realizes more than I could ever consciously grasp. However, He remains persistent. As I turn every moment over to Him, He continues to lead me away from my everyday stress to an oasis of peace. Our dialogue is beyond time, space, or place. No matter what the issue, as I trust to not conceal, the small, still Voice within appears and in no time, peace does reign. Even now, whole-heartedly, I desire not only to listen but also to diligently practice all I am learning from The Course and my Spirit companion. In fact, I am continuing to learn that I am learning.

Your Journey Begins

Now, I hope to maintain the reception of Spirit's gift through giving my experience to you. This book presents 52 of the hundreds of written communions I have had with the Voice of Love from within. I subtitled this book "One Year with Spirit" because these 52 conversations taken together can lead you through one year of self-awareness. I suggest reading one dialogue each week and choosing the subject headings that feel right to you. Following each conversation, prompts are included that will direct your own insight. In order to support a more personalized experience of this year's teaching, I encourage you to utilize a personal journal in conjunction with this book. As you respond to the prompts for insight, allow yourself to step aside from what you may consider to be your usual answers. Give over to another way of listening. I have also included weekly affirmations and concise tools for practice. They are intended to lead you through problems with attentive practice.

This book is a gift to you from our One Self. It is a guide to help you discover, use, and have a meaningful relationship with the Voice of Knowledge within your Self. God's Voice speaks to you throughout the day. I trust He guides you now, holding this book, as an answer to your intent. You are never alone. Now is the moment to begin. Spend the next year with your own Voice of Holiness within. Seek, learn, trust, and accept, just as much as I did, or more. All is perfect. Be willing to meet anything that shows up, not with judgment, but with consideration for your most serene desires. Never forget that God loves you more than you know. In appreciation, I bid you on your journey with these words from the One Source who knows exactly Who You Are in Love:

In deed you are in the process of opening your heart to your Self now. This is a time of great celebration, for you are welcoming the Truth within you, rather than keeping it at a safely concealed distance. The idea that you need to stay safe has been echoing through your life for centuries. This single idea has kept you from opening. However, I understand, for who would desire to open their heart when they fear it could be trampled upon and destroyed? Yet even now, as you read this, you are beginning to recognize that nothing True can be destroyed.

A wise man once observed, "Where your heart is, there is your treasure also." If your heart recognizes a need for fear, then fear becomes your treasure; vulnerability becomes your belief; and distance sadly acts as your savior. Place not yourself aside from Me, for I only bestow love upon you, love without malice. A heart that is open, knows of its strength.

This heart sees itself as happy and able; always does it welcome and shine to the entire world. Yet, if a heart keeps the world outside, it apprehensively filters what arises based only on its proven worth. Wait no more for proof of your Self. Free yourself now. The pain of the past must haunt you no more. I love you and hold your hand now, as always.

You can find all the peace you desire within you by simply exchanging your deceptive thinking for the Inner Light. Can you completely accept peace for yourself in this life experience? Say yes – and with this answer, God's endless bounty once again becomes known as your own. Could you potentially be hurt in the process? Ahhh . . . notice that thought. See how it justifies all the fears you still cling to.

Are you unsure? By waiting, are you choosing fear? Tell Me, what validates your hesitation? Are you seeking to authenticate my Voice by an experience within the world? Are you concerned perhaps that you may be vulnerable to investing wrongly? Dear One, this is fear, and it shall never result in your peace, only in more questions. That is why I tell you to set yourself free. See yourself as helpless, and able to be misled or destroyed, and surely, everything you see will be a reflection of that potential. Yet, never is this experience of fear a Truth.

Now, walk with Me and with each step, you allow an opening to strength. This is reacquainting your self with the One Self as God Created. Complete and whole, I see nothing ever as lacking; and no potential fear necessitates distance between us. Hold my hand accepting that there is nothing to fear.

As you open your heart, see how you do not have to go this journey alone, because never are you alone. God has not left you comfortless. Notice the door within desiring to be open. Is there a possibility that you will completely open it and walk through? Say yes to one step at a time. My Light is Your Own. I love you.

Spirit's Guidance for use of terms:

Truth

There is a difference between "facts" and "truth." Facts are things that your mind or the world believes it can define and prove. But most of what you experience, think, and believe is not "fact." Love, for instance, is not a "fact" that you can measure. It is not limited to your world nor rooted within the mind or life experience. Nevertheless, living without Love is impossible. Why? Because Love in Truth is Life. And Truth, with a capital "T" is used as a term to define all that is truly indefinable. This is why, our further discussions in this book, do not expect to find the facts here, as you would define them.

The word "Truth" is, for Me, a symbol. In fact, all words are merely symbols, representing in crude form. Just as the world thinks it knows facts, it assumes to know people or at least judge and define them. This is why I can say, that the only fact existing, is that you do not know Who you are. And so, in the search within, the word "Truth" then becomes a guidepost to Self discovery.

Who are You? If I chose to use words (once again as mere symbols), I could say You are limitless, boundless love, extending light. However, even after saying that, your real Self lies beyond. Whole and complete, your Self is beyond all words, images, and definitions. That is why I ask you to release your hold on facts, thoughts and words, and search for your Self. It is only through release and silence that a revelation of this Self can emerge.

I use the word "Truth" only to guide you back to all that is real. Truth beyond words is Reality. This Reality is simply being as God Created. It is the very complete beingness that You are, beyond all the conceived images you hold of yourself. Truth cannot be analyzed. Truth cannot be debated. Truth has no loss or gain. It need not be defended or defined, for it questions not the complete secure safety it has always been in the arms of God. All that desires to question does not know and therefore is not Truth. Truth simply is, as God is.

We are not having this discussion so that we can exchange beliefs of the thinking mind. Within this exchange, your questions are appreciated and loved, but we come together to look beyond questions. In Truth, we leave all thoughts and analysis behind in order to accept the wholeness that God Created. Is this impossible? It is impossible only if you use the limitations of the mind as your guide. Truth is far beyond the realms of a thinking mind. If you want to carry on thinking, use your mind to expand your sense of who you are. Allow your thoughts to open in peace to the stillness that is beyond understanding. Cease to speak. Resistance is futile as a path to Truth, for only as you release the limitations of your mind, do you then gain all Truth.

I am not here to confuse, argue or perplex, for all of those intentions come from a place of anxiety. I am here only to be a Witness to Oneness. I am the Oneness that Everything Is. It is so clear, if you can see it. In being this Witness, I know Love and I extend it to the Self that God Created, and this, Dear One, is You. If you desire to define Truth, step back, take in a long deep breath, close your eyes, and listen beyond the sensations of the body or the thoughts of the mind. Sink into the peace that emanates from within. Here is the first guidepost to Truth. Here is where we shall begin. I am with you always. I love you.

What Is Mistaken Identity?

Your Mistaken Identity represents every conceived thought declaring you not to be as God created You. It is mainly experienced through beliefs in limitation and feelings of unworthiness, abandonment or distress. Most of the mistaken identity's feelings and thoughts lead to destructive, unproductive, or depressive states. This struggling-self strives for immortality in body and/or mind. It is the only identity that has needs and fears. Only the mistaken identity believes it exists within time and is destined to die. Therefore, through this reasoning, it justifies every effort to protect all that one day will be lost.

Those who suffer from this mistaken identity see themselves alone, in pain and trapped within a world of suffering. They see themselves as a separate personality within a world of billions of other separate personalities. In this understanding, the mistaken identity thinks, feels, and expresses the self it recognizes through separation and journeys through life identifying those others it can justifiably befriend or hurt for its own interests. Generally, a state of victimization appears to rule all areas of the mistaken identity's existence. Lost and unknown, destined to adhere to confusing and contradicting rules in order to realize a shallow form of fleeting love, the mistaken identity resides, perceiving its prison scenery impossible to change.

Most arrogantly, the mistaken identity projects a god in its own image. This god being one also of judgment, fear and separation, it operates by insane rules of bribery, jealousy, dependency and favoritism. Seeking to pay homage to this god, the mistaken identity uses terms such as sinner and martyr to describe and encourage the worshipper into subservience. Here, all wishes to know god result in only confusion, trepidation or fleeting acceptance with the fear of potential loss. Equivalently, since the mistaken identity interprets this god to be its aspiration, this deluded representation of god is reflectively used to define worldly love.

Overall, identifying through the mistaken identity is like suffering from amnesia. Here, a deep forgetfulness has fallen on the mind, so pervasive, that it has no idea who it is or where it belongs. As amnesiacs these self-proclaimed individuals wander through the world, looking for answers to who they are and what they should do, but are rarely satisfied. Since the mind has completely forgotten, it incessantly questions but is suspicious of all answers. Consequently, it runs through states of confusion, abandonment, vulnerability, defense, and anger. Yet this is only because it is afraid, does not know, and has forgotten everything that is real.

At the very best, the mistaken identity settles within a temporary state of happiness. However, fearing the worst, it cannot fully enjoy this happiness or feel complete gratitude, because it senses that it could all be lost, at any time. In fact, the struggle for gain whilst remaining vulnerable and fearful is the essence of mistaken identity. This fear drives and represents everything you have ever thought or desired your individual self to be in this mistaken identification. However, never could this self ever be true. I repeat, never could this self ever be true.

Week One: **In The Beginning**

Spirit, I yearn to start a conversation with You. I ask that you guide me through the areas of my life experience that need healing. I have faith that we are here to heal, and I open myself up to Your guidance to teach me all I need to know now. Please, take my hand and direct me. I give all thoughts and distractions to You. Help me to seek Your love rather than my frustrations. Assist me to learn that there is a better way. Thank You.

Well come, Dear One.
We begin simply in stating the One Truth that is always.

You are as God Created you.

That is all. You have hoped to accept this Truth within you, which is why you have been led to this moment, to read these words. The journey apart from this Truth began when you chose to forget the certainty of your Self. It is only the attempt to continually forget which has led to your experiences of limitation, disconnection and unhappiness. But I tell you sincerely, to completely renounce your perfection is impossible. Therefore, you are still as God Created You.

This statement is simple enough in words, yet words cannot define You. Words rely on judgment in order to be accepted in understanding. This is why I do not ask you to accept this Truth in words alone. We are here to step beyond all judgments and concepts. And so, during these conversations to follow, I ask you not to judge. I ask you to release all need for worldly proof or intellectual understanding. Sink only deeper into the desire for peace which has brought you this far. My requests are never to restrict you, for that has only been your intention. Instead, I only witness to the Truth about You that has never changed. Now, in this moment, I ask that you allow yourself to step beyond the realms of every constraint. Here is the only awareness where peace shall be known once again.

Far too long you have accepted an entire world of limitation before God. I delude you not. Within the world, the search for happiness has you exhaustively seek outside yourself. You seek to continually stretch your limitations; inventing and experiencing newer, faster and more creative ways to express your limited self. Too often you will go to any lengths in the attempt to find personal validation, power, freedom or happiness, even if it is at the expense of another's thriving, happiness or freedom. And so the pursuit of happiness becomes a battle. This is why you believe your freedom must be constantly defended. You fear it can be lost. In fact, you fear all you are can be lost. But truly, I ask, if You are as God Created, would He Create a Child doomed to lose or suffer? Gathered from all that I know of You, surely not. Therefore, with this awareness we begin our journey of True Self realization. I will guide you to find the peace you have been seeking. I will guide you to the true oasis that will quench your thirst.

True happiness is to be in perfect connection. It is complete and this is beyond all inadequacy, judgment or fear. True happiness is perfectly free. This state of perfect being differs from the freedom defined by the conceptual mind. At best the conceptual mind defines freedom. In this classification, freedom is seen as fleeting, limited and able to be violated. To the conceptual mind, freedom needs to be protected for fear of loss. God does not extend in states of contradiction. Therefore as You are free, You cannot be restricted. In fact, perfect freedom is without need and rests simply as it is. Here you shall find all the desires for acceptance, wholeness, safety and trust you have longed for.

God reigns within a kingdom of Peace.
He is Perfect Love.
That is all.

God does not exclude, divide or limit. He gives all completely in extension of the Perfect Love He is. The one extension we shall come to learn about in this communion is the extension known as You. Therefore, to be truly happy is to be perfectly connected to every thought God has ever given You. Most importantly, this experience is never limited, divided nor kept from the entire creation of life.

I say, *YOU* are as God Created, because this You never changed. This You is of Spirit and it has remained at peace and in joy from the moment God extended Himself. This Spirit is and always shall be changeless. Never have You been anything the mind of judgment has placed before your eyes. And here we reunite in Truth once again. To say You are as God Created is to say You are Love. This Love is perfectly free, in joy, always innocent and wholly complete. Here is the first clue to the one witness that I hold for you, and extend to you for your consideration during this joining. You are led to learn as you are ready. This means that now, I know and have guided you to read these words. Seek not proof or reasoning within your thinking mind. The answers you desire are not to be found within the boundaries of the world. The purpose of our time here is to step beyond all limitations.

To be perfectly happy is simply to accept yourself completely as You are. Additionally, it is to accept all others in your sight completely as they are. In accepting such, no longer are you attempting to live in opposition, because only this restraint has brought you unhappiness. It is from this thought we shall begin, and it is here that the desire for peace is reawakened.

Is this impossible to do? No. But it does require significant release on your part. It will require the release of all thoughts which currently keep you prisoner to the darkness of your thinking mind. This includes all thoughts of judgment, condemnation, guilt, blame, victimization, and punishment. None of these are of Truth, nor will they ever be. It is only these thoughts which have brought a continuance of fear and pain between you and your brothers. First, I will call you to release these misunderstandings in exchange for simple reason. Here I beckon you to remember the light of Spirit, as God Created. I will call this the release for peace. In this release, you accept all that has never changed.

Surely, you question this as you read these words. Yes, I understand your resistance and need to analyze. However, I do not judge nor expect anything different. All is accepted as appropriate for where you perceive yourself to be now. Nonetheless, notice how focusing on these questions still does not result in happiness, satisfaction or peace. Each question only leads to more questions. Now we choose to bring an end to all questions and judgment. They have only convinced you of the impossibility of being good enough, smart enough, beautiful enough, loved enough, rich enough, and free or powerful enough. Have you not had enough of this despair? And so enough it is! Peace is not found in endless desire to have and attract more. It is not found in aimless temporary accumulation. Peace is accepted in the desire to be endless.

I call to you to witness now. This witness shall be called simply being. If you desire to accept this you choose to return to the simplicity of your Self as God Created. Here you choose to awaken and come closer to the peace which has never left You. There will continue to be times when you see a world of constraint all around you, our progress will not be revealed like magic. Do not fear. You have made an important choice now. This choice has you stir in your sleep and beckons you beyond dreams. I celebrate with you. In completion of this experience, all you saw yourself to be will not be the same again. Here you come closer to fully embracing your Self. Be joyous. Celebrate. You are freer than you have ever known before.

Here, as one, we accept the one Truth. This Truth, although described through mere words, is a description of all You are beyond each and every perceived limitation. Here we exchange misery for boundless love. Here we exchange limitation for perfection. Here we accept our innocence instead of judgment. In choosing perfect freedom we accept only that which is and always shall be the Self God Himself smiles upon throughout perpetuity. Here we call an end to all that has seemingly led you astray and welcome once more all that has never left You. This is why I refer to it as simply being. In this moment we choose to simply be beyond all distraction. Now we choose God instead and allow ourselves to discover our Self once again. Welcome.

Week One: Prompts for Insight:

1. Write out your most desired intention with Spirit. Most fervently, what do you seek within?

2. In releasing your thoughts and intentions to Spirit, what concerns remain? List these concerns.

3. At this beginning stage of your journey, what do you expect? List the expectations you have for your self-practice and those you have for Holy Spirit. What do you hope to find or learn from this year's experience with Spirit?

4. What is the most significant question you have about yourself, your life, or the world? How do you hope to receive help with this issue?

5. What do you feel is the most significant distraction or obstacle to your practice of peace?

6. What are other distractions or obstacles that fill your mind with confusion? Take a moment to notice any interruption that rises to the surface of your consciousness now.

7. If you were to describe your Self as God Created, who or what would this be?

8. Describe the Self that you believe Holy Spirit sees you as. How does this differ from how you currently see yourself in form?

9. What is one belief that you absolutely need to release?

10. What do you feel you have most forgotten about your Self? Make a list or write about any way you feel disconnected or under the ruse of the mistaken identity.

Practice:
Write a letter to God and / or Holy Spirit. Express everything that you have ever hoped to know or learn. Try not to be afraid. Be conscious of anything that you desire to hide or hold back from this intimate communication. Remember, God does care to listen. He hangs on every word you write. Yes, He loves you that much!

Affirmations:

> I am as God Created Me.
> I allow my True desire to lead.
> I am the Self that Spirit knows.
> Love is and this is perfect.
> I choose to be beyond distraction.
> I choose God and allow my Self.

One Simple Thought:
Your innocence is your inner sense. It is seeing the Self God Created as perfectly free.

Week Two: **Seek First the Kingdom**

As you begin to release all that which is not of Spirit, a deep belief in meaninglessness shall begin to arise. This belief is based on the identity you are most acquainted with feeling purposeless and alone. Do not allow this to deter you, for it is a sign of a greater awakening. There was a time when the mistaken identity appeared to have made a world for itself. Now you are willing to accept new realizations. Now you seek to reawaken from all self-imposed limits. Through this stirring, the persona you cling to interprets the new awareness as confusion and feels alone. Yet, no matter the insolent feelings, you are permitting all former attachments to be undone. Truly, this is a sign you are settling within Truth. Be joyous.

If a denser cloud of fear appears to arise, see this as the smoke rising from an extinguishing fire. To the eye, the smoke emerges denser than previously. It feels more choking. Yet this is only distraction from the fact that destructiveness is coming to an end. Fear not, for you have made significant progress and are well on your way to complete peace of mind.

Once your investment in the world as your definer starts to fade, you may begin to believe that you are nothing. Of course, this is not true. Only a mind lost in itself could perceive this nothingness as its reality. When values appear to have been torn away, anger is a normal result. This is only because your fearful beliefs are challenged. All anger is only a defensive reaction to fear. In fact the only two perceptions that can result in anger are:

1) *The perception of Fear or Threat*
2) *The perception of Powerlessness or Being Out of Control.*

When any of these perceptions occur, remind yourself that you are seeing with fear and not with Truth. This is accepting a life of vulnerability with death as your only eventual result. I know this may sound difficult to release, but truly the willingness to expand your current thinking will lead to your freedom. There is no purposeful reason to see yourself as being doomed to nothing.

Again, I say, it is impossible for you to be nothing. To be nothing would require you to have the ability to change your Self as God Created. It would require your ability to usurp God and destroy His Holy Creation. It is impossible for you to be unsafe. This is why I say to be joyous.

Realize that you do not know what anything is for. Every thought is reliant upon your underlying judgment and beliefs of limitation. All your thoughts are extensions of your mistaken identity. Every form or thought you have ever relied on is nothing in comparison to your magnificence in God. Yet, you do not accept this and so you ask, "What then am I left with? Am I all alone? Can I be apart from God? Does He know or recognize me?" These are the root thoughts of separation identity. Here you are seemingly stripped down to the ideas that arose at the beginning of your free choice to forget. Yet now, instead of attempting to formulate a world in which to hide, you may choose the opportunity to release these thoughts as being the idle wishes they are and settle into the stillness. In stillness, my Voice affirms clearly that you are incomprehensibly loved beyond measure and not alone.

Call this The Great Undoing. It is beyond all concepts, because at this moment you are beginning to place all concepts of a lone individuality aside. You are simply allowing, rather than making a distraction or struggling for meaning within yourself. Love is recognized within you now, and a mind once bent on self-delusion or self-destruction is now awakening to Self-acceptance. Welcome this Love as the Source of Creation, it is a power beyond measure. Allow it to place aside all confused thoughts. Choose to bring darkness to light and re-establish the fact that ONLY light exists.[1]

The words of Ecclesiastes reflect the thinking of a man who felt confused and challenged in releasing his belief in an isolated self. Here the writer began to realize that nothing was satisfactory for himself within the world. He felt alone and abandoned. From where he once sought (and found) power and control, he now realized not one thing had lasting purpose or gave solace to him. He was crying out for his own meaning. He was begging to find

out what everything was for and from where its purpose came. He
believed the world had abandoned him. He felt nothing, not even
power, was worth having. He was exhausted and crumpled within
his perceived self. Here it is shown that you can become king of
civilization, without truly finding happiness or any Real
Knowledge. You can value all substance, celebrating each moment
of "toil beneath the sun" and every possession. Yet nothing of
worth will be found or given you unless it is extended from the
heart of Truth.

Ecclesiastes further teaches how the impassioned pursuit of
wisdom can be meaningless. The pursuit of merely learning facts
and figures about the world does not reveal your True Self. Nor do
these facts or figures alone give you peace. This search uses
wisdom as a shelter and protective device. In it you hide so as not
to recognize the emptiness perceived within the mind or heart. The
meaningless "wisdom" I refer to is the wisdom of the world, not
the Knowledge of Truth. You shall not know truly until you Truly
Are. Man's thinking mind goes through life seeking an explanation
of itself. The writer is seeking for his very survival as well as a
purpose for being, while the unthinking "fool" may lose intellect,
but gain the idea of peace. The writer's mind strives through a
devotion to the intellect, making mental power his savior. The
thinking mind studies all that it believes it has made and seeks
complete self-satisfaction within its own limited knowledge. Here
the mind itself is seen as God, and the more the thinking mind
appears to understand, the more it feels it is in control and ruler of
the known world. Here the identity plays itself out in form,
through thought, feeling and experience for shallow fulfillment or
self-destruction. Thus, all the fears of the mind result in the
embodied self being renowned as ruler.

Look upon your world. What is most celebrated or envied? Is it
not achievement of intellect or accomplishment of body? This
temporal self sings psalms "Glory to the god of possessions, for he
rewards through tax-free shelters!" But all kidding aside, is not
power often found in your world among the most seemingly
brilliant achievers or possessors? Do you not celebrate intellect,

influence or the establishment of vast material collections at every turn? Do you not yearn for it and reward it as a glorious jewel to be admired and envied? Why do you value a thinking mind that cannot feel peace within the world where it appears to live? Does this intellectual understanding bring you a permanent joy? If so, look upon this moment, right now, book in hand and ask yourself if you are completely peaceful amidst your accomplishments within the world? But truly, of the most intelligent and accomplished within your world, who among you is ultimately the most peaceful?

Whoa . . . Wait right there. I can understand the aimless seeking for material goods without purpose, but are you saying that we are supposed to remain stupid too? That education within the world has no purpose? I could have saved a lot of time, stress and money there.

No, stupidity and ignorance are different. Why do you measure intelligence by the knowledge gained only of things within this world? Again, I ask, do you gain peace through delving deeply into the qualities of the world? Do you find your true nature? Or do you find a complex emptiness? Is it not "a chasing after the wind" that you find? The more you look within humanity and a materialistic life, the more ways you will find to busy your body and thinking mind. The more you will find another way to seek, never to completely find and be satisfied. Truly, I testify to you that every revered spiritual Master applied no value to complex theorems or masterful works. Each teacher was a Master because he or she found and applied the Master of Being rather than the mastery of doing. In fact, each teacher fully recognized how they were a pupil first. They lived rather simply and when called to intellectual discourse by his or her peers, they always answered with the simplest of words. In their experience, Love was always the centralized lesson. To their thinking mind, there was nothing of greater value than the value of God, and it was here that he or she rested.

The modern mind may say that this is not practical. But truly what is more practical than investing in the one foolproof identity? What other identity shall bring you peace? As long as you see yourself solely within this world, seeking only meaning and reward from within it, you shall be chasing the wind. This world can never give you your true identity. Your identity has never changed as God created it. There are no fools in Heaven. God did not create anything foolish. It is only the individualized mind that judges in terms of foolishness and then chooses to defend these beliefs. It is only this foolishness that need be awakened from. Do not renounce the world, but renounce merely your imprisoning absorption within it.

Distraction is the key for a mind lost in ideas of the world. That was the dream's purpose from inception. These dreams distract the mind into forgetting its True Self. Through forgetfulness, a need for separate self-validation is conceived and sought for through striving for happiness perceptually apart from its Self. This is what the book of Ecclesiastes teaches. Here a man who has been King, and has had all the wisdom and pleasures of the world, realizes the emptiness of it all. For in truth, he realizes, nothing of the world replaces the Love of God. Nothing of the world satisfies because nothing in and of itself lasts or truly defines him. Truly, there is not anything within the world that would make you more pleasing or loved by God. God loves you wholly and completely now, no matter your ways or means of a worldly existence.

It is this recognition that challenges you the most. "When?" you ask, "when will I finally know love as complete as you speak?" "When will I have enough or be enough for myself?" "When will I finally be loved and accepted by the world and be happy?" Thus the chasing after the wind continues. You will never truly be happy until the moment you realize that happiness is already within you. You are not served at all by distraction for All is given you only in Truth.

You continue to ask, "How can everything I have ever relied upon be nothing? How can everything within the boundaries of the world, as well as its very essence, have no real or lasting value? How can this be?" Dear One, these questions reflect only the fear that you have identified with for so long. Truly never did I say that the world has no value, but I have said that it does not serve you best.

I have a difficult time believing this, because the world fervently witnesses to the opposite. As a child I learned that the only purpose of life is to find happiness within the world, and all pursuits and studies were my key to that. The lesson was obvious that if people did not succeed materialistically with power or scholarship, or make this achievement their goal, they would suffer a lost and defeated life. How can I release all that is so deeply ingrained?

Isn't it interesting that if individuals do not profit within the world, they are either highly evolved spiritually or complete failures? Do you see how your search for personal validation has obsessed your thoughts and worldly objectives? This is because your mistaken identity is so occupied with itself as an individual and its search for meaning that it cannot fathom being without this venture. When you seek value, there has to be a duality. As you seek to divide and conquer within the world, there has to be a "we" and "they" which can classify the right and wrong, good and bad, valued and insignificant. Therefore, the individual identity has convinced itself that only this searching for fulfillment is its function. Without this, it could not be special, successful, right or purposeful. And it is from this value that so too does all your misery form. In fact, without this belief you could not be wrong, a failure, stupid or rejected. Do you see the double-edged sword of self-destruction here?

This is the same for believers in sin. If an individual does not make judgments or see guilt, surely they are seen as irreverent or diseased. Is it not seen as necessary to distinguish that which is most wicked, fearful, and destructive? In agreement with this, do you not then wish to punish, victimize, and lavish with guilt? Which of these practices has brought you joy? And if the God of Your Fathers is a God of Pure Joy and Perfect Happiness, where then has this God gone? This is why I tell you truly that a belief in anything other than the truth of Who God created is diseased. It is this belief in everything that you are not, and searching for fulfillment in everything that you are not, that is insane.

Consciously renouncing the world does not guarantee either failure or sainthood. Consciously renouncing your attachment to the world leads to peace within the world. This is because, through a practice of renouncing attachment and outer identification, you finally free yourself from the cycle of wanting. Remember, you cannot have wanting unless you believe first that you are incomplete. And so, renouncing attachment and want has you fully accept your completion. This is seeking first the Kingdom.

A mind that seeks first the Kingdom of God, does not seek to understand itself for it is not in confusion. Simply this awareness yields to release itself having finally realized that it IS as God is. Perfect and whole, always being and never lacking, You are. You are not to be judged by mere situations within a world of delusion or misperception. It is impossible for you to live only to suffer and die, possibly to suffer eternally. You live as God. You are forever loved, never changing from the One Self that God extended You to be. This is the only You that can ever be.

Is this heresy? Is this blasphemy? No. The only blasphemy that exists is your continued denial. But even this is not seen as guilt-worthy. This is seen merely as the simple mistake it is, and only love fills its seeming void. Truth is found in the acceptance only of the One Self, through the One God, for nothing else exists.

Seeking first the Kingdom is an experience that brings peace to the mind only when an inappropriate judgment is not placed there in its space. Here you recognize that you know not what you are, but allow only Truth to tell you. This is wisdom beyond all other wisdom of the world. Too much emptiness is found in a mind that believes it knows, and this can only lead to further delusion. What would be better is to give all openings to God. Every opening that you give to God is an opening to your Self. Here in the stillness do you find your guide Home. Here in the stillness do you welcome and listen to Truth beyond all identities of misperception. Here you think not with your mind, but with the very Will of God alone and are finally set free from endless seeking.

Notice in Ecclesiastes 3, the man declares there is a time for everything. Here he sinks from realization of nothingness to the ordering of the world. This is the mind's futile attempt to seek understanding within itself once again. A misidentified mind will always do this before giving itself over to God. "Maybe if I could just understand," it begs. "Maybe if I could just find the answers within the world, I would be happy." But, still all it finds is the chasing of the wind.

The thinking mind believes that if it can order the world, some sense will be discovered. However, there is no hierarchy within the Kingdom of God. Only Oneness exists. This is confusing to the thinking mind, because it functions only within ideas of separation. This is why ideas of hierarchy, individualization, and judgment are repeatedly projected onto God. Simply, you equate your limitations with an imperfect God.

But wait, I've always found Ecclesiastes 3 to be rather inspirational. Can you help me understand if it has a deeper purpose?

To the mind seeking understanding, order appears to be purposeful. This is the purpose of time construction. Time not only appears to keep experiences in order but it gives reason and structure to the mind in experience. In this order, the past has purpose for the present and the present opportunely defines the future. This is the reason you cling to the past, as it appears to help you gain a sense of understanding now. However, you can gain understanding from so much more than your dependencies. Therefore, your clinging to the need for order only depletes you.

God does not function within time. God is. There is no moment that God is not. There is no process of being more or less God. There is no past, present or future God. There was never a "time" when God was not, nor is there ever a time that God waits to be. God is always, and this "IS" is always by your side, in fact, within and all around you. Listen and welcome this awareness of the ONE Truth that never changes. God has never left you, and your time of aloneness has never been real.

All time is a perceived time of aloneness as long as it is seen through the mind of individuality. Think of this: has it not always been "your past" and "your future?" Has it not always been "your life" and "your guilt" and "your identity"? It is the perception of identity that leads you into needing mistaken hierarchies and seeking solace through self-definition. These mistaken opinions have become projected all about you, and you see yourself as separate from your Brother, separate from God, and left to figure it all out on your own. This is the mindset behind Ecclesiastes 3. Although its lyrics may bring peace to a confused mind, feeling alone within a world without order, you would not find it inspirational if you truly knew your Self.

I have mentioned before that I can use every idea within the world as a device for learning. Let us use this lyric in the same manner. See now how it is not the words, but the meaning which gives you temporary peace. See how with the ideas of order, you feel you can predict placement and purpose within the world. However, if we were to release our self from a need to have order and instead accepted that the true message is to see how God gives all to all in all manner of completion, each of these phrases would simply give way to gratitude.

The mistaken identity will eventually recognize that not even its own conceptions can bring it peace. This is especially realized once the desire for awakening is accepted. Likewise, this is what the phrase "For with much wisdom comes much sorrow; the more knowledge the more grief" refers to. Here it is realized that nothing the mistaken identity has ever thought has ever resulted in permanence. In this realization, you can see with eyes wide open, recognizing that all you have ever conceived and believed has never begotten contentment. I point this out to you as you begin to realize that every thought you ever treasured about yourself and the world needs to be undone. Every value must be questioned, for every value you treasure within an isolated self- identity is not equally cherished by God. Be not afraid of opening to God. In Him is the one place of Truth and Peace. Understand, then, that your only goal is to simply be. Not to do or be lost within the tasks   of the world. For this will only bring you, at best, ideas of meaninglessness. There will be a moment when you will see your identity existing beyond its human comprehension. This Self-realization is not acknowledged within time, yet within Truth. Although the Self God knows is already existing, you are unaware of this knowledge through your current state of experience.

Is there a simple way that you would recommend I use to release my feelings of anger?

Yes Beloved. Begin with simply noticing why you feel angry. This is always the initial key. If you don't begin within, it will be most impossible to gain a change without. We have already discussed how all experiences of anger stem only from within your own perceptions. Take a moment to notice these perceptions and observe what you are thinking. See what you believe. If you notice that you are feeling powerless, allow yourself to send love there. Allow yourself to reacquaint yourself with your True Strength, and this strength always lives in God. Your Father does not desire for His Holiness to be ruled by limitation. This is why He has Created You limitless! And do know, that the limitlessness that You are is unchangeable. It is not determined by outer circumstances or differing judgments from yourself or others. Your limitlessness is beyond time and space, forever living in the grandeur of your True Self. If it seems that you cannot see that awareness in the moment of anger, all is still perfect. Forgiveness is always the key to freedom. Forgive yourself for what you seem to believe and offer this love to the self you do see. As you offer love to the self of limitation, you consequently offer love to the Whole. This means that you can embrace the mistaken identity in all its varied images and allow yourself to know Truth once again.

Essentially, a clear way to guide yourself to Truth is to practice awareness, acceptance and alternatives. In this application you choose to free yourself from predetermined beliefs, that most likely only keep you wanting, wishing, woeful and worried. Again, the Holiness You are does not want, nor has it a need for wishes, woe and worries. In Truth you are perfect Love, accepted and aware of the Truth you are in all ways. Therefore, as you practice awareness, you come to accept this True Nature and realize how all is indeed more than your physical eyes may be perceiving. Finally, once you allow yourself to become more aware of the reality beyond the perception, you can seek out alternatives or practical problem-solving to assist you and your brother with realizing peace. Here you do not waste time on past wishes or shoulds. Here you allow yourself to welcome only the greatest knowledge, my Knowledge, that will guide you Home. As you surrender your conceptions and needs for control or intellectualization, you rest. This is an essential rest, for as you rest, you choose to simply be. Beloved, indeed in this rest, is your True livelihood. Trust in My Knowing and you shall always know the genuine Truth of You. I shall never leave you comfortless.

Wow! Thank you so much! That just knocked my socks off!

You are welcome. In fact, you are always welcome in peace, for it is You. Concern yourself not with the ordering of time or impassioned frustrations within the world. I have given you this lesson only so that you may see how there is purpose to releasing yourself from clinging to all attachments. Essentially, this is truly the only teaching from Ecclesiastes and the only wisdom helpful now. Simply continue to open only to the space that shall bring you True peace and True Identity in God. Here you shall be at Home. Allow yourself simply to accept the Truth that God is with You and you need do nothing for His Love. Sit in stillness upon this and purely allow your Self to be. I love you.

Week Two: Prompts for Insight and Practice:

1. What most matters to you right now? What does not matter? Seek within as to how you express these values within the world and permit them to construct a separate self-identity. How many moments do you spend focusing and acting on all that does matter as compared to all that does not? Write your insights.

2. What arises within your thinking or feeling experience when you consider renouncing all fears and values?

4. Read Ecclesiastes in the Bible. Write your thoughts on its content and insights.

5. If you were an advisor to the author of Ecclesiastes during this conflicted and confused time of his life, how would you help him? Identify what you would tell him to bring wisdom or solace through his moments of uncertainty.

6. What does it mean to "chase the wind?" Ask Holy Spirit for His explanation and how you currently exhibit this behavior.

7. Is it truly possible to be apart from God? Can you be a part *of* God? What feelings and thoughts arise when you consider either of these conditions?

8. Pay close attention to moments this week when anger arises within you. Identify which thoughts link to perceptions of threat and which stem from your own feelings of powerlessness. Write on your experiences and discoveries.

9. Choose five experiences that have led to anger. Next to each incident write down one personal recognition that has caused or incited these angry feelings. Are you feeling powerless or threatened? What are your beliefs about yourself or another? Are you having judgments based on past experiences or fears about the

future? How did you feel threatened by these experiences or the people within them? How did you feel powerless? Did you wish you could change the situation? Do you still wish you could change the situation? Next, identify if you feel you can accept this situation as it is. If not, why not? Finally, write down one positive alternative to anger. Review these thoughts and feelings with Spirit and write down any further insights you receive.

Affirmations:
I am as God Created Me.
I am never apart from God.
I need do nothing to be my Truth.
God is not an angry God.
I am not powerless.
Anger cannot define Me.

One Simple Thought:
Anger cannot exist in a state of non-judgment, release and full acceptance. If anger is only a narrowing of pain, can you realize the full liberation that waits you in forgiveness?

Resetting the Balance of Anger

Our feelings of anger and discontent have little or no real connection to the outside world.
All anger depends on our own personal interpretations to exist and thrive!
We set the balance based on our own inner perceptions.
This is good news, because we can always change our mind!
Simply Being© is recognizing where your true power is and living from within.
Here we use Awareness, Acceptance and Alternatives to reset the balance and feel better.

Week Three: **One Thought**

Dearest Holy Spirit, it seems that I'm having a difficult time trusting and letting myself go completely into peace. My mind seems to believe in multiple levels of struggle, and I get frustrated with what seems to be an endless process of confusion, release, and forgiveness. There are times when my mind literally feels tired. I know this is not how this process is supposed to be. Please help me find peace. Thank you.

If you cannot trust, this means you struggle. A struggle with trust requires an adherence to something else being the truth apart from you. This is a belief in the probability for purposeful deception. Furthermore, in recognizing this deception, you (in your human comprehension) must judge what is true from what is potentially false. God does not purposefully deceive, nor would He leave it up to you to judge Truth. Truth never relies on judgment to be known. God is only truthful, and it is this certainty He has bestowed unto you.

Now, if you see the option of deception, this is only because you still recognize the possibility of something else being "out there." This idea of innocent foolishness has led you to your current experience of forgetfulness.

Therefore, if you feel unsure in your trusting of God, it is only because you are unsure of whom you are, and so you invest in the guesses of the mind to teach you.

Some part of me still invests in ideas of the angry God who will punish me for not "doing it right" and trusting Him completely. I also fear that I am not realizing and practicing quickly enough. I desire to let this go.

God cannot be angry with you for searching. In fact, you have His complete blessing. You search only for a memory of yourself. God knows that there is nowhere else to go, for He has extended it all and keeps you safe in His knowing. To trust in God is to trust in His knowing and not your own. It is to release all ideas of who you think you may be. Release these ideas and return to the only Truth that ever was.

This is what I teach when I ask you to see beyond images of your body or mind alone. I ask you to be willing to be acquainted with your ultimate freedom and innocence. Here you can never struggle. I will always be here to remind you of your constant Truth beyond all images.

Your completeness is unalterable. Truth remains beyond all the images you think you have been or still think you are. See this Truth beyond all appearances. You are still as God created you, there can be nothing else! Nothing! Nothing! Nothing else. Hear Me well, I do not ask you to deny who you believe yourself to be, but to awaken in peace through it. Rather than succumb to dreams of limitation, you can know freedom. Call this a conscious awareness, but no matter it shall give you peace beyond your understanding.

You are no image outside of the Image God created. No matter how you see this creation, it remains the same. You are love, freedom, sanctity, joy, wonder, happiness, creativity and eternal brilliance. Even all of these words are merely symbols attempting to describe the Indescribable! I can understand how it is difficult to conceptualize or intellectualize these concepts. Here is a hint, perhaps it is not within concepts that you remain. Seek to feel this truth with your heart and not your mind.

It is important to recognize that you are not merely a mind thinking these thoughts. Investments in intellect can hinder you. Peace will not be found in the mind, or consciousness, for this also was formed by a belief in separation. You are a peace BEYOND understanding.

Okay, so if I can't find you in my mind or find peace through any thought or experience or through everything that I think I know now, then what??! That seems like an impossible task.

Do I hear a bit of edge in your tone?

Yes!!!! I feel frustrated by thinking that I cannot understand this.

That is because you ask your mind to be the teacher of Who You Are. You seek to place Me within a function of your understanding or worldly experience. I am beyond all of these thoughts. Beloved One, do not fear that you can be lost.

Yes, I do fear that. I don't think I can let go of every thought – every experience – every idea of everything. It just seems so impossible. The hurdles appear to stretch on for miles upon miles . . . almost as if I'm going in circles forever . . .

Remember, there is a difference between letting go and sacrifice. Only sacrifice experiences struggle. Sacrifice sees the request for letting go as a command. Sacrifice believes only in loss. Likewise I am not asking you to turn a blind eye to any belief you hold. This is not true. We are not running from anything. Nor are we acting in pretense. Do not forget the world, but release yourself from your binds within it.

Relax, Dear One. You cannot go in circles forever. In fact, you are at a significant turning point within this moment. Finally you have stopped your investment in experience as your teacher and chosen Me. This alone sets you on a pathway to peace within, which can (and will) bring you Home. Truly, I do not mean to yank the carpet from beneath your feet.

That is what it feels like sometimes . . .

I know. Hear Me now; you are blessed in every moment. However, peace is most profound in the moments when you choose to release a thought of darkness or struggle. Give these thoughts to Me and we shall celebrate each one, rather than fear them.

I ask you only to simply surrender to a deeper peace within. I ask you to be gentle with yourself or else it would not be love. I only desire you to love yourself. I could ask for nothing more.

To love yourself, Dear One, is a key to coming Home. It is part of the guide to recognizing the Truth of there never having been a need for a journey at the start. Here you reclaim who You Are beyond every possible other thought. Here you welcome peace and end the seemingly ceaseless battle of seeking definition. You quite literally release into the Arms of Love and remember this is Who You Are.

Any moment that you feel you cannot trust this, I ask you to simply breathe and give yourself space for peace. I do not desire you to struggle. It is only for your release from yourself that I pray.

Spirit prays?

My very existence is prayer. Prayer is an extension of Truth. It is the communication medium of Oneness. It is the rapture of welcoming the Will and Presence of God within your mind and extending that to all, knowing You are all. True prayer is to be still within this presence of peace and oneness within You. True prayer is simply allowing all that is to be.

There is just one thought that seems to separate you from God — only one. This one thought has the entire world built up around it. Whenever you feel you have to dismantle the entire world in order to step forth towards home, therefore making the journey seemingly impossible in form, remember this. It is only one thought that you need to correct. Only one thought needs to be recognized and released. This one thought is the key to the door of a dream world appearing to go madly awry. What is this one thought?

I am not as God created Me.

An intellect can see this as the teenage rebellion of eternity. Surely nothing in this thought was real and God knows this. That is why He stands by you completely in acceptance of Who You Are while you recognize this Truth once again.

There is a part of my mind that feels it is easy to say, "I want the Peace of God" or "I desire only Truth" or "Heaven is my Home." Surely, I feel that I can say these statements, yet honestly, I also recognize a part of my mind that remains confused as to what these statements really mean. I feel as if my saying of these statements is not always 100% genuine, that it is a going-through-the-motions type of response, and this saddens me.

> Grieve not, Dear One, for what you do not know. I know you as you are, and I sense the fear that you have convinced yourself to be real. I am with you and do not judge any part of this journey that you see as many exhausting steps. Sacrifice is not real, nor is this journey. I stand with you and offer solace to what seems to be. Really, it was only within your forgetful mind the entire time.
>
> It is okay to recognize where you think your mind resists. How else could we face these feelings and thoughts together to set them free? Do not grieve, Dear One, for you have lost nothing. I am with you and I love you. My love is not given only when you seem to attract moments of success, nor is it withdrawn when you seem to have moments of uncertainty. My love is firm and ceaseless. I do not limit or judge, ever. I will always see you as you are, not within your own mind, but within Truth, for that is all there is.
>
> Only one thought needs correction. Only one thought seems to have brought you here to this moment of conflict, and only one thought asks to be released for your own freedom. Time, separation, and the many faces you seem to encounter have no meaning here. See with Me how only one task is necessary and step forward towards your glory. I am with you.

You say that a lot.

> You need to hear that a lot. (Smile) This mind of yours, with whom you have aligned, has convinced you deeply that you are alone and homeless. It has told you many lies, all of which originate from the one thought which allowed you to believe that you were not as God created you. And in that one moment, you fell into a deep

sleep and dreamed a million dreams. None of these dreams could ever harm you, yet none of them could ever bring you back to peace.

Recognize from where these dreams arise, and you are more than merely stirring in your sleep, you are stepping forth into the Light of Home. None of these lies can bring you Home, nor can any of them truly affect you. You are free beyond any dream image they may present. So instead of believing that each image is another hurdle you must exhaustively throw yourself over, risking life and limb, I ask you only to release the struggle and surrender to peace. Permit yourself to recognize the one lie and the one solution. And in that may you also see the one Creation. And here Love does reign.

I love you. I am with you. I love you.
I am with you. I love you. I am with you.

Now, say slowly with Me and listen, truly listen to the feel of every word as it comes from every perceived level of your mind.

"I am as God created Me. I am as God created Me.
I AM as God created Me."

Close your eyes and embrace every word with an open mind and dedicated heart. Recognize how this is your call Home.

"I am as God created Me. I am as God created Me.
I AM as God created Me."

Continue this until you feel you have welcomed once again the peace of Truth. Remember that True Oneness is not found within any idea formed within the split mind. True Oneness is beyond any idea of who you think you are. True Oneness is being One with God in His Perfect Beingness. And so this awareness is beyond any idea of any correlated thought. This Truth is beyond any idea that sees you in relation to anything.

True Oneness is stepping beyond all ideas, concepts, and wills of your own mind. It joins with the only Truth there is, not as Self and Brother, nor as Holy Spirit and Self, nor even as God and Self. All ideas of relative being are two-ness. As you desire Oneness, you shall truly see that which is apart from nothing. In this, once again, you shall desire to meld with the ONLY knowledge. This Dear Beloved ONE is all that IS! That is why I say...

My Light is Your Own.

Week Three: Prompts for Insight

1. Ask Holy Spirit to please expand His teaching on how to live in "peace beyond understanding."

2. What do you deny? How does denial affect your current experience? How can denial be used appropriately and inappropriately?

3. What do you feel Trust is?

4. How do you define, ritualize or practice prayer? Is there any manner in which you would like to change this practice? How and why?

5. What is your most deep and intimate prayer? Do know that nothing can be withheld from or judged by God. He accepts you always and in all ways. Take a moment now to completely, without hindrance or self-judgment, share with Him your deepest desire.

6. If you were to communicate with God today, this very minute, one on one, what would you say?

7. What do you struggle with? How do you define struggle and allow it to affect you?

8. Ask Holy Spirit to lead you through your greatest obstacles to knowing love.

9. Ask Holy Spirit to please expand upon His teaching of "innocent foolishness."

10. Ask Holy Spirit to please tell you about awakening to peace through your ideas of self.

11. What is freedom? How do you define freedom? How does this definition differ from being perfectly free as God Created?

12. How do you express freedom in your thoughts, feelings, and experiences? How do you give yourself and others the gift of being free?

13. How can you establish more trust in your life?

14. Ask Holy Spirit to teach you how the "one thought" leads you to peace.

Affirmations:
I am as God Created Me.
I need not struggle.
I am free always and in all ways.
I rest in Spirit for peace.

One Simple Thought:
The awareness you seek is not complicated. Complication arises only out of confusion. However, God is always certain. Remember this truth and all confusion shall simply disappear.

Week Four: **Dancing With Yourself**

Dearest Holy Spirit, there have been several moments lately where I've been dancing in the darkness of resentment, judgment frustration, and apathy. I do try to give these feelings to you, but often don't feel immediate result; in fact, it seems like my mind obsesses about the result of these feelings from time to time. Help me understand why these feelings come up and what would be the best solution. Thank you.

First off, Dear One, when your mind obsesses about anything this is a sign the mistaken identity is involved. I've mentioned before that it is the mistaken identity that believes it must conceptualize, qualify, and measure all things. To this forgetful being, everything depends on a definition, a place, and a purpose. To Me, the only purpose is love and oneness. If you see your mind obsessing about any idea, thought, concept, need or judgment, this is a sign that you have merely forgotten to yield to the peace within. To notice this tendency to forget can set you free. In your practice and recent mental observations you have noticed your tendency to forget, but then you jump immediately to analysis, judgment and personal chastisement. As long as you hate, analyze or judge yourself for forgetting, the forgetting will continue because none of these thoughts are of your True Nature.

There is no need to dissect the dissection. Understand that to dissect is to separate. I never have any need to separate, for I only know oneness. If your mind desires a dissection of its thoughts, this is because it desires a separation. What *within you* has the desire for separation? (Yes, that was a rhetorical question.)

Listen now and hear clearly. If you have a desire for separation within your mind, you are seeking out an understanding within beliefs of the mistaken identity. This is why I tell you to release all need to qualify, quantify, measure, and judge. Forgiveness is accepting the willingness to yield your point of view to God's knowing. Here you accept that the only knowing and power is His. Yes, resistance is futile! Not because God's Will overpowers you, or has a defensive need to prove anything, but because there is no true success in any other will. Your little will has proven the extent of its success already. And how is that going for you?

You've really got a sense of humor going today.

Well, I figured you needed it. Because if you can't laugh at your own futile struggles with yourself, what can you laugh at?

I'm not really sure if I want to laugh at that.

And your other choice is???

Hmm . . . you have a point there.

Once again, listen and do not wrap yourself up in the futile struggles of self-judgment. I've noticed that you expect some sort of immediate result from your ritualistic chants of "I'm giving this to Spirit."

Okay . . . now are you making fun of me??

(Laughter) No, never . . . truly, my love for you often outshines your own perspective.

Ewww . . . yikes.

Indeed. But let's stay on track. A ritualistic chant is not a giving over to Me. It is a conscious reminder of exactly where your struggle is. Your struggle remains in the convincing of yourself that you are able to be free, but even as you speak, you still do not believe it. That is why you need to repeat it again and again. So what the ritualistic chant becomes is an outwardly expressed verbalization of the inner struggle. Similar to the child who holds her hands over her ears while all her peers mock and taunt her. She chants, "I'm not listening to you!! I'm not listening to you!!!" But in truth, both you and I know she is hearing and believing the taunts loud and clear.

Wow . . . true.

So, the next time you find yourself wrapped up in the moment of experiencing such feelings or thoughts, all I ask for you to do is notice and breathe. Do not feel the need to say anything. Do not feel the need to argue or rationalize. Simply notice the thought and breathe. If you become angry because of these thoughts it is only because you judge yourself. Welcome instead the peace from your breath. Relax into the truth, rather than bounce back and forth between what you may think needs to be said or heard. This is what the passage on "you need do nothing" partially means. Choosing again seems to be a needful conscious choice, but truly it is not. Choosing again in truth is about release of your own will and the acceptance of God's Peace.

God is not seeking a laundry list of tasks, created in your consciousness, judged by your mistaken identity, and then returned reluctantly to Him. This is an activity of resistance. Remember it is only in your forgetfulness that you believe that a qualification or designation must occur first. This is how you choose to value your own intellectual or perceptual power, before God's Will. This is you attempting to maintain control over all that has no need for your direction. It is I who know that God's Will is really the only being. The banter of the thinking mind will never give you peace. Release yourself into the acceptance of All That Ever Is. To do nothing is simply to accept. Here, you open your eyes and truly see, not through your own mind, but through the ever- present Truth of Who You Are as God Is.

Reluctance occurs when subconscious fears are brought to the surface. The reluctance you felt the other day was merely the tip of the iceberg of all the fear lying deep within your struggling-self. All judgments you have (even that one – I catch everything).

Now . . . wait a minute, come on!

Dear One, understand this well, every judgment and belief in separation must come to the light. Not one, but EVERY ONE.

To be honest, that makes it feel like this is an impossible task.

That is because you judge it and assume it will drive you insane. From where I'm sitting, you already are insane, because you consciously and repeatedly deny the very truth of all You are. This insanity has you repeat these lies to yourself every moment. Here you see yourself as nothing when in Truth you are everything! Now, how insane is that?!

Okay, you got me there.

Let's just be honest. Let's look at each thought and allow ourselves to be free despite any judgments. See my strength with you. See my freedom as a witness to all that you are. Dear One, you are not alone, nor will you ever be abandoned in this dream. Your enlightenment is not dependent on time. Try not to limit yourself to time by feeling you can fail or repeat lifetimes. Feeling that you must achieve perfect awareness within a certain time frame, fearing that you may otherwise be lost forever, is a judgment that God does not make. He does not penalize you by adding more lifetimes. Only the mistaken identity thinks in terms of prison sentences. Enlightenment is not measured in years and you can never be lost to your Father. He knows exactly where you are, it is only you who do not. My love is within you. My light is your own. Use these words as your guide and nothing can ever go wrong. Nothing can ever be lost within your desire to practice the truth. You cannot do this "awakening thing" wrong.

And what about the resentment?

Do not feel guilty over this; it is part of the process of release. If you were not to allow the resentment to come to light, it would still be suppressed within. I know it surprised you when that belief popped up. I know it seemed to make you feel guilty for daring to think such a way about Your Father. But honestly, it is not Him you harm; it is merely your ideas of yourself. When you notice these feelings, once again, breathe. Allow each thought to flow forward through your consciousness. Notice each perception and judge them not. Allow yourself to welcome the release that you now know is there. Allow yourself to welcome the peace that is the only truth. Do not feel the need to struggle or say anything. Simply relax into the arms of God. And if you feel so reluctant that you cannot even relax, simply breathe and allow yourself to be still for as long as necessary. Then finally set yourself free. Designate yourself to love in whatever form you feel most comfortable with in the moment.

Dear One, I do not ask for you to struggle with yourself to find your freedom. Your freedom is your natural state. It is not to be found through a dance of resistance, reluctance, and "ping pong" thoughts. When I say it is your natural state, I mean it is all that truly exists; anything else that you perceive about yourself is false.

Notice this next time, and allow yourself to be free. Accept the truth of your freedom, peace and love. Accept the oneness that you are, even when the world or your mind appears to be offering many opportunities for contrary desires. Permit Truth, not within your mind or intellect, but by resting into the Arms of God. Relax into His Grace fully—not as someone who needs to designate a truth through a debate within your mind, but truly as someone who knows that there is no other true resting place. Forgiveness of yourself will help you release. Here you recognize that only fear keeps you from forgiveness. See the strength of God within you and you can only be a survivor, strong and loved in the Oneness of God's knowing. In doing so, remind yourself that I have not absolved you of any wrongdoing; instead, I only witness to the fact that a wrong-doing could never occur. It is only your mind that perceives otherwise. I am here as you accept the light of Truth.

My Light is Your Own . . .

Week Four: Prompts for Insight

1. Obsession means "to besiege" or "to set against." List your needs and obsessions. How do they affect you? Ask Holy Spirit, how your obsessions keep you sitting against your Self.

2. Ask Spirit to help you look at where you withhold peace from yourself. Breathe and allow His response to flow beyond the judgments of your thinking mind.

3. Is it possible to just "go through the motions" of awakening? What is the difference between genuine awakening and "going through the motions?"

4. Ask Holy Spirit to please expand upon His teaching of "I need do nothing."

5. Write on acceptance and freedom. How do you perceive these ideas? Offer all thoughts to Holy Spirit for His guidance.

6. What do you resent? Can you seek peace beyond your resentments?

7. Holy Spirit teaches, "Freedom is your natural state." Ask for His help in recognizing where you withhold or limit true freedom from your awareness and how to be perfectly free within your life experience now.

8. Write on your thoughts about forgiveness. Seek Spirit's guidance on all these ideas.

9. Ask Spirit to lead you through the release of any thoughts of resentment and struggle.

Practice: Make a GRUDGE Rock
Find a medium to large weighted stone (approx. 5 lbs. or more).
Personally, I use a 6 x 4 inch marble slab of 2 inch thickness. Designate
this as your "grudge rock." Every time you have the desire to hold a
grudge or focus on guilt, picture yourself carrying the rock around. Or
if you desire, write your grudge on the smooth surface with a dry
erase marker, and carry the rock around for an hour. Attempt to
continue your usual daily tasks with this rock in hand. Can you feel
the weight and burden of holding grudges? Is it comfortable? Is it
really worth it? How would forgiveness set you free?

Affirmations:
I am as God Created Me.
Freedom is my natural state.
I choose to forgive, release and heal.
I need do nothing and be safe.

One Simple Thought:
Resentment is an attachment to judgments of the past. Brooding
means to "incubate in the mind" and literally has you feel again all
thoughts of ill-will. Here you project forward your beliefs in
separation for repeated experience. However, you need not blindly
resend any idea which presents itself in your mind. Forgiveness clears
your path and sets you free.

Week Five: **A Question of Perception**

Dearest Spirit, I have heard many spiritual practitioners state, "There is no one else out there" or "There is only one of us here." These statements infer that all people are a reflection of my mind. I have noticed a difficulty accepting this idea. Could you help me explore and clarify this idea? Thanks.

Blessings, Dear One. When I teach that there is "only one of us here," this truth does not concern bodies. Of course, to the physical eye, bodies cannot be overlooked. You are not being asked to overlook this seemingly obvious state of existence, but you are asked to see beyond its perceptual limitations.

Essentially this concept asks you to recognize how you constantly judge and project each judgment onto the people and circumstances encountered. No one is out there because you never truly see anyone. The central point is to help you notice how you merely see through your judgments and not how you identify yourself in the flesh. In Truth, you are whole, and despite who or what you see with your eyes, this wholeness is changeless. However, in thought, you often see what you believe. Therefore, you do not ever see truly.

But if you cannot seem to see this concept now, I only ask you to call to mind what you do see. If you do see bodies, what do they represent to you? Can you notice how you value and define these bodies? Can you recognize from where these definitions arise? Can you accept that it is not what you see, but how you perceive?

I do not ask you to deny a body or cover your eyes in play, expecting the world to disappear before you. You have invested in a world for so long (in terms of your time) that it would be silly and purposeless to deny such a thing. Obviously you believe it is real, you do appear to be here, correct?

Well, yes . . . I do appear to be here. This is why I have difficulties with accepting this concept. Whenever I hear the concept of "no one else is out there," the resistance within is tremendous. "How can they say that??" I think, "Are they blind?? How can they ask me to deny the world??"

I do not ask you to deny the world, nor do I even ask for you to deny its effects, for that is what you seem to see. This would be empty denial, or seeming foolishness. But I do ask you to openly recognize what you believe. To accept the concept of "no one else being out there" is about the content of your thoughts, not the forms of your world environment. Confusion will arise when you seek solely to compare my teachings to the world in form. However, the content of this teaching can show you how all creation of God is interconnected. All is one. Likewise, all that is believed within is seen without and all that is seen without connects within. If you are unable to realize or feel your interconnection, then perhaps you are attempting to accept something else in its place.

This world witnesses to a belief in separation, for that is how it is perceived to be. Since all that is without stems from within, your experience seeds from a belief in separation. Do you want to reveal the Truth about You and make peace with the world? Will first, then, to have all misperceptions arise so that they may be set free. In this willing for Truth, all that is within becomes peaceful once again and all that seems to be of the world simply fades away.

Does this mean that the earth-bound world will disappear?

No. This teaching has nothing to do with the physical experience you impression. However, what will occur is that no longer will you be attached to former perceptions and judgments. Essentially, you will come to know yourself clearly without any previous projection. Here you will come to forgive and forget, simply because sin will no longer be at the center point of your story.

Seeing yourself alone within a world of other alone bodies affirms the belief in separation. To see Who You Are in One Spirit will require you to see beyond separate identities in physical form.

Listen now. Your existence within Spirit is the only wholly true one in eternity. Surely a body appears to be separate, and bodies are never able to wholly join. Yet, separate identities are nonexistent in God. When you are being asked to see all as one, you are merely being called to affirm yourself with Spirit's Identity. In doing so, you align your mind with the truth of Who You Are and do not get lost in presented images, individuality, behaviors or other devices witnessing to separation within the world. When you center yourself here, recognizing only the Spirit through your Brothers, you set yourself free from all beliefs which are determined to have you be limited and not as God created. It is only from this limited belief that all ideas in perception, judgment, sin and condemnation have occurred. And it is here that you have suffered.

If you choose to recognize the aspects of how you see the world, you will quickly notice how separation has become your judge. Here, the struggling-self's ideas of fear and vulnerability have authority. Here, you live a life simply to perpetuate an individualized existence. Yet, I am here to help you realize that in order to be, this judgment requires your own investment in weakness and fear. You cannot see fear and weakness unless you allow fear and weakness to define you! Therefore, all ideas of separate identities were made to instill a sense of safety within the mind seeing itself as alone and afraid. The world is not your problem. Truly it only plays out what you perceive about yourself. Conflict within produces conflict without. A belief in vulnerability within projects a justification of fear outside.

But what am I to say to all the people who can witness to the atrocities within the world? What of all those witnesses to pain and fear?

Yes, if I were to say to the mind that only perceives through the world, "You are mistaken, you do not live within a den of fear," only mocking laughter and further denial would occur. This is because the mind that sees within the world is seeing itself backwards. And it is this backwards thinking that has you see yourself as a body first and not God's creation of One Spirit. Spirit does not rely on bodies, and so they mean nothing. Alternatively, a perception that is confused and does not know even itself, will rely on any thing to help its seeking.

No matter how many separate witnesses you call to prove the wickedness of the world, to be amassed in delusion is still to believe you are vulnerable, requiring separation and not peaceful. It is to see yourself apart from God's creation of One Spirit. Yet truly if you were willing to step beyond these ideas, only Truth would arise. So, my only question then is, "Do you want to see beyond your fear?" You are as God created you, nothing else. The point I am now gently but repeatedly stating is that you must intend to see what your mind believes, before you can see all that I know you to be.

The mistaken identity is not a stupid belief (albeit a foolish one far from how you truly are). It is well invested in what it seems to see. Recognize the content of each experience and you shall see more clearly. Truly, all that you see in the world begins and ends with you. This is the only reason why no one else is out there.

But as I choose to see the world differently, and begin to notice my thoughts about the world, am I not metaphorically required to pretend not to see with my physical eyes?

No, I only ask you not to judge. The image within the world is not the problem, only the judgment of it. This is why it appears many can feel differently within the same situation. It is never with your eyes that you see, but only with your judgments. This is why I say you already pretend not to see . . . and that is your only problem. Truly, even this problem has been solved, because your True Self only exists as Spirit or as God's Holiness would have it be. Your blindness is nothing but a foolish game of hide and seek. It cannot last. Do not close your eyes to images, yet accept these images as being mere guideposts to the beliefs you hold beneath them. As you look upon each image, allow its outer shell to fall away and reveal the Spirit of Love within. Here, through your images, you shall gain your greatest gift, and this is the gift of Truth within all.

Let the outer images fall away. Let yourself remember the Truth within and let yourself see more than what is in appearances.

Being that I know you still as God created, I do not argue with nor condemn your perceived reality. I know that the world does not contain problems or solutions. All is within and only within. Again, I say, you do not see truly at any time, for it is only through the projection of your beliefs that formulation occurs. This is what makes the world seem more real to you than God. For you painstakingly choose to see with your eyes of judgment first and not the eye of Spirit. You do not see your brother with Love's Vision; therefore, you do not see your brother at all. Your images are made through ideas you have about yourself, your fears, the past, and your world. You are quite literally living in delusion and all delusion is simply a false belief. You then live these false beliefs because you do not see wholly.

Listen now, any idea based on limitedness is false. Any idea based on separation is false. Any idea based on fear, victimization, vulnerability or need is never true. You see only what you perceive about yourself, judge within, and then project this belief onto the canvas seen as "others." Thus your brother becomes the expression of your worldly ideas.

Do you want to see yourself as a victim? Surely then you will see your brother as victimizer. Do you want to see vulnerability? Surely then you will see your brother as attacked or attacker. Even if you desire to see pleasing images of your brother, they are merely images. Remember this, not even pleasing or happy images of your brother (or yourself) are complete. You are beyond any image. You are indescribable as God created you, for no words or images can begin to grasp the expansion of ultimate reality you are.

None is real as long as separation is perceived. To see with God's knowing is to see wholly. You cannot see wholly until you release all ideas of separation both in body and mind. When you are asked to see that there is "nothing out there," you are not asked to institute another form of denial, but you are asked to call to attention the beliefs that you hold and choose to see through.

When I say you are as God created You, I intend to bring you back to the recognition of True sight. Your brother, too, is changeless as God created, for you were created as One Spirit. This Oneness is not in body, nor restricted to bodies, for these forms do not represent anything true. Neither were you created as an individual mind, for an individual mind thinks and perceives on its own. In this perception, private thoughts appear to occur, but truly these are nothing but your own conscious reflections of limitation, and Spirit minds them not. To be an individual body or mind, and not Spirit, would require you to be separate from God, and although you may perceive this, it is impossible.

A desperate attempt to engage yourself on the level of the mind alone has led to beliefs of your personalities being united in this imagery. This is not true. The forgetful mind is a divided mind and has made a world reflecting that. Therefore all identities and personas were made to function within this paradigm of separation. Hereto, the personality cannot see itself as One as long as it perceives itself as an individual needing to validate its individuality. However, this does not mean that you personality outreaches your current understanding. Together we will enhance your awareness so that you may come to see yourself as so much more than this limited identity. To reach beyond all thoughts and seek only the experience of Truth is to walk up to the gates of Heaven.

But when I hear this, I feel afraid. I feel that my individuated personality will disappear, that I won't be anything anymore. How can I begin to understand this, even as a concept, if I feel that I will become nothing?

This can be called the "identity death." Never did I say that you will become nothing, Dear One. Never can you be or ever shall be nothing. To believe that you are nothing is a mistake. Because it is then that you believe only your individuated personality makes you who you are.

Yet, let us look with Love at what your individuated

personality is. As you believed yourself to be separate, there were certain masks of identity that a conscious mind decided to express. You can call these masks of expression your individuated personality. In fact if you look at the literal definition of personality it does mean "masked identity." In distinguishing which mask to wear, the perceptual mind (already seeing through clouded vision) decided to divide itself even further. All its grandness (as well as depravity) stems only from a Spiritual Self-denial. In this denial it has divided, magnified and placed within a limited or mistaken identity.

To lose the individuated personality is only to lose the denial of Spirit. Therefore, in releasing yourself from this imagery, you gain a complete Self awareness, which compared to an individuated personality is incomprehensible. Nonetheless, the personality you think you are is not you. Nor can the complete Self awareness be appropriately described within terms that a self-centered identity can comprehend. Trust Me; all that You are is nothing like what you think. Remind yourself of this as fear appears to sneak in here. Dear One, there is no loss possible; only a gaining of what once seemed to be gone forever.

To say that there is "no one else out there" is simply to say that you do not see anyone as their Self. It is also to say that you do not even see your Self. This is because you do not know your Self as God created you. You only seem to experience yourself through this mistaken identity called individuated personality or body. You then use this as your guide to judge the appearances of others. Others become Brothers when you begin to see with Spirit's vision. It is here that you begin to open, away from the fear and division, to a unified sense of awareness. It is here that you begin to welcome your Self once again, not as a mistaken identity, but as Holiness alive in God. You are never divided, never apart, never wanting. You never need and have always been All One Spirit. Your peace and truth are beyond understanding.

Your Light is My Own . . .

Week Five: Prompts for Insight:

1. Where do you define and limit your experience by concepts of the body or identity?

2. Ask Spirit to lead you through to a deeper insight about your experience of the body and your perceptions of others.

3. What do you have a tendency to most judge?

4. What feelings and thoughts arise in hearing "you never truly see anyone?"

5. Ask Spirit to share more on denial as compared to true perception.

6. What does the statement: "Who You Are in One Spirit will require you to see beyond all separation" means to you?

7. When you consider Spirit being the One Truth, you feel:

8 Ask Spirit to elaborate on the statement, "All separation is nonexistent."

9. Write down a list of all thoughts of fear and weakness that occur to you and ask Spirit to help you release these thoughts.

10. What does the statement "The image within the world is not the problem, only the judgment of it is," mean to you? How can you build on this thought? Explore with Spirit.

Practice:

Draw two pictures. First, draw your body as you see yourself now. This does not have to be a picture perfect portrait, yet can be symbolic (images of a body of rocks, balloons, prison bars, etc.) Next, identify a minimum of five judgments you hold about your self. These do not have to be specifically body-centered judgments, but they can relate to your life experiences. Place these judgments on the body picture. Where do these feelings reside within your body? Do you feel them as headaches, stomach pains, tension or fatigue? Where does your body carry these judgments?

Next, draw yourself as you would like to see yourself within five years. Identify all the changes you have made beyond the previous images. Identify what areas of your body have been set free and how. Write all thoughts and feelings. Share these thoughts with Spirit and seek internal guidance. Take note of all arising.

Affirmations:

I am as God Created Me.

I and my Brother are changeless in eternity.

I receive what I perceive, why deceive? I am the strength of God.

Separation is nonexistent.

I choose to see all with Love.

I am the strength of God.

Week Six: **True to My Self**

Dear One, the greatest challenge to a mind believing in separation is to undertake the so-called journey of remembrance. You are not able to be lost. It is most important that you remember this. There is never a time when I am not with you, and for you to believe that you are alone is self-deception. Such a self-deception can last a long time if you remain unaware of your Heart. This is why I feel it is important to speak to you today about being true to your Self. It is only natural for you to want to know Who You Are.

It is only natural for you to want an outer experience that will verify the whisperings of remembrance you hear. However, these whisperings have often been mistaken as appeals for journey within the world. They are not, but instead are a calling beyond it. Completeness cannot be expressed in an experience of limitation, and so there is no material comparison. No compromise or accomplishment must you undertake. Therefore, do not fear, you cannot fail to be your Self.

Your struggling-self has you convinced you are something that You are not. This is why, every time you seek to know, you first look for understanding or proof within the world. Who You Really Are, requires no proof and surely is not dependent upon measurements within the world. If you truly want to experience the Real You, then allow yourself to simply rest. This rest is best accepted through the ultimate release of everything that you think you are now. And I mean everything.

When you are true to your Self you are embracing all that is Real. You choose to dedicate yourself to releasing all thoughts and beliefs that do not represent the Truth of Who You Are. This is not a task or chore, but a rest in release and trust.

You literally will be delving into the stillness and the silence of the mind. Yes, you will feel distracted when you do this. But that is because you are looking for experiences to occur that will involve a bodily or environmental response. We do not settle our minds for change within the world. We settle our Selves in God for knowing our Truth. As long as you ask to receive or see through the body, this wish limits you from letting go of the body. Likewise, in asking for proof within the world, you are reconfirming your belief that only the world can be the support and the witness to reality. Do you understand? Yes, you quite literally are working against yourself in these moments of seeking measurement and an experience of spiritualized form instead of simply releasing for peace.

So how do you let go? First, you need to recognize what it means to let go. It means to embrace the stillness in full, to consciously let go of all things you believe you are. You practice this by simply noticing anytime a thought or definition or limitation appears in your mind. As you notice, see it without judgment and then release it to Me. In this practice, you begin to consciously let go. Here, we join together to openly reconsider all wayward considerations. Yes, this work can unearth resistance. However, attempt to not allow this resistance to define you. Try to ask these resistances Who You Are and why you struggle. Are you a body? No. Are you a gender? No. Are you a religion? No. Are you a career? No. Are you a homeowner? No. Are you a businessperson? No. Are you an artist? No. You are seeing only surface distractions if you label yourself as any or all of these.

The practice of letting go may sound harsh or impossible. But liberating these self-definitions and attachments is a means to help you recognize all that which God created You to be. You may believe you live to express these worldly thoughts and labels and follow their lead to experience yourself in several unique ways. But, I reiterate, these roles were made by you as distractions. These experiences came into being only in the moment you believed you could choose to express a limited self-will differently from God's Creation. You are, truly, none of these things and never will be. Please know though, you are not a sinner or judged for valuing these ideas about the individual self. All is perfect and you remain innocent. Spirit is the nature of you, and this Truth never has changed.

To say "I am" is to claim a self-creation in the name of the Father. The remembrance of this sense of your True power is why the words "I am" are referenced with such authority in the Bible.

Every expression of human creativity is an answer to the subconscious call to remembrance. When you call into being all that you believe you are, you intentionally are attempting to create as you remember the Father Creates. Yet, there is one problem: you do not make things as the Father Creates them. You make within a prison and not within an extension of pure Truth. What you make and value within the world is dependent and impermanent. Is it not variable and prone to destruction? As you define yourself through these images, you feel sorrow when they do not last or meet your needs. Thus, the illusions you make become the bricks in the walls of a perceptual prison.

You are free beyond all these bodily, intellectual, and emotional limitations. You are still as God created you to be. See that? You are still. You are still. God created you still and simply complete. When I ask you to let go, I ask you to breathe this stillness into you. Take a moment now and do this. Simply bring peace to your mind, place all questioning and idle thoughts aside and focus on your breath. In stillness, there is no movement. There is no desperation to be in a busy mind or a restrictive body. Stillness of the mind resonates with the One Reality that is. In stilling the mind you step back from a consciousness of busy thoughts. Simply release all of the thinking mind's chatter and distraction. Step back. Accept how there was never a need to be anything else. You feel lost only when you think you need to express or experience what you are through masks. Take the masks off, and then you will see the truth about you. Take the masks off and embrace the stillness.

The moment that God Created You to Be, you were Complete. Any other thought is unnecessary. This completeness remains wholly available at this moment. God does not see His Holiness in the roles it plays. He loves your ability to extend in playfulness. He gives you this ability through All You Are. However, it would only be the tail wagging the dog if you settled within these roles and believed them to be the reality of You. Therefore, do not only settle within these mere conditional roles. Employed or unemployed, you are promoted. Mother or father, you are fertile. Rich or longing, you are supplemented. Healthy or ailing, you are infinite. Beloved Holiness of All That Is, you are so much brilliantly more than any idea of limitation.

If you think of all the busyness of the world in terms of illusion, it is important to note that the base word of illusion is "ludere," which means, "to play." These deceptions - that you see with eyes, ears, hands, and heart - are merely playful imaginings of a self desiring to be apart from God in form. They are nothing. Guilt has no place in this per-form-ance. All is a playful idea overflowing with God's Laughter and Blessing.

Guilt is one of the greatest deceptions, since it can have you believe that God wishes for your banishment. Never, I tell you, has this separation ever occurred; so, as you idle here, recognize you remain within the One Love which has never changed. You never could be anything other than what God expressed for you to be. You are an extension of His creative energy, and surely this energy could never change.

If you feel imprisoned with regret, due to a behavior or experience from within the world, please accept that God sees you as innocent beyond judgment. Accept and express this innocence through all your interactions, as this is expressing it to the whole Self. Even within time, the past is irreconcilable. However, any shadow that lingers can be brought to the Light of Love. Express this Light in whatever manner feels most appropriate and healing to all involved. Express a deeper knowing of yourself by enacting a blessing for healing now. This appropriately can be extended to all who took part in the event for which you mourn. As you choose to offer repentance, offer Love. Offer this love not out of requirement or insolence, as that is not love. Simply reach out to embrace your Brothers from the realization that you and all who join with you here deserve so much more than suffering. This is being wholly *true to your innocence* beyond form.

Again, the only mistake you have made is the continual adoption of this illusion. You allow each deception to rule over you. In giving these deceptions authority, you adhere to them as your values. You only value these deceptions because you do not know yourself without them, or shall I better say, you do not know yourself without the fear of not having them. It has become a cyclical inversion of Truth. The downward spiral of fear witnesses to your adopted deceptions and you then cling to them because of your fear. Is it not better, you ask, to have a false image over a perception of vacancy? However, I must retort, which of these choices bestows a remembrance of Who You Are?

I ask you to remove yourself from all worldly values, only so that you can learn to stop investing in a perception that accepts the possibility of self-destruction. As long as you see yourself as this destructible being, you make a simple error in judgment and temporarily turn a blind eye to Who You Are. These temptations only lure you into investing in a whole treasure chest of counterfeit monies. Although your experience of bodily life may include many wonders and mysteries, the Truth is incomparable and indestructible.

What is it that you are? You are perfect. You are peace. You are infinite loving kindness eternally expressed in all ways. Can you imagine yourself embracing the value of these words and becoming as such? Can you, if only for a moment, allow yourself to bask in the glory of all that God values you to be? Use your imagination now to escape your imagination. Close your eyes, settle in your thoughts. See a brilliant Light of Love dance across the inner-space of your eyelids. Feel its vastness embrace you. Joyful warmth radiates beyond your body's limitations, yet is clear from the inner recesses of your heart center. Breathe this loving presence deeply within. Inhale and rest contained by it. There can be nothing greater . . . because there is *nothing* greater. Here we know ourselves.

When you are true to your Self, you know this and doubt yourself not. God's Love is All You Are, and you bask in this radiance, knowing your Value intimately.

Can we pause here a moment? Truly, I find your guidance amazing! You are so deeply profound; however, my head spins from attempting to comprehend it all. Foremost, I wonder why I have such a difficult time believing this. Why do I hold fast to all these exhausting deceptions of the thinking mind?

You hold fast to illusion because you cannot conceive another way. However, the perfection You are is beyond any belief the conscious mind can comprehend. That is why you have such difficulty! Try not as much to figure out this guidance, as to see its overall golden thread. Secondly, you find the comprehension of this teaching difficult because you bind yourself to worldly comparisons in order to find proof. The seeking of Holiness within the world will always provide a paradox. You cannot find Truth in illusions. Do not expect the illusions to reveal Truth to you.

But what about the revelations of Light I hear about? Aren't there many spiritual gurus who see edges of Light within the world? If I were to practice all of these teachings, would this not be my reward?

The seeing of revelations of Light, like many gurus and spiritual teachers speak of in their own experience, is never meant to be a measure of your ability or divine progression. Furthermore, the Light episodes are not revelations seen within the world; they emanate from an enlightened awareness beyond your seeing eyes. These revelations expose Your Reality *beyond* the world. Worry not; there is no real progress to make. You are measured against no one. Awakening is instantaneous and is accomplished, despite your own measurements. Only the forgetful mind perceives this not to be true, and so it is in the mind that the correction must occur.

Okay, so how do I release the values or deceptions that I invest in?

Begin by recognizing your beliefs. Has not every belief you have held — up to this moment — brought you pain? Has it not led from divided and opposed thinking to shadows of separation and judgment? You believe that what God created can be changed by your own mind, so you constantly change your mind about yourself.

Truth is not about belief. Instead, accept (even if for only a moment) the radiance that is your Self. See God as your Master and not your thinking mind. Trust in Him to show you all You Are. Dear Beloved Holiness of God, invest not in the emptiness of a dark and abandoned stage, set up with false props distracting to the eye.

Only perfect Love exists. Beloved Child of God, you are an extension of only the good, the beautiful and the holy. Do not forget this. You are Love in Truth; it is your very nature. Holiness is in you, and where Holiness is, God must be, for Holiness only extends from Him.

To speak briefly about feelings, all of your emotions are vibrational echoes of thoughts stemming from either truth or deception. If you think that you cannot unearth the root of what you believe, become aware of your emotions instead of your thoughts.

You cannot silence the clamor of the thinking mind with intellectualization. Emotions, comparatively, allow the perceiver to become aware of his or her deeper connection to each thought. Emotions breathe a life into your thought. Thoughts are mainly one-dimensional, which is why they can be rapid and senseless. All feelings reach beyond flat dimensionality into an expression. Truly, do you "think yourself sad" or do you say, "I AM sad?" Fundamentally, emotions contain breadth and are multifaceted, reflecting your beliefs. Therefore, to be peaceful is not to construct thoughts adding up to peace. Peacefulness expresses in the knowing of your wholeness. Consciously this wholeness may be felt through physical sensations of tranquility. However, it is a feeling beyond all limits of body or mind. To be peaceful is an opening through your loving nature and allows you to bask in God's Light.

Here we step from mere beliefs into reality. Follow this very same pathway in releasing your beliefs. Seek first to settle your mind. Next inhale deeply and let your awareness notice any emotion that appears to surface. As the emotion surfaces, breathe again and ask to let Me know this sensation for you. I will always lead you from mere belief and emotional sensation to revelation. Let our bond clear these passing clouds. Indeed, we are the sun that shines away every shadow.

Yet, there is another key. Dear One, as long as you believe that any part of your world is not an extension of you, you will not find true peace. I know this sounds difficult to accept. But all darkness stems from the same wish, and all peace will occur from the same healing. You awaken united, just as you sleep as one mind. Do not see yourself as just a singular expression in a sea of faces. Peace is not found in any form of division.

Honestly, all you desire is a remembrance of Truth. That is why forgiveness exists in the first place. If you did not hope to find peace, forgiveness would not be possible. Echoes of reality weave within the world of dreams. Find these echoes, and embrace them. As you do, you slowly begin to stir in your sleep. Slowly, you begin to remember what you hope to remember.

Your Oneness within God exists because
His Oneness encompasses all.

I can make no clearer statement for the integral realization of your awakening. To be One with God is to claim all that is yours within Creation. It is to see yourself as an extension of the Truth. Accept everyone you encounter in wholeness. I cannot emphasize enough that there is no more holy way to see you. Join with all. Remember their innocence and bless them wholly. Every blessing you extend is a grateful acceptance of God's restorative power. Glory is to You, Child of God. Glory is to every moment that you embrace the Truth about your Self. I say be True to your Self because in being so you welcome awakening.

You are worthy beyond measure! God lives in You. He is of YOU and you are of Him. Yet, even as you play within this world, temporarily forgetting, you remain as God Created.

A mind perceiving limitations cannot comprehend being boundless. Nonetheless, you need do nothing in order to reclaim all that is holy and wholly your Self. Simply accept my guidance and be willing for peace. Here you are willing for Truth. Use this strength of realization to actively recognize how all deluded beliefs support fear. Listen and practice my guidance. Notice these beliefs and set yourself free from them. Choose and accept all that is One in God. Be willing to choose the Truth beyond the shadows and sink back into the arms of God. In trust and faith you will remember all He created You to be. For that is all You Are! I love you!

Week Six: Prompts for Insight:

1. How do you see and experience complete innocence? Ask within to see the innocence within all others you encounter this week, rather than any other thought or judgment. Watch your mind for all it seeks to represent to you.

2. Explore with Spirit, how you can see mighty companions within the world. How could you offer these brothers love with equal innocence?

3. Write down a list of your values. How do these values affect your experiences within the world?

4. Openness is...

5. Ask Holy Spirit to show you where you remain closed or restricted in your thoughts, feelings or perceptions. Ask Him to show you how you can be more open. What needs to be released?

6. To be true to your Self is to embrace all that is Real. How do you experience this?

7. Ask Holy Spirit to elaborate on seeking "proof" as compared to having faith?

F.R.A.M.E. Method:

Observe this week where you can practice these five components of being true to your Self. In your journal, or on a separate sheet of paper, identify a minimum of one way you practice each of the following principles through this week.

Forgiveness: Be true to your innocence. Forgiveness sets you free. The practice of forgiveness allows you to release every false idea of guilt. Ideas of guilt only keep us feeling separate. Here we live in the shadows rather than the Light. Offer forgiveness to yourself and all this week, and know you are Love.

Respect: God knows Who You Are. The word "respect" literally means, "to see again". Allow yourself to see your Self through your self. Look again and accept the brilliant Being You are.

Affirm: The word "affirm" literally means, "to make steady, strengthen." Let God be the Strength you trust. See this Strength within you now. It is. Be True to your loving nature. Remind yourself in words and deeds.

Mirror: In ancient times, mirrors were used as tools for divination. When you look within, do you see the divine? Now is the time to be true to your Oneness. Be the mirror of remembrance. See your divine nature. See the Light of Truth reflected in all.

Empower: Let the choices you make communicate the Love, power, and strength You are in Spirit. Empowerment is permitting the Truth within yourself to motivate all your thoughts, words and deeds.

Affirmations:

I am as God Created Me.

It is only natural for me to want to know who I am.

I value my Self in God.

I release all that does not represent the Truth.

Week Seven: **All Reality Has Purpose**

All reality has purpose, and this purpose is love. It is extension. God's purpose is one of extension, and this is the fulfillment of Truth. Read that slowly, *full-fillment*. In God's purpose, you are *fully filled* with Truth. You are filled with Love. You are complete and whole. To be as God Created You is to be fully filled. Here you realize the completeness that You are.

God did not create a meaningless world. To give meaning, in the exact sense of the word, is to give a purpose, wish or intention. Hear Me well, God's intention is fulfillment of wholeness, therefore His purpose expresses this desire always.

The world you experience is merely a world that does not accept this wholeness. It acts out the inverse belief through limitation. You can witness this through looking upon every idea of separation conjured in the thinking mind. Therefore, in your own extension of these beliefs, your world has become a detailed expression of separation. This is not reality. Separation is not an idea of God. Why? It cannot be God's idea because perfect freedom withholds nothing. God is that perfect freedom, and being so eliminates all possibility for restriction. Yes, it is impossible for God to be restricted or limited in any way.

To be of God is to know, truly know in being. It is the having of all and being of all, given to all in perfection. He is fully filled in every way and only expresses in every Creation as Fully Filled. Therefore, if the world is not expressing as a fully filled expression, it is not of God and not reality.

The true definition of the word fulfillment is "shared by all." It derives from languages that gave ultimate value to all things connected and shared. God's purpose is to extend from His Perfect Mind to Your Own. Therefore your ultimate meaning is found in God's sharing of all with you, through You. He gives wholly and completely in the thought that you are as perfect as He is. There is nothing else. Claiming to be lost within the world is a claim counter to your Truth. It is the same as denying your Creator. I say this not in judgment, but simply to point out where you deny the

Truth. You can deny and forget all you desire now, but this does not affect the Truth of You. Again, I say, no freedom is restricted in You, pretend all you like. Yet the Truth remains as God Created. Therefore, in this perfect freedom, you play, you dream, and you experiment with all thoughts that have you express limitation in temporal form. Never will or could you make yourself not whole, for that is impossible. Love is and always will remain as God Created, for it is changeless.

If you are to seek out meaning within the world, I ask you to see the limitation that this represents ("pre" "sends") or sends before you. See that if you realized You were complete and that your True meaning shares all with God, there would be nothing within the world needing to give you meaning. In fact, there would be no reason for seeking meaning outside your Self, for completion already knows it is all in all. It recognizes it is complete, and this becomes its only meaning. Only the mind in limitation asks for meaning. It is only the mind in mistaken identity that asks, "Who am I?" and "What is this for?" To ask alone is a declaration that you do not know. Therefore, merely to ask is to deny.

In today's experiences, see where you allow yourself to step into denial with every thought. See where you have substituted your own limited reality for what is changeless. I ask you to notice every moment where you substitute presumption, judgment or condemnation, instead of simply being. See where you judge yourself and your brothers. See where you believe something different should have happened rather than what is truly happening. See where you believe you know what other people are thinking and why they do what they seem to do. See where you attempt to predict the future or mourn a fearful past, rather than simply live in the moment at hand. See all the areas where you resist or struggle, and thus exchange life for suffocation.

Do you feel alone? Afraid? Purposeless? Depressed? Limited to the commands and needs of your body alone? If you see these ideas, whether or not they express in form, recognize how they speak of you. Ask if these states of being are comparable to all I have said You Are. Allow yourself to sink into the content of each belief. Not just to discover what they mean (although that is essential for your learning) but also to realize the wholeness that is being overlooked when these beliefs are being accepted. You are as God Created You. Again, I say, this is changeless. No matter how many seemingly separated forms you look upon, remind yourself of this one fact.

You are FULLY FILLED IN GOD.

In addition, since you are fully filled in God, there is no room for victimization, lack, loss, disease, helplessness or powerlessness. Fully filled leaves no room for anything more, for there is nothing lacking that therefore has a void. To be seeing a meaning in anything apart from God is to believe you are apart from God. It is aligning with the mind of self-definition. Simply, you deny all you are. Remember that all definition is to see within a boundary; it is to be "of finite," and of restriction.

How do you desire to restrict yourself? Is it by disease? Is it by powerlessness? Is it by victimization or lack? Where do you wish to hold yourself back from completion? Essentially, this is the only question to ask your thinking mind, since God does not hold you back in any way. It is only you (within a mind seeing itself as limited, finite and restricted) that chooses to express this mistaken identity within what you now call a world of physical being. Dear One, how do you choose to restrict yourself? Why? Be honest. Where do you see your mind going when you inquire? Where do you see your mind defending and defining yourself?

It is this fear and this fear alone that you need to release. This fear stems from your belief in not being as God Created You, which simply is from your acceptance of the void. This void (and you keep thinking "voice" for a reason) was made by the mind in the decision to play. The void speaks in a voice, heard and repeated by the wayward thoughts of your mind. There is no judgment here, for yours is a conscious decision to play within the freedom that God extended to you. As we pay more attention to this, we can appreciate and let this wish go.

The only restriction that you needed to accept for your play was to place knowledge apart from your mind, for how else could there be anything to pretend. Therefore, you willingly covered your eyes, counted to ten, and in an instant, you were transported to a world of imagining. This was for nothing more than an instant, whereupon you recognized this play was meaningless. Do not feel you can be stuck forever. You are already free. We are only working together here and now so that you may remember this freedom.

The lessons I guide you through are imperative. They make or break you of the wayward patterns of your thinking. You are recognizing the meaninglessness of the play you have agreed upon. You are calling back into your mind the fact of your willingness to place knowledge aside in nothing but play alone. In fact, that is all you desired in that instant, to play alone. This is why I guided you to the etymology of *purpose*. The word literally means "to put forth and design." The mind in play chose to design a world and put itself forth within it. It was an extension of your perfectly free mind to express, as it desired. It was a purposeful making of what it desired to experience. Therefore, seemingly, here you are. There is no guilt here, as it was a simple choice as part of your own intention within your own recognized freedom. As part of your recognized freedom, you chose to forget this very freedom. Therefore the original sin is really nothing but a mere mistake, long forgotten in the mind of a God who knows your Truth. Again, I say, the game you chose to play never would have worked otherwise. And so you have forgotten your true knowing and the fantasy has worked!

Now, if you desire to recognize once again how you chose to forget, all you need do is remember. To re-member is to join again. This joining may be in thought, as the remembrances of your mind, but essentially the joining you are recognizing is the joining with the reality beyond the forget*fulness*. I choose to use that word specifically because I intend to help you recognize that even as you forget, you cannot be without *fullness*. The next time you align with fear or limitation on any level, simply remind yourself that you are merely forget-*full* and focus once again on the memory of fullness deeply within you. Breathe and align yourself with the fullness that has never left. Align yourself with the fullness that you simply placed at the back of the mind for a mere temporary experience in playfulness. Again, as you play, fullness too has never left you.

Design: 1548, from L. *designare* "mark out, devise," from *de-* "out" + *signare* "to mark," from *signum* "a mark, sign." Many modern uses of *design* are metaphoric extensions.

The physical world is a metaphoric extension of the reality you once knew completely. You have designed it as such to express the limitation you chose to play out. Even as you design, you mark out the meaning of which you desire to put forth. You design in purpose. This is your memory of how God Creates. The only difference is the Father extends Love in Perfect Freedom, but you simply chose to forget it through temporary experience.

This entire purpose is the belief that you choose to make it.

Never was there any intention for guilt here. Guilt was a result of the judgmental voice that filled the void through your forgetfulness. Forgetfulness was never meant as an actual condemnation, for in truth there is nothing to condemn. Even you know in truth that you are playing. Rest in this knowledge, and rejoice in your freedom.

As you recognize the meaninglessness that your mind extends through its designs, forgive. Simply breathe, forgive, release and rest, as I will guide you through these imaginings like a passing breeze. Never is there a need for you to blow over or collapse in the process of recognition. Truly, this serves no purpose, other than to languish in a guilt that never was intended to be. Again, I say, guilt is a designation of the limited mind. You use the mindset of guilt simply to wallow in all beliefs of limitation and mistaken identity, perceiving yourself apart from God. Dear One, THIS IS NOT TRUE. You are not as you designate in your loneliness. Awaken and embrace the Truth of Love that has never left you. Be fully filled NOW.

You may need to breathe here. In fact, I ask you to take a moment to do so and allow this Truth to sink you into stillness. Repeat within your mind, "*I am as God Created*" and be still. Rest in God, Dear One. Rest in God. You are Fully Filled with the only meaning that could ever be. Truly, this meaning is LOVE. Yet, in Truth, love has no meaning for it simply is. Here all defining ceases. Here, only peace reigns. Here, you step beyond all limitation ever playfully imagined by a mind in simple child-like curiosity. Within this awakening, you find the Self that never lost its fullness through forgetting. Be at one with this peace, and be at one with the Self that remains solidly fully filled in all the grandeur God extended Him Self out to be. This is changeless. I love you.

Week Seven: Prompts for Insight:

1. Purpose means "to place forth," what do you place forth within your life? How do your experiences originate from your perceived purpose?

2. Where do you project your purpose onto others? Where do you give away the power and strength that You are? Write all your thoughts of blame, powerlessness, and guilt. Ask for Spirit's guidance to release these projections and shine a Light of Truth.

3. God and all His Creation are unlimited. Where do you see limitlessness within?

4. The original meaning of the word "fulfillment" is "shared by all." Where do you seek to withhold only for yourself? Where do you choose to limit and isolate yourself within the world and your thoughts? How does this affect you?

5. If you could design the world or yourself over again, what would you create, knowing all you do now?

6. If your life experience was perfect it would contain: _____. How do these wishes for perfection affect your current experience? Identify where in your life, body or feelings these wishes show up. Are they ever seen as resentments or disappointments? Ask Spirit to lead you through the process of release.

Practice:

Spirit encourages us in this reading to seek to notice the moments where we substitute presumption, judgment or condemnation, instead of simply being. "See where you judge yourself and your brothers. See where you believe something different should have happened rather than what is truly happening. See where you believe you know what other people are thinking and why they do what they seem to do. See where you attempt to predict the future or mourn a fearful past, rather than simply live in the moment at hand. See all the areas where you resist or struggle with accepting Your Truth." Write any thoughts, feelings or experiences that arise in the practice of this mindful realization.

Affirmations

I am fully-filled in God.

God did not create a meaningless world.

My true purpose is Love.

I design the meaning of everything I see.

I am limitless.

Completion already knows it is all in all.

Week Eight: **True Gratitude**

As I've said before, the only problem you have is your mistaken identification of Who You Are as God Created. This one problem has led to numerous misrepresentations within your world and continued beliefs about separation, judgment, vulnerability, destruction, death, and the like. I say, "The wages of sin are death," because if you did not accept the one error that has you perceive yourself apart from God, you could neither accept nor have any perception of death. Death is always the end result of all perceptions of limitation and separation. Without these beliefs, no other identity could be valued or played out. Likewise, without sin or its corresponding beliefs, this other identity would not be limited to a temporal life resulting in death.

I would like to take a moment to use the American holiday of Thanksgiving as an example for your learning. According to tradition, it is a holiday (which can be interpreted as "holy day") set aside for all Americans to express gratitude. Ritually, you give thanks for the seeming blessings you believe God has graciously bestowed upon you and those you love. Essentially, this holiday honors those blessings and freedoms perceived and considered within the world to be "good" (requiring your appreciation to validate their value) in comparison to those seen as "bad." When you choose to celebrate in this sense, it is a celebration of duality, rather than an expression of true gratitude. I say this not to admonish your perception of gratitude, but to assist you in birthing a truer gratitude honoring all you are.

Everything you experience rests in gratitude. Everything here is your wish. Remember, I have said before, that you experience your self in this world only because you have chosen to forget. Since you have chosen to forget, you experience a myriad of ways to express this wish. Yes, even the experiences of war and pestilence are mere manifested experiences of this wish to not remember the truth of You. If you ask to stop war, seek first to remember all ideas that support war, long before it is played out on the battlefield. Do you seek to know your brothers as separate from you? Do you seek to experience good as compared to bad? Do you seek to see yourself as vulnerable or commanded by needs of a body or in competition for expressing a "better way" than your brother's way? All you see is then a manifested experience of this wish. You HAVE been given all you wish to see; therefore here you can be grateful. Peace is found when you notice this gratitude. The dream is likewise released when you simply choose to remember, release your wishes, and still be grateful.

In looking at the symbolic history of this holiday, we find it exists to honor the receipt of a New World. The inhabitants of this New World see themselves blessed for their freedom to receive despite struggle. Additionally, they celebrate in honor of having a new religious freedom. Surely we can see much symbolism within this story. There is a belief in sacrifice, suffering, entitlement, survival, punishment, banishment, loss, vulnerability, and separation, simply to name a few. Yet, these pilgrims celebrate blessings they have received and the freedom to simply be in the ways they seek.

Is this wrong? Absolutely not; but it is based on a dualistic principle of happiness, which should be noticed for learning purposes. Everything is for recognition of a more loving and peaceful way, for that is my only witness to your seeming journey. In the traditional story of Thanksgiving, happiness is found from surviving a wrathful God and xenophobic followers, rather than from the recognition of a loving certainty and changeless freedom extended to all. The God of the pilgrims did not desire their perfect happiness. The God of the pilgrims expressed a variable nature where requirement and sacrifice were exchanged for blessings.

The mistaken identity's thought system celebrates its own world and its ability to survive despite many dangers. Within your mind it lives to fear the effects it has made out of guilt and misperception of self. Likewise, it projects this fear upon seeming others who can then hurt, kill, destroy or steal "freedom" at any moment (and if you recall, these pilgrims were escaping the wrath of the church). Essentially this story is about freedom not being free. It is a story telling of a limited brand of gratitude, where everything has strings attached and is honored and celebrated only in comparison to death. Do you see the insanity of such gratitude, for rarely in this do you truly feel grateful.

If you research the word *gratitude* itself, you shall find that it is rooted from the words meaning "freedom" and "grace." To the mistaken identity, freedom is not free, therefore thanks is not given from grace, but solely from being able to survive. Additionally, to the mistaken identity, freedom is dependent upon sacrifice, luck or elitist blessing, rather than an inheritance as God's Beloved Creation. To the mistaken identity, freedom or blessing is temporary, it always has strings attached and is rooted in God's variable nature, which could never be questioned nor understood. Dear One, this is nothing to celebrate. If you feel you must be thankful as a requirement of God, surely you are mistaken, for requiring is not a trait of God, but gratitude surely is.

True Gratitude results when you accept the only peace ever bestowed. True Gratitude is the acceptance of the one Truth of being as God created you. True Gratitude is grace and freedom endlessly extended with no restrictions or dependence. It is the bestowing of this memory upon your brothers, in glory of their own remembrance. Truly, this is not of requirement, yet of full extension and appreciation for the changeless glory that you are. God gives His Son everything as He asks, knowing that in His Extension, Love is known. Therefore, yes, Love is known even in your most horrifying experiences. I know this may be difficult for your mind to accept conceptually, but do accept this: every moment you are cared for, and for this you can be grateful.

Do you desire to seek celebration on this Holy Day? Do not use this time to be thankful despite all other seeming perceptions, for that would only be a celebration of grief in disguise. Use this moment instead to remember that truly there are no other possibilities, and you still remain as God Created. Bestow this acceptance of Truth on every Brother in memory of what you are and will always be. Use this moment to remember with Love's Clear Vision. Seek the peace, joy, and perfection that are yours and have never changed. Remind yourself of this Truth while you are gathered with your family. Remind yourself that your family extends beyond the reaches of any table and that every face is a reminder of your completion as One.

Wow . . . I think I'll need to have a few more drumsticks . . . (giggle)

Yes, to serve the family of Holiness, you would have to go beyond all limitations, for there are none. To honor your family in Truth is your very saving grace. For it is here that you recognize the one seeming problem has been solved, and all remain in peace. As you recall the Truth, connection through the eyes of others, see the many faces of the One Truth. Love your Brother, for He is as God created him. Use every moment to remind yourself of this Truth and to remind yourself of your Holiness. A day dedicated to this practice could be nothing but a Holy Day, and here your celebration could be no greater.

A day of True Gratitude is a day of remembrance and extension. Here you stand as a witness to the One glory. Here gratitude becomes your natural purpose. In Truth, gratitude is never based on requirement nor is it limited. Never is it separated out as a task of dependence or self-validation. Gratitude is, because God is. God has given all that He knows of Himself, and He is Grateful (meaning He extends his Grace freely) to You. God's Son is free to dream all that he desires, and nothing can take that away. True freedom does not operate within a dualistic nature. True freedom expresses openly. It only gives and loves all without restriction or dependency. You can refer to this true freedom as an echo of God's knowing. He knows no other possibility than the Love that has formed through grace. God knows nothing else.

In your time, you may come to learn how all things are connected at an energetic level. At a centralized level, this energy will be seen to express itself with all the same properties of thought. I know you don't want to get too scientific, but I bring this up because in your celebration of thankfulness, it could be helpful to remember how all effect (and form) is nothing but thought at an extended or magnified level. As you dedicate time to discover the properties of all form, notice how these properties are nothing except what you have discovered about yourself. Use your mind in dedication of this discovery, and true perception shall naturally follow.

To be Truly Grateful is to remember that there is nothing True that demands requirement and validation. Truth does not see through the eyes of comparison. It cannot be destroyed. Be in remembrance of Who You Are as God Created You and remove yourself from all ideas of sacrifice, loss or vulnerability. See the true gratitude that remains.

You have all in perfect abundance, and nothing can take that away. The Truth is always there, it has gone nowhere, and you have remained as God created you in every seeming moment. Accept this Truth for yourself and extend True Gratitude for all you are. Call this a celebration of what is. Celebrate your desires as you notice them and extend love for all being possible. In this celebration, gratitude becomes the fullness of what you remember, rather than the need for perceived thanks to out-maneuver dependence and deficiency. God does not require your ritualistic thanks in order to feel fulfilled. God simply extends in His knowing of all that is. Your conscious gratefulness is merely a reminder of all you have accepted and allowed. This is why it is said that to give is to acknowledge receipt, for what could be extended that is not already known?

One could say that if you are grateful, you are recognizing you have received and now accept all these gifts from God. This reminder can be helpful, for to be grateful in this manner is to call conscious attention to Truth. Here you call attention to all that is your own through the very act of extension. This gratitude is an echo of a song of Love. Likewise, you awaken to all your desires and in gratitude accept peace beyond all surface impressions.

See this moment of gratitude, and see your Self dancing in the light of your own radiance. Likewise you may choose to extend this joy to all you see, witnessing for them the only truth that has always been. Accept this, Dear One, and you accept your Self in Truth, no matter how many sets of eyes you fall upon. There remains only One, and that One accepts its love in gratefulness for all it is always. In confidence you stand strong in your acceptance, graceful in your reflection, and joyous in your Truth. Here you are truly thanking FULLY. This is the way, the truth and the life. I am with you always.

Wait . . . okay . . . I think that I got it. Or, more likely, I feel that I got it. (Smile)

Well then, I yield the floor to you.

Okay, here we go. True Gratefulness is graceful freedom. In my gratitude I accept in grace and freedom all appearances without judgment. I realize all are blessed as a brilliant component of Unified Being. This blessing also includes all things, accepting that all is in answer to my initial wish for free expression. There are no requirements or definitions that restrict gratitude. There are no needs in Truth. There is only complete and full expression.

If I am to be Truly Grateful, then I am to yield to this ever-present flow in all. This is wholly living as God created Me, nothing else. Likewise, I will easily forgive. In fact all I offer is forgiveness, seeing how this is the same as accepting the miracle and affirming how no restriction can delay grace. This is expressed more through a feeling or being, rather than thinking or acting experience. True Gratefulness is expressed in the realms of knowledge. It simply IS, rather than defined or described. True Gratefulness is the awareness that God only gives me gifts no matter what may appear to my mind! When I fully extend and express this gratefulness to my Brothers, I only see the fullness of Truth in them.

In acceptance of Truth, we remember the Grace that Created all, which can also be described as gentle Holiness, which lives and breathes beyond words. This Holiness is our very Being. God does not require a "thank you," nor will He smite us for not recognizing Him. His Creation is so free and clearly seeing that it is not dependent on anything! I say thank you only so I can remember and gratefully accept all that I am! So one could say that gratitude is the very expression of Creation extending!!! It is the very Being of God!!!! Wow, wow, WOW!!! How's that???

Perfect. I could not have said it better my Self.

Week Eight: Prompts for Insight

1. Write on the thought "the only problem you have is your belief in who You are not."

2. Spirit guides, "Everything within the world is your wish." Write a list describing both frustrating and peaceful experiences you had within the week. Think of as many as you can. Who are some people you spoke to? What made you smile or laugh? Who seemed to get on your nerves? Did you get stuck in traffic? Did you feel invalidated or overlooked or under appreciated? Did someone really push your buttons? Attempt not to specifically withhold any particular event from your list, but do not over analyze. Especially, include all the ones that felt uncomfortable, confusing, stressful, or challenging. Consider how you have wished for each one. Write your thoughts and feelings surrounding this idea.

3. Gratitude is graceful freedom. Where do you see yourself as free? Where do you see yourself within the Grace of God?

4. Make a list of all areas that you withhold gratitude from yourself and others. Within your mind see yourself giving these withholdings to Spirit. Write on your experiences.

5. Quiet your mind and listen within. Ask for Spirit to lead you to recognition of True Gratitude and how to apply this graceful freedom to your life experience.

Practice:
Be mindful of all the opportunities you have to say "Thank You" both verbally and nonverbally. Practice these daily. Aim for saying "thank you" a minimum of 25 times during each day. Say thank you to people in stores or check-out lines. Say thank you to your boss, clients and co-workers. Say thank you to your neighbor. Say thank you to the postal worker. Say thank you to your spouse, friends, and all loved ones. Say thank you to all who smile or catch your eye. Say thank you to each person that rouses a judgment within you. Say thank you to your pets. Thank yourself as you look in the mirror. Be creative and mindful. Especially notice if you desire to leave someone out of your circle of thanks. Continue with your practice of thanks all through the week.

Affirmations:
    Everything I experience rests in gratitude
    I and all my Brothers are invulnerable.
    I see myself dancing in the Light of my own radiance.
    I am as God Created Me.

Week Nine: **Limitlessness and Illusions**

Help me understand limitlessness as my truth in comparison to the acceptance of illusion. Thank you.

The only mindset that affects your acceptance is judgment. To accept limitation is to judge that you are not as God created you. It is to believe that you are vulnerable and the world is your master. To be limited is to feel you are not able to have or be anything beyond your individual self. All ideas of limitation are rooted in fear and mistaken identity.

When you see yourself as limited you do not see truth at all. You perceive yourself as lost within the false images and judgments. But remember, truly, you can NEVER be lost. You may appear to be lost to yourself, but God (and I) always knows exactly who You are as Created. Truth-seeking is simply only the awakening to and acceptance of this changeless fact.

With focused silence or stilling of the thinking mind, you are able to begin to perceive truth. Yet as long as you align with beliefs of limitation, opening and inviting these thoughts, you let these beliefs be your guide.

There is no purposeful reason for you to experience feelings that keep you wanting, isolated, and/or afraid. As long as you believe yourself to be a mere victim of the world, you react defensively, convinced there is no possibility of happiness. In this thinking, a feeling of aloneness settles in. Aloneness is the ultimate belief in separation. As you perceive aloneness, every peaceful thought and comfort is exchanged for a darker idealization of your self. In this darker idealization, you conjure many witnesses to support this substitute truth. This is called pain.

Originally, the word pain referred to punishment. This is literally what the word symbolizes. Recognize the true meaning of pain and you will see how it represents all the isolation from God you are perceive yourself to be guiltily responsible for. The belief in guilt could not but lead to a justification for self-imposed punishment. Consequently this wish for deserved penalty is experienced through temporal pain.

However, hear me well, the experience of pain is not always a choice consciously conceived and experienced. Therefore, do not blame yourself or another for its experience. To do this would be nothing but foolish judgment either against yourself or Your Self. Truly, I have said before, that sickness and pain could not exist without a unified investment in distortion. This means that it is not merely the individualized mind that chooses its condition, but the entirety of the mistaken identity. Therefore, if you see your Holy Companion as sick, the judgment of him or her resides equally within every conscious mind, including your own. The debt you hold against him or her is to see them not as God Created. See within the constraints of the body and you see your debt. Do not make pain or sickness an individual experience, it is not. All beliefs in separation are a belief for the whole mistaken identity. Surely you may invest in the individual experience of pain or sickness, thus declaring your agreement with this limitation. However, your beliefs in guilt and separation reside far beneath the surface constructs of your personality or thinking mind.

Yes, all pain does represent the conscious and/or subconscious belief in being limited, dependent and apart from God's Love. Without this investment in self-identification there could be no body. Therefore, each experience of bodily pain (or any bodily attachment) is merely the remembrance of your perceived separation and forgotten self. If you were to choose a remembrance of wholeness, breathing – releasing — resting, and coming to see yourself disconnected from the pain, surely with focused being the agony would miraculously cease. Remember a miracle is simply a healed perception. Likewise, all miraculous healing is the acceptance of Truth despite all limits of the mind.

However, as this dream of pain is permitted to exist, it is in its grasp you stay. Pain is solidly determined to live only as a mere shadow of Who You Really Are. Pain's shadows only project darkness forward. To see your Self as limitless is to see none of these shadows of pain as being true. See yourself as limitless and claim, once again, your truth as God created You. Join in truth, beyond pain, and see not with the body's eyes, nor with the mind's perceptions, but with the Spirit's essence. Here, love becomes your accepted understanding, and this becomes expressed in all manner of your experience.

To say you are as God created You is to say you are free no matter what the world presents. To say you are as God created You is to say you are pure, for God Himself is pure love. To say you are as God created You is to say you are endlessly able, for God is the true Source of power and bestows only this to His Son. Joy shall be to every mind that sees the Self as God-created. Although merely considering these truths is not your permanent Being, it shall be the door to your acceptance of true joy and awakening. Here you welcome the idea that you are limitless, as compared to every former idea of illusion made possible.

The next time you notice that you are feeling limited, I ask you to simply question the thought by inquiring, "What is this that I believe overpowers me?" Settle your mind on that which you perceive. Seek out the content of the thought rather than suffering or surrendering to its effects. Reconsider your false identity, rather than settle within it. Sure enough there will appear to be discomfort here, for the mind does not accept inquiry well (especially after being invested in falseness for lifetimes).

This is why a significant process within the awakening is the recognition of not knowing. In realizing that you do not know, the mind is able to release itself from its perceptions, mistaken identity, and former judgments. You may not be able to understand limitlessness, but truly an understanding is not the final goal. As you find yourself seeking only concepts, remind yourself that pure truth cannot be contained within a thought system. Sink instead into acceptance of stillness rather than the seeking of concepts, for here you become willing to discover peace. You can learn to release all thoughts that you once used to define yourself. Forgive yourself for accepting that which is not true! Recognize that you and your brother have done nothing, only your perceptions claim otherwise and they are mistaken. You have projected your mistaken identity onto the face and actions of your brother. Without this projection, no guilt could ever have been found, nor sin seen. Forgiveness is the process of reawakening to the only truth that is. It is the opening of the eyes of fullness rather than clinging to the mind of incompletion.

To define is to isolate or separate off into a limited understanding. That is why the very act of attempting to define yourself is error. This can only lead you to see yourself through images and not your True Self. To say you are as God created you reclaims wholeness and this wholeness then absorbs any preconceived concept or definition, setting you free.

Holy Spirit, I've noticed in your promptings to research the origins of the word *definition* that its components literally mean "of limitation." WOW!! So does this mean that whenever I attempt to define myself, I engage in the act of limiting myself? I also see that the word *definition* means "impermanence."

Yes, exactly. You are beyond all definitions, for you are infinite. You are eternal. Therefore, any limitation you place on yourself presents a pretend idea of vulnerability. Your entire universe was made from ideas of impermanence. This belief is symbolically played out through ideas of death and destruction as well as separation, body identification, and time.

Therefore to be in definition is to be unknowing of your True Self. Any definition is not knowing your True Self. Place not within words (and worlds) that which is expressed purely only in Truth. The only whole, or pure, experience that you could have within this world is stillness, yet even this is not complete. The mind cannot have wholeness and definition in the same moment.

Similarly, you cannot be happy and sad or angry and peaceful in unison. Every definition and identity you hold must be questioned and set free. All ideas of yourself must be released in order for true knowing to be welcomed. Serving two masters is an attempt to have both limitlessness and illusions. It is proverbially having your cake and eating it too.

Seek not to exchange God's Glory for shadows. All shadows

must be placed aside for wholeness to be known. As you desire to know yourself, recognize where you have placed yourself asunder. See where only stillness of your thoughts will permit you to discover the one viable witness to your Self here and now. This witness is Me.

Stillness opens the door to knowing yourself through my witness. I am not mainly speaking about stillness of the body, truly the body is inconsequential. However, seeing beyond the mere thoughts of the mind will assist you in the awareness. Therefore, the stillness for which I speak is mainly expressed within the mind. Stillness is most representative of your true nature, for in it you are aware of your Self as God created You. In stillness, you silence the mind that seeks definition and focus beyond distraction. Here you release and surrender wholly to God beyond all limitation, beyond all time, space and seemingly separate identity.

The most significant mistake that has been made in seeing is to believe that to be, you have to be something. This being of something is most often seen in comparison to other "things." Therefore it stands to reason (from the split mind) that if you were to be something, there would also have to be something else in order to comprehend what you are. This is dualistic seeing in a nutshell.

The forgetful mind contains itself in perception. It hesitates, limiting itself to beliefs of never being good or worthy enough to know God. Rather you are whole and complete now; worthy not just to know God, but to embrace Him. Define yourself no more by your fears. Wait no more, for all You are dares not be delayed in Truth. Hear Me well, there is nothing greater than to be your Self as God created you, and this you already are. This has been changeless since inception.

Whoa. Wait a second there. You said "since inception." I have to ask, does this mean that time exists?

I speak in terms of time because that is where your understanding currently appears. I use symbols to assist your acceptance. If I were to be wholly in truth, words could not be used at all, for symbols serve no purpose in Heaven. All is without any limit, definition or description. This is known. Consider this conversation a playing out, so to speak, of a translation process between true perception and knowing. As long as you perceive yourself in time, you can hear Me with your words. Here we are using symbols to release ourselves from our dependency on symbols.

That is why a translation is helpful. Limitlessness is your True State of Being. This is incomparable to anything the mind sees now. As you begin to accept your Self more deeply, I am introducing ideas of eternity and how you are in Truth. Now all I ask is that you listen, not as a thinking or questioning mind, but as an allowing one. Be still now. Churning your thinking mind with concepts will not set you free.

Your Truth has always been and will always be. Embrace yourself as you are now, and release all bonds of time and limitation. Your Father hinders no one. So, yes, now is the only moment to get out of your own way. Use time for this purpose and put one of your greatest misperceptions to healing use. If you desire to see through the eyes of time, apply it for expansion rather than your limitation. Communicate [which, by the way, means "to express or share in wholeness"] with those you may have once seen as others. Be a witness to your Self as a loving being, rather than, a limited being. Again, I say, You ARE as God created you, and to express this is simply to become the way, the truth, and the life.

My Light is Your Own . . .

Week Nine: Prompts for Insight

1. Where do you invite and open up to thoughts of limitation? Write down as many ideas as you can conceive. Explore these thoughts of limitation with Holy Spirit, asking Him to guide you beyond them.

2. "The only mindset that affects your acceptance is judgment." Explore within where and how you judge the most. How do these judgments affect relationships and experiences?

3. In what ways have you considered the world to be the master of your future? In what ways do you feel master of your own world? How do you practice this awareness?

4. In what ways do you give Spirit's guidance mastery over you?

5. Where do you attempt to serve two masters or seek out a compromise between limitlessness and illusion? Seek within for how you choose to build your house on sand. Ask Spirit to lead you through the construction of a more fortified foundation.

6. What do you believe overpowers you? Make a list and explore for further insights with Spirit.

Practice:

Recollect moments where you have seen yourself as lost. Imagine placing all of these moments into a box for delivery to Holy Spirit. See Him accept, sign for, and begin to open the package. Now, instead of shadows, a brilliant light pours forth. Miraculously, the very intention of giving these thoughts to Spirit, has transformed them into a most glorious gift. This is the gift of healing. This is a gift welcoming surrender, faith and trust into your heart. Truly, without giving yourself this gift, you could not affirm the Truth of You. Be willing to accept this affirmation now. Breathe in its Self realization. Allow yourself to rest in its peace. Write your thoughts and feelings resulting from this imagery.

Affirmations:

I am as God Created Me.
I am never lost.
I am unlimited in all ways.
I see with the eyes of Love.
I am not my fears.
God extends through Me, now.

Week Ten: **Attack on God**

I trust in God.

> Do you say this to remind yourself, Dear One?

Yes, I think I do. Today appears to be one of "those days" where I feel conflicted and frustrated. Today's feelings are not as intense as other days when I felt myself to be at the end of my rope. No, today's feelings consist of only a mere yearning to remember despite the outer condition. Maybe this is a sign of respite. Maybe this improvement is because I have permitted peace to settle in more; I do not know. But, fear still appears to be available in my sight, as well as beliefs in rejection. It doesn't feel perfect yet. I feel far from perfect. I still have several questions that churn within my thinking mind. I feel like I have multiple choices. On one hand I could pay attention to the resistance and questions. However, if I were to do this, I feel like I would be consumed and defined by them. I don't want that result. Therefore, on the other hand, I see You as being someone Whom I can give this frustration to. I guess, the truth is, overall, that I would rather have peace than this, and so here I am.

> Settle your mind, Dear One... breathe. I appreciate your willingness to join with me despite the shadows and inconsistencies of your thinking mind. This desire is to be celebrated. Indeed, I am always and in all ways here for you, my Beloved. Therefore, release your frustrations to Me. As you surrender to peace, I accept each perception of frustration and shine the light of Truth upon it. Here, in the miracle, you accept the gift of Self realization. Here, we rest in peace.
>
> Perfection has no measure. It is the release of all measures. As long as you measure yourself through an ideal of spiritual perfection in form you are not accepting Perfection as God Created. It is essential to be gentle with your self. It is helpful that you are able to observe when you have these thoughts and feelings. You may not see the original idea from within which

makes every experience. Yet, give yourself breathing room and peace will begin to arise as you are able to notice and observe the thoughts behind the feelings.

Yes, I do notice the thoughts, although I often first notice the feelings.

Dear One, there is no right or wrong way to do this process. You cannot change the changeless. You are not actually changing your Self here, only accepting your Self. If you place a judgment on your process you only hinder your peace. Notice that tension in your chest now? This is a feeling of fear coming up for release. Allow it to come to the surface. Do not block or judge it, for this will keep it within. See the thought for what it is. See your belief and the feelings that then arise. Allow yourself to release these feelings. Accept that they are perfect for your current beliefs.

Okay... well, I feel angry and disappointed. I feel rejected and disillusioned. I feel that others do "crappy" things to people and excuse their behavior. I feel that separation continues to get played out in this world and no amount of forgiveness will make it go away!!! Oh, and I also feel like spiritual practice is a "load of crap" sometimes, because people don't change. Some so-called "spiritual teachers" use spirituality as a way to project their judgments onto others!

There you are. Great! Feeling better?? Sit now and breathe for a moment. Then re-read the sentences you just wrote. Look at all those thoughts. Accept them. Do not belittle or judge yourself for having them. Instead, give yourself permission to feel these thoughts. Allow each thought to run its course through you. Then, close your eyes, wait a few moments, breathe again, wait for the feelings to become lighter. This may take a few moments. When you feel your body more calm and your mind's thoughts releasing through the breath, seek out the willingness to make a clearer observation. Breathe again. Now, I would like you to go back to your statements. Now, objectively read your statement and see all the judgments. See the assumptions and beliefs in separation.

Observe where there is an "us or them" and "victim or victimizer" mentality. Ask yourself, "What brings peace in these beliefs?"

Okay... yes... I see. There is no peace there. There is no love there. It is only a mind believing that separation is possible and defense is necessary.

Disappointment is only possible when you feel that guilt and vulnerability are real. Disillusionment requires the making of illusion. Separation requires an identity apart from God.

Defensiveness requires a belief that attack and vulnerability are not only possible but necessary. An "amount of forgiveness" would require you to not truly forgive. In your surface forgiveness you make yourself dependent upon this seeming other's behavior to change. Therefore you still define yourself through them and feel more powerless than ever. You cannot expect peace from a brother as long as you refuse to give yourself peace. You cannot find freedom as long as you perceive yourself to be controlled and dependent upon others to make or break your peace and self-worth. And how can you recognize a gift from your brother when you feel unworthy to accept such a gift?

When you notice these beliefs, remind yourself that you still are as God created you and nothing else. Do not feel that this is something that you must accept, only allow yourself to hear the Truth. Be gentle and breathe. Take in all that you are feeling, without rejection of yourself or any other. Only allow yourself to be. In doing such, peace will come, for you are opening yourself up to trust, rather than judgment. Mistaken identity occurs when you invest in false ideas about yourself, not by merely noticing them.

Therefore, do not think you can go wrong by noticing these thoughts. Honestly, as you notice, you bring the false to Truth. Noticing gives you the ability to choose again and set yourself free from any thought of powerlessness that may be present.

I recall *A Course in Miracles* stating how this world was made as an attack on God. If I invest in the world, or even placate my thoughts of

the world and its seeming disappointments, am I then attempting once
again to attack God?

You ask, this question only because you still see attack as real and
worthy of a punishment. You never truly did attack God; therefore,
there is no "once again." You have just turned an attack on your
brother to a judgment and attack on yourself. This assault will
serve you no purpose. Over and over again you can play out ideas
of all you "have done" or "could have done differently," but this
does not make these ideas reality. Likewise, they only make you
believe in the possibility of creating a better past. This of course is
impossible. Now and always, you still remain ONLY as God
created you. The past does not exist outside of the realms of your
mind. Truly, only YOU keep its dream alive.

Listen, you were completely innocent at the moment this dream
took hold and you remain completely innocent now. All ideas of
the past, present and future, only reflect your own beliefs in
powerlessness, for so much of time is seen as being out of your
control. You are not a victim of the world you see, nor can you save
yourself through mere concepts alone. Accepting Love and seeing
it within all is your only savior. Here you choose peace over
powerlessness. Here you rest in the arms of God and not time.
Again, I say, attack can only occur when a mind believes in
vulnerability. Guilt is seen as a consequence of judgment.
Judgment is seen as a consequence of attack. Attack requires you to
believe that not only are you vulnerable but that you have someone
else (apart from you) who can be attacked. God cannot be attacked.
God is not apart from You.

God knows only the purest Truth as Created. Notice what you
are thinking now and realize how it is only because you believe
that guilt and separation are possible. As long as you believe you
or your Brother can attack or make you disappointed or unhappy,
you believe you can be guilty or separate. To believe that God sees
this in You is mistaken identity to the highest degree.

As long as you believe you can be attacked, you believe also
that God can be attacked.

Whoa . . . wait a minute there . . . I don't want to attack God.

So why do you attempt to separate His Son from Him?? Any belief in attack is a belief in attack on God. If you choose to see that God's Son can be guilty, can be hurt, can be anything other than what God created him to be, you attack Him. Yes, this attack on your Brother is likewise an attack on your Self, just as much as it is an attack on God. You are ONE. What you do to the least of me, you do to Me. Yet, here is your saving grace... this attack is only all within your mind. Truly, you are free and truly you can attack only nothing.

Remember, any thought outside of the One Will of Truth is denying that any Truth exists. Here you willingly accept only the false. And through your insistence of seeing with a little will, you thus accept the false; you accept death; for it is to die when you refuse to live as God created you. But truly this is impossible.

You cannot live apart from God, for God is as You are. You can do nothing to change this, ever, neither in dreams of delusion or concepts of reality. This is the perfection extended to you. Unchangeable means just that. In fullness You are, with nothing else in between. Nothing else. You have not created your Self. Therefore this guilty separated self you see is mere illusion and never reality. In fact it can never be reality. You are as God created you, and this is more magnificent than any other thought. This is Life truly.

You cannot truly live apart from God. It is impossible to make separation possible, which is why you are dreaming. Think of the metaphor of Snow White. Not but ONE bite from the poison apple put innocence into a deep sleep, waiting only to be awakened by the embrace of True Love. This True Love is before you right now. There is nothing left to do but awaken to it through your own acceptance of being nothing else. No one can attack you but yourself. God cannot be attacked outside of your mind. And this attack is only an attack on you through the first belief in guilt, vulnerability, and separation. It is impossible to accept this otherwise. Notice this. Look with unwavering eye upon what you believe you have made. See how this has affected your feelings about yourself, as well as your experience within this world. If you can call this peace, then surely you are insane. Do you want the Peace of God, or do you instead desire delusional grievances against a separate identity never truly known?

Not really a choice, is there?

Only a choice between delusion and reality, which could be truly seen as no choice at all, for Truth has no opposite. Remember, as A Course in Miracles so perfectly summarizes, "Nothing REAL can be threatened, nothing unreal exists, herein lies the Peace of God."

Wow . . . you really know how to call me on my stuff, don't you??

It is merely the loving answer to a desire to see Love. To say this world was made as an attack on God, does not mean that God sees it that way. God sees His Son only with Love and honor. The mind you think with sees attack as possible, which is why a belief in sin fell upon the Son immediately after the belief of seeming separation. Yet, in Truth, there was only freedom and peace. God does not mourn his Son. It is only His Son who appears to mourn him Self.

The mistaken identity believes it can attack and believes it has attacked. Remember attack is only possible when defense and vulnerability are deemed as possible. God has nothing to defend, for He is not vulnerable. God has lost nothing. God only continues to see wholeness in every way, for God knows there is nothing else. God is your strongest Witness to your Self, for He knows that nothing has ever changed, or ever could be changed. I am in remembrance of this Thought. I am as a Witness to the One Truth that has never changed.

Peace is His only Self. He has bestowed this eternal Peace unto you, but you do not realize its presence or value. You have made something else to distract you from this Truth, and so you dream a dream of nightmares and delusions. Just because you are distracted does not mean that this Truth ceases to exist. You remain as God created you. Nothing else is possible. To believe that you can and have attacked God is only to see that something has occurred different from Truth. The mind investing in its mistaken identity will do whatever it deems necessary to continue a belief in its vulnerability, for it sees itself as dependent upon the world it has made.

God only knows Truth and Freedom. This freedom He has given eternally to His Son. This world can be a blessing for your healing and not a curse. Within it you can see every mirror of your true freedom. God has given His Son the freedom to express and Loves Him endlessly. This is the blessing and why no curse could ever come upon you. Dear One, you are free beyond your imaginings. Embrace this Self and accept once again the only Truth that ever is. My Love witnesses to this Truth all ways and always.

My Light is Your Own . . .

Week Ten: Prompts for Insight:

1. Spirit teaches, *"No one can attack you but yourself. God cannot be attacked outside of your mind. And this attack is only an attack on you through the first belief in guilt, vulnerability, and separation."* Identify five moments in your life when you felt attacked. How have these experiences progressively affected you? What lasting judgments have you held against yourself or others? What thoughts or feelings of discouragement and victimization have lingered? How have these judgments affected new opportunities, achievements, and relationships in your life? What thoughts and feelings come to mind when you now learn that you can only attack yourself? Write each of these thoughts and ask Spirit for a clearer understanding.

Practice:

On a blank piece of paper, list your judgments. Write however many that now come floating to you consciousness. Let your mind run wild. Do not hold back. Allow yourself to think of all the people, places, situations and experiences where you judge. Use multiple pieces of paper if necessary. If feelings come forth during this exercise (tension, stress, anger, disappointment, etc.) take mental note of these feelings and where they resonate within your body. Accept these emotions and sensations. Make sure to breathe deep throughout the practice and keep an open mind. Allow all thoughts, feelings and sensations. Catch yourself even if you judge this exercise and yourself for how you do the exercise.

Next, after you have completed your list, place it aside and sit in peace for a moment. Breathe deeply. Continue to allow all residual feelings from the making of this list to flow through you. Notice all sensations within your body and yield to them, accepting that each is a perfect witness to all inner observations. If needed, express these feelings in a safe, nondestructive form. Punch or scream into a pillow, throw a soft object to the ground. Clench and release the muscle groups of your body. Do all that you feel is appropriate and necessary to allow the expression of these feelings safely.

Now, say aloud for each thought, *"I accept this thought and know I am free to think it."* Repeat the same for your emotions and sensations. Say, *"I accept I am loved through this feeling."* Continue to breathe as you notice and feel all sensations, thoughts and experiences.

Finally, when you feel all has appropriately cycled through you, rest your mind and ask Spirit for the willingness to see another way. Say aloud:

> *"I am invulnerable. I cannot attack myself, another or God in Truth, all are perfect, safe and free."*

Breathe deeply for a few more cycles, and return to your list of judgments for review. Be as objective of as possible, noticing where you choose separation, powerlessness or vulnerability. Using your insight journal, process these judgments with Spirit, asking for him to lead the way.

Affirmations:

I am safe. Attack lives only in my mind.

I am as God Created Me.

I trust in God.

I am accepting all with Love.

Week Eleven: **Littleness Versus Magnitude**

You are the Holiness of God.

Spirit, sometimes a sense of fear overtakes me when I attempt to imagine this as being true.

> You need not imagine, Dear One. This is the Truth. In your graciousness to accept this glory you offer gratitude to the Father and to your Self for all You Are. Here is the acceptance of holiness made aware.

Thank you Holy Spirit, but I seem to have a problem when I seek to offer gratitude to God. Part of me feels that I can't offer gratitude to God, because I don't identify a personality with God, nor do I have a clear concept of who God is relative to me. I ask myself, "To whom am I offering gratitude?" Not necessarily why or for what, but mainly to who? I think it was important that I recognize this resistance. It appears to be a significant block to peace for me. Mainly the block stems from a continued fear associated with the enormity of God compared to my small self. Second, it is difficult for me to conceive that personally I am important to God. Why would He care to hear my thankfulness?

I can recognize these uncertainties as beliefs in unworthiness. Yet even in my recognition and attempted forgiveness, I feel distanced from the gratitude I hope to offer. I thank you Holy Spirit for helping me recognize how even when my resistance seems strong, it cannot interfere with God's Love for me. Your assurances promise that all I need do is forgive myself beyond my fears, and all that is my Truth will be restored.

> Yes, you are correct, Dear One. It is only your fear that shades you from your acceptance of holiness. It is the only darkness that blinds you to the light of God. In Truth, nothing can block the light of God, for there is nothing that is more powerful than it. This is why I say "blinds," because to be blind in your world is to have a limit

on your abilities to see. In your world, blindness does not change the fact that what is not seen exists, but it does limit the perceiver from tangibly knowing the reality.

To say something could overpower the light of God would be to say that a creation by the Creator was more powerful than the Creator. This, of course is impossible. It is only your imaginary blindness, your blindness to the Truth about You that keeps you blocked. Your resistance witnesses to the illusions of the separated mind. It convinces you that you are unworthy and unable to offer the Creator the only gift that is yours to give. Surely this is not true.

Just because you are unable to align with certain words within your mind, or fully conceive the acceptance of the Truth of You, your gratitude is not vacant.

I have seen and heard you offer gratitude to Our Father in many ways. Do not dismiss these ways even if they cannot come to mind now. Thankfulness need not be accomplished through certain rituals and routines. Thankfulness is a vibration from your True Self towards your Creator. In fact it is all vibration in and around God. He knows your "heart," so to speak, and cannot see the illusions that you hold against yourself. God does know your gratitude. He adores His Creation. Your tiny beliefs in illusion cannot change what God knows eternally about You. He witnesses and accepts your joy. Yet, even if you cannot perceive this joy, do you not have true determination to return to full awareness? Is this not why we communicate now? Could you not call this longing for return to your Father gratitude? Would you not first need to recognize and accept God's Love as being possible before you can desire to align more fully with it?

Yes.

In deed Dear One. Fear has you construct walls in an attempt to keep yourself in deception. Yet God's Light streams through the walls and knows these walls are mere dream figures. Even if you attempt to quickly plaster over every crack, God is with you. Now is the time to loosen those bricks. And as you give direction to Me,

I shall do so. Fear keeps you from wanting to see Truth. It convinces you that Truth is impossible or that Truth is pain. It may even suggest Truth is fear. This is not true and only a reflection of your resistance.

Pain is not a component of Truth and never will be; that is why it is mainly felt within the limited body or mind. Pain wants to remind you of limitation and vulnerability. It can never speak for Truth. All that is Truth is pure and eternal. Truth knows you are invulnerable, safe, and unlimited. See not this with the eyes of the body, but with the acceptance of the Spirit. And as you do, pain will be no more. Again, do not resist pain. Do not judge or fight with it. This resistance only prolongs your discomfort. Instead, allow your mind to rest through the experience of all pain. Allow your own acceptance of the experience, rather than embattling yourself. Pain cannot persist without resistance. It will leave your reality by your choice to accept and rest. Truly, no emotional or physical pain can thrive when you choose to step beyond all ideas of vulnerability and limitation. Again, be gentle with yourself. Rest your intentions, judgments and expectations. Focus fully on rest and opening up to the glory of your True Self. In this rest you choose to see Truth over illusion. Although this practice may appear to take time to master, do not judge yourself by the time. Do not ask, "When? When?" or judge your progress. This anticipation is resistance. Release all ideas of limitation and direct your mind to only the present experience of rest. Here peace is your own Self and cannot be overtaken by deception.

Wow, thank you. I will remember this the next time I feel pain or separation.

Even if you choose to remember then, I ask you to seek acceptance now.

It looks like you are asking me to choose between the world and God.

I ask you only to choose between Reality and illusion, fear and Love, your Self as God created you or some deluded belief that has you entrapped in pain.

That seems like an easy enough choice.

But it is a choice that you have been refusing to make since the beginning of time. Unceasingly you hear the voice of fear speak its lullaby. You listen and become entranced by the dance of lies. You have allowed yourself to sleep from its melody and dream only nightmares from its whispers. Therefore, when I ask you to choose between the world and God, it is only a choice to awaken you to the only Reality there is. Surely no choice really exists, because that would be equating the lies of fear with Truth. Yet if you see that you have another way to see, outside of the present distortion of your mind, you begin to turn towards the Light that has been beckoning for you always.

I felt urged to go into the Bible and review a selection of the Psalms of David. Beginning with 21, I read each one up through 25. Noticing the significant change in tone and fervor through these psalms, I was touched by the obvious progression of David's own acceptance of Truth.

I asked you to begin at Psalm 21 because that is the psalm of the mistaken identity. It presents the story of misplaced fervor through beliefs in a God of wrath. David scribed this psalm before choosing to give over his will to God. He saw through the eyes of separation and likened that to God. He invested in enemies and war with his Brothers. But by the next psalm the enemies appear to turn on him completely. He has no friends and writes of fearing his own suffering and destruction. Even though it is a psalm to God, it begs for the survival of the personalized self.

David is having a difficult time in accepting his own divinity. He struggles with himself and sees this struggle through the eyes of rejection from the world. In Psalm 23, David gives his will to

God and rests (if only for a moment) in the graciousness and
gratefulness of his love of God. Surely this was finally a moment of
peace for him. He accepts his divinity and loves the Lord for all
He has to give.

As I said, it only takes a moment of gratitude to reacquaint you
with truth. A moment of forgiveness is magnanimous within the
realms of Spirit, for it finally allows you to open the door that has
been secured tightly for too long.

Notice the progression through the psalms? Notice how David
went from cries of fear and self-destruction to acceptance of peace.
This journey is important for you to acknowledge because it is the
journey of you. Before you invested in fear, now you find yourself
beginning to trust. Now you embrace hope, where before you
embraced pain. Every journey of remembrance experiences these
hills and valleys. None are more True than another, but it is the
mind that uses them for its own learning and awakening.

Be not afraid of the journey, for in truth it does not exist. Yet use
each moment you encounter fear to lead you back to the light
within. Every moment you find yourself investing in the world,
remind yourself of how only love is real and guide your mind back
to truth. I am here with you as you do this. I am here assisting
you in your reclaiming of your light. I am here through your
remembrance, assisting you in your acceptance and always
witnessing to the pure truth that you are. For this has never
changed.

Wow . . . okay, so if I am to live truly I am to accept my magnitude and
the magnitude of all I encounter?

Yes, but you have no choice of whether or not to live Truly, you
only have the choice of whether or not to recognize it within this
moment. God created you in Truth and continues to witness to
your Truth through every perceived moment. I too join Him in this
Will. Yet, as you believe you journey, you often invite mere
reflections of littleness through your experience. What this means
is that you make your limitations, embrace them as yours, reflect

and seek to find them within the world. Then you once again accept them through the witnesses who return with the very same gifts of littleness you bestowed. Do you see the cycle?

Yes, I do. But how am I to embrace my magnitude when it appears that the world is only sustained in littleness?

Are you asking if it is acceptable to belittle yourself as God created you so that you may fit in within the world?

Well, when you put it that way . . . I guess not.

{Smile} Dear One, you are your magnitude in every moment. Nothing can change the fact of Who God Created You to Be. This will exist eternally. But if you desire to seek treasures within the world, so be it. Nevertheless, understand that as you do, you will only find the limitation that the world can witness. Nothing, no thing, can give you the equal magnitude of God within this world. To ask for such would be to ask for an illusion to mock the Truth. It would be as if you held a teddy bear up to a grizzly and expected it to be an equal comparison.

Yikes . . . I don't think that would work . . .

And neither will your attempted satisfaction with this world in comparison to God's True Creations. But you can choose as you wish for as long as you desire. Choices do not put you at risk. This is the freedom that God created for you. He keeps you safe, although you dream. If you desire anything within this world, at the very least, embrace it with all the wholeness that you can accept as yourself in this moment. That way you are transferring an idea of love into the moment, which will instill a happy dream. Share this happy dream with all of your brothers, and at the very least you gift them with a witnessing of the truth within them. See their magnitude and celebrate all you can see within this world. Embrace your brother with the truth you hold about yourself.

Praise his glory in all moments, and like Me, you hold the light for All. Although circumstantially you may appear to be experiencing a dream, live with all of your and your brother's glory in mind until you fully awaken. This can be done in many ways. You may offer peace, comfort, compassion, joy, laughter, honesty, support, love, hope, fulfillment, and/or forgiveness. All of these, although taking place within your world, witness to the echo of your True magnitude within the world of littleness. It is not a compromise, but an opening of the door to full acceptance. Offer peace to your brother and offer remembrance to yourself. I repeat, you ARE the Holiness of God. You are. Here in accepting your divinity you welcome the only Truth to accept.

Peace is yours from the moment you see your Truth. Peace reigns both within the stillness and in the graciousness you offer your brother. Here you welcome Holiness for yourself in all ways. I am glad to bring you these tidings, for they once again permit you to embrace the Light of Oneness. And honestly, Dear One, that is all I could ever ask to give. Heaven is not complete without you.

My Peace is always with you . . .

Week Eleven: Prompts for Insight and Practice:

Search within for where you feel unworthy in the presence of God. Where do you accept judgment, fear, guilt, or separation to be your guide? Is it really possible to feel unworthy to be your Self? How can this denial be justified as real, except in delusion? Our One Self is Created in the Holy Image of God, as a complete extension of God. It is impossible to be unworthy. We are as God IS and God is continuously willing for us to see and accept this One Truth. Take several moments today to remind yourself of this Truth. Upon rising every morning and retiring every evening say:

"I am a Holy Creation of God. I am worthy of this Image. Amen."

Process with Spirit all under*lying* ideas of unworthiness that arise during the week's activities.

Spirit says, *"Only your fear shades you from accepting your Holiness."* Make a list of your fears. In these fears, what false evidence or assumptions do you accept about yourself, others and the past, present or future in place of Holiness? 99% of all fears are based on assumptions extended outward ("what if" thinking). A "what if" thought wishes for what you do not want to happen. It gives you the trauma ahead of time, similar to paying a mortgage on a home you will never live within.

Use these steps to help you release these fears:

1. *Notice the fear.*

2. *Accept the fear.* Do not judge yourself for having these thoughts. Recognize that fear is normal for your current perception, but can be released.

3. *Yield without resistance to all its sensations within your thoughts, emotions and/or body sensations.* If you feel fear, safely allow yourself to

express it for a certain period of time. Recognize this fear experience to be a choice and not against your power.

4. *Finally, breathe and choose to release the thought by honoring your self in the moment.* Involve yourself in a peaceful activity, quiet your mind or engage in a fun activity. Use an affirmation or remember the moments where you truly felt magnificent. Remember that in order to believe in fear you must first believe in vulnerability. God has made no creations that are any less than perfect or eternal. Remember.

Affirmations:

I am my magnitude in every moment.
Pain is not the Truth.
My very being confirms my gratitude to God.
Fear only deceives, peace always relieves.

Week Twelve: **Failure Is Impossible**

Help me understand the feelings of failure I went through today. How do I stop it?

Dear One, failure is all within your mind. Only you can accept it and only you can make it possible. Failure is simply the fearing of all being lost. Remember that – Fearing All Is Lost Under Real Existence = failure. It completely depends upon time and a belief in personal constraints. Centrally it is rooted from your under*lying* beliefs of abandonment from God. Here you feel unworthy to be your Self as God Created.

Deep within your struggling mind you hold a memory of completion. Here you recognize that once you had complete peace and felt always comfortable. This is your memory of Heaven. It is this memory that has resulted in your willingness to communicate with Me. Yet, to the deceived part of your mind, this memory is a far off echo perceived only through confusion and lost within time. In this loss, it does not know what it is or from whence it came. Truly, anything that the mistaken identity does not understand, it looks upon with fear.

Now, let's look at time. Failure always measures itself against something. You see yourself as a failure because you are not who you think success is. Although it appears you are quantifying success, truly you only define it by time. You literally deny success because your current condition does not align with your presupposed perceptions. All that you see emanates from your perceptions. You cannot perceive yourself to be different from what you are unless you believed that different possibilities could be. Are not these mere possibilities only fantasies of your mind? Are they not mere arguments with your current condition? Truly, how productive is that? Your perception of failure stems from this confusion. Peace only accepts - it never resists. This is not because it denies. Peace accepts because it only sees acceptance of itself as Truth. Peace cannot even begin to align with fear or time, because it knows these things as being mere illusions. Here, in peace, it is happy. Here in peace it accepts fully. Therefore there is nowhere else to be than right now.

This means that fear must believe in both separation and resistance. In feelings of failure, you haplessly scurry within your mind attempting to find out why you don't feel at peace. In this scurrying, you refuse to relax or accept. You only cling to beliefs of things being different. Therefore peace becomes some far off idea apart from now. "I will be at peace if…" or "I will feel like a success when…" this is the mantra of dependency on time and resistance of now. Therefore, in this scurry, peace is never given the opportunity to come forth, for the mind is too busily consumed with ifs, ands and buts. Here the mind then agrees it must be lost, unworthy, or both. This is the feeling of failing, and it is not but wholly based on your confused ideas of self.

Hear Me now, you cannot fail. All failure is impossible, because you cannot change Truth as God Created. Does this mean that you can never feel like a failure? No. You can feel in accordance with all of your accepted beliefs and wishes, but surely they are nothing but mistaken ideas of yourself, and do not ever reflect Truth. Next time, when you fear failure as possible, notice your feelings and see the confusion within. See your desire to not live in the moment. Then, take a moment to breathe and remind yourself that you are simply fearing all is lost and nothing else. Recognize the presumptions you put forth in time, assuming a fearful future based on your current dissatisfaction. Notice the resistance to see what can be used and learned now. This is projection to the nth degree. Focus beyond your thoughts and fears. See beyond your investment and expectations in time. Accept the reminder of Truth deep within you *now*. Here, recognize how it is not the measuring or judgment that makes you whole, but the full acceptance of Wholeness simply is. Question or compare no more. You cannot be anything or anyone apart from Truth at any moment. God has never lost His Son. He knows you and embraces you in His Holy Home now. Rest in this certainty and rest in peace. I love you.

Week Twelve: Prompts for Insight:

1. Holy Spirit teaches, "*Failure is all within your mind. Only you can accept it and only you can make it possible.*" Where in your life have thoughts of failure (past, present, or future) affected you? How do you feel now that you have been told that these ideas are all within your mind? How do you seek to release yourself from these feelings? Take several moments this week to purposefully notice where you keep yourself in thoughts of limitation or loss. Process these observations with Spirit's guidance.

2. Holy Spirit teaches, "*When you feel like you have failed it is merely because you fear all is lost.*" Is it genuinely possible to be lost? Take a moment to observe the thoughts you perceive within and how you see yourself as lost from God's Love and protection. Afterwards, take a deep breath and consciously give these thoughts to Holy Spirit. Ask Him to lead you through to a deeper knowing.

3. What do you need to succeed? Is it True that the Holiness of God needs success, or needs anything? Take a moment now to notice your attachment to measuring or quantifying success. Observe where within your mistaken identity these beliefs are fed. Notice where you judge yourself or your life experiences because of these attachments. Process these thoughts with Holy Spirit.

4. What does it mean to be dependent? Notice where within your life experience you have acted or invested in ideas of dependency. Identify some fears you use as your "mantra for dependency." Process these fears with Spirit.

5. Holy Spirit teaches us, "*Peace accepts because it only sees acceptance of its Self as Truth.*" Where within your life are you able to fully accept your Self? Where do you extend complete acceptance towards others? Ask Holy Spirit to show you where your Peace always exists.

Practice: Storytelling Your Future.
Write a story of exactly how you would like to see yourself and life experiences ten years from today. Describe fully all the characters, scenes, and plots. Be conscious about all you see yourself seeing, doing, and feeling. How will you be (physically, emotionally, and spiritually)? Where will you be? What will be most important to you? Visualize this as the perfect story of your dream life. After you finish your story, say a prayer and give this script in mind to Spirit. As Creators we are creating as One. If this is perfect happiness for you, trust that God only desires this and more for you. Never mind how it is going to happen, but use this exercise to unearth the trust and awareness of perfection God promises to you in every moment. He will lead the way as our inheritance from Him is greater than our imagination.

Affirmations:
All that I see emanates from my perceptions.
I am as God Created Me.
Peace accepts, it never resists.
Failure is impossible.
I cannot change the Truth as God Created.

Week Thirteen: **The 23rd Psalm**

The week before this conversation took place, I was filled with intense moments of sadness, challenge, and judgment. Personally, I felt like I was nearing the end of my rope of tolerance. Although, I tried to clear these feelings up with my usual ice cream binges and coping mechanisms, nothing appeared to be working. Saturday evening passed with me crying once again and praying fervently to Spirit to help me see another way. Sure enough, I awoke on Sunday morning with phrases of the 23rd Psalm in my mind. Particularly, the phrase "though I walk through the valley of the shadow of death, I fear no evil" kept repeating in my mind. Now, I have to admit, I am far from a Bible scholar. Case in point, I originally thought the above phrase was from "The Lord's Prayer." It wasn't until I researched the prayer online that I discovered that this phrase was actually from the 23rd Psalm. In preparation for the discussion with Spirit that follows below, I released all ideas and judgments about biblical text (It's a good thing that I didn't have many to begin with!) and truly let only the words flow from within as I received the commentary from Spirit. Now that this disclaimer is in place, enjoy the powerful teaching that Spirit gifted me with today.

"The Lord is my shepherd."

If you focus on the title of shepherd, you may equate a judgment that God sees you as an animal creation or that you are belittled in His presence. This is not true. You are not God's pet. This has been misunderstood in this prayer in the past. To be a shepherd is to guide, nurture, and provide wholeness. A shepherd nurtures his sheep. They become like children to him. He provides for every one of their needs and watches over them with love and endless attention. He does not let even one of them wander off but keeps equal care, love, and mindfulness over every member of the flock. This is the same with you. God guides you endlessly. He always provides for you through His attention and nurturance. He never leaves you, for He is within you.

"I shall not want."

To want for something is to believe that God has not already given you everything. Realize your completion now and know there is nothing to want. In the True Kingdom of God there is nothing but completion. This phrase is not meant to imply that if you want anything you are a sinner, but it is meant to correct a misperception of where your true value and wholeness reside. You are complete, and there is nothing else for you to desire. If you do find yourself wanting at anytime, use this prayer as a reminder of where your Truth lies. Allow it to guide you back to right-mindedness.

"He makes me lie down in green pastures."

Welcome the peace that is yours as you release all resistance and struggle. Peace is yours to have because peace is you in all ways. To lie down in green pastures is also to rest in the arms of God's endless nurturance. Returning to the sheep metaphor, these animals eat, sleep, and thrive within the green pastures. So to say that you can lie down in green pastures is to say that you fully accept, thrive, and rest happily within all that God has given to you. You do not need to worry or search for provisions. You rest, knowing that whatever you need is all around you. You rest, knowing that there is no need for worry, doubt, or concern in the least for you are literally surrounded by all that you should ever need.

"He leads me beside still waters;"

In Truth, you are still. You are peace. *A Course in Miracles* states: "I am still as God created Me." You are still. God leads you beside still waters. He shows you exactly what you are: peaceful and without any disturbance in the least. Also, the still waters are a place for the shepherd's flock to drink in and quench all thirst. God knows that you have nothing to thirst for, and so even as you may believe that you have need, He leads you beside the waters, helping you to remember that all is given to you eternally. Even as you have a desire or yearning, you are reminded that all is still and available to you. In addition, let us talk about stilling your mind. This is also a way to interpret or teach this passage. God leads you to stillness within you. He helps you to recognize, through your own witnessing of stillness, that this is where you will find your peace and quench any other longing.

"He restores my soul."

Now your soul has never been injured or apart from you, yet your perceptual consciousness may not always see your soul as being available to you in Truth. God re-establishes the link between a confused mind and Soul Truth. He witnesses for you and He created Me as that witness as well, to help you recondition the Truth about you. He guides you back to Oneness without the possibility for any other state of being. And it is through your restoration that you recognize that you never left His presence. Here, you realize that to return is only to remember the "place" which you never left.

"He leads me in paths of righteousness for His name's sake."

God's Name is Your Name. Love has begat Love. As you embrace the peace found in aligning with your clearer identity you recall Your Name to you. In stillness, the peace that is your Truth becomes a vibration so clear that you are deaf to the awareness of all other experiences. This vibration of Truth is Your Name. It is a sound so sweet, true, and peaceful that when it is heard, nothing but Love is radiated. In describing Your Truth, words are too limiting. In Truth, the utterance of Your Name instantly awakens you from the dream. Dreaming cannot continue in the Presence of Your Name. This Truth is full of boundless Love. God knows Your Name, for He bestowed it upon You. He knows its power, for it is the power of all creation, as is His Purity. To be righteous is to be clear-minded. Notice the synonyms listed in your thesaurus as alternatives for the word righteous: "virtuous, moral, just, good, blameless, honorable, upright, decent, and respectable." Also notice the one antonym that this reference book provides: "sinful."

When you are righteous, you are moving beyond any sense of sin. To be righteous is to recognize where your Truth is centered. You are blameless, virtuous, and honorable beyond belief. To embrace this Truth is to live as God's namesake. That is why it is clear-minded thinking.

"Even though I walk through the valley of the shadow of death, I fear no evil;"

Why do you fear discussing this line? Is it because you believe in the notions of death? Is it because you equate death with loss, fear, abandonment, or uncertainty? A mind who sees itself as disposable would know only fear. See and hear clearly now: you are safe. God cannot dispose of Him Self and you are His Extension. My presence is with you as I teach Truth now. I have brought you to this moment only for gentle release of these notions. Dreams of death have ruled over your mind for all of time.

They are nothing but fearful projections from within the mind who has forgotten its Source. They know nothing except the potential loss of their identified self. However, never do I judge your beliefs. I honor your freedom, yet know of your Truth. And since there is no doubt that this dream is quite real to you, I therefore, in gentle recognition, proceed. Read this phrase slowly. You walk step by step, one experience at a time as you process the journey Home. The valley is the darkness within you, but notice the valley is called the "Shadow of Death." You can rewrite this, as it is simply a name that you have given to this valley. It is called "Shadow of Death" valley. See it.

The valley is named after illusions. It is a valley of illusions. Shadows are only illusions. They distort an image and stand behind the truth. They stand away from the light. The object that casts the shadow stands in the light! You stand in the Light of God.

It is only the focusing on darkness that distorts you and has you believing in death. You can see this valley as the Valley of the Distortion of Death. Death is a distortion of Truth. It is the mistaken identity's belief system that makes illusions of truth. Therefore, having forgotten that you stand in the Light of God, a distortion may seem to form from this, a distortion which witnesses to images that are not true. Dream figures cast shadows of distortion. Death is a dream figure; it is a distortion of Truth. Therefore as you walk through the Valley of the Shadow (illusion / distortion) of Death, fear not evil, for that too is a result of distortion and illusion. This one line bears witness to the truth behind death, fear, and all shadows, calling them exactly what they are. These illusions are not you, and so fear is not a truth within your awareness at any time.

"For You are with Me;"

I am. I am here to help point out the shadows that seem to keep you walking in fear along your journey to awakening. Yes, remember that in Truth you travel nowhere, but since you believe that you progress, I am with you on your way. Also, to say that there is no real journey is to call attention to the fact that you have never actually stepped foot in any valleys. The valley is an illusion along with the shadows. I am with you through every belief that you hold.

"Your rod and Your staff, they comfort me."

Returning to the sheep metaphor, a rod was a device used for guiding the sheep. A staff was for support in this task. So to say that God's rod and staff comfort you is to say that His guidance brings comfort, protection, and security to you. He has given Me to you in order to point the way, for I am God's rod. We can even go as far as to say that God's staff may be seen symbolically as His personnel, His "staff". Who is the "staff" of God? See them as the community of One Spirit with many accepted names. All within this community have already remembered and call witness to you with God. They act as One Voice, One Guidance and One Comfort. Some may see these personnel as so-called ascended masters, but in Truth all are your Brothers and You. There are no separate entities within God's Kingdom. As we delve into the metaphorical meanings behind this psalm, you can consider yourself equally guided, comforted, taught, loved, and understood by God's staff. We are open 24 hours a day / 7 days a week.

What's that—a little humor??

Who said I always have to be serious? Laughter is the key to lightness.

"You prepare a table before me in the presence of mine enemies."

There are certain recitations of this prayer where this phrase is omitted. This is partially because it was added later from the original scripture. Yet it is a continually inspired component of the overall message of the prayer. David (in writing this originally) had an inspiration of Oneness. He accepted the understanding. So, you wonder how someone could have "enemies" unless you believe in separation.

That is why this phrase was included in later versions, as the focus on mistaken identity beliefs still continues to have its moments of speaking louder than truth. You can look at this phrase in that way. It witnesses to the understanding that although there may be a belief in separation, God brings you to understand that you are safe within the presence of perceived "enemies." He prepares a table for you before them. It is this table which is representative of the feasts that would occur when an ancient people desired to seek peace within a war. At these feasts, a truce was celebrated. Where before there were battling peoples, now there became one civilization. If you were to have a feast before your enemies, it would show that you were celebrating a healing. Notice that God cares for both you and the enemy that you perceive equally. No true division actually exists. God nurtures both of you, sustains, and provides for you even though you may divide and embattle yourselves. He sees your peace as eternal and celebrates this with you.

"You anoint my head with oil."

This phrase too is a cultural component from the origins of the psalm.[2] God offers His protection, knowing that you are eternally safe. He honors you as His Son, blessing you with His touch and care. The "oil" is His blessing from His caress. He washes you in fragrance, letting you know that you are beautiful in His sight. He wants you close and chooses to speak to you intimately. In addition, at a banquet, this ritual was enacted upon all guests, even those who were once enemies. Therefore, this ritual further expressed appreciation to one's guests as brothers (even if they may have been seen previously as separate or enemies. This particular phrase points to the banquet that occurred on the night when a truce was made between kings who were former enemies). What was once seen as two who were divided against each other have now become One in God's sight.

"My cup runneth over."

Here, you again are reminded that you do not need to want for anything. God welcomes you as the prodigal Son. He bestows endless celebration and gifts of His Kingdom upon you. You shall want for nothing, and all that you have is yours to give. It quite literally pours out from inside of you, neither ceasing or with any limit imposed. In giving then, too, you receive. Recognize your receipt and joyously share all with your Brothers, seeing that they too are deserving of all as ALL. There is always enough to share, and all are worthy of this sharing, for your desire to give reflects your own acceptance.

"Surely goodness and mercy shall follow me all the days of my life."

This is the acceptance of truth as you open yourself up to the Truth within you. Goodness and mercy are your natural inheritance. As your inheritance, these blessings are with you every day. Mercy is in Truth only a reminder that you are never guilty. God's mercy is not an overlooking of perceived sin. Rather, God in His Mercy knows that you have never sinned. Thus, God is not merciful in the face of sin because God knows that you are righteous (blameless, virtuous, etc.) [3] This is how He Created You, and nothing can deter from this unalterable truth.

Yes, God's fortune is always with you. His kindness and compassion are within you. He has given you the gift of forgiveness for as long as you invest in idle wishes. With gratefulness you receive this mercy. Gratitude always affirms your reception of any gift. You cannot be grateful if you did not recognize your gifts. Accepting God's gift of forgiveness returns a measure of appreciation to God because when you accept something it is inherently valuable to you. You accept mercy, forgiveness and God's fortune "all the days of your life," noting that there is no alternative to life. Life is all that God is, and as His Son, Life is all that you are. Oneness is the very quality of Life, which bears witness to the powerful unity of eternal Creation. This is our only True reality.

"and I shall dwell in the house of the Lord forever"

When you recognize the Truth about your Self, you clearly see your One and Only Home. In Truth, there is no where to go. God placed you safely within His House at the moment of your inception. It is, always has been, and always will be your One and Only Home. To know you are in The House of the Lord is to accept every miracle that witnesses to your Truth. It is an acceptance of Oneness (notice there are no multiple houses, developments or residential communities of the Lord). Yes, there are many mansions, but this was a metaphor expressing the equal abundance that you are within God. He is accepting of all and honors all. You are never separate, and therefore, you dwell together with All. His walls of protection encircle you. His "roof" protects you. His "staff" serves you. He is the Lord and Master of the House, and you are His Son forever. You are cared for endlessly.

You are My Light ~

Week Thirteen: Prompts for Insight:

1. *"To want for something is to believe that God has not already given you everything."* How does the statement relate to your life experiences? Are you willing to accept that you have everything? Remember this is not a material gain, but a Spiritual fact. For what have you wanted and for what reason have these desires been of importance? Process the list of all that you want with Holy Spirit, and ask Him to lead you to your deeper desires.

2. Spirit guides us to *"release all resistance and struggle. Here we welcome the peace that is our own."* The word "struggle" literally means, "ill will." What will within you have you notice to be ill? Can the Will of God struggle? What does struggle mean to you? How have your struggles of the past, led to peace in the present?

3. *"To be righteous is to be clear-minded. It is to recognize where your Truth is centered."* Think of all the ways you desire to be clear-minded. How do you intend to practice these desires for clarity? Write a routine for clear-thinking with Spirit.

4. Spirit guides us to recognize that no Truth is found in dreams of death. Process this thought with Spirit. Share how thoughts or experiences of death have affected you.

Practice: Reading the Bible

Ask for guidance within the reading of the Bible. Choose whatever version of the Bible is comfortable or convenient for you. Say a prayer for guidance and trust that Spirit will lead you to exactly the right section for your understanding. Next, randomly open up to a section within the Bible that you feel most guided to explore. Do not worry if you feel slight uncertainty with the section revealed. Do your best to place uncertainties aside. Breathe. Read the section and while you read, take note of anything that crosses your mind and needs further explanation. Make note of any confusion, tension or fear that you have within mind or body. Afterwards, say another prayer of appreciation and ask Holy Spirit to guide you through each note on your list. Trust that His explanation will always lead you to the greatest and highest knowledge of your Self.

Affirmations:

God guides me endlessly.

God holds me in equal care and love with my brothers.

God provides me with His nurturance and attention all ways.

Love begets love; I am the Holy Namesake of My Father.

Peace is mine to have; I release all resistance and struggle.

Week Fourteen: **Beyond Attack**

Holy Spirit, what would you have me learn today?

Let us look today at the reasoning behind your attack thoughts. It is essential for your learning that you recognize every contradiction. Seek safely with Me today, as to why you vehemently align with ideas of illusion. Why do you perceive yourself to be limited and at the will of the world? Likewise, why do you feel these thoughts can be deterred or ignored through a superficial choice to "be spiritual." Who is this mask of spirituality that you choose to wear if it is not the truth you feel within the moment? Truly, it is impossible to be apart from your Truth, for you never have changed from what God Created you to be. A choice to "be spiritual" is a pretense. Here you mask your attack thoughts rather than release them. If you wear a smile or blissful façade, does that make the terror within disappear? Surely not. If you believe in separation and judgment, you believe it. Never will turning a temporary blind eye to the beliefs held heal your mind.

So, am I supposed to allow these negative feelings to come to the surface? Am I supposed to be angry and interact with others this way?

Listen, words are not always necessary to notice thoughts. You need not declare or act out your thoughts in the world for them to be realized. Before a word is spoken, you are well aware of the thoughts supporting and what you believe. I am not asking you to restrain your feelings or to deny them. Instead, bring to the surface the recognition of what you believe. Notice these fears. Reflect within rather than project without. Here, you can no longer be a victim, but instead you walk towards the light of knowledge and awareness. Choose to see every way in which you desire to limit yourself. The opportunity for peace is always within you. It is You.

It will be helpful to ask within, "What evidence do I see that makes my brother or me guilty?" Follow up with: "Who is the one believing these thoughts and why?" Is it more peaceful to believe these thoughts or can you release your condemnation and extend your peace? And yes, no matter how much you feel that this "other" deserves your condemnation, the origin of peace is always within you and is beyond these images. Questioning your thinking differs from self-condemnation. Insightfully and without malice, take responsibility for the way in which you see your brother. See where you judge, justify and demand that your brother change himself for you. All of these are only products of your mistaken beliefs. This simple inquiry into your thoughts will call to your mind what you truly desire to see in yourself and all others. Likewise it will help you to decide where you choose to go from this moment. You can choose light and inclusion, rather than shadows of fear, defense, and exclusion.

As you observe these beliefs you can choose to release them. You can choose to surrender each judgment to Me. However, even if you feel unable to surrender, suppression and denial of the feelings will only delay your opportunity for correction. Becoming aware of your feelings will give you ample opportunity to bring all errors in thought and self-identity into the light of Truth.

All of your ill will, stress and anger come from your alignment with wrong-minded expectations, perceptions, and choices for limitation. In recognizing this you have the first key for your retrieval of the Peace of God. Without recognizing the expectations and divisive beliefs, which limit your experiences in this world, it may be impossible for you to accept better possibilities.

Notice whether your thoughts include a desire to question or condemn your brother. Notice where you see a need to judge or attack. Notice where you do not see yourself free and at peace. In each of these examples, you see yourself commanded by the world, rather than nurtured by God.

These thoughts only lead you to adopting an identity apart from God. This truly need not be. Therefore, recognize these thoughts. Allow them to flow up through your mind. Observe from where they emerge and what their declaration is to you and to the world. Finally, breathe and align yourself with the stillness once again. Once you accept a deeper desire to see your Self and the world more inclusively, you may say: "I am as God Created Me, and so these judgments are not true." Or "I release these judgments, knowing they make me suffer." Then, you may choose simply to rest in the quietness of your mind until you feel the love flow freely.

If you notice a choice to be sympathetic or helpful towards your Brother, realize first that this belief need not emerge from judgment. Love always sees itself, rather than a need to correct or alleviate. Then, as you choose to reacquaint yourself with the Love within all, recognize that this love can be extended in any manner. Often support or joyful remembering is most assistive through silently listening and simply being an attentive witness. It is always most helpful to extend the hand of love rather than correction. Mainly the wish to correct a brother is rooted in the initial wish to judge him or her. If there is any doubt in what you believe your brother needs, seek to extend love before judgment. Choose first to be an ambassador for peace within your perception, and all you encounter will come to see this love in you. Here the door to true perception is opened with a willingness to see through the eyes of Love to God's completeness.

By the way, I laugh at the characterization of "being spiritual" because you never need to be anything, especially a characterization that you use as a cover up for distorted beliefs. You need not wear a mask of any sort. God created you free to be as free as you are. Hiding or putting forth a persona that is not true, is choosing not to be true. Being aware of the choice not to be free is much more helpful to you than choosing to hide beneath the label of "being spiritual." Here you at least have the opportunity to recognize where you have perceived in error. Breathe, and align yourself with the judgments that fuel the mind's perceptions, instead of choosing to suppress or delay healing.

We are here simply to recognize all errors in our thinking and release them in reclamation of all that never changed. Your focus will be necessary in order to notice all the ways in which you erect obstacles to peace. But remember that our goal is not to think ourselves into paralysis, but to recognize the doors we have constructed. See these doors only so that we may choose to walk through all barriers and into the only wholeness that exists. *You cannot make this journey incorrectly.* You can merely delay or deny the inevitable. I already know you as you are, and so my only desire is for you to recognize this gracious magnitude for yourself. Limit yourself no more, Dear One. Present yourself to the light of Truth, and be free. I am with you. I love you.

Week Fourteen: Prompts for Insight:

1. When Spirit shared "*I laugh at the characterization of being spiritual,*" what thoughts and feelings surfaced within? What does "being spiritual" mean to you? Have you ever felt the need to "be spiritual" instead of express your preferred feelings? How do you expect other "spiritual" people to act? What images do you assume they need to uphold? Process your thoughts with Holy Spirit.

2. Make a list of five ways you choose to limit yourself or another. Think of grievances, grudges, judgments or even minor opinions for correction. Next, for each one ask within:

"What evidence do I see that makes my brother or me guilty?" Follow up with,
"Who is the one believing these thoughts and why?"

Notice any insights or arguments that rise in your thinking. Use your journal to process these feelings if you wish. Finally, when you are ready to see these thoughts differently, inhale and exhale deeply and say:

*"I am as God Created Me, and so this belief is not true.
I release all judgment and will for peace."*

Now reside in the quietness of your mind until you feel the love flow freely. Continue this process for every limitation you identified. Write your thoughts and feelings from this experience with Spirit.

Affirmations:
I am as God Created Me.
I am not my fears.
Attack is never justified.
I trust in God.

The Five C's of Anger Management:
Use the following steps when you find yourself answering a "call for love" with anger. Seek not to throw fuel on the fire of misperception. Choose instead to calm down and be a bearer peace instead.

Calm Down: Anger clouds our thinking and narrows our views. Breathe, release and rest your thinking mind from judgment. Try to see the situation in a different way.

Control: Get control of your behavior and reaction. We can't control other people's choices or behavior! However, we can control our choice to perceive ourselves as vulnerable, powerless or threatened. The goal is always to arrive at solutions instead of creating more problems.

Cope: Coping skills help us think or feel better. They are practical problem solvers. Take a deep breath. Take a walk. Write in a journal. Meditate. Laugh. There are a myriad of healthy ways to respond to the situation or your feelings rather than suppressing anger or causing more problems. Find a healthy and safe way to express the energy of anger now. You will solve more problems in the end.

Communicate: What expectations, justified defenses, and fears do you communicate to yourself? How many unrealistic expectations have you carried and not spoke about until you felt disappointed? How many self-defeating messages do you bottle up within? Consider where you can lovingly share your thoughts with calming respect rather than belated defense.

Change: Is there something that you can do to change? We can't control what other people choose to do, but we can control how we react to these experiences. How can you change yourself? Here the power and freedom of decision is always your own.

Week Fifteen: **Purpose of Love**

Dearest Holy Spirit, recently I've found myself having feelings that conflict. Sometimes I feel bored with life and don't see why I'm here, or understand how to make something of it. At other times, I desire to make the "dream" of life a fantastic one, but then wonder if that is a waste of time. Help me to understand these feelings, find a better purpose, and heal. Thank you.

Dear One, if you are seeking your purpose, I will always be consistent. Your purpose is to awaken. This is your purpose for Truth and Reality, accomplished through forgiveness, clear thinking, and release of all mistaken identity. This will never change. Nor would I ask you to settle into the world of dreams just to make the best of it while you are here. Your purpose is steady and shall be accomplished. Be not at a loss for this, as its truth is changeless.

Now, as for being in the world you see, stay aware of how this world is of your mind. What you make can be made for satisfaction within the realms of time or suffering. What you desire is up to your mind's thought system and all beliefs you seek to uphold. Seeking beyond the world at hand may appear to be a futile attempt from where you currently seem to stand. Therefore use the experiences of the world to seek out the Truth. When used as tools for your awakening, you make the world's experiences worthy ventures.

If you desire a purpose within the world, share the love you seek yourself to be. Align yourself with the Truth you desire and naturally express it within the world. Share and give with love to all. Become as the treasure you choose. This goal reflects a desire for a happier dream, but as you learn that this dream is not your final goal, your mind will be enlightened and search deeper to find the Truth. Happy dreams remain only dreams, and dreams should not be your final goal, so do keep your eyes on your readiness for Truth rather than on a desire for more pleasant dreams. Our practice together is not in order to gain silkier pajamas or a more restful mattress. You aren't here to remake your bed for more pleasing sleep. Rather, through our communions, you are destined to know your True Self with a greater clarity. In this way, you come to accept your Self in God's Holiness. This awareness is a great blessing to all you encounter and can only rain Light onto every aspect of living experience.

Do you want to write a book? Go ahead, write a book. Represent the truth of Love to your world and reinvest this Truth for your Self. Is it not only for that purpose anyway? Desire as you choose, Dear One. This shall be your adventure and hope. If you want to dedicate yourself solely to the awakening process, you may need to be gentler with yourself rather than having concerns about doing it right or worrying when you feel that you have gone astray. I would rather you not judge yourself. Instead seek peace, and claim a kind awakening and genuine acceptance of Self as your purpose.

Being the presence of Love is being your Self. It only is the pure accepting of the All that God created. Surely this is your only goal. Clear Vision is Love. Clear Vision is Peace. Clear Vision is full acceptance of only that which is. And so why is this being yourself? Simply because there is nothing else to be.

See only the Truth, even as you seem to be surrounded by multiple forms. Seek only the Clearest Vision. Allow your mind to release all thoughts of illusion's permanence or power. Open your heart and permit yourself to settle there as in a cradle of love. Permit yourself to know love, to be love, and to extend love. In doing so, you radiate the presence of Your Holiness. Jeshua and all spiritual Masters live centered wholly in this awareness, which is why they appear to radiate peace in all ways. From mind to body, you become whatever you embrace and accept, and so that quality is seen through you. You stand as a witness to Reality, and here only the Truth is remembered and extended to All.

Again, I say, judge not your wishes within the world. Ask yourself what serves the purpose of True desire, and nothing shall be a waste. Do not torment yourself if you find a yearning to be within the world. This is never wrong because the Holiness of God can never be wrong. Yet, you can be misdirected if you use the forms and moments of the world to replace the Truth of Heaven. Does this mean that you should completely and adamantly resist seeking in the world? No, resistance is never helpful. However, you may choose to blissfully use every tool at your disposal to settle into a deeper peace. Again, I say, you cannot do this journey wrong, for you are already Holy despite actions.

Try to find love and peace through every experience, and allow this clearer Vision to be extended through you. See your brothers, who you will have plenty of interaction with, as a glorious reflection of Love. Look into the considerations seeking separation, for this judgment does not serve your purpose. Choose instead to offer all that you are in the willingness to know all You are. Use every interaction for this greater function. Witness to the Holiness of God in all and you shall know it.

Do not allow yourself to feel guilty for wanting anything. Instead, simply notice why you feel this wish is wanted. Remind yourself that you are whole despite appearances. It is true that no accomplishments or possessions outside your Self can replace the Truth; however, does this mean that you must live in poverty, absolution and obscurity? Again, no. Write a song, perform on Broadway, be a billionaire, win a Pulitzer Prize or erect a monument to your greatness. Any of these results is acceptable. Nothing is unacceptable for God's Holiness. No matter the wish, if you desire to find the clearest function, simply ask Me how these ideas serve you. I will always direct you to what is most truly helpful and blessed. If you notice a belief in need, once again, give this to Me and together we shall use this recognition to bring your mind back to a clearer Vision. Truly Beloved, no correction is impossible to undertake.

The purpose here is to know your Self.
Remember this Truth
beyond every imagining you hold.

This can be accomplished through the open embrace of one or one billion people. It is not the amount of Truth that you offer which defines Truth, but rather the completeness that you offer in wholly extending it.

You are as God Created You, and this fact spans far beyond the reaches of time, actions, experience or notoriety. Truly, they alone are not you, yet as you wish for them, you may heal them. Again, I say, you cannot fail nor can you fail to serve your purpose. Love is with you always because it is you. Accept this and step into the light of full being. Here we step beyond any idea that does not align and extend the peace of God's Love. Remember, do not judge or reject anything. Simply step beyond every thought of limitation in an everlasting desire for peace. Truly the purpose of Love is to be extended and not limited by any imagination. Here is the certainty that can never leave you. Here you are simply in Love. My Light is your Own. I love you.

Week Fifteen: Prompts for Insight:

1. *"Dear One, if you are seeking your purpose, I will always be consistent. Your purpose is to awaken. This is your purpose for Truth and Reality, accomplished through forgiveness, clear- thinking, and release of all mistaken identity."* What is your purpose? Write down a list of your desires. Do not judge yourself for any desire, because each one is an ideal expression of your perfect freedom. Process your desires with Holy Spirit.

2. Spirit guides: *"Your purpose will never change. Nor would I ask you to settle into the world of dreams just to make the best of it while you are here."* Recall times when you have felt the need to just go through the motions of life by daring not to rock the boat. Where have you tried to just fit in or make nice, even when you have felt yourself struggling? Process these thoughts with Spirit.

3. Spirit guides: *"Your purpose is steady and shall be accomplished."* Where within your own experiences of yourself, others, and the world have you doubted your purpose? Doubt is only an obstacle to love's awareness because it only witnesses to the reality of fear and limitation. The word "doubt" literally means, "to have to choose between two things." Therefore, as we feel doubt, we believe in our own will over God's Will. However, our one purpose is always certain. Observe any thoughts of doubt you have within. Ask Holy Spirit to show you where you use these doubts to invest in the split mind or fearful self. Finally, give these doubts to Holy Spirit.

4. Spirit guides: *"Therefore use the experiences of the world to seek out the Truth. When used as tools for your awakening, you make the world's experiences worthy ventures."* Make a list of ten ways in which you interact with the world. Include family, friends, career, love relationships, parenting, socializing, etc. Review this list with Spirit and ask how each of these areas can be used as tools for your awakening.

Practice:
Write a list of your dream desires. With Holy Spirit's guidance, ask how you can use each of these goals to know your Self in Truth or to bestow a greater knowing of Love to all. Be willing to surrender to Spirit's guidance, accepting that it is not with your own mind that you are meant to see. There is no sacrifice in peace and all expressions have a perfect purpose. Nothing can be withheld from you.

Affirmations:
I am Holy beyond every desire.
My purpose is accomplished with Love.
My purpose is always to awaken.
Love is with Me always.

Week Sixteen: **Victim and Victimizer**

All aspects of victim/victimizer beliefs are fueled by beliefs in fear, abandonment, and guilt. In other words, they are all mistaken identifications concerning Who You Are and Who Created You. God does not abandon you, but the forgotten belief in Who You Are will play out this scenario to justify its thought system. With this mindset, either you blame God for abandoning you, or you see His seeming abandonment of you as a necessary punishment for your sins. Of course, both of these beliefs would make sins and separation real, but since they are never real, these thoughts are never true.

Guidance will arrive when the mind readies itself for acceptance. You are ready. You desire to allow a new thought; one not of your own mind, but one of Truth. This has allowed you to manifest an open mind to healing rather than making a victimized self. Your experience always reflects your determination to receive. That is what "ask and it shall be given you" means.

In order to believe that you can be victimized, you must first believe that you are not as God Created You. You must believe that you are not whole, complete, and loved beyond measure. All of these beliefs are necessary in order to accept anything apart from Your Truth. You must fully accept all of your "sins" before you invest in a belief in "punishment" or "guilt." Is it possible to see guilt in the innocent? Obviously, only lies would make this possible. Therefore, every moment you see your Brother as guilty, you exchange truth for lies. Isn't it strange that a "sane" mind passionately informs you of who is to blame for the misery it perceives and why he or she is to blame, without knowing anything but its own thoughts? Is this conclusion from the mind really sane? Hear Me well, only insanity begets insanity. Your thoughts may appear to be clear and well-informed in their justification of attack, but truly, any justified thought of attack is only lunacy in Truth. This is not sane.

Wouldn't it be better to seek for peace of mind rather than concocting insane attacks on yourself and others? Truly, as long as you seek meaning outside your Self, you will only prolong these hapless fabrications. Seek forgiveness instead of dreams. This is always the key idea to peace of mind. You have no personalized direct control over the forms in the world. It is only through the practice and purpose of forgiveness that you will discover your true power and freedom.

One cannot disprove an illusion with another illusion. Recognize this fact when you find yourself muddled in inquiry. Your thinking can weave questions for infinity. These "how's" and "why's" are not as purposeful as asking "what now?" This is always seen as a difficult premise to accept. It is a fact that questions keep you hesitating rather than opening to the fullness of Truth. This is why I ask only that you still your mind and settle your thoughts. Increasing thoughts will never assist your peace. Only stillness will. Stillness is the only "experience" that gives you the openness required for peace to be welcome. Without stillness, accept that you are struggling against God. Just as Jacob metaphorically struggled with the angel, you struggle with your most True Self. Instead, allow stillness to awaken you to the fact that your struggle is unnecessary. Truly, it only stems from a limited perception of Self.

Stillness is not the place for "why's" and "how's." As long as you ask questions about the purpose of the dream, you are clearly implying that you do not know God. The Father has never for one moment made your dream real. To seek meaning within a delusion is to believe sanity can be found there, as if through conscious effort, delusions could be transformed into reality. Truly, such compromises could never exist if you truly were your Self as God Created.

Notice your anger now, Dear One. Hear the tearful cries of a belief system challenged at its very core. This is only because you dearly desire to control and prolong a self-struggling will where no clear-minded Will of God would ever exist.

Settle your mind, Dear One. Breathe. Release. Do not make the past real for to do so is merely the exploration of a mind seeking its own meaning in beliefs of separation and abandonment. You cannot place a rational distinction within a thought system that is fully based on deception of Self.

All I ask you to realize now is that you are Whole as God Created You. You are not your past nor shall you ever be. You are not your self-struggling will. This is not a moment in which to enter confusion; this is a moment to instill peace. And this is my only reminder for the loving witness I know as God's Holiness.

Whenever your mind reels with questions, especially over "why bad things happen," notice that this process is only fear attempting to justify itself. I understand that this response (or shift in perception) may seem difficult to accept. But, to this again I say, stillness is your own key to peace. Notice if you desire to listen and release yourself from pain. Notice if you desire peace. Allow yourself to trust and sink into stillness rather than into confusion. What is your wish?

"But I do not understand. . . . But I do not know. . . ." These are the thoughts of a struggling separate mind that seeks its own identity. These are the thoughts of a mistaken identity that recognizes its own potential for destruction. Again, settle your mind.

Notice how these thoughts only take you further into feelings of fear and frustration. See how their very essence is based on confusion, separation, individualized will, and mistaken identity. God is inevitable. He has never left you to suffer, Child. He has never left you alone. You are indestructible and loved beyond measure. Rest in this Truth, rather than furthering the thoughts of a confused mind that seeks meaning where there is nothing. Dear One, notice from Whom your peace truly emanates and where it resides. Notice the space where all thoughts are still and only love remains. Then, if you notice fear's attempts to interject, simply decide again for a peace beyond your confused understanding. The more you allow, the more peace will settle in your mind. Yet a settled mind is not your final goal, remembrance is, and this is beyond your thinking mind. Only invincible Truth exists. Love is beyond the mind's measure. This invariable Love is your only life — in the One from who you can never be apart. Never vulnerable, never afraid, never alone, you are still as God Created You.

There are no victims and victimizers in Truth.
God would never create that which is bound to suffer.
Fear serves no purpose for Love.
Never can there be deviation.
Your Peace is eternal.
Your Truth is unwavering.

Whenever you seek understanding, where there is none, simply remind yourself of the One Whom You Are, settle your mind, and permit only peace to be. This is your Truth. For My Light is Your Own and only this is True. You are as God Created You . . .

Week Sixteen: Prompts for Insight and Practice:

1. Write down your feelings relating to Spirit's sharing: "*Guidance will arrive when the mind readies itself for acceptance.*" Do you feel you are ready? If so, how? Ask Spirit to show you.

2. How does the belief in separation perpetuate all ideas of suffering and victimization?

3. Where has the belief in separation caused you to see yourself as a victim? Attempt to reverse each of these beliefs by seeking out where you have observed yourself to be strong, supported and complete.

4. Can you find moments in your life where you have abandoned or victimized yourself? Where you have chosen not to love or appreciate yourself? Process through your thoughts of blame and past hurt. Seek out deeper insight with Holy Spirit's guidance.

5. What feelings and thoughts arose when you read, "*In order to believe that you can be victimized, you must first believe that you are not as God Created You.*" Is it possible then to be an innocent victim? What do these beliefs cause for you in your experiences? Can you see peace instead of this?

6. Write your insights on "*fear serves no purpose for love, other than to make lies where there can never be deviation.*"

7. Make a list of ten ways in which you have felt disappointed by others. Make a list of ten ways in which you have disappointed yourself. For each of these, take a deep breath, release and say aloud, "*I am not a victim. I am free. I cannot be lost in God.*" Process your thoughts after this exercise with Holy Spirit.

8. Make a list of five ways in which you desire to release the roles of guilt, blame, victimization, and shame in your life experience.

Make a list of five people who will be released from their roles as victimizers once you choose to release yourself. Envision yourself standing hand in hand with each of these Beloved ones. Together, you are free.

Affirmations:
Life lives through love.
God never abandons.
God Creates nothing bound to suffer.
I am as God Created Me.

Week Seventeen: **Confidence**

I see you led me to the word "confidence." What message about confidence am I to know now?

The idea of confidence requires more clarity. Self confidence is not faith in the mistaken identity or personality. Lo, instead, Self confidence is a state of Being that reflects beyond all illusions. It arises from the willingness to leave your judgment and fear behind. Quite literally, the word *confidence* means "with trust." As you have already realized, the cornerstone of faith is trust. Without trust, there can be no faith and without faith, you stand guard over the door to healing the mind.

Ask yourself in whom do you desire to have trust? If it is your ideas of self-limitation, than surely only fear will result. All invitations for accepting the miracle have you choose between love and fear. When you choose to trust in God, you open the door to allowing His Holiness to reflect through you. Accepting this brilliance can be done only through the release of all illusions since there is no compromise between Truth and illusions.

Confidence is a feeling that extends as you discover the wholeness of Who You Are. To know your Self is to be confident in Truth. It is to accept the wholeness of God within you and to extend this wholeness in all ways. Here, you place your faith in a clear and present state of Being, rather than a fearful restricted humanness.

Trust is always certain. Truly, who could fully accept anything without certainty in what they were receiving? Therefore, as we allow ourselves to yield from fear and doubt to trust and acceptance, we are gaining the entirety of Heaven. A lack of trust is merely the sign of a confused mind. This mind is uncertain and so has no clear awareness of Who it is or where it belongs. You belong in God. It is only the uncertain mind that does not know. Therefore, when you notice experiences lacking trust, remind yourself where you belong and seek to regain this awareness with Me. Give all uncertainty to Me and I shall always lead you Home.

Too often the thinking mind attempts to figure out a solution to uncertainty. This wish to control is doubt. A doubting mind always asks questions in search of its own reclamation of certainty. Doubt never finds what it is seeking simply because it does not know what it is looking for. Doubt is always a blind search. In most states of doubt, the mind will ask questions and seek evidence. However, these questions and evidence are always rooted in a pre-existing fear and uncertain understanding of what it truly seeks from this proof. This is why I am unable to answer most of your questions to your satisfaction.

Let's take the example of the most popular question, "how did the impossible occur?" This question is simply unanswerable for the very reasons shared above. Any answer given would require not only making the impossible possible, but an answer considered "acceptable" would affirm the possibility of more impossible. Can you see the contradiction here?

When you choose doubt over certainty, you choose not to know your Self. Truly, it is that simple. However, remember, there is no sin associated with this choice. It is all merely a misunderstanding, corrected by forgiveness. Hear Me well; I do not judge your progress towards faith or dances with uncertainty. Truly I only see and know the Self-confidence in our Being. Indeed, I already know Who You Are. Do not hinder yourself with projections of guilt or attempts to judge. My love for you outshines all mistaken identities. As you choose to believe in fear no longer, accepting that fear is not Who You Are, you shall desire to release for peace naturally.

A perfect example of this transformation is seen through the story of Doubting Thomas. Oh, and by the way, it is a story. This parable was actually written and relayed by Judas himself. It is his story of affirming faith beyond the ego's perceptions. Here, Thomas was unwilling to accept the appearance of the resurrected body of Jesus without proof. Symbolically, this is representative of how Thomas invested so firmly in the belief in death (loss, limitation, ego's perceptions) that any ideas of being the Holiness of God beyond his thinking mind seemed impossible. "I was always demanding proof only because I was uncertain of my Self and where Jesus was going with His teachings." He continued, "Fear seemed so much more willing than peace. It presented louder within my mind and stated question after question without respite. My rest occurred when I was willing to yield to faith and trust beyond the doubt that sought proof in form. Here, I finally stepped out of my own way, yielding to God and accepting Holiness as the only way, truth and life. This indeed was my own witness of resurrection."

The mistaken identity always believes that illusion is more real than Truth. Again, this is simply and innocently because it does not know. Therefore the acceptance of trust and faith are necessary. Trust and faith initiate from your willingness to admit that your best thinking got you as far as you can currently identify. This is the acceptance of forgiveness for all, recognizing that indeed you do not know. In this moment, of clear recognition, you gain awareness of Self-confidence emitting beyond illusion. Indeed this is the realization of light beyond any thought of you.

This Self-confidence awaits you now. However, it is not anything apart from Who You Are in Truth. Trust in this and you trust in eternity to lead the way. Trust in eternity and all we are as One becomes known. Remember Beloved. See Me reaching out my hand now. I invite you to the Light of Self-confidence. This is the Light of Truth. Let us stand in our glory as One. I love you.

My Light as it is Your Own.

Week Seventeen: Prompts for Insight:

1. The word "confidence" means "with trust." Spirit shares that we feel truly confident when we seek to remember our Strength in God. Guide yourself within now, and ask to see how you can increase your trust in Self and Spirit as well as accept strength in God.

2. Take a moment to write down all that trust and trusting in God mean to you.

3. What does faith mean for you? Is it possible to have faith in your Self? The Self, in which we have faith, is not limited to body or identity. This Self is the One who knows. Take a moment now to quiet your thinking mind and ask Spirit where you can realize faith in your Self. Ask Him to help you trust and know your faith in God. As we have faith, we embrace the wholeness of our Self with complete love and happiness. We not only come to realize this Self through our self, but we begin to see our True Self in all we encounter. Indeed, here, life becomes a realization of True Perception. Ask Spirit to take your hand and guide you to this faith now.

4. Write down your thoughts about faith in love over fear. What do you feel keeps you from loving in every moment?

5. Without confidence we doubt. Thomas' story is a metaphor for where we all deny the Christ simply because we have a limited faith in this True Self. Doubt is always a belief in lack over limitlessness. It is an investment in the divided will. Here we deny the Holiness of God because we are blind with fear. Write down where you see yourself believing in lack or denying the Christ in you. What do you feel must happen before you can accept your Holiness as it is? What keeps you from seeing the Christ in all? Seek to give these obstacles over to Holy Spirit now. He is waiting to show you the Truth You are.

6. Focus your mind, and ask: *"Spirit, help me realize how I can come to You in certain trust when I feel in the midst of fear."* With confidence, wait for His response.

Practice:

Confidence arises from within us. Identify ten areas within your life where you feel strong. Identify ten areas within your life in which you feel weak. Review each of these lists. How does each of these thoughts, assumptions, or judgments impact your experiences within the world? How do they affect the way you see your self and others? How do they affect the choices you make? Further explore any idea of guilt, separation, or fear identified on the "weak" list. How can you heal these feelings? What needs to change within you? Process both lists with Holy Spirit.

Affirmations:

I am far beyond my doubt.

I choose to extend forgiveness and be still in mind.

I choose to accept peace.

I have confidence and Trust in my True Self.

Week Eighteen: **Judgment**

All judgments made from your mind are those of limitation. This is because your entire thinking mind sees itself incorrectly. You do not see your True Self, nor can you think of yourself as being whole. However, God's judgment, as well as my own, always initiates from Wholeness. This Holiness is Who You Are and is never limited. Likewise, this Holiness cannot change. In summary it is best to state clearly: Your judgment is always false while God's Judgment is always True. Notice if you feel afraid or offended here. In fact, it would be purposeful if you were to notice offense, because then you would realize how your judgment seeks only to protect its own false images.

I have said before that all ideas of defense stem from a belief in weakness or incompleteness. Therefore, as you seek to defend yourself against the statements I make, do realize that these defenses exist only because you do not know. And hence, my point is proven. (Smile)

Trust me, Beloved. My statements are never a judgment of you. They are merely a gentle call for realization. The more you hear the Truth of all you do not know, the more willing you become to step from the investment in shadows into the Light of True Being. Yes, this is a good thing. I only speak for Love. Always be sure of this. If it is fear you sense, it is only your own uncertainty. Again, this is not a judgment, yet only a call for realization. I always love All You Are, and this includes your dreams. Surely, I know you are not your dreams, but I love the joy you find from wishing them into experience. This joy I have is truly a celebration of your freedom.

When judgments are made from your mind, they are in recognition of the perceptions you hold. For example, the judgment you make that inspires worry, is only a strangling upon your mind and experience. In fact, this is literally what the word "worry" means: "to strangle." Likewise, each worry you have plainly sees yourself as constrained and chooses to instill more restriction. As you choose worry, you choose an adherence to the belief in limitation and powerlessness. In Truth, this is not True.

Therefore, every worry only has you lie to yourself about your Self.

However, you can use all judgments and worries to one advantage, and that is to recognize how limited you see yourself and others within your world. Here, these thoughts are transformed into devices for unlearning. If you desire to see beyond judgment, pause and look at every declaration that crosses your mind. Hear clearly what each statement proclaims. Notice how it reflects upon you. How does it make known your worth? Ask, can that which is whole in Truth, represent itself in such a way? Perhaps you want a more practical question for self-realization. If so, ask yourself simply, "Can this situation be wholly true? Where is my evidence?" How do you factually know anything, if you do not know the whole of all thoughts and experiences? Truly, you do not know the past, present and future. You do not know other people's thoughts and experiences. You do not even know your Self. Therefore, these judgments that you make only further distort your current perceptions and convince you of a false, substitute, and dependent reality. Here you see yourself not as God Created, but as some vulnerable entity, who is doomed to live and die in enslavement. Now truly, does this thought system help or hurt you right now?

The word "represent" means literally "to send forth before you." Are your thoughts sending forth an acceptance of wholeness or limitation? If it is limitation, ask yourself again, "Is this what I perceive myself to be in God?" In this thought, you bring the belief in limitation to the Truth and ask it to declare itself there. In this revelation of Light, all limiting beliefs are shaken loose from the mistaken identities they inhabit. Through this introduction of Truth, the awareness of your shadows cannot be avoided. When a choice is made to bring the false to Truth, the Truth will naturally dispel illusion, and your sight is healed for Clear Vision.

The best question that can ever be asked of the mind is "what does this thought represent of me?" Since you do not know your Self, it is essential to bring all thoughts to Light. Your healing will not be within the analysis, but it will bring the mind to a place where it recognizes a desire for healing. Here, forgiveness is seen as a necessity if you surrender to an appeal for Truth. In this simple mindfulness, the will for peace does shine. If this will desires to see another way, henceforth forgiveness will be extended within.

Consequently, this is why I speak your language and present my teaching clear for your understanding. My teaching style or symbols will not bring healing. However, the will for being taught realizes health You are upon you. Do you see the difference?

Yes, I think so (smile). You cannot give me healing, because that would interfere with my own freedom. It would impede the law of cause and effect. This cannot be done if there is to remain perfect freedom. Also, you see me through the Holiness of God I am. Thus in Your eyes, my Self does not require healing. It only requires its Self to know who it is once again. This is why you cannot induce healing, but you can introduce a way to help me see my Truth once again.

Well, someone's been paying attention. (smile). The explanation you just put forth is perfect for where healing remains and knowing is. I know Who You Are; therefore, no need for healing exists from my point of View. If I were to see you as needing healing, then I would see you not as You are. To see error is to see in a state of lack. Since this is not True, and I see you only as Whole in God's Image (as Created), then I represent to you only this knowing. The healing occurs when *you* recognize (not Me) where the misalignment is taking place in your own witness. This way you engage in the process of healing with Me to standing as a witness to the Truth.

Dear One, I shall always witness the Truth for you. There is nothing else that I can place before you. You are the Truth in every way. Once again, I say that this is changeless. To be as God Created is to know this.

True perception is to call into Vision as God Created. Within this perception, you see through the illusions. Choosing to forgive (and consequently seeing through illusions) provides an entry way to the experience of Self. The mind cannot remain within a perceptual realm and know the Holiness of Truth. As long as you identify yourself with the thinking, individuated mind, you remain in perception. Does this mean that you are not whole? No. It means that you are only simply fooling yourself. Here, you perceive yourself not to be Who You Are, because you think of yourself as different from Who You Are. Through forgiveness and, thus, acceptance of your Self as Whole, perfect and free (despite presentation in form) this mistaken thinking is released; and you align with the Holiness that never changed.

When you release the mind completely and ask only to welcome God within the Self as You Are, your bodily form will simply fade into the mists of perception's illusion; and we will join wholly on the level of awareness. What I mean here is that the body form will no longer have the specific purpose that you have designed. It will be accepted as merely a tool and nothing else. Truly, as you awaken to your True Vision, the body (and all its accompaniments) will be seen as merely just another costume or component of scenery on the set of Holiness' playful imagining.

Therefore, beyond the form, True Vision has you walk in the contentment of Who You Are. This is Love without ceasing. You may describe this as enlightenment.

Basically, enlightenment is the release of all illusions and their effects within form. Although this may sound like psychosis, it is not. The difference between what you would describe as mental illness and enlightenment is that in enlightenment you see in Truth. Mental illness is the distortion of illusions, and therefore cannot reflect spiritual reality.

Enlightenment does not mean that you are out of touch with the practical nature of your world. God would never leave you to wander disorganized or amok and call this peace. Yet, in this state of complete contentment, you are unattached to the world of judgment and its perceptions of limitation. Here, in this peace beyond description, is where God shall meet us.

Wow, okay. That sounds really good! I was worried for a minute or two there that, if I was to become enlightened, I'd be seen as a nutcase in the world. I feared that I would never be able to hold another normal conversation with another friend. I feared that I'd be left to be isolated in public living. Truly, that does not sound like any fun, nor does it sound attractive.

Beloved One, there is a Zen saying, "Before Enlightenment: chop wood, carry water; after Enlightenment: chop wood, carry water." What's the difference? The everyday jobs are the same. The need is the same. What about the frame of mind? Who is chopping? Who is carrying water? This statement represents the continuance of livelihood that you will feel when you realize a state of True Perception in this world. As you interact with all in a state of Enlightenment, you shall stay awake. Within this simple Being, you shall exist within a purer and most loving frame of mind. With this knowing, you shall interact with all as the Love You are beyond every image.

Enlightenment releases every conscious attachment to fear, worry or limitation. Here you free your adherence to all wayward judgments and simply know your Self as You are. This awareness shall likewise be seen in all interactions. As an enlightened Being you shall definitely be able to carry on a normal conversation. In fact, you will even be able to joke and speak about any and all topics. However, in these interactions, you shall not be speaking from a fearful or limited state of mind. In this state of Being you will clearly see the illusion as it is, and still Love all You are.

Trust Me, Beloved. Jeshua was far from a wet blanket. He laughed and loved with all. He enjoyed simply being and appreciated conversing publicly and privately. Never did he choose to judge or sit on the outside of a heated conversation, but instead, he simply witnessed to Truth without condemnation. In fact, he often helped people laugh at themselves and seek another clearer way of seeing despite their own judgments. He let them come to their own conclusions. He sought to see the peace and joy in all manner of experience. When someone appeared to be presenting him with a disagreement, he merely allowed the Truth he knew to lead the way. Rarely did he correct. Never did he act like aloof or impersonal. He did not sit apart at gatherings or have a spaced out, uncongenial presentation or wear a vacant smile. Always did remain perfectly alert and interested in all His Brothers concerns. Likewise, he witnessed for what was most clear in every situation. This clarity was most often found in simply being a witness for God's perfect happiness, support and appreciation, no matter what the outer presentation offered. This was literally seeing and being the Truth. Jeshua did not separate himself from his beloved companions. Jeshua lived in complete happiness and openly, willingly shared this limitless joy with all. This is the Being of Enlightenment.

Therefore, yes, you can still watch the Super bowl, eat chicken wings with jalapeño cheesy nachos and put your feet up while being enlightened. You can still attend cocktail parties and have the benefit of ordinary conversation. In fact, I recommend it. However, all these experiences may not have the same meaning as before. Now, they may actually become better and more delightful. Why? As you are enlightened, you no longer feel the need to act artificial, seek approval or fearfully perceive possible harm within these experiences. No longer will you be judging yourself or another within the experience. With an enlightened awareness you will be fully aware. You will be fully present and completely able to simply thrive in every moment, enjoying all you have to be.

Wow! That sounds great!

It is! Now pass me a chicken wing. (Laughter) Beloved One, do not worry that you can ever lose your happiness. God bestows this Truth (which has never changed) within His Holiness, because He knows nothing else. God is happiness. To experience the Wholeness of this Truth is incomprehensible within the imaginings of a limited mind. This is why I say it never can occur with an adherence to perception. That is why you can worry about enlightenment, and fear it, all without actually knowing it. To fear your own Self is to reaffirm the existence of the mistaken identity. However, no matter what you believe, you have your Self known in Truth. Seek your peace here, and you will strive to be aware of the Truth You are without hesitation.

Before we can begin to introduce the mind to Truth, the mind must accept itself beyond all judgment. Let us once again look at this important practice of surrender. To judge is to say, from within a limited mind, that you know. This is often why you hear the words "I know" when a judgment is occurring. If you ask the perceiver how he or she knows the seeming facts supporting their judgment, either uncertainty or threat arises. Usually, at best, they can give you proof based on assumption, hearsay or perception. Remember, an observation gained through sensory perception is not a fact in Truth. If aware of this contradiction, the foundation of the perceiver's judgments may begin shake. However, usually this judgment rests on a deep investment in limitation and past identification. Therefore, the recognition of fear and threat often only leads to more judgments. Surrender, on the other hand, releases the perceiver's attachment to fear and threat. Without surrender, the battle seeking proof of limitation will continue all through time.

This is why a specific process is outlined in the workbook section of *A Course in Miracles*. If you were to be told simply that your judgments meant nothing, there only would be resistance in the form of denial and eventually anger. Why is this? Because you see as you believe, and your beliefs have already been fully accepted as your reality. The entire world witnesses to this seeming fact. Therefore, denial of your perception is useless. I am not here to inspire more perceptions of separation.

Letting a "righteous" judgment descend and separate is a common mistake made among brothers who find themselves seeking healing. Here, they choose to see the ego as evil and consciously engage themselves in a battle to survive beyond its sins. What occurs then is a seeming battle of separate wills. Truly Love knows no battles. This is why I ask for you to release all judgment, stilling your mind, rather than seeking to engage in a judgment of judgment.

When you encounter a brother in need of healing and you appear to have been given the role of healer, understand this is a role being played out in two seeming bodies, but only one mind. What could you desire to offer this mind rather than the one Truth that it is? I refer here to Love, not superior concepts of your own perception. Therefore, you are not asked to proselytize or change the mind of your brother, for this would be to identify with separation. You are asked only to LOVE your brother and be this love in full extension. Here is your most opportune moment for healing the one mind. Here you are only being the love you are and nothing else.

Always strive to see your brother as he is in Truth, not as you perceive him to be in judgment. Allow him to be your savior for showing you the mind that asks for healing. Here you allow yourself to accept your Self through a seeming different set of eyes, yet only of one Truth. Permit yourself to see your Self and choose Love as your Source, rather than perception as your battle cry.

You cannot ask someone to release perception as long as it is seen as real. This is why the call for Love must be met with a love extended, not denial. If you desire healing to occur, do not extend judgment of how the individuated mind judges, haughty piousness or devaluation of your brother's perception. Instead, extend your own willingness to see his or her reality, thus asking to join, rather than separate. A skilled healer is one who asks to see as the patient sees, not to judge, but to bring peace. To extend peace, then, becomes the unified goal, and here is the recognition of love beyond form.

A Course in Miracles guides that the one who is the saner of the two will recognize his indebtedness to the other and, therefore, desire only an extension of love. Questions can be used to assist in the recognition of what is perceived (to assist with the joining). However, notice if these questions bear the image of accusation, sarcasm or denial; for these judgmental qualities do not remember love, they seek only fear and a prolonged belief in separation.

Truly all healing is a desire for joining above all else—be it a desire to join with God or with your brother. These essentially are the same. You are asking to see as God Created. Here Truth alone becomes your guide and remains the content of your desire. Very simply, all mind healing can be accomplished through forgiveness. Here we release for peace, rather than restrain through judgment. Truly, I say, Heaven joins with you when two ask to become one, for here I am.

Again, I say, be gentle with yourself and be gentle with your brother, for both of you are from the same Source. Neither of you are truly limited. Forms and appearances will always deceive. Therefore, keep in mind your brother's nobility, and choose to honor this through your witness to Truth. All judgment shall fade from sight when your True state of Being is recognized as Who You Are. I am with you all ways. I love you.

Week Eighteen: Prompts for Insight and Practice:

1. Write down five positive and negative thoughts you have held about yourself or others recently. What do you feel these thoughts send forth before you? What does each represent to you? Identify a minimum of one feeling for every thought. Write down one possible experience that could occur because of this thought.

2. Holy Spirit teaches that, for the most part, when we judge and say we "know" we are: *"Usually, at best, [utilizing] proof based on assumption, hearsay or past perception. Remember, an observation gained through sensory perception is not a fact in Truth."* Take a moment to identify and write down five judgments you have held lately. Next to each judgment, ask yourself, "where is the proof?" Where did the proof you have utilized emerge? Is it supported only by past perceptions, assumption or hearsay? Are your observations supported only by sensory perceptions? If so, look again and reconsider each of these judgments. Better yet, take a moment now to surrender them to Holy Spirit, accepting that you do not know.

3. Spirit outlines in this writing how all thoughts are rooted in your beliefs. Write a list of 3 recent situations. How do you feel your thoughts influenced your experience of these situations? Attempt to trace these thoughts back to your initiating beliefs. What do you believe this situation reflects about you? Write three or more ways you can see this situation differently.

4. Is there any experience that you have feared losing because of enlightenment? If so, write down a list. Follow up each listed event with at least one way that you currently experience yourself in this activity without wholeness. Do you still hold onto judgment or seek separation? Do you feel dependent on this activity for your completion or self-satisfaction? Truly, these dependencies could not exist in genuine enjoyment. Now, imagine how this experience could be expanded or enlightened through your own illumination. How would a pure mind engage in this activity? Have fun and see

yourself enjoying this activity without limits. Write down what you feel would change in the activity or your experience of it, with an enlightened frame of mind.

Affirmations:

I am as God Created Me.

Love knows no battles.

In Enlightenment, I have and am All.

All judgments exist only within my mind alone.

When I choose to heal, I choose to know the Truth of Me and All.

Week Nineteen: **Extension**

Holy Spirit, can you help me learn how to make better choices for myself? I would like to choose to see Love first, rather than always come to it as an after thought. Thank You.

Wonderful, Dear One! We begin by looking at *every choice* you consider.

Whoa! Did you say EVERY choice? Is that even possible? Sounds like I'll be wrapped in analysis paralysis.

Every choice you make holds a key to a greater acceptance. But honestly, there are fewer choices than you recognize on an intellectual level. The intellect shatters one belief in separation into a myriad of effects and possibilities. However, the only two options existing in the split mind are a belief in fear or the acceptance of Who You Are in God. This is the choice between Love and fear. That is all. When you ask to see Love, you ask for the ability to see your Self in Truth, without the distorting influence of fear. You are seeking a clearer-minded path to Love, rather than a path that chooses to pass through fear's distorting lens. This power of fear need not be overwhelming. All I ask is for you to find the willingness to look within and seek a more serene awareness.

Do not deny anything. Look with honesty and try to remain aware of your incentive as well as potential roadblocks. Ask why you want to see this obstruction. Each roadblock represents a heightened value you ascribe to fear. This belief has you justify a separation from your brothers. Every fear mimics your beliefs. If you choose to bring every belief to the light, you will see yourself choosing to absolve yourself into Love.

For the focus of this teaching, I will refer mainly to the conscious choices you make on a day to day basis. Although each of these self-made choices is a feature of dualistic thinking (or individualistic thinking, meaning thinking that seeks only to place itself in division) each choice symbolizes an idea seeking healing on a subconscious level. Never will I ask you to deny your thinking nor will I attempt to force an idea of Love in its place; but, I *will* ask you to notice what every thought or choice reveals to you.

A mere *idea* of Love is not our goal here. Our one goal is the complete awareness of Love and True Being. This extension is a genuine desire, not a wish for mere temporal displacement.

The complete awareness of Love is accepted when fear is released in favor of an ever-growing knowledge of Truth. And although your life experience may stand witness for your practical need of fear, the complete awareness of Love is the Real You. Through our application of these insights, these calls to awareness, we will slowly begin to acknowledge our True Self.

Do not concern yourself now with the inevitable totality of awakening. These goals are beyond your temporal form and current state of consciousness. Truly, you cannot conceive the grandeur that You Are, when you are bathed in Truth. Therefore, it is purposeless to try and intellectually define this state of Pure Being to a mind that does not know. I say this not in belittlement. I say this only so that we can use our joining most productively.

First, we shall gear our practice to recognizing what thoughts, feelings or actions are helpful to your healing desire. As this is accomplished, your willingness for release and rest will expand. This expansion results in peace being consciously known with greater clarity. Truly, this is a most perfect purpose in time. Joining in awareness for the remembrance of Love on the conscious level is true perception made manifest. Therefore, still your mind of questions and concepts, for repetitive analysis or metaphysical intellectualization does not lead to peace. So yes, envision yourself now settling into the grassy plains before the gates of Heaven. Be mindful of your peace and allow all to simply be. Trust Me, Beloved, this awareness is a much a greater gift then intellectual satisfaction.

Once a conscious peace has been established with a greater clarity, the choice for love itself will be accepted into the One Mind. In this we welcome a further extension of love's Pure Being. This love is beyond choices and beyond all definition. Simply, it flows from within the One Mind and has no restriction or control.

Therefore, the practice of conscious choosing is only our initial application. It differs from One Mindedness. Choosing to make or not to make a choice is still accepting that a choice is available. This is to work within the realms of your accepted boundaries. Our eventual goal is to reveal ourselves beyond our consciousness and therefore no longer rely on choosing. This is surrendering to a greater knowing.

Concepts are not the key to peace. Complete release from all divisive ideas is the experience of Truth, but this can only be accomplished through release not redirection. Redirection is the thinking mind processing options and suppressing its beliefs. Release is the full acceptance of all beyond limitation. In release, you do not struggle. You do not fight to figure out or understand. In fact, you let go of all need for understanding and completely rest in trust.

This is why the idea of limitation must first be looked at. Again, we start here only so that we may reach beyond all limitations of the conscious and subconscious mind.

I will stand with you as you realize the role your mistaken identity plays in your suffering. Then, as you hold my hand, I shall guide you through the release of these scripts into the accepting of another way. This way can be called the Content of Wholeness.

I recognize this communication seems difficult for you to understand on the surface. Do not judge yourself if you don't get it yet. In your dedicated desire to see more clearly, we shall break through the distractions imposed by your thinking mind. Don't worry, Dear One, you will "get it."

From a thinking mind's perspective, change is not an easy task. I repeat, no change is an easy task, especially to a mind trained in dysfunction. The mind must be untrained of its destructive impulses first. This will take discipline. Surely, this too is why *A Course in Miracles* is not as easy for the mind to comprehend, on the first read. It usually takes years of practice to successfully implement.

In the process of unlearning, your consciousness will continue its projection of confusion. This is an attempt at resistance. However it will also effort to convince you that your savior is the intellect. Yet, neither of these is purposeful or true, not in the least as much as you'd like to think.

I guide you now to recognize your Self beyond your thinking. Here, where once thought was seen as your Source, peace is embraced as truly being you.

I am not asking you to devalue or deny anything, *but to notice when you ask to deny or devalue any reflection of your Self.* Each of your experiences, thoughts or feelings is beholding a gift for your own release. Notice when your thinking mind wishes for control. In this moment allow your mind to sink into a state of full noticing. Follow the thought back to its foundation. What is it that you really want through that control? What is it that you really feel? How does this feeling affect you? What does it say about you? Furthermore, what do these thoughts and feelings say about your True Self? Freely allow your mind to observe. See where you feel restricted and see where you desire to feel free. See how you believe that one choice allows for the gift of freedom, while another seems to represent imprisonment. Notice and allow each discovery. Each thought discovered and released honors your desire for awakening.

Every thought you have is a manifestation of LOVE being free to see its Self without limits. In other words, God has Created you so totally limitless that you can even go as far as imagining limits without true consequence. Be grateful for every opportunity you have to express. Each one is indeed a blessing from God Himself.

Are you saying that eventually I am to learn how to never make a conscious choice?

I am saying first that you need not BE your conscious choices. To become the choice is to see your self as limited to self-identity. It is to identify with need. Here you feel the necessity to control or survive only through your thinking mind. Here you feel "I must

choose in order to live, thrive or be happy." Rather as we come to
practice the release of our dependency on choice, we will extend to
all beyond all mere definitions. In this you welcome the grandest
extension of being through you. In this, you come to a peace that
steps beyond the requirements of choices. Likewise, you step
beyond the fear of making right or wrong choices. In releasing the
choice, you rest in trust and acknowledge how all that is IS. But do
not fear, this will not be done impractically. I will force you to do
nothing outside of your comfort zone.

Good, because I'm thinking this sounds impractical, at least for day to
day living.

Honestly, Beloved, you are so much more than your day to day
living. But, I shall never take anything from you. I will use
every thing as a device for learning. However, tell Me, is it your
practicality within the world that you desire, or peace beyond all
that binds you?

That doesn't sound like a fair question. Can't I have both?

Can you have both the world of limitation and the peace of perfect
beingness? Dear One, all is yours, or shall I say, all is within you
for nothing can change the peace of perfect beingness. Yet, when
you see yourself in limitation, relying on practical successes for
sustenance, rarely do you realize the peace of perfect beingness. In
limitation you attempt to exchange unlimited peace and love for
boundaries that are not your Truth. Therefore, although you can
HAVE both, you cannot KNOW both. In fact, you have both now,
only you have forgotten that your freedom to express brought you
here. You have forgotten that this limitation is merely just an
imagined wish gone mistakenly awry. Therefore, you have
forgotten your peace. And so what I am guiding is the release of
your forgetting and nothing else.

Do not feel that your freedom has to be sacrificed in order to
receive or reacquaint you with peace. Again, in Truth there are no

choices, only the full extension of your Holiness. Wholeness is yours and has always been yours. That is why this game you play has no real consequence outside of the world you play within. It is only your forgetful mind that has chosen to engage in this game of hide and seek. It alone has allowed the availability for all choices. However, you are still free. Release your thinking and see beyond what you think you need. This reawakens the peace of perfect beingness that has always been. This naturally releases you from the beliefs in fear and need. Sharing this forgotten memory is my only intent. Again, I am not asking you to deny anything, but simply to allow yourself to flow love through it.

Boy! This really sounds complicated! But I also am beginning to recognize how you are only guiding me to remember that I do not need to control anything. Although, I'm okay with that, it will require a LOT of trust on my part.

An intense amount of trust is only necessary if you believe that fear has equal power to love. If you feel resistant to trust, you perceive another possibility to trust. This is doubt. The word "doubt" literally means, "to choose between two things." Now, be honest. You doubt only because you are not certain in your desire to trust over your craving for fear. This is okay, but also it is important to realize what you crave for your healing. I guide you to release the self-will and sink into the extension of love. Do this only so that you may strive for certainty. Certainty is acceptance and thus the relinquishment of all illusions. Here we simply step into the realization that you are free to extend beyond all false identity. Love extends and does not deny. Its essence is one of expansion and completion. Therefore, Love refuses nothing and is all inclusive. Likewise, as you choose to live this essence of Being, you seek to be the love to all from the wholeness that exists in Truth.

Again, Dear One, do not confuse your mind, but be gentle with your self. Read this communication several times if you still feel confused. Try not to solve or decipher its teachings with a thinking mind, but ask for my guidance to show you the one thread of golden teaching.

You have functioned within the world of time for as long as you can recognize. In this world you have repeatedly relied on your thinking and feeling in place of God's knowing. Although, yes, it seems that God has not shared much of His Knowledge with you; now, I am here to hold your hand while we remember together. I ask you not to deny, but simply to notice and allow love to be where the struggling-self sees need and fear. We begin here. Do not concern yourself with doing this right or wrong. It is impossible. Nor am I asking you to perfect this as a process or to scrutinize every thought. I am not looking for paralysis of thought, but extension beyond it. Extension simply is acceptance. It is the deep breath felt and released where restriction and fear once were chosen. Remind yourself that you are free and cannot fail. I am with you, and my love is ever present in wholeness. I witness willingly to all you are. I love you. My Light is Your Own.

Week Nineteen: Prompts for Insight:

1. Choices are dependent on a belief in duality. We are always free to make these choices; however, a healed mind uses this freedom as a key to expanding true perception. A healed mind is always first aware of its Truth and then seeks only to extend its desire for sharing strength, certainty, and trust. Inversely, an unhealed mind chooses out of fear and the need to control. Write down a list of the choices that you currently see before you. Seek to see how a healed mind would see each choice, as well as an unhealed mind. Then, in a prayer, give these choices to Holy Spirit, asking Him to guide you to the choice for true perception over fear. Write your thoughts and feelings through this exercise.

2. Spirit shares, *"Every choice you make holds a key to a greater acceptance."* What does this guidance mean to you? How do you feel it would affect your life experiences? Do you feel you could give every choice to Holy Spirit? What fears surface when you consider this? What anticipations? Write down your thoughts.

3. The desire to see all in Love is the desire to see with a clearer vision. It is the desire to see in the eyes of Truth. What, in your life experiences or self, do you desire to see more clearly? Try to identify these desires with Holy Spirit. Write your thoughts and feelings.

4. Spirit asks us not to deny anything, but instead to look with genuine openness upon all our thoughts, feelings, and wishes. Are we asked then to bring every thought, feeling, and wish to Truth? Spirit teaches, *"The very act of resistance witnesses to an investment in fear."* Take a moment now to consider what you deny yourself by seeking fear. Identify as many thoughts and fears that you desire to hide. Process these with Spirit.

Affirmations:

Love in Pure Being is my True Self.

I release fear for an ever-present knowledge.

There is no practical need for fear.

I am as God Created Me.

Love knows no fear.

Week Twenty: **I Will There Be Light**

I will there be light. Holy Spirit, sometimes I feel confusion over the terms "my will" and "God's Will" and how to merge the two. Could you help me clarify? Thank you.

First off, there is only God's Will. Your will is merely an imagined idea of separation. This belief in being apart from God is definitely not True. Your beliefs are mere distortions. Never would I ask you to merge a distortion with Wholeness. Merging is impossible because it would be asking to compromise delusion within reality. There is only One Will, and this needs simply to be accepted for your peace.

Dear One, for the most part, your will has been expressed in ideas of fear, guilt, unworthiness, need and control. All that you perceive, experience, and idealize centers on these thoughts that perpetuate your belief in the self-will. Without the self-will there would be no need for competition, requirement or comparison. It alone devises and uses phrases such as "I should...," "I need...," and "I must...." Furthermore, only the self-will extends these desperate cries for completion out into the world, demanding "They should...," "They need to give me..." and "They must...." For example, let us look at the many circumstances where you frustrate yourself with feelings of powerlessness and disappointment. Are not these disappointments simply stemming from not receiving the expectations you have intended? Now, tell Me, why do you feel the need to expect anything? What would happen if these expectations were not met? Truly, are you that vulnerable? Can you see how all expectation is unrealistic and only leaves you wanting? Only the distorted traits of the self-will motivate such thinking. As long as you continually invest in these traits you will not only experience fear, guilt, unworthiness, need and control; but, you also will believe that your life is vulnerable and has no meaning unless you receive affirmations of love, appreciation and recognition from the outside world. It is only this wanting that can lead to loss and disappointment. Therefore, it is the belief in the self-will that begets all struggles. Honestly, none of this struggle is of God, nor can peace ever arise from such thinking. Without investment in the self-will, you would fully know that you have and are all in complete perfection. There would be no other possibility. As I have stated before in *A Course in Miracles*, truly, only your thoughts can attack you. Be willing then to see your true power and strength in God, and not the self-will. In this, the door to peace for all existence is opened.

God's Will is beyond all limitations. He Wills only one expression, and that is Complete Perfect Love. To completely know the fullness of this Will within your mind is unimaginable as you harbor and idealize a self-will. This does not mean that His Will must command over your own. There is no struggle for power here. Lo, instead, as you harbor and idealize a self- will, the very idea of limitlessness is unperceivable. This is why our practice is a guide to stepping beyond all perceptions of limitation. Together we yield illusion and return to the light of Truth. In this guide we come closer to full acceptance and in full acceptance we know.

First, let us recognize that the self-will does not desire the light. The individual body and thinking mind abhor and fear the light. Seemingly, they would never choose it over the self they tentatively recognize. To the self-will, the body, personality and thinking mind serve its best interest. Contradictorily, the Light simply is and cannot even begin to conceive a value or need apart from God. Yet, this does not mean that we cannot unlearn the self-will's investments in order to see more clearly. Truly, it is your present use of this will that can help set you free. Therefore, I use all ideas as learning devices. Let us then use your ideas of a self, to release you from the self.

Choose now to rest your thinking mind and will for an expression beyond the limits of perception and limitation. In this lesson we use your understanding of perception to recognize a deeper thought of Truth. Here we settle within. In consciously choosing to remember God's Will, you are using your own awareness (your will) to step beyond it and find once again what has never been truly forsaken. This is the conscious act of giving your will to God.

Fear may seem to select its words with persistence only because it is afraid. Fear operates within a realm of self-made identity and feels threatened by the release of all it does not consciously control. Never is your Identity in God at risk but merely your idea of an identity. Fear sees all loss in self-will as threat. Truth knows its Self and knows nothing apart. Rest and accept your Self beyond every bound.

Do not fear the release of an identity, as if to think that you will be left with nothing you know. You never were who you think you are. Instead, allow yourself to simply rest and judge not. Peace will come to you in all the ways. In willing there be light, you realize a desire beyond darkness and distortion. In this desire, you ask simply to rest and release from your dream. In willing there be light, you will for sustenance beyond your present confusion. In willing there be light, you will to know your Self once again, rather than continue to sit within a blind man's dream, merely perceiving reality through symbols.

God's Will is not found in words or images. His Will is not found in meaningless expectations or investments in time. God's Will has no needs or fears, nor does He project His Will onto others, fearing a disappointment from a wayward dependency. God's Will is found in the release of all things and is a knowing supplement rather than a sacrifice. It flows through all without limitation or need. Accept His Will, and release into the stillness of all that simply is. Here you become your Truth, rather than tease yourself through impossible riddles and hapless demands for limited satisfaction.

Never ask for a distortion to define your truth, for your Truth cannot be defined. Truth is a witness to its Self. Seek not knowledge through the world's understanding, yet allow yourself to see the binds of this attempt at understanding, so you may loose them. All that sees itself as incomplete cannot call an accurate witness to completion. This would be as if you had asked a blind man to be your guide. Deception can only define deception and speak its only known language.

Here is one significant error that the seekers of awakening project. Their first hope is to find a compromise within the world to prove their inner beingness. This is impossible and will only lead to disappointment. Nothing within this world (no experience, no person, no idea, and no words) can accurately describe your Holiness. These symbols can but merely lead the way to your own imagining, but surely you cannot settle there.

Once you have recognized the need for awakening, ask not God to describe yourself to you. Ask Him not to prove your existence or His Own. He IS existence itself and has no part of your doubts and knows nothing of proof. Instead, allow yourself to see where your own eyes have betrayed you and kept you believing in a dark representative of yourself, and then simply choose to release this image back into the nothingness from whence it came.

This is the will for light. This is the acceptance of God's Will over and beyond anything else. This is the removal of all obstacles to peace and resistances to love. Here you accept your Self as God Created and simply become a peaceful presence of Truth unlimited. Here your treasure shines bright beyond any world to see or call its own.

A sign of God is not your goal, for mere signage cannot detail the wonder and majesty of your Glory. You may consider yourself to be insignificant, if it is merely the perceptual self you see. Yet to God, you are magnificent and created in the sight of angels' splendor, and this light is unimaginable to your mind alone.

Hear Me now; do not concern yourself with meeting an accurate image of the Will of God. Just allow yourself to be. Rest your mind in stillness and release all desires for doing a task "right" in God. He has no bounds for you and insists on no requirement. Experience is for your mind alone; magnificence is gifted through His. And Beloved One, this light is your own. I love you.

Week Twenty: Prompts for Insight:

1. Holy Spirit teaches, "*I will never ask you to merge a distorted self-will with Wholeness. This is impossible because it would be asking to compromise delusion with reality.*" Identify where you have wished for and sought to compromise your self-will with God's Will. Write your discoveries and share these with Holy Spirit.

2. The self-will expresses only in ideas of separation. Some of the ways this separation is communicated to our brothers is through expectations, needs, dependency and yearnings for love, appreciation and recognition outside our selves. Take a moment to look within and see where you have had these yearnings. How have past expectations, needs, dependency and yearnings for love, appreciation and recognition served you? How have these same yearnings challenged or frustrated you? What most concerns you in choosing to release these practices?

3. Identify 3 needs you have and process them with Holy Spirit.

4. Identify 3 fears you have about losing your identity. Process these fears with Spirit.

5. Where do you feel most powerless in life? Where do you feel most disappointed? How have these experiences and feelings affected you? How do they continue to affect you? Ask Spirit to help you release these shadows upon your awareness. Write your guidance.

6. Identify one way you can fortify Self appreciation. If you are unsure, offer this in a question to Holy Spirit.

Dealing with Disappointment

The next time you find yourself experiencing disappointment, use the following steps to recognize how your thinking mind can appear to be your maker or destroyer.

Stop! Calm down. Breathe. Give yourself some time before jumping to conclusions. Remind yourself that you do not know what the future will bring. Assumptions are never reality!

Acknowledge your feelings. Express your emotions in a way that doesn't hurt you or anyone else. Do something healthy and positive to relieve your tensions.

Inquire. What thought or belief are you currently exchanging for peace? Ask yourself if the anger or resentment will help you cope or move on? Will these grievances give you what you want?

Release personal investment. Notice if you are taking the situation too seriously or too personally. How do you allow disappointment to devalue you?

Plan and learn. What can you learn from this experience? Write down a plan for self-sufficiency rather than dependency. The conditions that appear to rule your life only rule your mind.

Surrender. Our time is not God's Existence. God does not place His Holiness in limitation, nor does He judge. Accept that you already have all as needed in perfect peace now. Surrender to God's Will and release your struggling self-will. God always knows better, because He alone does know.

Week Twenty-One: **Practice of Peace**

Being the love you are requires only one conscious action: release. In your release you permit yourself to let go of all that has kept your mind preoccupied in self identification. To release is simply to relax and no longer consume your self with fears. In my asking you to release, I do not ask you to struggle. This is not an act, it is a non-act. The breath is its main tool. To release in breath is to allow oneself to breathe out the mind's pursuit. It is to turn one's thoughts from search to acceptance. See yourself as merely purposefully blowing out the mind's distortions. Focus not on judgment but on the desire for stillness and permission to let love comfort you. In being love, you center yourself in comfort rather than confusion. Thus to breathe freely is to be free, resting comfortable in the arms of God.

A practice of peace is not an action that needs to be actively monitored or ritualized. These actions are all restraints of the thinking mind seeking control and understanding. Stillness steps beyond all of these desperations and rests. Seek not to obsess yourself with the many questions or dissections the thinking mind persists. Seek respite in stillness now. If you recognize any discomfort within, this shall be your guide to the need for release. Do you experience a self breathing? Attempt to release any identification with the tasks the body does. Simply close your eyes and feel the breath blowing through you. You may breathe more voluminously and listen, as the sound of the ocean appears to flow through you. However, all interpretations are not necessary. Focus only on the desire for release is now.

Preoccupation with the mind has caused you much stress. Truly, all of your discomfort arises not from the situation but from how you occupy your mind with judgments about the situation. This is why I say; do not desire the world to change, but focus on changing your mind about the world. Here we return to what is within our own control, and truly what is causing our most pain. There will come a time, through mind training, that you will no longer need to identify your beliefs. Once the thinking mind is trained, its obsession with distractive beliefs naturally step-aside. Here you rest in God and choose to simply be. But for many this conscious rest is not experienced until after many years of dedicated practice. Do not let these judgments deter you. In every moment of practice you come closer to full realization and release of all distractive beliefs. This is the only reason why we focus on discovering our beliefs first. How can we release what we cannot identify? Therefore, consider this practice of belief realization to be the mere gateway to complete liberation.

As you recognize your beliefs do not assign blame or guilt. This confusion often arises when I mention responsibility for sight. Simply recognize responsibility for where your thoughts are taking you. There need not be any further processing. Specifically attempt to refrain from assigning projections to the past, present or future, victimization or psychological analysis. Is it a journey into peace or a descent into hell that you seek? Be aware of where your thinking mind leads. Use this recognition as your opportunity to allow another choice. Again, I say, in this practice, minimal time shall be spent on the thoughts or interpretations of the thinking mind. Use these thoughts merely as your guide in remembering that serenity is needed. Align yourself with the tranquil feeling emanating from within and the desire to let go of all discomfort. This is not as much of a routine or ritual, as it is a simple acceptance of stillness. Proceed in whatever way brings you the most serenity, rather than the most structure. Allow your core focus to be obtaining peace above and beyond the mind's interpretation.

In fact, I purposely do not detail any potential result of success or failure here. This practice is not about any sort of evaluation or prediction. It is about releasing all preoccupation with the mind. Do not obsess yourself with any strict instructions for doing the practice, and how it will feel to succeed. Simply align yourself with the breath, release any and all attempts to distract and choose silence. Rest in this now. I am with you. I love you.

Week Twenty-One: Prompts for Insight

1. Spirit guides, *"Being the love you are requires only one conscious action: Release.... To release is simply to relax and no longer consume your self with fears and willful assumptions."* Make a list of five stressors you have had this week. Identify ways these stressors can be viewed differently. How can you accept or understand the other persons involved? Can you identify limiting beliefs about yourself that led to your stressful conclusions?

2. *"Release is a non-act. It is to breathe out the mind's pursuits. It is to turn one's thoughts from search to acceptance."* Is it possible to practice a *"non-act"*? Is Spirit asking that we stop thinking all together? What thoughts come to mind in your consideration of this week's lesson? Set aside a minimum of five minutes each day this week to simply sit still and allow yourself to be. Write down your experiences and challenges, offering these to Holy Spirit for further guidance.

3. Spend one week applying the Practice of Peace Method as guided by Holy Spirit. Write your thoughts, feelings and experiences.

Affirmations:
I am Peace.
I am Love.
I release all to the Spirit of Love I am.
I am as God Created Me.

The P.E.A.C.E. Method

The genuine Peace of Self always exists beyond appearances. This peace is realized as we choose to surrender beyond our thinking and struggle. In peace, we take Spirit's hand. Here, He guides us in the recognition of all obstacles that keep us investing in the illusion. Use the following steps to help yourself realize the Truth You are:

P = Perspectives: Can you discover another way to see a negative situation? Your perspective depends upon your judgment. Judgment is always seeing in limitation, and thus you become blind to complete reality. Now is the time to remove the darkened glasses you wear! What you believe is often what you get. Take notice of the meaning you apply to life's situations. See the stories and judgments you are telling yourself. How do you judge yourself and others? Who owns your power? Realizing our perspectives has us begin within.

E = Expectations: Disappointment cannot occur without pre-appointment. What rules do you project onto others, yourself and the world? What do you feel "should" or "should not" happen? Can you change or control the world through these beliefs? Is it purposeful to dispute the current state of experience? Disputing the outside image only affirms resistance within. Take a moment now to realize the baggage you are carrying and how it seeks to define the world. Drop your bags, release expectations and choose instead to seek a clearer acceptance.

A = Actions: What can you do now that brings you the most peace? How can you accept life without constant struggle or resistance? How can you practically problem solve? Pay attention to how you may wish to choose the easier and more destructive way to solve your problems. Take mental notice of when you want to blame or punish others instead of find a better way. Decide now on what is a more purposeful outcome for your current experience and future well-being. Give yourself the gift of peace.

C = Consequences: We are always choosing our own adventure. There are no eternal victims. Why? This is true because we always have the opportunity to embrace healing from our difficult experiences. The past only lives within our thoughts and depends upon our personal investment in its stories. Therefore, be the cause and not the effect. If you are unhappy with the effect, look within and see the choices that may have contributed to your current experience. Now, gently allow yourself time to choose peace, heal and accept inner guidance for a new way.

E = Environment: Be aware or beware. Be aware of the company you keep. Take notice of how you may place yourself in destructive or self-defeating situations. Take notice of the people, places, circumstances, judgments, grievances, thoughts and emotions that you value and entertain within your sacred space. Who do you invite into the bed of your mind? Take a responsible look at where you put your and to what extent you may suffer thereof. You always have the freedom to decide!

Week Twenty-Two:

Sharing in Perfect Oneness

Okay, I've been having quite a few moments within mistaken identity lately. It seems that I see myself wrapped up in almost constant judgment and comparison with others. I don't want to feel this way, nor do I desire to justify these feelings. Help me to stop seeing the separation and accept all that is mine in Truth. Thank you.

> Dear One, you have all. You are all. It is not your True Self that perceives with the body's eyes. The body's eyes only communicate beliefs in separation. They show to you the witnesses you desire and allow you to project forth all the images you believe are to be seen. The You that is all is the You as God Created. Do not fear to see beyond what your eyes present. I can use every means concocted for separation as a learning device. You ask Me for a homecoming by abandoning all justifications for discord and accepting peace.
>
> Choose again when you find yourself seeking a rationalization for conflict or divisions within your mind. If you catch yourself judging inequality, realize that you do not see clearly. If you feel jealous, realize instead how all are equally blessed beyond mere appearances. The Holiness that God extends through you reveals the grandeur of the entire Kingdom. Therefore no one can have more or less within God.

I guess part of my problem is that I don't always see myself as part of the Kingdom of God. I can conceive this thought and occasionally hold onto it I feel lucky if I remember to practice it! Yet overall, there still remains a very well established idea of division. I, especially now, want to get past these obstacles, as I'm beginning to become sick and tired of feeling resentful.

> I understand that sometimes you see with the eyes of limitation. This is normal for where you perceive yourself to be. You can go as

far as to call your world, the theme-park of Division Land. This is when forgiveness of your thoughts is essential. Listen. You are not a mere part of the Kingdom of God. There are no pieces of God, only The Peace of God. His Kingdom expresses and extends through all life. It simply IS the force of life itself. The Kingdom of God is within you, as the life force of God Himself. Do you really believe this life force could be wrong? Or that it could be so vulnerable to misperception and iniquity? Truly, you are as God Created you. That is why I say forgive yourself for all that you have not done.

Sometimes when I think of forgiving, I still think of it as an afterthought. It seems that I still have this tendency to recognize an error and then choose forgiveness, which as *A Course in Miracles* teaches, is not True Forgiveness.

Yes, True Forgiveness is when you recognize that Your Holiness cannot be erroneous in any way. Here you see beyond your identification with the body and your experiences within it. Truly, as long as you see your life as ruled by a body, this investment in identity apart from God will only lead you to believing you are vulnerable. This is why I do not ask for you to forgive on the level of any form. To limit yourself here is not only dependent forgiveness but reaffirms the belief that forms can overpower you. Instead, what I ask for you to do is to forgive the idea of your vulnerability. Accept instead how you are perfect in God's Holiness, as are all your Brothers. Find the peace here and you will never want again. In this moment you align with the Truth as God Created. Temptation will have you contort illusions into temporal deceptive truths. A temporal deceptive truth usually is decided upon by your intellect and often contains some form of disquieting compromise or suppression. Do you really feel that God would ask your mind to be disquieted or suppressed? Surely not. Therefore, this is not true forgiveness.

As I have said, the Kingdom of God is within you, expressing as the force of life itself. Beyond a body or any imagining, this Self is invulnerable and changeless. Therefore, to align with this knowing, welcoming its wholeness within you, as you, cannot but command all illusion to fade like mists before the sun. Recognize that Truth cannot be changed by bodies, perceptions, behaviors or any idea of limitation. As you do this you will simply laugh at every attempt the mistaken identity makes to define you. In this moment, you see the light as it is. Here you accept peace for the sake of accepting your Self. This, of course, differs from relegating to temporary or compromised considerations because some Voice in your Mind told you to do so.

Sometimes, you really crack me up!

All that I teach is meant to be used. I do not teach for concepts alone. I teach for your awakening. Your awakening is found within the practicing of what you hear, now.

Sit now and listen. Listen to your thoughts and search them (you won't have to look far) for all ideas of separation. Look where you perceive others to be more special or gifted than you. Look everywhere that you see yourself as standing apart from someone else's light. Look where you see any division within the body, mind, talents, perception, identity, beliefs, communication, possessions, experiences, etc. See it all.

Notice everywhere you see others as having or being more than you. Notice where you judge some to have or be less. Although this is not as much of a problem for you, it is a separation identity you adhere to in your viewpoints of the world and all its material and socio-economical divisions. Judgment is to see some as having more and some having less. This is separation and an enacted substitution for the One Creation God has extended in perfection. It is to claim a mocking vulnerability as an alternative for wholeness in Truth. Although the world may show you its witnesses through claims of multiple differences and delineations (be it educational status, capitalistic versus poverty stricken countries, social classes or relationships and/or all the limitations human beings appear to be innocently born into) you remain changeless. The world tells you that some appear to just have been dealt a bad hand, right? To invest in this belief is to justify an image of victim and victimizer. Never does judgment bring you peace. Recognize this now, so that all images testifying to the justification of division can be released.

There is nothing of the world that is True. No one is divided within God. No one receives apart from the belief they allow within the moment. This is why, for some, poverty is seen as a blessing; while for others it is seen as a torment. I know this appears hard to accept, so let us just simply look at what beliefs you see within this moment and cease.

If you believe that any brother has a greater gift to understand the Truth than you, you extend separation and hide yourself within its illusions. This is the same for when you judge any brother as superior or inferior to you. Each of these is simply an attack upon yourself and furthermore and attack on God's Oneness. Choose instead to see your brother as only witnessing to love, which is truly your own desire. See everyone as only speaking and being the truth for you. Here, we recognize that wholeness is beyond images and peace is in perfect expression all ways.

Watch every thought that attempts to steal your peace. This is the diligence with which I have spoken time and time again. It is only your belief in separation that has you see yourself as having more or less. It is only your belief in separation that has you yearn for validation and attention from others for anything. Instead allow yourself to accept the purity of Truth and creation with which you choose to acquaint yourself. See this as the gift that is available in all moments. For it is for all.

There are others who do not ever perceive themselves to have any share of wholeness, although this is only for their own understanding. Do not be grateful or disparaging for what your Brother seems to, or not to, have (because remember they all have all). Embrace the joy within each moment you have chosen to see. Celebrate the same for your Brother. This is your step forward into the light, and you and your Brother do this together. You are never healed alone, for that would make separation real. There is only ONE mistaken perception, and this has been resolved in Love as You are.

There is never a need for jealousy within the Kingdom of God. God has all and gives all equally. Only your mind perceiving separation sees it otherwise. You try to distract yourself with justifications even as you hear this because these are thoughts you do not desire to see. This is not a moment for guilt. It is a moment for reacquainting yourself with your Self and has been our theme of late.

We had spoken on bringing the false to the True, and there you noticed many thoughts you had that needed the light of Truth to shine upon them. I use this moment to reacquaint you with all that still asks for healing.

I am here with you as you choose to see healing. I am here with you as you choose to welcome forgiveness within your mind. I am also here with you every moment you choose to see separation or special stature within your Brother, isolating yourself off from the Oneness which is You. I see all that you ask for and extend only love.

You do not need to leave anything within the world to receive this Truth. You do not have to physically dedicate your life 24 hours a day to this awakening in form. As we both know this will not be a choice you desire. One of the basic thoughts of your jealousy and fear is that you wish you had more time for spiritual practice. You wish you could dedicate your entire life to it, but then you worry about mortgage payments, job security, your family's opinions of you, and all the other judgments that once again reflect fear and division. Remember, Dear One, the process of awakening is not dependent upon anything within the world, nor is it dependent upon an image, persona or body.

Let us not concern ourselves with these ways of thinking. These thoughts are attempts to prevent your healing through fear. They attempt to make your world real and a feasible opposition to peace. Thank goodness this healing is not of form. Wherever you are, there you shall heal. Healing your thoughts does not require a place to be. It does not require a retreat center, guru, or special surroundings. Healing your thoughts does not even require a body! Imagine that! You can do all that you desire within and still be as God Created You.

Your perceptions of separation are only played out in form, but remember that the content, Content, CONTENT of your beliefs is the key to all you see! Use each moment to see differently. Seeing differently can be done while physically sleeping or awake. It can be done in traffic or at your place of employment. It can be done at the dinner table or with your favorite bowl of ice cream afterwards. It can be done as you enjoy the company of your friends, pets, family or favorite book. It can be done in every moment, for time or space does not determine your progress. There is no judgment… there is only progress.

Remember this every time you need a reminder. Call attention to every thought of separation. Breathe and open yourself to healing. Remember there is no better or worse; there is only love. And this love is you!!! I am calling out for your awakening and loving you in every moment, no matter how you see yourself. You are the Love of God eternally. You are all your Brother is. You are changeless, flawless, boundless light. This light is Our own and I love you.

Just as a whim, I decided to start writing down some of the thoughts of more / less in my mind. I started with just some of the things that I recall have tripped me up repeatedly. By the way, there were names in the — spaces, but I have erased them to protect the innocent.

I see — as having more clarity and wisdom.
I see — as having more money, material goods.
I see — as being more valued at work.
I see — as being more attractive.
I see — as being more respected.
I see — as having a better family life.
I see — as having more time to be "spiritual."
I see — as having more understanding.

I see — as having more intellectual knowledge.
I see — as being more aware.
I see — as having more love in their lives.
I see — as having more like-minded friends.
I see — as being more appreciated by others in their life.
I see — as being more cared about.
I see — as being more validated, more recognized.
I see — as having more Peace.
I see — as having more freedom with their time.
I see — as being more willing to extend friendship to others.
I see — as less afraid.
I see — as less concerned.
I see — as more gifted.
I see — as being more interesting.
I see — as having a better outlook on life.
I see — as being a more skilled writer and speaker.
I see — as having a nicer, cleaner, and more affluent home.
I see so much unfairness in life!
I see so many struggles between myself and life's progress!

Oh my goodness, I see divisions everywhere!! And I can't believe how this list reflects the loneliness I really feel within. I see divisions in talent, abilities, life styles, money, social classes, homes, education, personality, behavior, politics . . .

Wow! I really do see a lot of judgment. I see a lot of limitation. It's amazing how each of these has been a shadow upon my sight. Every one of these thoughts has kept me waiting and wanting for the Peace of God. I have believed every one of these thoughts and felt jealousy, division, anger, misunderstood, loss, sacrifice, disdain, resentment, greed, pain, hurt, loneliness, rejection, etc. even this list seems to go on and on! Every one of these thoughts keeps me from truly seeing the Love of God within my Self. Every one of these thoughts sends a message into the universe that my nature is divided, separated from my Brothers and not worthy. It's amazing, though, how hard it seems to see Truth sometimes.

That is because all you need do is open your eyes. Any idea of separation is blindness to the Truth you are. You extend a shadow over the light of Truth and call this an image of yourself. Too much time has been spent on diversion. As you use this world and time it becomes a diversion of division. Now, if you desire, you may instantly return to the peace you so desire in Truth.

Well, yeah! Is that even a question??? Hit me! (Smile)

I cannot do this to you, but I do this with you. I guide you through your own awakening, because I honor your freedom to be as you wish all ways. Yet, in the expressed desire to see all anew in Truth now, I thank you for extending yourself beyond fear. No longer need you play victim to these whispers of delusion.

Gosh, more like a booming voice of delusion!! Yes, there have been many times when I have used fear as my divider. I have allowed it to settle as a distraction within my mind. Yet, now I do ask for another way.

And so it shall be. Quietly, as you discover every thought of separation, focus on your breath and repeat, "I am limitless, boundless love, extending light. I am free." This shall help you remember the Truth of Who You Are. This practice of remembering is calling into your consciousness the very beingness which God Created you to be. Here you find your freedom from all limitation.

Another good exercise in remembrance involves the next time you are gazing into a mirror. Look yourself in the eyes and say, "I am limitless, boundless love extending light." Continue to keep this thought in your mind as you look. Truly LOOK into your eyes. See your Self through yourself. Continue to repeat, not necessarily in spoken word, but in thought as you see all the limitless, boundless, joy upon your face. This is your Self shining through. Stay with this thought for as long as you desire. Yet attempt to keep it with you throughout the day and within every moment where an idea of separation pops into mind. Now is your opportunity to look again at each of these shadows upon the mind and literally choose again. Choose and find the peace that has never left you. Choose and find the Love that has always been and always will be. Choose and regain the responsibility for sight and embrace the wholeness of you! My light is your own, and I love you.

Week Twenty-Two: Prompts for Insight and Practice

1. Where do you see separation in your life? Write a list of at least thirty-five (you'll see how easy this really is) ways you see separation within the world, relationships or yourself. See where you perceive some as having more or less than you. Call up all beliefs of victim and victimizer. Don't forget the numerous ways we divide people through social-economic strata, religion, education, age, appearance etc. Now, with your list in hand, focus on each device of separation and say, "*There is only wholeness here. This image is forgiven.*" Write your thoughts, experiences, and feelings afterwards with Spirit.

2. Consciously stay connected to all within your life experience this week. Smile at people you pass while walking down the street. Greet people in the elevator or on the bus. Say thank you to anyone who provides a service to you (postal worker, waiter or waitress, and the clerk at the convenience store). As many moments as you can remember to keep each of these people in mind, and say within: "*You are limitless, boundless love, extending light. You are free.*" Write down all surfacing thoughts and feelings with Spirit.

Look yourself in the eyes and say: "I am limitless, boundless love, extending light. I am free." Continue to keep this thought in your mind as you look at yourself in the mirror. Truly look into your eyes. See your Self through yourself.

3. Practice the eye gazing exercise each morning for two weeks. Write all surfacing thoughts and feelings with Spirit.

4. Ceremony of Release: Cut one piece of paper into six strips. On each strip write down one thought or image you would like to forgive. These can be images of yourself or another in the past or present. They can be thoughts which have a lingering shadow of guilt, projection, hurt or anger. Now is the moment of self-forgiveness and release of perceptions. Once you have all papers complete, take a walk to your favorite natural spot; perhaps a body

of water or your own backyard. Choose where you feel most quiet and comfortable. One by one take each strip of paper, read your thought aloud, and follow it with:

> *"In the name of my Truth, I choose to release [read paper]. I am innocent. I am loved. I am free. I am as God Created Me."*

Now, heartily tear up the paper and discard it. This is a fabulous ritual of release for all situations. Use this ceremony for healing before a new season or year, or ritualistically act out your wish to release unhealed events from the past. NOTE: How you choose to discard your papers is your choice. I suggest using recycled disposable paper and burying or safely burning each paper in a fireplace, so as not to leave unwanted waste. The form of the ritual is up to you, yet the meaning is tremendous.

This is a fabulous ritual of release for all situations, including healing before a new season or year, or simply to act out forgiveness beyond form.

Affirmations:
I am limitless, boundless love, extending light.
I am as God Created Me.
Truth knows no comparison.
Love is always One in All.
There is no separation or limits in God, nor in Me.

Week Twenty-Three: **Stillness**

Stillness is the gatekeeper to peace of mind. For it is here, in opening beyond restraint, you accept Love as your Self and release all thoughts of a mind in mistaken identity. Here you answer the call. Just breathe and release. Allow your mind to come to rest in my awareness. Here is where stillness is. Here is where you allow the gate to open for your awakening.

Stillness is You. It is the call stating that you remain as God Created. To say you are still as God Created is to declare your changelessness beyond all mistaken identities. It is a calling to be at rest, to be changeless, to return to the All that never became anything less than wholeness. Be still and settle the mind that asks to witness in limitation, rather than wholeness. Be still. Knowing this perfect tranquility is resting your Self in Truth. Breathe, rest and release. One awareness, one peace, one being throughout the Kingdom of God is You.

Stillness is as You are. These are the simplest words I can use to call you Home. Here I witness to your serenity in Truth and call you to bring to light this wave upon the infinite.

Stillness is as You are. Settle your mind here and let us listen. Listen to the call in the vibration of Your Holy Name. Let us welcome the serenade to Holiness. Extending, expressing, and enjoying the grace of Truth, you harmonize in glorious awakening. Rest in this stillness and be witness to your Self in the symphony of One. Enrapture yourself in your Self and simply be.

Not a memory or echo of that which is apart from reality, this song calls out from deeper than your limited mind. This song and sounds are waves of God's Beingness, harmonized by the Angelic Choir, gently resonating beyond all space and time. Here you witness your own sonata to Truth. Rest here and allow the intonations to swell up and embrace you. Hear the call. Listen in recognition of your divine melody. Dear One, be in praise for the glorious appearing of the Love that You are. I am with you as I love you.

Week Twenty - Three: Practice:

There are a multitude of suggested methods for deeper inspiration and connection. One of my favorites is the easiest and follows the guidelines received through Supplements to *A Course in Miracles: The Song of Prayer.*

First, find a favorite place to sit where you can be undisturbed for at least five minutes. Wear comfortable clothes and sit without constriction of body or mind. Now, with or without music, settle your thoughts and quietly focus within on the words *"Stillness is as I am."* Breathe deeply and guide your mind only with these words. Focus your mind on receiving your connection to God in perfect awareness as You truly are. If a distracting thought arises in your consciousness, simply breathe, release, and rest. Focus your desire on embracing the stillness that you are. Imagine the entire Kingdom of God surrounding you.

Continue to repeat: *"Stillness is as I am."* Allow a deep feeling of gratitude to swirl through your heart-center. Picture yourself reclining on the supple grasses before the Gates of Heaven. Feel the presence of Light all around you radiating in the Love you are. Sit quietly in this space for as long as you feel comfortable. Here we come in the companionship of God Himself. You are Loved.

Practice this meditation once a day upon waking and once more prior to retiring for bed. Supplement other moments through your day as you feel is guided.

Affirmations:
Stillness is as I am.
Stillness is the gatekeeper to peace of mind.
The Kingdom of God is within Me.
I am as God Created Me.
There are no obstacles to God outside of my own mind.

Week Twenty Four: **Surrender**

Dearest Holy Spirit, I don't understand what anything is for. I give this moment to you.

Thank you, Dear One, for recognizing our connection. In realizing that you do not understand, you choose surrender. Sometimes it appears to be surrender for genuine release of the self-will. While other times you give up from a desperate cry for help and desire to escape from futility. No matter the type of surrender, I honor all calls for love with love. In our goal for the turning towards Truth, we behold your innocence and thus extend Love rather than fear. As you surrender, accept your Self beyond the world. Welcome Love as your guide.

What impedes surrender? You wish to escape and have a need to control. In a wish to escape you see through the eyes of restriction, guilt, and victimization. Here you determine yourself to be an effect of fear. Prior to this desperate cry for escape, the thinking mind may try to "work its pain out on its own." Here you feel the need to control, in order to protect yourself from a world gone mad. In this, you claw at every possibility your thinking mind can conceive. Here you battle with the world and do not rest. Eventually, you frustratingly quit in defeat. Does this not sound like the product of the self-struggling mind? Better yet, do any of these sound evocative of the peaceful Holiness You are?

Quitting out of defeat is not surrender, but merely it is an acceptance of a belief in victimization or sacrifice. In it you acknowledge an entrapped self concept. And thus you ask to escape from all that has or can hurt you. Here you claim to give up in exhaustion from the abuse of your innocence, not because of Who You Are in God, but because of how the world has affected you. You stand alone and afraid in a world determined for your inevitable destruction. You may cry unto the heavens, "God help me!" Yet you never do believe He cares enough to listen. Thus, the futile desire for escape masquerades as resignation, all the while your self-will reigns.

The more beneficial desire for surrender occurs when the will of the self is faithfully retired as folly incomparable to the Will of God. Here you completely release yourself from the need to control, predict or plan. In True surrender, you have no pleas for escape or separate agenda. Rather you allow yourself to rest in God.

True surrender is yielding completely in certain Trust. It is acceptance and appreciation for all You are beyond images. Here you acknowledge that you are not of the world, nor your mistaken identity. Here you allow your True Self and desire to only serve its knowing. In this surrender, you release for peace.

I was guided to research the etymology of the word "surrender" and found: "to give (something) up," from *surrendre* "give up, deliver over" deriving from: *sur-* "over" + *rendre* "give back" (see *render*). The reflexive sense of "to give oneself up" relates to imprisonment.

This definition of surrender exemplifies the two specific components of your current beliefs relating to it. The first type of surrender is associated with either loss or sacrifice, which as I've said before is really not releasing, but only a reaffirming of the belief in suffering. Here you resign because of an identified loss from either the world or yourself.

In the initial stages of healing, the self-will defines the process of surrendering to God as a sacrifice. This stems from the need to control for your own security and validity. The concept of sacrifice is not possible without fear. Only fear believes that it can lose anything. But, in Your Truth, this is not the case. Until the identification with fear is released, through your willingness to trust beyond this identification, true surrender remains impossible.

The second definition of surrender directly relates to Truth. It states that surrender means, "to deliver over, to give back over and to give oneself up." Consider this to mean that you choose to yield over to God what has always been His beyond time. To give one's struggling-self up, to receive, and deliver over to God are truly your goals in surrendering. In this choice to surrender, you accept the peace and joy that has always been yours and see all else as being merely misleading.

Surrender is never a practice of denial within the world. However as you practice, you will see how it is a realization of reality. In surrender, you accept the One Self in exchange for service to your mistaken identity. You choose trust in place of imprisonment. Notice how the above definition states that you "give oneself up, especially as a prisoner." This describes the acceptance of Self over self-will.

Dear One, surrender and see past your brick and mortar boundaries. See beyond all fears and needs that have never expressed any idea but limitation. See all that God has declared for You. I am with you in your perceived return to Truth. My love knows you have never gone anywhere.

My Light is Your Own.

Week Twenty-four: Prompts for Insight

1. How have you wished to escape from life's situations? When? Write down a minimum of five situations when you have wished to escape. Review this list and identify the emotions you felt in each situation and whether these emotions stem from beliefs in powerlessness or threat. How does feeling powerless or threatened continue the role of playing victim? How does each reflect the shadows of judgment and mistaken identity? Finally, quiet your thinking mind and consciously give this incident, thought or feeling to Spirit. Complete your prayer by saying, "*I accept I am as God Created Me for there is no other Identity I am.*"

2. The word "escape" means "to take flight" or "to get out just in time – leaving disaster with just one's clothes on their back." How does this explanation affirm the role of being a victim? How does it progress the role of limitation in your life? Identify ways you have felt like a victim and process these thoughts and feelings with Holy Spirit.

3. The word "surrender" means "to deliver over, to give back over and to give oneself up." Therefore, in terms of our practice, it is to give up the areas where we struggle and choose instead to Trust beyond fear or doubt. Write down a list of the circumstances, thoughts and feelings you would like to surrender to God. How have you sought to control this circumstance with your own thinking? How have these solutions worked for you in both the short and long term? Where have these actions not succeeded? Please realize that surrender differs from apathy, it is a trusting in our ability to see merely beyond our own thinking, rather than struggling for control. After you identify all that you wish to surrender, take a deep breath, quiet your thinking mind and say, "*I deliver [name situation] over to God, knowing I am free.*"

Practice: What I Give to Serenity
Create a list of all the situations in life you feel you cannot change in relation to the past, present or future. Continue this list with all situations you can change. Envision yourself giving this list to the Holy Spirit, trusting He will heal and lead the way to deeper guidance.

Affirmations:
Repeat the following prayer in all noticed moments of frustration, stress or anger:

The Serenity Prayer

God:
Grant me the serenity to accept the things I cannot change.
The courage to change the things I can,
And the wisdom to know the difference.
Amen.

Week Twenty-five:

Surviving an Ego Attack

Dearest Holy Spirit, Wow! The fury that came over me last night was intense. At first I found myself recognizing many destructive thoughts. Following your instruction, I took a few deep breaths and then tried to reintroduce a truthful thought. Yet, to be perfectly honest, I didn't feel any better, and the distractions appeared to persist.

In fact, it felt like my mind was mocking my attempts. All attempts at changing my thoughts felt shallow and useless. Worse yet, a belief in peace seemed impossible! Eventually, it did get to a point of over-flow. I couldn't sit still and had to get out of the house. I wanted to run somewhere, anywhere! Then of course when I did, all I saw were opportunities for attack, criticism and projection. Consciously I knew what I was doing and why but it seemed like my mind had a spite of its own. I don't understand why this fury seemed to persist so strongly, even when I wanted otherwise. Can you help me gain some insight in retrospect? Thank you. I love you.

First of all, Dear One, it is essential that you remain gentle with yourself. This judging of your reactions is not helpful. Yes, you did feel as though you couldn't take it and sit through it. Yes, you did find reasons to attack and project the destructive ideas of your mind. Yes, this was the thought system of a mistaken and fearful self. You even sought justification for these ideas through assumptions of knowing what these others "were really up to." Yes, you really did not believe the attempts to replace the ideas with peace.

It is all okay. I repeat, it is all okay. I see and know you for Who You Are and never judge. This situation is not an opportunity for further condemnation. Condemnation is only appropriate to the self-will who thrives in judgment. However, although these thoughts were present within, you are never without your Truth. Each ego attack is an opportunity to learn. In fact, all experiences are opportunities to learn. Accept this witness to forgiveness and receive an awareness of more peace.

Let's go through this together. I would like you to breathe now and attempt to step back into your belief system at that moment.

Do I really have to???

(smile) I am only here to be truly helpful.

Okay . . . (smile)

Now, as you breathe, I would like you to reintroduce some of the ideas that were appearing within your mind last evening.

I definitely perceived myself to be limited. I saw myself as feeling snubbed / rejected by someone I really respected. I jumped to a conclusion that I wasn't liked and also that I was being used. My thoughts supported all the evidence of how this was true and how I was once again being victimized. I sank into many ideas of fear and attack.

Yes. And do you notice the closed feeling and tension around your throat and heart centers as you say these beliefs?

Indeed!

Now, continue to breathe and close your eyes. Cease from typing and breathe out this closed feeling. Try not to swallow too much, but forcefully breathe if the sensation for swallowing arises. Gutturally direct the breath through your mouth and feel yourself pushing all emotions and impulses through the breath. Do not judge. But instead allow yourself to sink into only the thought of release. You may say simply, "this is not Who I Am," but truly words are not necessary. Now breathe slowly and notice how I shall introduce a feeling of light around you. Feel my presence and love within. Sit and breathe here for a moment. Quiet the mind and just be.

One of the keys to this practice is releasing all distracting thoughts and settling within the feelings, urges, of your body. I am not asking you to identify with or value the body, but to use the force that appears for your conscious release. When a feeling of tension slips to the surface again, allow yourself to forcefully breathe through your mouth. Take these breaths slow and do not focus on any words or thoughts. Focus solely on release. Allow the rate of your breathing to slow and deepen. Allow your mind to be open to light. Focus yourself deep within and use your breath as the metronome.

Simply allow yourself to release and rest through an open awareness. Guide your inhalation and gently pass through this moment with a more determined purpose for peace. Use as much time as you feel is needed, until you palpably feel the sensations of body and mind settle. When they do, there will be a merging of stillness within both.

During this experience I felt an increasing of physical releases in various forms. I coughed, belched, sneezed, and even passed some gas. I felt a tension desiring to be released from my throat, and so I forcefully breathed through my open mouth. I also began to notice an increased tingling feeling around my crown chakra. This tingling was a comfortable feeling that allowed me to settle more deeply within the releases I was feeling throughout my body. I often had a buildup of saliva in my mouth. Instead of swallowing, as guided, I spit it out, almost in a guttural nature. Each time I cycled through this forceful breathing, coughed or spat the saliva, I felt more free to relax and more inclined to focus. I cycled through this process multiple times, attempting not to allow tension to settle within, but instead, releasing it through the body. I allowed feelings to release however they desired, focusing on the process within rather than what my body was doing.

Eventually my breath began to feel freer and more settled in my body. Tension had dissipated, and I could focus within on the tingling, peaceful sensation around my crown chakra. I allowed this tingling to spread and felt very comfortable and lighter. I continued to breathe slowly, resting in this sensation. The entire process took about a half- hour, although time was not my focus. Eventually, I felt the desire to breathe deeply, both in and out of my nose. A deep relaxing and cleansing breath flowed through my lungs and the tingling in my crown chakra expanded fully. I chose to rest in this state with eyes closed for about another 10 minutes until I felt prompted to open my eyes.

Wow! That was an interesting experience!

> Yes. Here you used your body, rather than your mind, as a channel. With My assistance, you were able to guide the energy block through an expressive, physical release and settle yourself once again in peace. This practice was once an ancient yogi technique where the body was used to release energy blocks or restrained beliefs. Remember that the beliefs you interpret as being thoughts, can also be defined as energy. They can be represented as thoughts, words or even experiences, but all are erroneous.

It feels like a darker energy.

> You can describe it as that, but it is only restraint. You interpret that which is not You as an opposite, and this interpretation has led to a definition of darkness or evil. Yet, since this "darkness" is an illusion, it really is only misperception that is mistakenly seen as something else. True Self is freedom and knows no boundaries. All illusion is inverse awareness of this. Your Self can be seen as an energy that expands from the Love of God. Boundless Love, limitless and free, You are continuously expanding light. Therefore any mistaken belief is only an attempt to restrain the Wholeness you are. This is why you feel restraint flow up, for you have literally unleashed the restrained energy of misperception within you. In this process you release the subconscious beliefs that have convinced you of your limitation.

That's really quite amazing. It is so simple to see these thoughts as mere distortion. Yet, I'm amazed because usually the actual practice appears so complex, fearful and mysterious.

Yes, the mistaken identity thrives by keeping itself in the shadows of enigma. The attempt to try and "solve the mystery of self" keeps the game going. Truly you cannot struggle to remember unless you have first agreed to forget.

Sometimes these unknowing thoughts emerge as opinions or judgments about you, other people, places or circumstances. Each thought speaks for the restraints you conceptualize yourself to be.

In these thoughts, the Light You are appears filtered and distorted into an apparent dark-energy. It is not apart from You, only merely another way of expressing. This is why forgiveness is essential. In forgiveness we see ourselves as whole, accepting that there is no limit to how Light can express itself. Here, in realizing freedom without the possibility for lasting distortion, you can stand back and choose again.

The key to healing an ego experience is not to think you must replace the restraint with another thought. If you attempt to, it will simply feel ineffective and incredulous. This is because the mistaken belief fueling the experience already perceives itself to know what the problem is. It perceives restraint and seeks only to find the cause through projection. It is seeking expression of its assumptions. Therefore, if you attempt to further restrain or argue with the already invested belief it sees this attempt as foolish.

Why? Because you already are agreeing that the limitation is real, long before the negative feeling is experienced. Merely replacing an ego belief with another thought would be similar to attempting to place a band-aid on a severed gangrened limb. How could this initiate healing?

Instead, see the belief for what it is. Expose the belief. See the ingredients within the recipe. Meet the thought where it is, and gently allow yourself to release the false belief. Logically, you could think simply accepting loving thoughts where there appears to be loss would naturally result in success. But truly, this method relies on the mind to attempt to heal what is far beyond the reach of the mistakenly identified mind. The ego is neither stupid nor naïve, but it is accommodating in its service. It always says "Yes sir" to all requests which appear valid from its judgments. As long as the forgotten self remains accepted, evidence shall be felt. In fact, as all disturbing emotions are felt, the possibility for limitation of Your Holiness has already been accepted. This is why we are not seeking to mislead, trick or reprogram any perceptions, but simply heal.

Here the body can be a purposeful resource. You can channel the release of ego ideas through a conscious healing process (as I led you through). This is one way to productively discharge the darker energy and accept peace can be beyond its illusion. Breath is a natural cleansing channel for the body. Through breath, you can assist yourself to increase focus, encourage release, and accept healing. It is a helpful intermediary between the mind still perceiving a body, yet seeking to reveal a peaceful Source within. Many ancient religions and mystics revered and used the breath because, throughout time, it has been recognized as a healing channel.

In a way, isn't this asking me to identify with the body?

Is it not true that you already do? I am not asking you to do or see anything that is not already perceived. Instead, use your perceptions for healing purposes. See this similarly to the learning opportunities I have spoken of before. I do not curse that which you perceive, although I know it to be incorrect. Love does not curse or condemn. So, instead, I gently allow you to recognize for yourself—through your own perceptions— all that you have already accepted as valuable for healing. Here all can be used as a learning device. Recognize the gift in all and you will simply accept healing through all.

Use this healing process any time you desire. Remain aware ideas that whisper restraint. See these beliefs for what they are. Observe the content through the perception. Then breathe, release, and renew. Remain awake at your post, not in defense, but in recognition. Here you shall see all that desires to be set free. Here you shall open your eye to your Source.

Through forgiveness you agree to see yourself once again as the limitless peace You are. In this acceptance, the limitation you once claimed is revealed as illusion. Beyond this seeing of the illusion, a channel to your peace is guided through Me, with you, to release. You call this healing. In this manner, your mind is set free of every illusion and awakened to your True Self. Set yourself free and know your Self once more. I am with you always. I love you.

Week Twenty-five: Practice

Schedule and participate in the conscious healing process three times this week, for at least one hour each day. Trust that the Holy Spirit is always with you and only in complete gentility desires your well-being. Find a safe place to express according to the following instructions:

1. Begin by settling within a safe and relaxed location, preferably with no interruption, possibly a bedroom or meditation sanctuary. Wear comfortable, nonrestrictive clothing. It most likely is best practiced alone, so as to fully engage in the activity without self-conscious restraint. Playing calming background music may be helpful in the process, but not a requirement.

2. Breathe deeply for five minutes.

3. Center your mind in an awareness of Spirit's companionship.

4. Allow yourself to think of a negative belief. If you feel you can, let this negative belief be one of significant influence in your life experience. Thoughts such as "I am a victim," "Nobody loves me," "I am all alone," "My life is purposeless," etc. are rather appropriate for this exercise. However, if you feel uncomfortable immediately diving in so deep, choose a thought that is less distressing and then work your way deeper. Yet remember, as *A Course in Miracles* states, "There are no small upsets, each are equally disturbing to my peace of mind."

5. Upon choosing the belief you would like to reveal for healing, let yourself sink fully into this belief. Accept the judgment, anger and/or fear this thought presents.

6. Identify exactly what this thought is telling you about you, others and your life experience. Do not muffle, resist or deny its statements and theories. Do you feel like a victim? Notice your thinking without attaching yourself to each perception.

7. Notice how your body reacts and responds to these thoughts. Be mindful of tension in your muscles or tighter chakras. Take mental note of where the restriction expresses in your body. Completely give your body over to these sensations without resistance.

8. Throughout this practice, continue to breathe and close your eyes.

9. Desire to transmute these thoughts out of your body through conscious breathing.

10. Picture these thoughts being swept up by the breath of your body. Purse your lips and with a forceful conscious breath, exhale.

11. Try to be conscious of the swallowing reflex. Swallowing can be symbolic of the subconscious wish to suppress these thoughts or feelings, keeping the restrictive energy within the body.

12. When you notice the yearning to swallow (or suppress / restrict), forcefully purse your lips and breathe out rather than swallow. If you are familiar with Lamaze style breathing, use a similar power of your exhalation.

13. Do not judge your progress or practice. Release all expectations for what should or must be in this experience. Completely give your conscious mind over to the body's expression.

14. If you desire, repeat as you release, "This thought is not Who I Am. I am as God Created Me."

15. After allowing the body to consciously and physically release for ten to fifteen minutes, begin to reduce the fervor and rate of your breaths.

16. Begin to breathe more slowly and deeply. Count 1...2...3...4 with every inhalation and exhalation.

17. When you feel more ready, less tense and restrictive, ask Spirit for the awareness of light to be known within and around you. Trust as you ask, it shall be given.

18. Feel / accept Spirit's presence of Light and Love. This may originate as a slight vibration over your crown chakra, flowing down your spinal column and settling within your heart center.

19. Sit and be still of mind and body. Allow the light to present fully to you. Allow it to flow through your body and mind, engulfing you in peace. Surrender to this Light and Love, resting in its peace.

20. Continue to rest in Spirit's presence. Trust all that shall be healed is now healed.

21. Once you feel ready to continue with your day's activities, do not immediately jump to your feet, but slowly rise, stretch and inhale slowly for 3 breath cycles.

22. If you desire, say a prayer of gratitude to Spirit and a blessing to yourself for this release.

Affirmations:
I am as God Created Me.
I rest in God.
The glory and Spirit is mine now.
Love is Who I Am.

Week Twenty-Six: **Suspiciousness**

There are many individualized aspects to the experience of suspiciousness. However, no matter the presentation, suspiciousness always supports your mistaken identity and simply is the resistance to love in thought.

In suspicion of abandonment, the mistaken identity declares that you do not deserve love. Therefore, even though love may present itself to you in form, relationship or behavior, you quickly deny, question, and challenge its presence. You assume your unworthiness and renounce even the mere possibility of deserving a lasting and invulnerable love.

When you suspect any form of disrespect, hurt or judgment from another, you judge this present experience from an investment in all past experiences of hurt. This choice is based solely on your own ideas about yourself, although the ideas appear to be focused on others. Dependent upon a belief in separate victims and victimizers, suspicion requires that you deny wholeness. In fact, all denial is *Self* denial, and the sooner this truth is recognized, the sooner the mind opens to its only options — forgiveness and acceptance.

As you notice yourself feeling suspicious, consult within as to why you are more willing to perceive separation than you are to accept wholeness. Why is it that the struggling mind appears to cling more to pain than peace? In other words, what do you fear?

A thought of suspicion appears to ready you for defense. Its lies prepare or make you wary of perceived attack. This would not be possible unless you first judged that attack is real and can be offered in secret or under the ruse of love. No matter the type of suspicion, it always makes trust impossible. The mistaken identity does not want to accept love in error, for that may lead to more significant hurt. It is suspicious because the mistaken identity would rather attempt to protect itself from potential forces of pain, than blindly trust. It chooses to see guilt now, rather than be left at risk for disappointment later.

Truly you cannot know genuine love without trust in your One

Self, which is extended through trust in your brother. To deny one is to deny all. To choose fear for one is to choose fear for all. Therefore, in fear and denial of its Self, the struggling mind accepts that all experiences must harbor rejection in disguise. It does not remember the unalterable and sees itself only as lost.

Listen, all ideas of suspiciousness are within your mistaken thought system. It is here that your imagination is placing a wall in resistance to its very Self. Through suspicion, you ask love to be proven beyond your fears. Simply this is impossible. Accepting the reality of fear denies love. Your shadows are the obstacles *you* have made and invested in. They are nothing more than that. To claim these obstacles as more powerful than love is to give the dream of the forgotten mind dominion over God's Holiness. Yet, in truth, you are the dreamer of the dream. You are the author of the wish. And there is nothing that can truly have dominion over your grandeur, for The Kingdom of God is within you always.

Notice when you find yourself being suspicious. Isn't the first inquiry a questioning of the other's integrity? Judging another only affirms a belief in your own uncertainty. Furthermore, do you not already feel yourself to be vulnerable and at the mercy of the world's opinions and activities? All of these ideas affirm only a more deeply held belief in God's abandonment of you. He is the only one that you feel can judge or banish you and only the world plays this out in representation.

These obstacles are of your making. They are given life and matter only within your dream. With recognition and acceptance of your truth beyond illusions, we laugh at each pretense. In fact, we will laugh hardily at all the distortions that once appeared to bring an endless barrage of nightmares and lost hopes.

Write a list of suspicious thoughts, and see how you claim each illusion by your own justification. Take responsibility for the thoughts that seemingly clog your mind and prevent peace. If you resist seeing the problem, healing from it will be impossible.

How often have you intended to look at the idea of resistance, when suddenly another alternative pops up in distraction? This is because you are afraid to see your fear. No, you do not have to alphabetize your sock drawer now. Fearing to see fear only prolongs the shadows. Here you reinvest in the distortion. Be willing to breathe, release and rest and your fears will be seen as the gifts for clarity they are. In order to allow yourself to welcome the peace that is, you will need to transcend your distractions.

Consider this; the mistaken identity can play both sides of the chess board. Suspiciousness may also be used to define itself. For instance, if you are suspicious that your friends may be speaking ill of you, could this not also be used as a way to stay in other's thoughts when you are no longer present? Could other's investments in you validate the worth of your existence? I realize that this may sound contradictory. Why use a perception of attack or fear for personal validation? Truly, the insane mind expresses in insanity and uses anything in support of its contrary mission for individuated value and discovery.

No matter the scenario, see the erroneous thoughts for what they are, and see that they hold no power over you. It is in honestly looking at your fears that you see how foolish they truly are when compared to the knowing Light of Holiness. Analysis is not the way, for that is another form of distraction. It takes you away from seeing the source of the illusion. Do not analyze. Seek instead for awareness. Look and will for a neutral mind, letting all the ideas that linger in the shadows to be freed.

Next, as you see the idea for what it is in simple observation, ask yourself if this suspicion represents Holiness. The Holiness of God cannot suffer or fear. The Holiness of God does not need judgment and is not vulnerable to it. With this in mind, all concerns can simply fade away.

Choose surrender to your magnificence rather than suspiciousness. The dreams you have used as your disguise will be left in the shadows that never held any power over you. These shadows have no substance in Truth, and that is why they must remain only within your thoughts and never within your true Self.

Try as you might to place your hands around fear, it slips from your grasp. Fear never can possess any substance except for the illusory traits assigned to it through your mistaken mind. Can you try to catch a shadow? Sure. But notice how as you slip within its darkness, it has nothing you can hold. Choose to truly look at the thoughts of fear, which appear to keep you hostage. In this choice you will clearly see how it is only they who have convinced you of your powerlessness. Only they desire an investment in fear, for that is their own awareness.

The mouse is seen as simply a tremulous creature more scared by you than you by it. Innocent in truth, it scampers off hoping to save itself from the mighty giant that it does not know calls it master by mistake. This is the same for all your fears and concerns. You are the one who has given them reality and power, and although you endow these shadows with the gifts of substance and cling to their distortions, they remain nothing.

So too can you not usurp God in Truth, for although He has bestowed upon you perfect freedom, He too knows only your Holiness. He knows this Holiness can never be clearly, knowingly exchanged for distortion. To give fear dominion over love surely would be insanity, and God does not bend to insane wishes.

Know that I love you and remember all for you, until you call into mind the remembrance of all that has never changed. My Light is Your Own. I love you.

Week Twenty-six: Prompts for Insight:

1. Process a list of your fears with Holy Spirit. Fully allow each fear to be written on the paper without judgment. Next, write down after each fear, what having this fear occur would mean to you. Follow with what that occurrence would mean. Continue with this train of thought. Ask yourself how you let these meanings affect you, and from where do they arise? Seek out the judgments you have assumed about yourself and your limitation. Have Spirit guide you to what this fear symbolizes within yourself. Is it a belief in death, rejection, judgment, loss of a body / identity, being unloved? Allow these fears to be the "*gifts to a greater clarity within.*" Each of your fears holds a gift for your healing.

2. What or who are you suspicious? Write down your story of suspicion, observing why you feel this way. Do not judge your judgments, but instead allow them to flow through your mind onto the paper willingly. Process this story with Holy Spirit, seeking the gift for your healing and the greater beliefs within it.

3. When do you feel most safe? Write down your story of safety, observing why you feel safe in this moment. Furthermore explore this image of safety and observe if it is dependent on yourself or the world. Process this story with Holy Spirit, seeking the gift for your healing and the greater beliefs within it.

4. Write about where in your life experiences, thoughts, or feelings you resist or deny yourself love. Ask yourself within why you are more willing to perceive separation and guilt than you are to perceive or accept love? Write your thoughts, quiet your mind and seek Spirit's guidance. Take notes on whatever comes forth.

5. Write a list of the assumptions you have made that keep the story of attack real and possible. Where have you decided that it is better to protect yourself from a perceived potential for hurt? Notice within, how do you play the role of vulnerable, lost, and

fearful Child of God? Write down all the thoughts and feelings that surface through this process.

Affirmations:
To deny love in my brother is to deny love in my Self.
I am as God Created Me.
Suspiciousness simply is the resistance to love in thought.
I am and deserve love all ways and always.

A Simple Reminder

If you have come this far in our year's communion, then surely you are becoming aware that Love is the ONLY way. There are moments when your mind appears distracted and you perceive yourself as apart from our teachings. No, do not see this as a failing, but do notice how this can be a temporary resistance to Truth.

You are unable to change your Self. You are unable to change your Creation. You are still as God Created You, and this is changeless, without end. Hear Me now and understand. Love is the only way. Recognize that ways which appear as apart from love are only simple mistakes. Truly there is nothing else to be.

So, you ask, do I always expect you to stay in meditation with Me? No, but I do ask where you believe you are when not in meditation with Me. Being One, we can never leave one another. There is no "apart," or times of separation. There are no seams, for we are one fabric of life.

Allow each moment that you align with my voice to be a witness to our oneness. Use every moment where you believe you are apart as a beacon to remember Truth. Invoke love in your heart in the moments where you feel most distant. Allow yourself to once again be warmed by the pure joy of our constant connection.

There is never a judgment or expectation, simply a calling. Love is the only way. That is why I say I am the way, the truth and the light, for love is all I am. There is nothing else. Joy is to you who remember and call your True Self back to awareness. Joy is to you who discover a Self beyond where shadows once appeared to speak for otherwise. And joy will be everlasting once you allow yourself to bring every false premise to light and finally accept your true inheritance.

This is merely a simple reminder of what I witness for always. Allow this reminder to speak to the corners of your resistance. Feel it lovingly guide you through your beliefs in separation. Recall this message whenever you notice yourself desiring a need to live "in the world for now" and speak to Me "later." I only smile at these comments, for I know that there is no time and later is only another way of saying, "I am not worthy of this moment."

Do not fear, you are worthy and I am always with you, whether you desire to recognize my witness to your Truth or not. As I said, your Self is changeless and is not dependent upon your perceptual mind to recognize when I'm around and may have something to say. Notice how even these colloquial inferences witness to a belief in separation. There is a moment now where all inklings of separation are nonexistent, even in your mind. You may call this moment enlightenment, but no matter the understanding, it is here and now.

Enlightenment is never dependent upon your constant recognition, for it is not of your mind. It is not something needing to be practiced or ritualized. It is simply itself always. You are the same.

Enlightenment is simply your acceptance. This is the acceptance where denial of truth is seen as fruitless and you rest in God. It is as much of a fact as your Eternal Self. Although you may need to remind yourself of this Truth, sometimes repeatedly, and sometimes over and over again within one day, do not fear. The place of peace within you is permanent. It is a calling similar to the instincts seen in your nature. You cannot "turn it off" completely, but you can hide its desire and then find confusion when you hear its call.

I know your True Self and can never call into mind anything else. You may pretend to, but even I know these pretenses as being what they are, skips in awareness, never permanent. You are as God created you. Again, I say, this shall never change. You are as God created you. Identify yourself with this, and there will be no need for another thought. Allow this to still your mind in every moment and welcome once again all that could never be anything else.

My Light is Your Own . . . I love you.

Week Twenty-seven:

The Guise of Separation

Holy Spirit, I felt a twinge of frustration just now in reading over something from one of my brothers. It appeared he placed himself in a position of specialness in comparison to others. I feel frustrated. I feel he was expressing spirituality in a form of separation. I feel this was a clear cut attempt to inflate his ego and abuse his role as teacher in the spiritual community. Basically, I feel he is a hypocrite and a ...

And you feel that this judgment now is spiritual? Tell Me, Dear One, does Spirit need your defense? Is there a need to defend the Truth?

(deep exhale) I... (Another exhale) Okay... yes, I feel like I need to defend the Truth. But I was mainly thinking, "Who the hell does he think he is?" Why do people insist on making division even within a thought system based on unity?

If I could answer the first question, I would interpolate, "Who in hell do you think you are?" or "Who in hell do you think they are?" These questions lead to the central core of the issue.

(A few more deep exhales) Okay, you got me there. (Slight pout) Yes, I can see that. I can see that I place my self in hell when I focus on division apart from God's Creation. All right, I give this judgment to you.

(Smile) I love you, Dear One, and I thank you for your recognition of this learning opportunity. Any moment that you focus on a belief apart from all which is the perfection and freedom God Created, you support a mistaken identity. This mistaken belief extends limitation where there is none. All limitation can be seen metaphorically as an opposite to Heaven, which would be hell. Are you not feeling tormented by these ideas?

Yes, I am. And I can see how I feel more separate from my brothers when I judge them. But, within this particular case, I feel a justified judgment because this guy is distorting and misrepresenting Truth. I don't like people using spirituality as an excuse for ego profiteering. I feel that profiting from another's ideas of perceived loss is wrong. "Oooh you're my hero, Mr. Spiritual Guru! Thank you for saving me and here is $500 for your troubles." Geez! Aren't they taking advantage of their brother's vulnerability and weakness?

And so you must defend these people you see as at a loss?

Yes. I think I do.

And so you defend these limited, victimized people by making yourself miserable, critical, and angry? You save them by justifying division among the Holiness of God and stating how the ego is up to its old games again.

I can see where you're going with this. First, I notice I'm seeing my brother as limited and a victim. I can take responsibility for that. And I'm seeing myself as the innocent protector of the world, thus continuing the belief in my own specialness and self concept — the very defensive ideas I'm blaming my brother for. And I also accept how being miserable, critical and angry isn't serving any purpose. But I do attempt something. I try to represent the Truth through my experiences with you.

And being angry is the key component in that? (smile)

(Another deep exhale) No, being angry doesn't help. Fine. You win.

Dear One, it isn't about winning or losing. That too is an idea of division. But it is about looking at what invites peace and what projects restraint in your self. And if you say you want the peace of God, which you do say, then it is essential that you look at how your mind is producing and projecting all ego beliefs. As long as you believe you need to defend anything, you align with beliefs in limitation. Defensiveness serves no purpose. It is wholly dependent on furthering beliefs in division and guilt. Neither of these is true or purposeful in Reality. As you become centered in the awareness of your True Self, all desire for defense and attack will fade away like mists before the sun. This is why I speak often about observing your thoughts. I do not ask you to hyperactively analyze yourself, but I do ask for you to seek out every obstacle to your peace.

I do see how these ideas about my brother are obstacles to my peace. So let's change *this guy and what he is doing*!!

Good try (smile). Let's not focus on change. Let's focus on acceptance and release. Here you shall find your true freedom, for here you extend in love, rather than depending on any change to be possible or necessary. In order to change your brother, you would first have to judge him to be wrong or not as perfect as God Created. Do you see how this would be lingering within the realm of seeking a limited self?

Yes, I do. But sometimes it seems so much easier to look to change things on the surface, rather than deal with the division and misery I hold within.

This is only because you align more with the outer world than your inner Truth. As long as you align with the outer world, you shall always seek the easy surface solution, but truly never will you gain peace. To only seek a change for the surface problem is to ignore the inner condition behind the problem. This strategy will only lead to further misery and another form of the problem later on. This dealing only with the surface presentation is done quite regularly in the world when people simply change their surroundings or relationships and are left wondering why they repeatedly attract the same situations into their lives. The faces may change, but the problem is the same. These individuals are left perplexed and exhausted, often depressed and wishing only to give up. They see themselves as innocent victims and are unable to release their illusions and find peace. To continue to focus on the form and ignore the content will only result in a continued experience of hell on earth. Why? Because hell has already been accepted as existing within, and this hell is only playing out in any way deemed necessary for its own survival.

Here, we need to ask within, what would love desire? Would love desire to starve in loss or thrive in peace? If you choose to accept yourself as love and desire to thrive in peace, you need to bestow peace upon yourself.

Okay, so what about those who say they'll just "do away" with themselves? If they escape from life they'll have peace then, right?

If you perceive this to be possible, my only question is, why would one perceive self-destruction to be a conduit for peace? More truly, the act of suicide is only an affirmation of beliefs in loss, powerlessness and loneliness. Peace does not come from seeking to escape an invested belief in fear. Remember, a thought does not leave its source. If you project fear, that is what returns. If you project loss, that is what returns. When an experience of representative body death results of this very illusion, the thoughts of fear or loss shall return if unhealed. I do not say this in judgment, only realization. However, no matter the worldly expression, you are never met with judgment. Lo, instead you are only met with a gentle acceptance and representation of your beliefs. Love thrives in all expressions. Therefore, you are always met with love. This love is timeless and always gives God's Holiness the opportunity to renew itself despite its imaginings.

Hear Me well; I cannot place peace where one refuses to accept it. That would be dishonorable to the perfect freedom I know you to be. I can present love and solace where there is need, for this is always my witness of You. Yet, you still have the freedom to even turn an innocently mistaken blind eye to this. However, you cannot continually play out this dream of fear, Self-denial and destruction forever. God will always call His Holiness Home. Realize then, that no matter what the surface presentation, You are never truly lost.

When a mind invests itself so deeply within every illusion of fear, it seems to know only limitation. Surely, limitation is not truly its Self. But it places this filter before the light and affirms a belief in darkness. Therefore, the illusion appears to block the truth, and such has resulted in no less than the making of your very world.

But can't you just give us the healing we want? Wouldn't that be most loving?

Are you saying that it would be most loving to deny you your freedom?

No... uhm... yes... maybe?! I don't know. I guess I want to believe my Loving Self is so True that you would go to any lengths to make sure I accept it.

All while you restrain yourself against it? I should convince you of your Truth against your will? I should force you to peace? Beloved One, that would not be love. Love accepts all and honors all.

A huge component of the seeming problem is the fact that you do not go to any lengths to remember love, but do go to many lengths to deny it. You do not know the glory that you are in God. I do, and never forget it.

You do not know the love and graciousness of every moment in your Truth. You do not know how this Love only seeks to extend its Self out to all in perfect acceptance and Oneness for the Love it knows its Self to be. And as long as you do not know this truth, you replace it with confusion.

This, and only this confusion about the Wholeness that you are, has led to every perception of separation held within the mind. Thus, it is only here within the mind that the problem can be fixed. This inward focus on Truth is the journey towards the peace you so desperately desire. Your peace is not found outside yourself. It is found beyond all dreams of perception. Your peace is found in your acceptance of Self, which truly is your acceptance of the Love God Created You to be. Here, and only here, do you rest and bask in the eternal joy of Who You Are. Here you have forgiven all. Here you have accepted only Truth as your witness to Self. Here you have allowed the Oneness you are to reflect through the faces of every seeming body and relationship, and so here do you align with the way, the Truth, and the Life of Wholeness.

Now, let's go back to your perception of the original problem. You perceived your brother to be violating or devaluing the Truth through how he chose to represent himself.

Yes, I did perceive this. Although I can now see this perception is a projection from my beliefs about the lack of value I see in myself. I see that I devalue him because I devalue myself. I question him because I question myself. What would be a solution here?

First, do not blame yourself for these beliefs. Do not jump on a bandwagon of further hell. These beliefs are a part of the dream the mind has extended in play. They are written into the script. Yet, despite the roles you play, always you are innocent, as is your brother. Therefore, the solution is always forgiveness. I will never be inconsistent here.

Do notice how interesting it is that your belief in defensiveness is placed under the guise of spirituality. You are willing to separate from your brother, under the guise of defending the Truth, all the while refusing to experience the Truth. Truly the Truth needs no defense. In Truth, you are not separate from your brother, and to say you are angry at your brother for projecting an idea of separation or hierarchy is also to say that you accept the reality of this for yourself.

Okay... you got me there. I did feel devalued. This is probably why I thought, "Who the hell do they think they are?" I felt they were saying they were better than I, more advanced or loved in God than I am. At least that's how my mind devised it.

Devised is the proper word here. Go ahead, look it up.

Devise: circa. 1300, from Old French: *deviser* "dispose in portions, arrange, plan, contrive," from Latin: *dividere* "to divide." Modern sense is from "to arrange a division" (especially via a will).

Is it not your self-struggling will that chooses to see all in separation? Truly, do you really know what your brother was thinking? Or have you projected your own beliefs in limitation through him?

Yes. I see that I did not know anything about him or why he chose to say and do all that presented. All I did is assume I knew and assign guilt, judgment, and separation.

Again, I do not point these erroneous thoughts out so that you can feel guilty. I only point out the places where you are projecting. It is in these places that you feel vacant and seek love. For your healing I will point out all obstacles to your peace if you permit Me. I desire only the Truth for You, for this is what I know you to be. I love you. This is changeless.

I can accept and understand the rationale supporting my healing. But does this mean that my brothers can say or do anything?

Do they not already? More importantly, do you not already accept all they do as either your "maker" or "breaker"? Here you have perceived yourself powerless in the face of a solid belief in victimization. Only this belief has you attacking your brother, nothing else. Here you see yourself as the innocent victim within an evil world. Through this self concept of powerlessness never shall a moment of peace arise. Is it powerlessness you want or peace? Is it self-concept or Self? The answer to this question shall help you recognize what is your most treasured belief. If it is healing you ask for, so too is healing offered. I only offer you the recognition of all I know you to be.

You never see your brother clearly! It is essential for your learning that you recognize this fact. Love is the only True Witness to Who You Are, and this is because it is ALL You are. If you see anything outside of Love, it is only because you do not know the Truth, and again, as long as you do not know, you align with restraint as your guide. This misalignment is seen in the form of displacement, fear, victimization, limitation, hurt, etc., and will continue as long as you perceive yourself to be who You are not. Remember, Dear One, the Truth is whole, and ANY attempt to separate it is a belief in guilt. Since you are innocent, take a moment and look where your mind has appeared to have turned on itself. Look where you use the excuse of defending the truth, for denying the Truth. Look at where you allow your own misperceptions to define you, project anger onto your brother, and give rise to your own belief in separation.

Listen well. You are not separate from your brother. You are One as God Created, and no matter how many dreams you have apart from Oneness, the wholeness remains changeless. Remember too there is no hierarchy within the heart of God, for there is none who is more gracious and loved than the One Holiness of God. There is no one else to be. There is no other place to be. There is no other.

It is only the mistaken identity that desires to see form. It is only this belief in separation that longs for specialness and illusions of advancement. In Truth, there is no identity. There is no self and therefore no possibility for division. Although your process of awakening appears to be occurring within the realms of time, this illusion cannot make separation where there is none. Therefore, a teacher of God is only as equally loved and aware as his seemingly least progressive student. In fact, it is through his least progressive student that he may learn the most truth. The greatest teacher is the one who sees his students and himself as one. He sees beyond every face, to faceless bounty. He accepts awareness without arrogance and with Certain Trust. In fact, he represents (places forth before him) the Love he accepts Self to be beyond all faces and places.

I have said once before, the process of awakening is not about *your identity* awakening. The process of awakening goes beyond all identities, processes, and forms. It is the release of every *thing* into no *thing*. As long as you perceive yourself to have an image to venerate, you only make a choice for dreams. I am not saying this for the advantage of anyone else, I say this for you. Every aspect of how you choose to separate yourself from your brother calls out to be examined. For each of these is a call apart from God. In denying your brother, you deny God.

Whoa... right there. Now that sounds like a thought attempting to make guilt.

You see guilt only because you see with projection. All guilt stems from investment in the dream of separation which plays out as a perceived rejection from God. Here is where the content of your thoughts come to light, and it is here that we can replace the loss with the acceptance of Truth. Accepting your innocence (and your brother's innocence) is the only route to peace. Here the perfection that has remained changeless is reintroduced to the mind that has lost its Self through denial of Truth.

God has not forgotten you, but you have forgotten your Self. Neither has God denied or rejected you, but you have. This Truth is the key to accepting healing. Notice this Truth and remember the lie at the core of the problem. Bestow acceptance, and the lie will disappear as clouded mists before the sun.

The tension you feel within is only the resistance you believe. I see and know you as perfectly free and innocent in God's Creation. Dear One, this shall never change no matter how many wishes you extend to perceive otherwise. Again I say, you cannot change your Self as God Created, for this is impossible. I could never see you as guilty because I know who You are in Truth. Like clouds, these mists before the sun contain pressured resistance. And like rain, it is only when this pressure builds to a point of intolerability that the rain does fall. Yet for you this is a rain of tears.

Now, when it comes to your perceptions about your brother, it will be essential for you to look at every assumption you make. These assumptions are judgments, and all judgments are misperceptions of Truth stemming from projections of the unhealed mind.

No matter what guise appears to be; no matter what excuse you conjure, your perceptions are your own beliefs extended into the world around you (notice LIE is at the core of the word belief). You are the hypocrite. You are the actor, not your brother.

As long as you choose to see with an "I" of division, rather than the Eye of Love, you are pretending to be all that you are not in Truth. This pretense continues to extend as you imagine knowing who your brother is, what he is thinking or doing incorrectly, and where you feel he needs correction from your seemingly more healed mind. Listen carefully, the mind that perceives itself as more advanced than his brother is the lesser of the sane. For this mind uses denial in the form of separation just as much as the ignorant one.

Ouch.

I love you and this will never change. But I also will, in our commitment to learning, point out all the calls for love you engender and make real. Again, I say, the Truth needs no defense, for it is not vulnerable to anything. There is nothing that can separate, define or devalue within Truth. You are not awakening to anything other than All that has never left you. Your brothers do not awaken alone, and there will be no door prizes.

But what about Jeshua? Isn't he mentioned as being our beloved elder brother who has already awakened and mastered the lessons? Is he not more advanced than we? Has he not already awakened and returned through *A Course in Miracles* to show us the way?

Only if you look at yourself within the illusion of time. Truly, I use every aspect of your illusions as a learning device. All identities within separation are used to your advantage so that you may remember and extend beyond them. Jeshua's example within time is being used to step beyond time. His seeming Self has agreed to play this part. You stand, side by side, with Jeshua and look on in glory of the Oneness you share. Jeshua has seemingly volunteered to be the guiding light within the illusion of time, but truly Oneness is all there is. He knows this Truth just as much as the greatest teacher knows himself to be equal to the least of his students. As Jeshua walked the earth, this equality was accepted by him and was reflected within all relationships he beheld. He saw only his equals within the eyes of many. This awareness of equality is what made his Love Truth. And so he continues to represent this Truth now. It can be the same with you if you so desire.

But if Jeshua can be used as a guiding light for ourselves, can't we be a guiding light for a seeming other?

You can see all identities and their uses as you choose, for it is your dream, your perception, and your freedom. Truth will be seen if you choose every experience as a guiding light for yourself to your Self. As I have already said, this Truth lies beyond all division and certainly in Love is extended equally. To say you are here to awaken your brother, or to point out all the areas where he needs to learn, is to say you are separate or special, and he is lacking. This is to say you (and your brother) are not in reality whole and perfect. This is to place you within a role that is separate from Truth.

Healing can be accomplished in many ways, but love is beyond all ways. Love is always a witness to Truth now. In accepting and extending this Truth, you recognize there is no call for love outside of your own. The fear and limitation you perceive on the faces or within the lives of others, is only your own fear and limitation re-presented to you. To see each of these situations as you own call for love (which truly it is) is to accept where love desires to be found.

Here all is aligned in the one way of love. Here you accept nothing else. If you appear to need a reminder to realize all that You are, so be it. But this is only so that you may remember the oneness beyond it all. It is not so that you may perceive to forget who You or Your Brother is in Truth through the playing out of misaligned hierarchies. To do so is only Self limiting, thus projecting further delusion.

Remember it was said, "The last shall be first and the first shall be last." You are one, and no personality can separate You. Your oneness is reflected eternally. All the separation that you see is not as You are. Therefore, do not allow yourself to be lost in lines of division, for these are merely hiding the truth of You. A Course in Miracles states, "all are called, but few choose to listen." I say this not to instill any lines of division among those who perceive themselves to be listening against those who put the call on hold within the illusion of time. Within Truth, all have already accepted the call, and it is only in time the mind has forgotten the answer.

Sometimes this feels like a practice in semantics. I understand what you are saying, but sometimes these conversations leave my head spinning. I'd rather not get lost in words.

Better yet, do not get lost in self. You feel confused here because you perceive the need for understanding within the mind, rather than allowing acceptance to guide your experience. Breathe, Dear One, and allow yourself to listen clearly. The most essential component for our conversation now is this: You and Your Brother are One. If any moment of confusion persists, come back to this one Truth and rest. Breathe in the Love of Who You Are, and allow your mind to welcome peace. Here you shall gain the experience beyond the understanding. Truly it is only this experience of Truth we seek. For here you simply rest in being your Self.

Let us release all beliefs by permitting God's Light of Knowledge to guide you Home. Again, I say You are not separate, nor can You ever be. Again, I say You are not defined by symbols, nor can You ever be. Again, I ask you to seek out the one idea that places a belief in separation before you, not as an exercise in analysis but as an allowance of Love restored. Offer yourself forgiveness and release for peace. Seek not to change the world or your brothers, but choose instead to see your brothers with the Eye of Spirit's Purity. Their calls for Love are the same as your own. Release the belief in division, and all perfection will flow forth through unimaginable light. This perfection is Who You Are.

Here your Self becomes the advanced teacher of God, not to anyone else, but to yourself from your Self. This Self is beyond any face, place or identity within the world. Here you accept the call for Love. Dear One, it truly resounds beyond any call of emptiness perceived within, for nothing can compare to the Perfection You Are. And here, only here, shall you realize all you sought was never lost from the start. I am with you. I love you.

Week Twenty-seven: Prompts for Insight and Practice

1. Spirit teaches, *"There is no division apart from God's Creation."* On a separate piece of paper, write down a list of all the places, people, thoughts, feelings and ways you feel or see division. For each way, try to identify a minimum of one commonality between you and this identified division. For example:

Where I see division and what we have in common:

Murderers:

On occasion, when feeling real upset, I've wished someone to be dead.
I've acted out impulsively without considering consequences.
I've (accidentally or purposefully) caused a form of life to end.

Hateful People:

I don't always see equality among all people.
I also judge others.
I also resent others.

This exercise is not meant to be a list to promote denial or guilt. Seek not to associate guilt or 'bliss over' your experiences. Use this exercise to genuinely discover how you can relate to your brother in content as well as form. Find the threads of connection running through all bodies and identities, victims or victimizers, and guilt or judgment. Try not to be so "spiritual" for this practice (e.g., repeatedly writing "We are all the Holiness of God."). Be practical and honest. We ALL have something in common and many of these are our investments in the illusion. After the exercise, write all the thoughts and feelings that surface and give them to Spirit's guidance. It can be shocking to see how alike we are to the ones we love to hate.

2. Spirit teaches, *"Defensiveness serves no purpose. It is wholly dependent on furthering beliefs in division and guilt."* To the mistaken identity that

sees division and attack on multiple levels within the world, defensiveness appears necessary and rational. Therefore, complete defenselessness may be a rather difficult concept to accept without judgment. How do you judge this statement? How would you like to live a defense-free life? Discuss thoughts and feelings with Holy Spirit.

3. Make a list of all the ways you practice defensiveness. Defensive posturing always affirms the preconceived belief in vulnerability and attack. Without a vulnerable ego-identity, there would be no reason to defend. Defensiveness may surface in our lives through the practice of denial, displacement, suppression, intellectualization and rationalization of seemingly justifiable anger or upset. Although justifiable to the ego, these states of being are never peaceful, healthy or productive. If you'd like, research further explanations of defense mechanisms through your own preferred resources. How does the practice of defensiveness affect your life experiences, feelings, thoughts and/or behavior? What do you defend yourself against and why? How do you desire to seek more peace instead?

Affirmations:
  My defenses only protect me from peace.
  There is no division apart from God's Creation.
  My Brothers and I are One in Truth.
  I release all Judgment in the Light of Truth.

Week Twenty-eight: **The Happy Dream**

Dearest Holy Spirit, help me to gain a deeper understanding of the Happy Dream. I feel I have misunderstood this experience. Is this relating to an experience within the world? In the happy dream will I live more successfully and more materially prosperous? Is the idea of the happy dream similar to the concept of achieving through the law of attraction? I thank you for your teaching.

The happy dream occurs as complete forgiveness. This is expressed as you accept the truth about your Self and extend this to all your perceptions. Here is the release of all illusions. Here is the acceptance of Self in God. The happy dream is not a reference to any material possessions or accomplishments in form or effect. It is beyond the mistaken identity's qualifications of self-achievement, power, and definition. Since it is an experience of true perception, you see with clarity. However, it is not Truth.

If you choose to use the law of attraction solely for the sake of attracting symbols of abundance, you ask to manifest illusion from within the mind. This was not the original intention of the law of attraction, however, now it appears to be a quick fix for an identity defined through loss or vacancy. Attracting an appearance of abundance makes your dream happier simply because of the symbolic nature you have assigned to money and power. But the goal of manifesting prettier material goods (such as silkier pajamas or a brass bed to sleep in) still does not have you awaken. Never could successful manifestation in dreams hold a candle to the light you are. At best, it can only express an idea of symbolic completion.

However, this being said, there is an echo of truth within the law of attraction. You can consciously practice the law of attraction by recognizing how the mind is able to make experience through its own projected thoughts. The law of attraction teaches you how powerful you truly are. It makes you out to be the god of your world and experiences. This is true. To learn this is quite purposeful to your overall goal of awakening from the dream entirely.

All form is symbolic and a mere shadow of reality. Take a moment to look around. Do not all the accomplishments, objects of wealth or achievement you crave express limitation? Is any object or accomplishment truly free and enduring? Is any thing complete without need or dependency? Now, ask yourself, "What of Wholeness needs anything?" Answer this and you will see why settling for merely attracting things or accomplishments has no lasting peace.

In Truth there is no limit to your totality. In God's Creation, you are permanently perfect and without need. God has already given you all. This means that you need not attract anything in addition. Surely, the only thing necessary for your actualization of this reality is the healing of your memory. If you would like, use the law of attraction for this remembrance. Actively recall how God has never made you wanting. Realize that Spirit's awareness flows perfectly through you now. Call this acceptance and experience into your world. Repeat and affirm this request, knowing the awareness of completion is your True Inheritance. Ask to see your Truth known in and beyond all things. Do this and you will finally recognize fortitude beyond mere images.

Likewise, you can also use principles from the law of attraction to recognize where you perceive yourself lacking. Take a moment to notice what you initially hoped to achieve through the worldly application of this law. Now simply ask why you feel this component of yourself or experience is limited? What do you hope to attract, and how can this yearning bring you peace? Using this noticing, you shall become aware of what you perceive yourself to be. Consequently, this discovery can then be given over to inner healing rather than seeking for outer appearances. All of your thoughts and feelings carry an energy. This energy literally extends the world that you see. Although all energy reduces to the energy of Truth, each use of this energy is guided by the purpose intended. Again, your purpose is what you place forth. Listen. As the creative and innocent mind of Holiness chose to experience limitation, the entire world you see was born forthwith. This world is not wrong or bad. It is not evil. Completely it is free in its expression, and that expression is not of form, but of content. This projective free experience is not limited only to your material world, but also to your feelings and thoughts. Innocently exploring, the Holiness of God (You) chose a veil of limitation to hide you from your Self. This veil of limitation so too permitted the experience of beliefs that remains impossible in Truth. Continually expressing, attempting to live out this dream of possibility apart from God, a myriad of bodies and personalities were born through time. So too have each of these continued to express. Now we have another myriad of thoughts and feelings that each of these bodies and personalities can express. Continuing, these thoughts and feelings express and now you have your experience of the world.

Remember, I have said that all of this can simply reduce down to energy of innocent exploration and still contains the Oneness of God Himself. Therefore, in Truth, all are blessed and within the ever present flow of His Love. As God's energy constantly expresses, not one of these expressions could be without the Love of God Himself. Ideas leave not their Source. Accept this truth and you accept your Self. Here you can see no other purpose than to fully accept your Self as God Created. This Self would be beyond any body or personality. This Self rests in God.

The happy dream is living by clear Vision and has nothing to do with outer conditions. Jeshua was living the happy dream as he allowed his body to be nailed to the cross. In the happy dream, no longer does this thinking mind need to judge, project, or control. Here the self-struggling will struggles no more. Simply it rests in its acceptance of True Self and gives this awareness to all it sees in form.

One could describe the happy dream as living the secret of the game. The secret is realizing. See this as looking through your "real eyes." In this vision you see why you see and how all experience aligns perfectly with your inner Vision. With this understanding, you can influence the game pieces so that each can be wholly reflective of the Love You Are.

For the Master, his or her awareness of influence is not used for materialistic gain as much as it is used to realize a deeper awareness of truer thought and feeling within experience. A Master will accept how his or her thoughts and feelings contribute to the perceptions of all. More frequently, he or she may desire to release all these thoughts and feelings to wholeness (Holiness). In this desire, the mind alive and unhindered by its abilities to bless sends out the new awareness of blessing. Here you live the miracle and come to know your Self both within and without. Surely then do you become as a fully aware being walking upon the earth.

If you ask now to apply the law of Self Awareness (you like the new title?) to experience, I am here to assist. Ask and indeed you shall receive, as the Holiness You Are always deserves to know Thyself. Sit back now and notice your awareness. If it appears to not be of God (not perfect and wholly joyous) surrender every thought that impedes your peace to Me. I am your Guide for realizing your True Self. I am always witnessing for your Truth beyond every shadow self of mistaken identity.

If you sought with your physical eyes alone, you could not wholly see the God energy in all. This is because your first innocent wish was to experience all ideas of limitation. Consequently, in time, every tool of your body was made for this communication. What this means is that if you were to use the evidence of the world alone, it would be impossible to fully know your truth within it. The world will maintain every image it was made to represent, and these images are not as clear as God or His Holiness.

Therefore, if your goal was only to seek pleasant accompaniments within the world, your seeing would remain in limitation. Yet, do not curse this world either. Listen clearly: God has given you this world to make because He always blesses His Holiness' desires. Realize the sheer gratitude which guides this expression for you and once again you will be able to know your Self through your Father's blessings of complete freedom.

How will I recognize the Happy Dream? Can I accurately describe it as a life experience?

Living the Happy Dream has you embrace and give fully without conditions. Here it is impossible to claim either limitation or illusion as your Self because you see Truth in all as God Created. Within the Happy Dream, you walk the earth as a hand outstretched. Love and joy become your only offerings. There is nothing to need and nothing to seek. Nothing threatens or can attack you. You are without anger, fear, judgment or questioning. As you feel the Happy Dream, certain tranquility beyond earthly existence radiates upon your face. Gratitude is abounding for all you encounter and all that surrounds you. Everyone is accepted as your Brother in Holiness and appreciated as your liberator. Indeed, all of this is, as the famous commercial states, "priceless."

Remember *A Course in Miracles'* essential components of form and content. The Happy Dream depends not on form. In fact, the experience is one where all forms, although seen through the physical eyes, are translated into a unified content. This content is complete acceptance of and oneness with all, for here you consciously choose to release all temporal substitutions.

The Happy Dream may have your body appear to be in form but in actuality Truth is perceived through your mind and so content reigns. It is essential to learn how all symbols within the world are only representatives of your mind's wishes. If you are aware of how these symbols are expressed, you are well on your way to releasing them completely. This release of all illusions is still necessary because even the Happy Dream is not the complete being of Truth. At best it is merely a bridge before allowing God to take the final step.

Awareness within the world can teach you your freedom, but, it is not being free. Therefore, to settle in a dream (happy or not) would be an attempt to settle within an illusion. Seek not your happier dream and call this Home. Surely, from the mistaken identity's perspective, a happier dream appears gratifying, yet all dreams are still dreams.

Your Source of Being is not the Happy Dream, for you have not been created from dreams. Settle here and you deny yourself the completeness of Who You Are. I have said that within the Happy

Dream you use the world of form for your experience of fullness in God's Light. But hear Me well: it is NOT fully being God's Light.

Whereas the Happy Dream may reflect content in Truth, it is not the Truth. Whereas the Happy Dream may use the wholeness of form to communicate beyond form, it is not Wholeness. Whereas the Happy Dream may experience Love as being your Source, it is NOT the Source of Love. Do you see that there is a definite differentiation here between dreams and reality? See truly that you are of reality, and no matter how many dreams you dream, this Truth remains changeless. For this reason, I say not to make your goal the Happy Dream, for that would be a goal of mistaken identity.

How can I find myself to be within the Happy Dream?

Simply, Dear One, allow yourself to recognize who is the dreamer here. Bless yourself through your Self. Bestow a remembrance of graceful freedom upon your presence in this experience. See yourself as the Love You are and extend this through real eyes to all. Accept forgiveness and live your genuine desire for Loving as God is. I know this Light within You as strong and willing. Still your mind and be gentle. Breathe, love, smile, dance, and enjoy. Whirl within the Light of Truth and feel yourself extending to all in joyous surrender. Breathe deeply and release all struggle. Accept the peace that can only be and always be yours eternally. Guide yourself to your Self, Dear One, and then guide your Self with Me to God. Allow forgiveness to be your guidepost to Self Seeing. Extend this Self to all you encounter and accept their offering upon your altar. Here you know and truly express your Self. Here we live, not as a dream, but in an infinite reality of simply being as God Created. Remember Beloved. Beyond all dreams you are. Beyond all dreams You ARE. I love you and join my Light with You. Here you truly express your Self, as God Created.

Week Twenty-eight: Prompts for Insight and Practice:

1. Make a list of all experiences or things that you wish for within the world. Next to each, write down what every one of these attainments would mean to you. Ask to see the deeper meaning you seek behind every image. If you seek to be a master of this game, first you must be a master of your wishes. Remember there is nothing wrong within your wishes. All is perfect in your innocent expressing. Ask to seek out where a wish may represent limited ideas of yourself, reflect dependency or could be used for a better purpose. Write down your thoughts and feelings. Seek inner guidance with Holy Spirit and take note of all that surfaces.

2. The Happy Dream occurs as complete forgiveness. This is expressed as you completely accept the Truth about your Self and extend this to all your perceptions. Is there anything that you feel would be difficult to forgive? What? Why? What do you feel this limitation represents to you? How can you learn to see this thought, experience, or feeling with realization rather than burden?

3. All your feelings directly influence the experience you have within the world. Write a list of ten negative feelings and ten positive feelings. Read each feeling aloud to yourself and search where and how its energy expresses within your life experience. See what influence this feeling has on your body, lifestyle, choices, self-esteem as well as your perceptions of self and others on a day to day basis. Seek with Spirit how each of these feelings is manifesting in your life now.

4. Identify when you feel most abundant. Offer this recognition to Holy Spirit for His further guidance.

5. Contradictory wants show up as negative experiences in our lives. They come forth because we are seeing ourselves through the eyes of fear and limitation. Write all the ways you feel

contradictory wants have been expressed in your life experience. Ask Holy Spirit to guide you through the belief hidden within these experiences.

Affirmations:
I hold the keys to the Kingdom of Heaven here and now.
I choose to know my Self in God.
I choose to express the Love I am within all now.

Week Twenty-nine: **Angry with a Brother**

Holy Spirit, I'm feeling the desire to be angry with a brother. Help me with this thought.

Every thought of anger is based on your own beliefs in limitation. There is only a narrowing of pain in all expressions of anger. In fact, this is literally what the word "anger" means, "to narrow". This pain is simply not true and reaffirms beliefs in powerlessness and threat. This fact cannot be altered in anyway. I understand that from your current perception you do not willingly desire to see the situation this way. However, remember a justification for anger only treasures illusions. I will never argue with or belittle your beliefs, because this condemnation is not Love. I am a witness of Love. As a loving witness, I offer you a few questions to seek out what you truly desire.

1. Would you rather be right or at peace? You are familiar with this familiar question from your studies of *A Course in Miracles*. However, you do not always accept the most logical answer. Too often the thinking mind believes that it will be at peace when it is proven to be right. Here we see only the conscious delay of peace until some future time. The conscious delay of peace is reflected through many life lessons, including all seeking outside yourself and the use of the past as a device to distort a present awareness of Love. To delay peace is simply to deny Who You Are as God Created. This delay has you temporarily lose touch with your Self in delusions of separation, denial, and limitation. To be aware of your peace now is to hear the call of Love within your Self and be willing to hear only this call through all images.

2. Who is the one that judges? Although this may seem more like a philosophical question, it really is a simple statement. Who chooses to place a judgment based on his or her own interpreted impressions towards his or her brother? Who is the one that makes expectations at the start? Even if you were to answer "well, they

deserved it," notice still how it is your mind that initiated the judgment that led to the displacement of peace. This question allows you to take the responsibility for what you see. Will for awareness and call back to your thinking mind the Self denial that has you believe in all deceptive presentations.

3. What do you desire from this judgment? This again is a simple question to ask. If you are insistent on judging your brother, even if feeling that this judgment is warranted, what is the result you desire from this action? Is it a definitive identification of guilt and limitation within your brother? Is it some feeling of being more in control or more worthy than he or she? Is it to feel that you have gained some clarity about your brother's seeming sins and can thus extend a blind eye upon your own? Of course I speak only in supposition. In Truth, no sin, guilt, or power can be gained by any recognition of limitation. Nor does separation exist. Since no True Light is in these judgments, surely your mistaken mind is seeking to control certain aspects of the illusion so that it can see itself as less fearful.

I remind you that the need for control is based solely on the acceptance of lack within. If you fully aligned with the Truth of your Self, you would neither desire power, nor would you conceive of questioning any idea about your brother. To accept only the Truth is to see your brother fully in Holiness always. However, if you would prefer an acceptance of limitation, recognize that the same measurement is applied to you because you project what you desire to experience.

Projection is the mistaken extension of creation's ability. In your reflection of the dream, you have designated projection as a way to communicate your beliefs. But neither creation nor projection could be without a Source, be it the Source of Remembrance in God or the seeming basis of your dreams. This is why the understanding of projection is imperative for your learning. For in recognizing its errors, you are able to unearth every misgiving belief.

Okay, so what I'm recognizing through these questions is that this anger, and all anger, stems from me. I guess my individuated mind doesn't want to hear that because its entire dream of self-denial will end.

> Exactly. One thought to keep in mind is that your individuated self both wants to be separate and fights its own feelings of aloneness at the same time. It literally is a mind in conflict. Knowing nothing, it attacks and recedes, lashes out and refuses to trust, hears its desire out in the world, yet runs feverishly from it all. The individuated mind can never find happiness unless it seeks destruction in the same moment. Here the calling is a request for more illusion, only desiring something, anything that can make its dreams appear more real. And it is this very thought system that keeps the mind in delusion and unable to conceive of peace. Can you see how self defeating this truly is?

Yes I can. It reminds me of having expectations. I have learned all expectations of others are useless attempts to control other people. They consciously choose to judge the world by individualized standards and do not accept any other way of seeing. Expectations all tend to set me up for disappointment or anger because I set my mind on ideas of how things should be, rather than how they are. Rarely do I share my thoughts with the ones I'm expecting the behavior from until after they've already "pissed me off" by not meeting these needs. Of course then, when my expectations are not met, I feel like it is their fault. Something must be wrong with them. Then anger occurs, and I feel justified in my upset.

> Yes, this chain of events only leads to a dungeon of imprisonment.

Yes, and even though I feel justified in my anger, I still suffer. All justified anger is merely justified suffering. And truly, who wants that???

You'd be surprised how many knowingly choose this road. Isn't that what brought us to this conversation?

Yes, it did. You got me there. So are you saying that all expectations and judgments are based on fantasies?

Everything in your world is based on a fantasy because none of it is seen through the eye of Truth and wholeness. Any belief in limitation is foolhardy because it outwardly denies the entirety God has Created. This entirety is known both in you and your brothers. Foolishness judges your brother as not only being apart from Love's Eternal Bond of Holiness but calls out to more illusions to prove witness for every so-called justified belief in separation.

All witnesses for separation are insane because all they value is the continual denial of your reality. But for this choice you are never guilty. The mind chose this experience with an innocent curiosity for all it was not. In Truth, you already have placed your toys aside. Now, we use these echoes of time to remember the unchangeable.

So we are already healed?

Beloved Holiness of God, in Truth you never were lacking wholeness, nor could ever be. We use these echoes as an acceptance of the fact that you never were in need of healing to begin with. For your perceptual mind, it is called healing because it is a gift you are willing to receive.

As you accept these offerings from wholeness, recognize that each one speaks only of the Truth that you are. Allow this gift to settle deeply within your mistakenly identified mind. Allow its restful guidance to bestow the peaceful breath of resigning to your holiness once more. Truly it is only in your resistance that you become exhausted. It takes much energy to fuel the fires of resistance through desired suffering and attack. I stand in the peace, awaiting your recognition of the battle being against no one but yourself. I stand ready to embrace you and tend lovingly to your perceived wounds, knowing that you are safe. Walk with Me through this moment now and see the smoke of all armaments fade like mists before the sun. You are free. You are Love. You are complete and not one illusion of ill will towards yourself or your brother can make this true. I only know the One of Holiness, and you are magnificent. I love you.

Week Twenty-Nine: Prompts for Insight and Practice:

1. Make a list of your recent thoughts and experiences that lead to feelings of anger. Answer the following questions for each and write your thoughts and feelings. Share these with Spirit and take notes on any guidance that surfaces from within you.

a. Would you rather be right or at peace?
b. Who is the one that judges?
c. What do you desire from this judgment?

2. Holy Spirit guides: "*I stand in the peace, awaiting your recognition of the battle being against no one but yourself. I stand ready to embrace you and tend lovingly to your perceived wounds, knowing that you are safe.*" Use this as a meditative thought this week. During your quiet time, take several deep breaths and imagine yourself standing with Spirit however you picture Him or Her within. Envision Spirit embracing you and tending lovingly to all your thoughts of pain or hurt. Stay and share all your thoughts and feelings openly as Spirit listens. See yourself safe within this space. Then with a thought of gratitude for this visit, embrace Spirit once again and return to your own space of quiet peace, accepting that although Spirit appears to be of mind, you are never alone.

3. The individuated mind literally is a mind in conflict. Where within your life experiences, thoughts, or feelings do you see conflict? Have you ever asked for one circumstance to come to pass but then chose procrastination or resistance instead? Where have you desired and resisted in the same moment? Identify all areas that conflict has played its role in your life experiences, feelings, and thoughts. Process these with Spirit.

Affirmations:

I choose to see with the eye of Wholeness.

I am as God Created Me.

I choose not to deny myself from my Self.

All anger stems from within my confusion.

Week Thirty: **Beyond the Wind**

Holy Spirit, I awoke today with many ego thoughts lingering on my mind. Help me be still and listen to the Truth. Thank you.

Mainly, Dear One, you are confused about your self-identity and what this whole experience of awakening means. There comes a moment in every awakening child's experience when he or she is unsure of what is the dream and what the reality. During this confusion it is easy for fear to slip in as a hypnotic weight appears to be shifting. Do not be concerned with these fears. Hear the words I continue to witness for you from *A Course in Miracles,* "Forgiveness looks, waits, and judges not." This awareness of non-judgment in every moment will be essential to you now.

You are now more aware of the confused thoughts within your mind. In fact it appears difficult to ignore them. Yet, all I ask you to do is to breathe and wait. Breathe and wait. Look at these thoughts without judgment or attachment. Hear what they have to say. Let their words flow as if you are standing in the billowing wind which now thrusts itself against your window pane. Yet, even as the wind gusts, even with force and might, fury and power, remember where your safety lies. Remember I am here, and you are never alone. Center yourself within an awareness of peace beyond the wind and never is your Identity obscure.

The identity that you feverishly wonder about — this human identity — will never be a waste, nor can it be used inappropriately. You cannot be in error, my Child. Not one of your imaginings can distort or disown the Holiness of God He created. There is no wrong way to be. Notice the tightness of your concerns, how they seem to constrict your mind with fears. Surely this is not your truth. Surely, you cannot reveal a greater peace through these judgments and concerns. Realize my guarantee of your innocence beyond these thoughts. You are free.

Fear not. You will not be required to deny your self-identity in order for a truer one to be affirmed. I never ask you to deny the self you think you know, but I do ask you to seek beyond it. Is it loving for a parent to physically struggle with his or her child, in order to grasp a toy away?

Of course not. A loving parent peacefully watches over their child and encourages them to release the toys on their own. He or she tenderly supports and teaches them to be wise. Truly, Beloved, I am there for you just as that loving parent.

It is only the limited self that believes it must lose to gain. God only desires your perfect happiness and sees you whole as you are. No loss is necessary or ever desired. As I ask you to reaffirm where your safety lies, I do not expect you to assume some spiritual concept that "seems right for what you have been taught." This forcing and guessing does not promote a true acceptance. The memorization of empty concepts is a pretense. Enough with pretenses, they will never set you free.

Beyond the wind there is a serene oasis. Here you can see the water, clear and crystalline. Here warmth caresses your mind as a deep stillness echoes throughout. This is the oasis of inner peace. This is the representative awareness for your Truth beyond the wind. See yourself here, resting upon the soothing comfort of a softly lined bed. Possibly in the far off spaces of your mind, you may recall a storm and continue to hear its fury. But alas, what is that? Where is that? Surely it is nothing worthy of disturbing your peace.

Invest instead in this quiet beyond the storm. Do not exchange one imagining for another, but simply notice there is another peacefulness that can be recognized. If this be a more welcoming transition for you, make whatever images you want to support the more peaceful dream, yet allow it simply to be a bridge to guide you in comfort beyond your dreams. Hear its beckoning beyond the wind's forceful thrashing. The peace you yearn for is there, in the quiet spaces in between. Breathe and become aware of this quietness. Seek not to put another image upon it, just let it be.

Seek not to judge anything. Do not concern yourself with how you are to be seen or what your name or workings within the world mean. No matter the outer image, you still remain as You are. The true purpose of release is to recognize this. Beyond all your imaginings, you remain as You are. This is your true inheritance. This is your Self, aware of its truth, quietly waiting in the wings of the stage, certain and sure of its beingness beyond every role played, costume adorned or drama enacted.

This Self is certain, resting solidly within its being. Here is the quietness beyond the storm. He listens to the "special effects" and whispers, "That was not thunder; that was just a man hammering upon sheet metal." And "That was not lightning; that was just the flicker of lights." Yes, it knows that these effects are mere illusions and walks quietly, centered in seeing the true Self beyond the wizard's show. Here you laugh, for you know the image is just a mere distraction from reality.

Yes, hear the wind blow, Dear One. Feel the fear within you as you picture yourself within its mighty grasp. Yet are you not sitting here within your Holy Home? Concern yourself not with any other image than this. Seek not excuses to share a concern for your fear or to share its identity. Yet allow all the bellows to blow past, as you remember the truth of where you are in stillness.

Imagine and judge no more, for these pretenses are nothing. Here, I am with you, standing watch by your bedside, knowing all nightmares are simple distortions of the mind in fear. You are still. You are safe. You are loved. And it is here that Your Truth reigns forever and ever. I love you.

Week Thirty: Prompts for Insight and Practice:

1. According to Spirit's guidance, the temporal self-identity is always in confusion and uncertainty. Rather, the Holiness of God is certain, resting solidly within its Being. What experiences, thoughts, or feelings are you most confused about? Start with a sentence such as "Within my mind (or feelings / experiences) I am confused about _____." Ask Holy Spirit how this confusion can be translated into certainty. What is the gift or the oasis of peace within this storm?

2. Do you have a fear of identity loss or personality loss through awakening? What do you feel or fear within about the "death" of the individuated self? Write your fears associated with the awakening process. What do you see as being the most difficult during the awakening process? What thoughts or concepts are the most challenging for your mind to grasp? Why? Discuss these with Spirit and be open for guidance.

3. Imagination practice: Create an oasis of peace. Using a paper and crayons (or the art supply of your choice) draw, paint, sculpt your oasis of peace representing your serene inner sanctuary. Within the creation place all the perfect tools for your serenity. What do you have within your image? Who is with you in the image? Where are you within the image? Be creative, listening within as you express. When finished, hang the image within your meditation room or fold it up and use it as a bookmark for this book. Keep it near and look at it whenever you desire to remember all you hope to accomplish in peace.

4. The movie, *The Wizard of Oz* is extremely metaphorical in its representation of our dream. If you have the opportunity, watch this movie during the week. While watching, write down all symbols you notice within the movie relating to the journey of awakening. Look within yourself for what meaning you can apply to this movie. Write down these observations asking for Spirit's

guidance about them.

5. Review the movie *The Wizard of Oz*. Now, using a personal journal, write down your own story of experiencing a personal Oz in your life. Take notice of how all the characters walked the yellow brick road seeking completion. Observe how many times they struggled, dealt with fear and even fell back to sleep. If you wish, you can use the same characters from the movie to inspire your creativity. For example, imagine the Good Witch Glenda as the Holy Spirit and the Wicked Witch as ego. Dorothy can be seen as the innocent sleeping Son, Scarecrow as the thinking mind yearning to understand all in its intellectualization. The Lion can represent the fearful part within us desiring only to know its self better and the Tin Man can represent our wish to know inner love. Overall, use this story to creatively transform your own inner observation.

Affirmations:

I am certain, resting solidly within my True being.

I choose to remember the Truth of where I am in stillness.

I seek not to judge anything.

No loss is necessary or ever desired.

God only desires my perfect happiness.

Week Thirty-One: **Choosing Healing**

Background Information: I am employed full-time within a psychiatric facility. Over the past ten years I've worked in this field, I've learned a lot about the chronic nature of mental illness. Recently, we had a client who completed the program to the full abilities of the treatment team, was successfully discharged, and then returned within 14 hours claiming to be suicidal once again. Within the past three months, this client has repeated the same treatment program approximately eight consecutive times without any noticeable signs of consistent improvement. To the staff, it seems that this client has become dependent on the program, and really only wants to stay in the hospital rather than face life on life's terms. This is evidenced through her refusal to accept other referrals and lack of motivation to be compliant after discharge. She just gives up within less than day.

During these experiences, both personally and professionally, I feel frustrated. Each time this client has gone through the program I've given her my all and desired for her to improve, only to feel it is not helping. I take responsibility for my feelings, which are often referred to in the counseling community as counter transference. Again today, the same client was admitted back into the facility (after another attempt at discharge this past weekend), and I felt myself hitting inner peaks of aggravation.

Although normally I am caring and empathetic, I noticed a feeling of exhaustion within me. Thoughts of anger churned within me, "What more can I possibly do for this person? How can I possibly help her if she refuses to help herself? I no longer know what to say or do! I should be cold to her when she arrives, so she will know I'm angry and finally get her act together!" Over a couple of hours, I watched these thoughts come and go, eventually recognizing that my ego's expectations would definitely not help her or me. It was obvious that this response was futilely inappropriate and not truly helpful; however, I still felt entrapped. At this point, I knew I had to go to Holy Spirit with this seemingly overwhelming issue.

(Sighhh) Dearest Holy Spirit, help me see this situation with X differently. I don't know what to do or feel here. Thank you.

Pray for her.

(Brooding silence) What?? NO! I feel angry. It is her fault!! We'll have to get back to this conversation later!

(About 2 hours later and less frustrated) (sigh) Okay, dearest Holy Spirit, help me see this situation with X differently. My sulking didn't help. Thank you.

Did you pray for her?

No. I still feel tension there. Help me understand why I feel so disturbed within this situation. Why do I feel as if I can't offer her compassion and love? Why do I feel so resistant to prayer?

Simply, Dear One, it is because you are identifying with all the errors you feel she is guilty of. Are you not choosing to see her through a perception of error, rather than the Vision of Truth?

When you asked me to pray for her, I felt immediate resistance – as if to say "anything but that!!" Truly, I don't want to feel that heartless, and it scares me. I don't know what this is about.

Remember I have said that every idea of anger is rooted in your own ideas of powerlessness and threat. These presumptions are always misplaced identifications.

Yes. And I can see how I do feel powerless here. I also can see the feelings of threat. You are right... as usual. These thoughts all are misplaced identifications. My thinking mind is telling me that she should have healed by now. I feel that the whole staff and I did everything we could to make her feel better. We have other clients that need our time and attention too! How much can I possibly give without result? I feel it's not fair to other clients for us to give so much time and attention to her when she's not getting any better.

So, you are saying that the decision to offer love and see your brother as whole is fully dependent upon the result it receives.

I... no.... I.... well, maybe it does sound like that . . . grrr . . .

Your resistance to praying for her has many beliefs attached. First, you struggle with seeing her as equal and unified with you. Next, you also resist forgiveness and removing all projected judgments from her. Remember, every grievance you hold (and yes, this does qualify) is towards yourself alone. These grievances are the same erroneous judgments you cling to against yourself and the entire Kingdom of God. These grievances indeed "hide the light" and are the only beliefs that deny your peace and True Holiness.

How come it seems that my life situations always so perfectly parallel the daily lessons within *A Course in Miracles*?

And how come you still refuse to use them? Listen, Dear Child, this is not an accusation, but a calling for your attention. I have given you these lessons as a gift. Your resistance to them is part of the gift. You just don't realize how much you don't desire to heal. In this struggle fear leads the way. It is the same with X. Can you see the same in her seeming behavior? Haven't you said this yourself, "She just doesn't want to heal"?

Yes. I have.

And so the blessing of your mind provides the perfect situation to reflect for you exactly what you need to learn through the seeming faces of others. This is your projected experience made for your own learning. Embrace this blessing.

I never saw it that way before. I thought it was all about her and not me. Gosh. So you are saying that my struggle with X represents the very same places of resistance within me? In fact, I should consider all the times when I refused to follow through with the "treatment plan" you have given me? Whoa. Sigh. That really hits the mark.

I know. Again, I say, there is only One Holiness of God, deluded within His mind to perceive a myriad of bodies and minds. But still, there is only one Love, One Holiness, and this brilliance is You. All experiences and interactions reflect your own mind. All you are receiving is a constant offering of the lessons most assistive for embracing peace. All opportunities are only offering you love. Do you desire to take it?

I want to say yes, because I feel like that is the best answer. But my behavior and thoughts show me that it is not always the most willing answer within me. Sometimes, I don't even feel like answering at all.

Yes, but judgment also will not serve you well. It is best in these times of uncertainty to offer yourself forgiveness. Take a time out. Take a breather to relax from the conscious resistance. Notice that there is a better way and simply change your mind. Through this surrender to peace you will see Heaven. Your True Home has never left your side. Only in your mind have you perceived yourself to be locked outside its Holy Gates. In fact, there are no gates outside of the perceptions of your mind.

But how about when I feel as if it is an "all or nothing" judgment? Sometimes I feel stuck between seeing errors and attempting to fight for peace.

Dear One, it is more like a "nothing and nothing" judgment if you see that you need to judge or fight. All judgment focuses on illusion. All battles are of the ego. Heaven does not operate in the realms of illusion. The All has no judgment and is beyond every bit of perception or judgment the thinking mind holds. Heaven has no acquaintance with disunity.

Also, as to the "all or nothing" judgment, it is not God who makes the judgment. He already knows you are All. He Created you in this Truth. Yet it is your perception that sees yourself and your brothers as nothing. You see this way when you feel that they are worthy of judgment. It is this alone that has made you focus on being miserable. Of course, your Truth cannot change.

The only healing you ever offer is to yourself, for you are all one. Remember this as you fear. Remember that all you fear is merely your own Truth. Remember that all you ever see is mistaken identity. Vow to look not with your own eyes but give gladly your sight to Me, and I will present to you the complete Vision. In this Clearer Vision there is nothing but rejoicing.

This is what I meant when I said to Peter that I would place him at the gates of Heaven. Peter is/was not a separate man apart from you. His struggles were the struggles of the confused mind. His story represented the constant conflicts of all who battle within for the choice of Truth. He struggled within, yet sought to see purely. His faith and willingness to see with Me were his most strong characteristics. Yet, his life seemed to be filled with many choices. Often he felt unworthy of this new found spirituality. He felt challenged by both what he knew he wanted and where his family and cultural heritage had led him for the majority of his life experience. His family was not proud of his choice to follow Jeshua as a disciple. They thought he was being foolish, irresponsible and deceived. In return, Peter dealt with significant bouts of uncertainty, fear and inner questioning. Especially when in moments with Me, although faithful, he personally felt embattled. Who was he supposed to be? Was he supposed to be as his family desired of him or as was his calling within? Often he wondered what the whole of life and faith meant anyway. Many a time he felt internally embattled. This is why I said that I saw him placed at the perceptual Gates of Heaven.

As Peter stood at these gates to inner serenity, he was unsure and felt placed in a position of judgment. Although he desired to see purely, he still knew of the opportunity for confusion.

Likewise, he also valued concepts first over trust and inner guidance.

This too is your intention. See how you too place yourself at the gates of Heaven and stand watch between peace and judgment. See how it is through your desire alone that you accept a blessing or perceive a distortion. Your intent is to see purely. You have the faith of Peter. This is your blessing, and so here I celebrate with you. Yet, be aware and do not sleep. Do not hypnotically fall to the lyrical whispers of your fears. Notice all that you perceive is of your own imagining and give your sight to Me so that I may guide you through all perceptions of distortion. I know you in Truth, and this Truth can never be wholly misperceived.

Your reluctance will serve you no purpose either. Listen well; here we recognize another obstacle to peace – the belief that there is more than one of us here. In this obstacle you live as not only a divided body but also as a divided mind. In all division is limitation, for you are embattled against your truth. Here you perceive yourself as not whole as God Created you. Here you think of every reason to hold onto only the dream and deny reality. Here you cling to illusion and make yourself aligned with what you are not. Always will this misalignment result in suffering, for here you do not express yourself in Truth. To not be True to yourself is to believe you are lost.

You are never truly lost except within the realms of your mind. In perceiving limitation for yourself and your brother, you keep yourself in the hell of your perception, consistently denying all that is your own. I stand with you and continue to witness to all that is real. Therefore, as I ask you to pray for a brother, I truly ask only for you to pray for yourself.

A prayer is a connection. Particularly, it is a remembrance of your True connection to Your Father. In True prayer, you leave all your illusions at the door and step beyond them. Again, you recognize your choice within and choose the only Truth. You are the one who has constructed a gate to keep you from reality. You have placed yourself in guard there, and you decide what your Truth is. Truly, Dear Beloved, there is no choice for Truth, there only IS Truth. Surrender yourself past these gates and know that Heaven reaches out to welcome you. Here you settle in the stillness and simply open yourself up to your Self as God Created. Here you are free and remember the all embracing Truth of Love never forgotten.

True prayer is an act of remembering the Love you are. It is an offering only to you. Here you connect to the Truth beyond all illusion. Here you remember. Here is your peace realized.

Do you dare see yourself as the All? Do you dare see yourself as the One? You have nothing to lose. Literally, you have nothing to lose, for only illusions are rooted in dreams of nothingness. But you are Whole. You are All. You are blessed as the Holiness of God, no matter what mask of dreams you wear. You are as Your Father Created, and this is your most wonderful treasure of Truth. As you go to workplace now, remember, Dear One, that all you see are merely faces of your Self. Choose to remember and construct no more gates to keep yourself from Heaven. Be aware, Dear Peter. Be watchful of all you allow. Give your Vision to Me and seek not to be confused again. My Light is Your Own. I love you.

Week Thirty-One: Prompts for Insight and Practice:

1. Spirit teaches, "*True prayer is an act of remembering the Love You are. It is an offering only to you.*" Dedicate five or more minutes each day of this week to experiencing True Prayer. Read *The Song of Prayer* from the supplements to *A Course in Miracles* and thoughtfully intend your prayers to include the following:

a. *Three prayers of unification.* Identify three people from whom you have felt disconnected or have judged. One by one, taking as much time as you need, envision yourself standing with each mighty companion in the Light. See past their appearances and join with them in the heart and mind of God's Love.

b. *Two prayers of acceptance.* Make a list of all you are grateful for in life, thought, and feeling. Put this list aside and now focus your intent on recognizing all that is not on the list. Your aim for this moment in prayer is to recognize how you have received all, all ways. God withholds nothing. Reach into full acceptance of all that God has already given.

c. *Two prayers of transformation.* These are the prayers of honoring your Self in God. Here, you leave all requests and needs behind. You are not your body but solely intent on joining in gratitude for all You are as God knows and extends. In this prayer there "*is no asking, for there is no lack ... without needs of any kind [you are] clad forever in the pure sinlessness that is the gift of God to you.*" (The Song of Prayer, p. 8) Sit within the moment accepting the Light and peace You are. Envision yourself reaching not without for God, but within. Accept all as completely perfect. Extend light from your heart center and feel its warm glow envelop you into pure beingness. Spend as much time envisioning this Light of Truth all around you.

Affirmations:

I choose to remember all I am.

All that I give to my Brothers, I give to Me.

I construct no more gates to keep myself from Heaven.

In unity I welcome all my brothers who are One with Me.

I have nothing to lose. I am Holiness.

Week Thirty-Two:

Grief and The Small Self

Your small self is always in grief. In fact, it depends upon grief in
order to keep searching for itself. To know grief is to know loss.
Since there is no loss within the Kingdom of God, an outside
fantasy must be extended for loss to be palpable and participatory.
The main character of this outside fantasy is the small self. It is the
hero of the dream. This small self is wholly dependent upon its
belief in loss and separation in order to perceive. Thus, it is a tool
for separation and a requirement for perception.

When I speak of the small self, I refer to the identity treasured
seemingly apart from God, born to live within time and die a
certain death. The small self always has grievances, for it lives in
constant struggle. In the struggle it seeks outside itself for
satisfaction, proof of its worth and happiness. It seeks value and
identity for all it does not know.

This small self sees, comes to know itself and the world through
its limited vision. You may call this loss-e-vision. In loss-e-vision,
you see only from a limited state of mind. Constantly you are
seeking to find out who You are. Again, this is merely because you
have forgotten. In this constant search, you mainly find the proof
of more limitation playing out within the world. You continue to
wish and hope for the discovery of maybe "just one place" where
you can find a brief oasis of peace from all this searching. Yet, even
with the best brief oasis of peace (temporary happiness or special
love), you still churn with dependency because loss (or its future
potential) has become your first sight.

I brought you to look at the stages of grief because they
contemplatively coexist as the stages of healing. Symbolically,
they outline your journey. This journey starts from a belief in loss,
continues through the willingness to forgive and leads to an
eventual acceptance of your Holiness.

The first stage of this journey is denial. In denial, you do not
recognize your true Self, nor can you begin to appreciate all of its

magnificence. Here, you live fully within the world and its guidance. Here you are your body and all its accompaniments. You deny the Truth of You and the Truth of your brother. You wish to know nothing else, because you perceive that there cannot be anything else except the small self. It is all you are aware of.

I have said before that this world is dependent. None can function successfully without expecting some result in return. At best and worst, your small self is dependent for its thriving. Within this, happiness within the world requires receiving your needs and the temporary displacement of your fears. In Truth, happiness cannot exist without the relinquishment of fear. However, to the small self the relinquishment of fear only arises from a sense of temporal security. Honestly, do you think this would be the gift of a loving God to His Holy Creation? Would He require a negotiation of give and take just to live? Surely not. This is why dependency is fully reliant upon all ideas of separation to prosper.

Give and take is significantly different from sharing. In sharing, all is open. Give and take relies upon the validation of incompleteness and need. All throughout this dependency you equate yourself with fear. Only when fear does not get what it needs does anger arise. Anger could not occur unless you first perceive threat, powerlessness, or pain.

Metaphysically, anger stems from the idolization of the world taking a tumble. All that you have come to value results in a flat, false sense of satisfaction. Soon disappointment sets in and you start to recognize how very much you do not understand yourself or the world. Sure, at first you tried to follow all its rules and make a home within in it. You did not disturb or disrupt anyone or anything, so why, you ask "couldn't I just be happy?" "Why is the world so cruel?" For some, these disappointments and insecurities are projected onto God. "What have I done?" "Why me?" "Why...why... why?" You pine to have happiness, fairness, and world peace. You fear death and see its miseries without understanding. What purpose is this grand and intricately detailed castle in the sand, if the raging ocean current sweeps it away?

Perhaps in your anger, an inkling of awakening comes to mind, not so much as a desire to awaken just yet, but more like a desire to no longer consume yourself in victim mentality. At first, you may fight back against the so-called "evils of the world," labeling this activism, martyrdom or compassion. However, even these are reactions are fully dependent upon the belief in separation and victimization.

Unfortunately, even in your pleas for amnesty the world still appears to rule you. You still recognize a definitive split. Sure, the anger may appear to give you an additional illusion of power. In its use you stick it to all the people who have ever stuck it to you. However, truly, there is just so long that this honeymoon of fury can last before exhaustion sets in. Soon you begin to fear the day you can fight no more and wonder "what next?"

Bargaining occurs when your uncertainties within the world and yourself approach a peak. You begin to wish for a compromise. Thoughts of awakening may have already introduced themselves into your conscious mind, but you far from understanding them. To desire them, you think, you must give up your control and identity within the world. The "giving up" is seen as sacrifice rather than necessity. Eventually the call for surrender is truly necessary. Yet, this surrender is only a rest in peace and has no fear within it.

Bargaining often plays itself out as an attempt to compromise all you fear of losing with an idealistic vision of the world. Some may call this the request for Heaven on earth. However this bargaining is never beneficial because it only agrees to its "side" so as to gain protection from further fears. Consequently, you hope to bring God into your dream. To bring God into your dream would save your treasures from sheer destruction. Only you see this as possible. "I recognize how this world is not ideal..." you think, "but isn't there something worth saving?" "How can it be wrong to want judgment and punishment for the obviously guilty?" "Can I not keep just one treasure for myself?"

Bargaining is the stage of judgment. It values not necessarily the judgment of others, but mainly the judgment of yourself and God. Here you metaphorically "allow" God to come to the table and talk. "Okay, 'God' tell me what you got?! I will give it a listen. But if you mess up just once, that's IT!" The judgment is merely a defense against all you fear. Loss remains a possibility, especially if you *must* release into the unknown. Soon this judging mind begins to question incessantly and thrive in doubt. If you do not receive the proof you feel is warranted, the stage of anger may be repeated.

Depression arises from the recognition that the self-will is purposeless. There is a saying in certain healing circles, "we leave deep claw marks in all we choose to let go." In this stage, you see the foolish attempt beneath the dream. "Whoa!" you may think, "God must really hate me for what I have done!" Moreover, in this, a deeper guilt and separation is felt. Some refer to this as psychic-pain. This inner torment is a pain of mind rather than of body.

Now, hear Me well, depression only exists because you judge yourself as guilty. That means that you judge yourself as separate and in loss. All references to guilt within the Course witness to the belief in loss or separation. Likewise, you cannot have depression without this belief. Call this the depression of the sleeping mind. Simply it is the conscious recognition of all you have perceived as loss. Yet now (which is why the depression stage differs from the denial stage) no longer do you see loss as a thought that can be anesthetized by glorifying the world. In fact, you potentially begin to despise it.

Unbelievably, depression allows you to stir completely within your sleep. It is here alone that you finally relinquish all idols and begin to surrender to a deeper yearning for more profound knowing. When depressed, you do not yet understand that God or I never ask for these losses or sacrifices, for they alone are within the dream's awareness. However, your relinquishment of the self-will has you begin to desire release over resistance.

In depression (clinical as well as metaphysical), all foolish and fearful thoughts come to the forefront of your mind. Here you always have a choice. This choice is simply to believe or not to believe these thoughts. This choice has you wish to invest further in the loss (claiming it to be real and you to be dependent) or not to invest, accepting Self as your true completion. Likewise, now you see all the dream figures revealed. The transition of depression does lead to the responsibility for sight finally accepted.

Within the later stages of depression, you begin to connect the dots. An identification of loss can be released for a desire to know your Truth. *The Serenity Prayer* is quite a purposeful prayer. Its words make manifest the desire to give to God all that is God's. You ask Him to show you the way, rather than the alternative (bargaining). "God grant me the serenity to accept the things I cannot change, the courage to change the things I can and the wisdom to know the difference." Truly, no matter the words, when you choose to ponder release, you ask God to show you the way.

The final stage of healing all grief is acceptance. However, before I fully explain this, it is important to note that there is no period of time associated with these steps. In fact, many moments of fluctuation will occur between the steps. In the experience of healing, you may alter acceptance with depression and depression with bargaining. Sometimes you may even spend a few months returning to anger or denial (but this is rare once the desire for your real existence has emerged). Essentially, your experience of these steps varies according to the amount of judgment you hold. Judgment is always a witness for loss. Therefore, as long as judgment is made useful within the mind, acceptance cannot be fully known.

Accept: circa.1360, "to take what is offered," or "to take or receive willingly," or "receive," from *ad-* "to" + *capere* "to take".

Acceptance is your release into God. Here you release all that you thought you once were as a dream figure, determined to live and die as a small dependent self. Enlightenment is acceptance. As you welcome God's Will to be your own, the awareness of one's Self in Truth flows freely. Seeing God now as able to lead the way, you ask for His Guidance and hear His Voice. There are many stages of acceptance, ranging from its initial awareness to surrender, revelation and completing with true perception. But no matter what stage of acceptance you are able to bring to awareness, the Truth of You is happily seen as real.

Now one reason I invited you to this teaching this week is because I have noticed how you have been offending yourself with fear lately. Granted this is the process of healing from your belief in unworthiness, but it is imperative that you realize how this dance of self-offense is truly not purposeful. Every moment you offend yourself you reinvest in your grievances of the small self. This is the same as holding a funeral service. You then may think that this is purposeful, to bury the small self, but truly it is not. To bury your small self is to invest in its vulnerability, guilt, and loss. This is not healing.

Again, you cannot invest in loss and call this peace. You cannot heal by burying (or suppressing) anything. You cannot heal by insulting yourself and doubting in the glory of God's Holiness. Remember Beloved, His Holiness flows through you and lights your Being. ALL MUST BE BROUGHT TO LIGHT rather than to death. This is essential for you to know now.

All grievances held from the small self are an investment in loss. It is that simple. Choose this loss and choose your denial of Self. This grief may even project onto God, where you feel rejected and at a loss for His Love, and so you choose to punish yourself through guilt / separation. However, even as you play these beliefs out, You can never truly be separate from your Magnificence. Whole Self-denial is impossible. As is any loss in God. Remember that I love you and desire not death to be your way, but only know of your eternal light and life. Take a moment now to rest in this light of peace and reacquaint yourself with the blessed pathway towards healing that you now walk with Me on. Never can you truly grieve in God, for only His Life and Light exist. This splendor is all You are. I love you.

Week Thirty-Two: Practice:

On a separate piece of paper, identify how the stages of grief and healing have played out in your own experience of awakening to the Truth of You. Use the following summary as a guide:

Denial: In this stage, we are living what we perceive to be a normal life. Here we don't recognize our True Self, but live completely defined by beliefs in separate identities and needs. Typically we justifiably engage in the usual life habits of searching for happiness, security and self-validation.

Anger: Here is where the first inklings of disappointment and broken dreams emerge. After much frustration, the idols of the world begin to take a tumble. Our search for happiness, security and self-validation is recognized to be exhausting and unsatisfactory. Consequently we feel lost and afraid. Anger arises from these feelings of threat and powerlessness.

Bargaining: This stage occurs when we wish to compromise between Heaven and earth. Although we are aware that our way is not giving us peace, we still feel that there must be special justified circumstances. We refuse to completely surrender to God, but seek to find a middle-ground. In this stage we cling to such compromises as "the Law of Attraction". Bargaining furthers our fears and attachments to the world. In it we hope to make the world into a better or more comfortable residence, instead of releasing our confused wishes for Holy Spirit's knowing. We may say: "Can't I just keep one grievance??" "But HE doesn't deserve forgiveness!" "I need a beautiful house or car for my security…" In this state we tolerate God, but we still yearn for control.

Depression: For many, this is the stage of decision. Here, we recognize that all we have previously invested in does not work. We see how human living can at best speak for limitation and further struggle. "Just making it through" is purposeless and we recognize our feelings of loss, fear and confusion. In this stage, many questions and conflicts from the subconscious bubble to the surface for our release: "What does life mean? Who am I really? What now?" At this stage we can permit ourselves to build bridges to hell or Heaven.

Acceptance: In this stage we finally yield to God's Way in complete trust and finally recognize that all peace is beyond our own ways of thinking and believing. This is the full release of our self-will to God / Spirit. Although we may filter through this stage briefly at first, as we continue to realize where our genuine safety resides, it becomes our final rest.

Affirmations:

God's Holy Son can suffer no loss and I am God's Holy Son.

I remember the Love of God in place of loss.

I accept the Strength of God now.

Beyond this world is a world of Love.

Week Thirty-Three:

Patience is a rest in Truth

Dearest Holy Spirit, I've noticed myself having an issue with patience lately. Although I am usually pretty laid back, I've noticed an attachment to time and expectations lately. This surprises me. Can you explain not only why patience is an important aspect for my learning, but also why it appears to frustrate me so? Thank you.

Dear One, you have found yourself increasingly impatient because you are persisting in your release of beliefs in limitation. This process has you begin to bring forth the deeper unconscious feelings of fear. As you continue to dedicate yourself to healing the mind, you become increasingly aware of the hell that has remained reclusive within time. Although it appears to feel uncomfortable and confusing, truly, it is a sign of progress. This awareness is part of the overall healing experience.

Only by bringing forth illusion to Truth can the release of illusion occur. This is not always comfortable, but it is necessary. Neither fear nor judge this process, but allow yourself to be more aware of what the thinking mind attempts to tell you. Hear its beliefs in limitation, so you may become more aware of its deceptions. Allow yourself to rest through these thoughts; giving yourself to faith, rather than frustration. Here, in this moment of faith, you find the peace for which you long.

The practice of patience releases you from identifying with time and need. The practice of patience allows you to identify beyond the limitations constructed that make time necessary and useful. In your patience, you allow yourself to simply be. Without patience, you allow yourself to be ruled by time, need, and all limited constructions within the world.

Now research the word "patience" and see what you find.

Patience: circa.1225, "quality of being patient in suffering," from Latin: *patientia* "endurance," from *pati* "to suffer, endure," "to damage, injure, hurt" (see passion). Subsequent meaning: "constancy in effort."

Whoa... I don't know how comfortable I am with this definition. I'm fearful when I think of being forced to endure suffering. Wouldn't that be using illusion to define me?

Remember, Dear One, all words are merely symbols of symbols, and you already use illusion as your core substitute for Truth. This is why you see yourself at this moment in time. Yet, I wouldn't confine the definition of patience to meaning solely the endurance of suffering (as if suffering were reality). Instead, accept patience as *the choice for you to endure beyond the thought of suffering*. Here, you choose to align yourself with eternity, rather than restriction.

In your aligning with eternity, you are settling into an awareness of your wholeness and releasing from the need to declare things to be different from what they are. Each moment you declare your experience should be different from what it is, you engage in suffering. This is because through these contrary determinations you battle with yourself. In patience, however, you do not judge experience but release into trust. Here you accept how there is no need for judgment because God's eternity is indefinable. Here you accept that nothing can restrict or contain pure expansion. Rest in this place of acceptance and you rest in peace beyond definition or embattlement.

Notice, too, that there is another meaning for patience, "constancy in effort." Surely, I do not ask you to struggle, but disciplining your mind will be necessary. Dedicate yourself with willingness. The undisciplined mind cannot be patient; it is too busy attempting to control, predict, judge and command the universe, rather than releasing all to God's care.

As I have said in *A Course in Miracles*, you are much too tolerant of a wandering mind, so too are you much too tolerant of judgment. Having no faith, the impatient mind uses judgment to contend with its constant dissatisfaction and fear. This mind is adverse to trusting and releasing its will. Instead, it chooses its own will over God's and commands this will to be its own special self-centered reality.

If you dedicate yourself to faith, trust and are willing to accept what is in Truth, you will soon notice that there is nothing you cannot be tolerant of. This is because you choose to rest in God and fight no more.

Are you saying that if I am impatient, I am fighting against God?

Dear One, you can't really fight against God, only against yourself. Hear Me now, all your confusion and mistaken identity is but an engagement upon a perilous battleground. In each limiting belief you seek to adopt a substitute reality. Here you resist God because you imagine you fear Him. What is this imagining based upon? Simply it is the forgetting of your Self and your Holiness. You feel that you cannot release to love because of an assumption of guilt and abandonment from God.

None of these are reality, but you assume them out of your insanity and the subsequent mistaken choice to align with the thoughts of limitation. God will always know You as You are. Therefore, in choosing faith you accept His memory of yourself over your own deception. The yielding to faith has you rest above the battleground in certain trust of All That Is, surrendering to all as God extended into eternity. In this surrender, the demand to control time and activity through your expectations passes away. In its place you realize the Truth through acceptance, timelessness and faith.

At times when you don't have patience, have you ever noticed that a resistance to fully accepting the moment as it is activates your discomfort? This is what I mean by the battle with yourself. In this battle, you feel out of control and threatened. Clearly, this is but fear attempting to command an uncertain universe consumed by mad delusion. In projecting limited beliefs, you use judgment as your tool to satisfy or justify the investment in fear. When you do not feel your expectations are met within an instant, an unsettling of peace occurs. Truly, without your beliefs in fear and resistance to faith, no battle can occur.

Consider this the next time you feel frustration because the grocery clerk has accepted too many items on the express line. Remind yourself of these facts when the traffic is hampered or the friend does not call on time. Consider this when the lines are too long or the clock seems just too fast.

Patience is always a rest in truth. It has you accept life on life's terms without resistance. Patience gifts you with the ability to see life's situations as they are, rather than through the individualized filter of judgment or threat. Truly, and listen well, not but ALL of your demands, justifications and judgments are unrealistic. Not but ALL of them are unjustified and punishing to only your experience of self.

This operating within the world, you may say, does not have very much to do with spirituality or Heaven. But truly, all that you see within the world is a reflection of your mind. Moreover, every idea of hell you see within becomes a projection of hell on earth.

To guide yourself with patience is to guide yourself by the permanence of Truth. It is to have complete faith and trust in God's Will, rather than your temporal and limited one. Truly, to not have patience would be to invest in fear. Only fear can support the idea of threat that a lack of patience would justify. Without your investment in fear, you would be free beyond your imaginings and would rest graciously in the eternal strength of God Himself. Here, there could be no temptation to invest in time's meager offerings. Here, there would be no reason that could be a greater master than Truth. Here, in this rest, would you recognize in faith that all is extended by all for all in all, and with this understanding you would know your Truth.

Patience is necessary as long as you see yourself apart from eternity but are willing to accept eternity as your Holy Home. There is no need for patience in Heaven, because all is accepted in the fullness of being complete. Therefore, as you seem to have experiences here and now, patience can be your guidepost to faith and trust. This alone is why patience is endurance beyond your thought of suffering, rather than a complete release. In the practice of patience, you choose not to define yourself by the limitation or mistaken needs you see expressed within time's determination. Instead, you choose to rest your will and accept what faith cares to see.

In the moments of experience, you fully recognize time; yet with patience, time becomes an erroneous guide for the Truth of you. Release your bind with time and release a limited perception of yourself. Therefore, look not in the shadows to measure your progress, but go forth into the Light to truly see.

Time cannot measure or validate the completeness of God. Fear not that you could or could not have what you need in experience. Truly, to have in experience is insignificant to knowing fully in God. All that you do through limited experience is incomparable to the completeness you are always.

See yourself through the knowledge of eternity and know yourself through Vision's eye. Rest and release yourself from all limiting requirements that you feel could define you, since all of these beliefs are investments in deception. God only sees perfection in you. His idea of happiness for you is your awareness of this completion for He knows you are complete. Surely only incompleteness could result in fear or sorrow, and this is impossible in God! Be true to your Self as God is True to You. Center your mind on this perfection through faith. Patience results from trust as you accept eternity for your Self. I am with you always, for my light is your own. I love you.

Week Thirty-Three: Practice:

On a separate sheet of paper or in your journal, write down a list of ten situations where you feel most impatient. Be honest, we all have them. Is it the traffic light when you are running late? Perhaps, it is the line at the post office or the grocery customer with more that fifteen items on the express line? What really gets your frustration up?

For each situation on your list, identify:

1. What do you most fear will happen or not happen in this situation?

2. Why do you fear not having your expectations met? Why do you choose a loss of your peace to enhance this disappointment?

3. Take note if you are projecting, assuming, or attaching yourself to unrealities. If so, how can you release this way of thinking?

4. Write down one or two ways you can appropriately release this fear and bring a more calming experience to the situation.

5. Once you have completed your list, take a deep breath and look upon every idea that you have acknowledged. Next, allow yourself to rise into a state of peace, quieting the mind. Stay in this moment for about thirty seconds and then say:

"I am still as God created me. Now, I trust in Him to lead the way."

Afterwards, return once again to your breathing and feel His Certain comfort flow through you. You are free.

Affirmations:

The Holiness of God is timeless.

Peace is always within.

I give this moment to strength over fear.

Holiness has no limitations.

More Thoughts on Practicing Patience:

Feeling impatient? Before you jump to conclusions such as "I will NEVER get out of here," and "This ALWAYS happens to me," take a moment to explore other options:

1. Self-Inquiry: Before allowing yourself to become controlled by minor irritations, ask yourself some questions about your current attachments and judgments:

What is the worst that could happen if you decide to endure this experience?

What are the real chances of that happening?

What meaning are you placing within this situation?

Are you centering on ideas of expectation, powerlessness or threat?

How is your impatience going to stop that result from happening?

What would you rather have right now, peace or conflict?

Impatience only projects fear into the future and keeps you feeling like a victim. Take a deep breath and allow your thoughts to stay in the now, rather than the then or maybes. Unless you are psychic you never really know what might happen.

2. Realize who is in control: Why you are feeling the need to be in control? Is this a realistic and helpful wish? If your best thinking has brought you as far as the frustration you are currently feeling, perhaps, there is a better way.

3. Be unattached: Our attachments have us drive mental and emotional stakes into the ground, limiting our movement. Are you

prepared to be burned at this stake? Here's a fact: the world, as we know it, is a reflection of limitation. This will never change. As long as you perceive yourself to be within the world, you will see time as your keeper. However, you can be willing to give this limitation your love rather than your fear. Do you stand over your garden and wonder why its not growing... NOW!!! Of course not. In the art of simple waiting, you allow nature to take its appropriate course rather than impose your own demands for instant gratification. The garden vegetables (as well as all things in life) usually taste better when they are given all the time necessary to grow.

4. Judge less, live more: Practicing patience will always give you the opportunity to let go of your judgments. How are these judgments benefiting you anyway? Do they bring you peace of mind? Judgments always keep you locked in the prison of your mind, denying life's current opportunities for freedom and peace. Choose now to unlock the door to your cell of misery.

5. Get off the battlefield: Practicing patience gives us the opportunity to practice acceptance rather than resistance. When you choose to resist reality, you are fighting a purposeless battle and shooting out your own eye! How can you find the strength to accept these seeming challenges rather than deny your peace? Now is the time to release your fear and embrace your freedom!

Week Thirty-Four: **Valuing the Body**

Help me understand how I am to value the body. There just seems to be so many questions in this idea. I think of all the experiences of sickness, death, maintaining a healthy lifestyle, vanity, etc. The list goes on and on. Therefore, I'm giving all these concerns to you Holy Spirit. Please help me see all ideas of the body in another way. Thank you.

Truly, Dear One, this is not about understanding your body. Surely, I can espouse many metaphysical teachings about how the body came to be and its purpose. However, let's minimally focus on these often misunderstood ideas, because concepts alone rarely yield to peace. Truly, it would be most helpful now to focus only on releasing the body from all thoughts you use to define it and likewise yourself.

The body is a representation of misunderstanding. All along your journey, within this realm of perception, the body has been a tool. Its job is to play out all ideas of limitation. Never can you be this limited identity. You are not entrapped within its physical limitations, nor can the Holiness of God ever be merely a body.

The body is a tool and communication device. Essentially, the body will act out every image that you wish to see through it. Therefore, the more you invest within thoughts of limitation this is what you will see. Be it pleasure or pain, the body is only a representative of the initial dream of limitation. In fact, no matter which way you choose to see yourself as the body, the thinking mind, personality, emotions and circumstances of the world will oblige to correlate with this wish. Does this mean that you are in complete control of everything experienced? Not exactly. Remember, part of the dream was to act out powerlessness. However, you are in control of your interpretations and how these thoughts are applied within the world.

Believe it or not, when it comes to your worldly experiences, the old adage, "What you see is what you get" often applies. If you focus on ideas of limitation, victimization, ugliness, inadequacy, insecurity, impermanence, suffering, poverty and all else, the body with all its accompaniments will gladly play these ideas out for you. However, although the willingness to accept these states of being emerges from your own perceptions, these ideas did not originate from you personally.

All possible states of being are mere echoes reaching out from their original source. In the case of limited state of being, this original source was the first wish for limitation that occurred within the playful mind of Holiness stating "I am not as God Created." Since then, let us say colloquially, all hell broke loose.

Okay, so sickness is a physical experience representing my wish to be limited?

No, not *your* wish. Sickness is one expression of the wish to experience limitation from the Holiness who forgot its True Self. The original choice leading to the form of sickness is not a conscious one. Although an individual can believe in sickness, and see him or herself as a current or potential victim of sickness (or death), he or she have not individually created the idea of sickness. The thought of sickness initiated from the first playful imaginings of a mistaken identity. However, an individual can use his or her thoughts about sickness to intensify or diminish the experience of sickness. The body and mind do work together.

Have you ever met someone who, although they were medically diagnosed as sick or dying, chose not to accept this condition for themselves? And do you know of others who have convinced themselves that a paper cut will lead to amputation? These are examples of how your personal thought system can affect the experience of sickness.

If you invest in a body, you see a body. If you make this body dependent, you will see dependency. If you see this body as requiring status, beauty and certain physical expressions in order to be valued, this too is what you will see. However, none of these ideas are really you. They are just mere ideas that the communication device called the body can help you experience.

This dream appeared to begin in time when the Holiness of God imagined a personification seemingly different than its ever-present awareness. This choice to personify led to the experience of individualized consciousness. However, in order for this consciousness to experience itself, a further expression of division occurred and was maintained through the limitation overseer called time and space. Eventually all of this playing out led to the experience of individual bodies, personalities and all their accompaniments. So yes, essentially the body is devised as a tool and nothing other than a tool. This tool is the puppet, playing out what the Holiness of God wishes to pretend.

This is the best explanation as to why some infants are born ill, appear to suffer and die. It is not their personalized bodies, minds or souls that choose such an experience, but the entire misperceived mind. This mistaken identity uses every expression at its disposal to continue playing out the ideas of limitation. Therefore, the innocent can appear to be victimized, the young can appear to die and humans appear to live only within diversity, judgment or luck. The baby or his or her parents did not make the experience of sickness or death. However, they can always use the experience for healing or further dissociation from Truth.

Consequently, I would never ask you to judge a brother based on his or her appearance of sickness (or, for that matter, appearance of anything else). Appearances always deceive. Likewise, all individual experiences deceive. Nothing that appears to happen to you is wholly of the you seen as body. What appears to happen is merely an adopted form for a mind choosing to see itself within appearances.

Miracles of healing often occur when individuals consciously choose to not personalize the experience of disease. For some, this is easy, for others, more seemingly challenging. However, there are no hierarchies or order of difficulty in miracles. You can accomplish all miracles when Truth is accepted as your Self. This acceptance, in and of itself, is the miracle.

No matter the miracle desired, give yourself completely to God and trust all is complete. Seek not to yield in fear, because this thought only has you reaffirm the realities of fear. Yes, this may take a dedication to inner focus, however never is release impossible. Remember, all thoughts of Love are your Self. Accept this reality as your Inheritance. Expect these miracles because of Who You Are. Honor your awareness for the very sake of Love its Self. Here you will know that sickness is not your Truth, nor is any idea of limitation for God's Holiness. Here you will clearly see that it is not through your individualized self that healing is known but by stepping into the Light of One Being. Give place to this Light to have you know it. Accept the availability of Healing Grace within you at all moments and truly no form or function is necessary.

Okay, so I am thankfully realizing what you are teaching. However, I'm wondering what attitude I should hold about the body in general. Should I dissociate from or despise it?

Beloved One, Love is always the way, the truth and the light. This is true for all experiences. Do not despise your body, but love it. Appreciate this tool for all the ways it can serve your healing mind. Come to love your Self not just as an experience of embodiment, but as an everlasting freedom to Be. Love your body. Love all opportunities for Self expression. Care for your body, treat it well. Keep your body in a state of perfect mind and physical health, if you so choose. You may even choose to wear adornments or eat chocolate without guilt! Yes, indeed you can do and be everything, without limit, in an expression of Self Love.

Guilt (or an idea of separation) has really been the only problem here. In guilt you accept a self apart from God, and this self is often seen as sinful, worthless and afraid. No wonder this thought system can spin off into a multitude of other mistaken impressions about yourself! Do you want to love the body? Go ahead; however permit this Love to be ALL encompassing. Permit this Love to be a representation of the limitless, boundless Light You are! In this realization you can dance, sing, and enjoy all foods or experiences without worry, concern or judgment.

Likewise, as you choose to live in a forgiving, loving and

healing state of mind, you will not over indulge. Everything will be perfectly welcomed in moderation, because you will come to know yourself far beyond all appearances. Here you will treat yourself, your body and every body with the Love it always deserves. An experience of health will also be known through this practice. However, this health is not reserved only to form. If your experience of health appears to contain physical sickness, remember that no matter what the form, you are Holiness beyond any other personalization. And through this simple beingness the miracle rests in our knowing. I love you.

Week Thirty-Four: Prompts for Insight:

1. Make a list of ten ways you describe yourself as a body, identity and/or personality. Next, make a list of ten ways you would describe your Self in Spirit. Although Spirit truly is beyond definition, use your imagination to envision what Spirit Self would be. Now, look at each definition of the body self and see where these definitions provide a limited identification and/or are dependent upon a separation or comparison. Would you like to release these images of yourself? If so, how? Write down your insights. Ask for Holy Spirit's guidance and take notes on all thoughts that come forth.

2. What does Holy Spirit's guidance of "*The body will act out every image that you desire to see through it*" mean to you? What do you feel you have acted out for your self? How do you feel this statement relates to all thoughts, feelings and experiences you hold about yourself? Take a moment to particularly consider how this statement can affect your self image and self esteem within the world.

3. The topic of sickness has always been a difficult one for our understanding. Holy Spirit shares in this reading several rather pivotal teachings about sickness. Take a moment now to review the teachings. Their combined call is asking for us not to seek an understanding of the why's and how's of sickness, but instead to seek the release of all such ideas through God's Knowing. Write all thoughts and feelings or challenges that arise from this teaching. Share these thoughts with Holy Spirit and trust in any response received.

Affirmations:
Sickness is impossible in the Holiness of God.
A mind perceiving limitation can only teach limitation.
I release for peace and settle into pure awareness.
I am not my body. I am free.

Week Thirty-Five: **Perfection**

Dearest Holy Spirit, I cannot conceive myself as being perfect. In fact, I have a lot of discomfort when I even try to think about it. I recognize this as a judgment of unworthiness within my mind. Will I ever get to a point where I can be without these judgments? What does "perfect" mean to God? Thanks.

Thank you for coming to Me with this inquiry, Loved One. I understand that it is rather difficult for you to be in this space. I appreciate all moments you choose to step aside from your own ways of thinking, as this is how you access a deeper knowing. In our joining, you are willing to place judgments aside. In this surrender, as one, we open to peace beyond your experience. Therefore, yes, continue to allow for release and you will find peace beyond these judgments. You are doing this now. Likewise, if you were to give Me every thought that appeared to trouble you, peace would always be your experience. Release and listen now. Let us welcome healing with an open awareness. My blessing extends to this openness in you.

Now, before we begin to speak about how God sees you, it is important to look at why and how you see you as you do. The struggling-self, through whom you identify, is always blind to its own True perfection. It is impossible for a mind functioning in limitation to conceive or accept wholeness. Surely, if you struggle now with accepting yourself as merely approvable or tolerant in God's Sight, do you really think you could fully accept the extent of perfection I truly know you to be? This endeavor would be similar to attempting to convince a fictional character of his or her reality while still within the story. Urging the identified self to accept all the wholeness it is in Truth is asking for it to give up all it seems to know and understand. This could not be done without an experience of fear. Remember, the nature of the mistaken identity is a belief in loss and limitation. It does not know itself and feels lost. If you were to force any idea of wholeness upon the mistaken identity, these ideas would be seen as at best alien, at worst a threat. Therefore, the ego cannot compromise or be cajoled.

Loss and limitation cannot coexist within the realms of Perfect Love. This means that you could not equally hold your wish to see flaws and still be fully aware of your Holiness. Simply all that is asked is for a peaceful release from all mistaken identifications. In this release you surrender from all justifications for judgment. Here you simply realize the pure innocence and folly beyond the ego's ideas and release all into peace. This surrender is opening the door and remembering Who You Are. Again, I will never tell you to ignore your beliefs or forcefully convince them to change. Instead, a yielding to the desire for release must naturally be the higher calling. Here you willingly embrace love with love rather than fear.

This struggling-self has been given value as part of the role you play. The forgetting mind has given it a specific purpose for a specific need. Feeling judgmental and limited is normal from where you perceive yourself to be. To ignore this wish would be only an inappropriate use of denial. It is not helpful to deny or curse these wishes. Therefore, when you notice a judgment, do not feel shameful. That is truly counter-productive. These experiences are only expressions of your initial wish to see differently. This is not to be judged and never will. Therefore it is perfectly acceptable to notice these thoughts and say, "ahh, look at the choice I am making." Next, from this awareness, allow forgiveness and love to take the place of the choice. An awareness of your perfection can arise when the thoughts of judgment are simply met with a deeper rest. Within the moment of timelessness, there is only laughter for the nightmares you currently insist are you. We are not laughing at you, but with you, as you express your Self in freedom. This is why your innocence remains intact. We know the Truth and nothing else. Beloved, this Truth is perfection beyond every moment of time. Therefore, as I direct you to know yourself as perfect, I ask you only to see yourself in God's Love. Keep this in mind as you welcome a release of your thinking from all erroneous attachments. Seek to settle within the Truth within you rather than judgments.

Now, go and research the word perfect as we normally do:

Perfect (adj.): Circa.1225 from Latin word *perfectus:* "completed," relative to *perficere:* "accomplish, finish, complete." From *per-* "completely" + *facere* "to perform."

Okay, so if I understand correctly, the word *perfect* means "completely accomplished or performed." How does this apply to my Self as God Created, as well as the personal self I seem to experience?

When I say you are perfect, it simply means that God has extended Himself in completion through your Holy Being. He has completely extended Himself and brought You into full development. In your True Beingness, there is nothing left to accomplish. There is nothing missing. In this state of Being, You are Wholeness itself.

Since, you are Wholeness itself; does this mean that your behavior will always reflect this Wholeness? No. Does it mean that you can think yourself to be this Wholeness? No. Your behaviors and thoughts merely reflect your belief in loss and limitation. This is the best they can reflect as long as they play their appointed role.

However, you always have the opportunity for release. The role you play is not the Self you are. Perceptions only arise from all mistaken beliefs you hold within the consciousness of separation. Therefore, for as long as you see yourself in this sense, all behaviors and thoughts will read from this same script.

Likewise, perfectionism is only an ego's defense to self-judgment, self-attack, and comparison. It strives to keep itself from experiencing the loss it perceives itself to be. It overcompensates for this perception of loss. The "cure" for perfectionism is release. Release yourself from all the ways and manners that have you choose to judge instead of love. Be aware of the thoughts that assume you will be judged, and so must portray an image of perfection for your own protection. Do the same for all ways you see your brother. Your judgments upon him are all a figment of your imagination. Not one of these judgments provides you peace, not even temporarily. Peace and vindication of the ego are not the same. Release yourself from defining your brother by his form and you shall find a Self-same. Extend Holiness towards your brother and recognize not only your brother's perfection but mainly your own.

Hear me well; a false image of perfectionism is not perfect. Any false image remains as it is: false. Therefore, if you find yourself "putting on a face of charity" in order to be seen as loving or kind, this is not a genuine being. Be mindful of this action, because it is time that you stop attempting to fool yourself and God. In the instance that you choose to be false, you are only fooling yourself. Here you are pretending not to judge, or at least present your judgments on the surface. This does not mean that you are not judging. Nor does this mean that you accept your own perfection. Truly Beloved, judgment will never lead to peace, nor will any form of pretense. Does this mean that you should share your judgments with others or act unkindly if that is how you feel? No. Because any wish to be unkind only stems from your own self-judgment. What you see in your brother is always first and foremost within your own deluded mind. Therefore, if you feel prompted to correct your brother, ask first for where you seek to heal yourself. Notice the fear or belief in limitation within your own awareness and place your correction there. This is offering love to the one place it truly belongs. Consequently, as you offer love and acceptance first to yourself, these gifts will not but only radiate outward towards all you meet. Here, you come to know yourself and then know your Brother. This is true healing.

Additionally, you would have no need to desperately seek completion in the outside world if you were to accept yourself as complete within. There would be no purpose to search for what you already possess. But then again, there are many who have sought for their sunglasses all the while they sit right atop their own head.

Very funny!!!

Truly, I only say this to help you recognize how you endlessly search for all you already own. Merely you have forgotten, and this fugue has you think searching is necessary. Hear Me now, Dear One, do not look about you, nor toss and turn in worry. Simply look up and you will find exactly what you have forgotten.

A bit metaphorical there?

Symbolic as you desire it to be, loved one. (Smile) Realize that your own Self is complete, beyond all its perceptions, and you will have no need to seek for validation of this perfection within a world of limitation. Likewise, as you associate with your brother, you will have no need to either judge or be upset over his or her variant behavior. If you were to see with love, there could be no variant behavior outside of love. Yet, I do understand how the thinking mind will analyze and judge this statement, so it is best said that as you seek, see the loving Self beyond appearances. If you are unsure, ask Me to be your guide.

Jeshua spoke while upon the earth, "*Be ye therefore perfect, even as Your Father Whom is in Heaven is perfect.*" (Matthew 5:48) Truly this comment has challenged many a theologian for centuries. However, the answer is as clear as is the true meaning of perfection. As I ask you to be perfect, simply I ask you to remember your Truth and make this your way. Again, the true meaning of perfect is complete. That is all, literally. As you seek to practice perfection in your experiential world, seek only to remember the Truth of You. Allow all your interactions to mirror the remembrance of Truth for yourself and all you encounter. This quote from Jeshua is merely a reminder of all You are. Jeshua's words are not commanding you to be behaviorally perfect. This is how the ego would see the phrase because the ego is constantly judging itself. In Truth, You are not judged; nor are your behaviors considered any less than normal for where you perceive yourself to currently reside. Therefore, do not perceive this statement to be anything but a call to remember who You are. You are complete, even as your Father Whom is in Heaven is Complete. You need not seek for anything else. You need not be dependent while you move upon this earthly experience. You need not judge yourself or your brother for any idea that appears to need correction. Lo, instead, all that is asked of you is to remember. In this remembrance you will feel no other prompting but to share this remembrance with all. And so as you do this, sharing the perfection You are with all, helping them remember their own perfection as you stand as a clear witness to their Light, you will know yourself as God knows you.

In fore-giving, you bestow the awareness of perfection previous to the experience. Here, you give perfection to the world and recognize only perfection's messengers in return. Here, there can be no mistaken identities because there are no recognized errors in thinking. This would remain consistent even in moments when your brother approached you with anger, disapproval, or discontent. There have been times where it has been asked for you to see your brother as love or fear; yet, I clarify, to see your brother in fear is to see your brother apart from love. This existence is impossible.

Feel no need to offer compassion through judgment. That is pity and this is not of Love. To see your brother in fear is to see your brother as incomplete or at a loss. Truly, is this point of view most loving if these two cannot coexist?

Hmmm… I guess not. I've never really thought of it that way. I can see how there is a space in my mind that would want to say, "Awwww, my poor, poor brother, it is so sad to see him see himself this way." You are right, that does not sound like love.

Yes, it is not. Imagine if I saw you in this way. Do you think my sympathy would be rather helpful? In fact, take a moment now and look up the origins of the word sympathy.

Sympathy: circa. 1579, "affinity between sorrow," from *syn-*"together" + *pathos* "suffering, feeling, emotion."

Wow. So when I have sympathy for someone, I am only aligning with a belief in sorrow or suffering? I am only multiplying the experience of suffering?

Yes. To align with sorrow is to align with loss. To align with loss is to see through the eyes of deficiency. This is to perceive yourself AND your brother as being incomplete. Now, does that sound like love to you?

Wow. Gosh. No, it does not.

Beloved One, do not pity yourself or your brother for one more moment. Choose instead to offer only the love that is deep within you as One. Choose to see only the completion, that is, the perfection that you are in every moment. Here you find your truth beyond all images. Here you know your peace.

Furthermore, call a witness to your completion. Accept that God requires nothing of you. He sees you as Him Self, Holiness in all ways. He has extended you as complete, and there is no question of this certainty.

So, if I recognize that I am perfect, I am simply recognizing that I am complete and that God requires nothing of me as His Holiness.

Yes . . . perfect. (smile)

Okay, and then if my brother's behavior seems to be erroneous, I should not join him in a perception of this error through judgment OR pity, but I should only offer him Love. Here, I offer up all judgments for release, beyond appearances and settle within the love that is most purposeful.

Yes again. Perfect. This is the same for your behavior too. Do not pity or judge yourself, for that is only to join in suffering as well.

Wow... I really like that. However, wait, I have one more: In forgiving (or shall I say "fore-giving") I choose to offer once again the memory of completion. This is the memory of who my brother and I are prior to any other perception. In choosing to accept this memory as my Self, I am free from all barriers built in deception of Truth. How's that?

You got it, my Perfect One.

Gosh, stop saying that.

Why? Do you feel uncomfortable with my reflection of Truth to you?

I ... uhm ... no, it is just that I think I am still seeing that word through the eyes of the struggling-self.

Do not worry if you do not realize all of this right away, Dear One. You have been putting yourself through these definitions for as long as you can imagine.

Cute. Okay, I'll cut myself a break.

Better yet, love yourself a healing.

Boy, you are on a roll tonight! (smile) So let me clarify some more. My behavior and thoughts will continue to reflect only the perceptions I accept for myself, until I decide to release my attachments to the thinking mind. Right?

Yes. However, do remember that the thinking mind plays out all your beliefs. There is nothing here to be averted. There is nothing here to judge. So do not judge the judgment of the thinking mind. Its thoughts merely support the awareness of this dream and have served your wishes well.

Okay, so don't judge my judging or judge the judging of others who appear to judge. (smile)

That will help you see your freedom, as well as your brothers'. See yourself beyond your thoughts, feelings and behavior (likewise, see your brother beyond his or hers) and you will begin to know yourself with a more significant clarity. In fact, once you notice how much you can release from these choices to express limitation, you can wholly give your awareness to Me. I always guide you in return to all You are.

And here I will see myself as perfect? When?

Peace is yours; perfection is now. God perfectly extends to You. You are complete. You need not anything but realize this Truth. As I guide you to recognize your perfection, recognize that this perfection is beyond time and requirement. Your perfection could not be complete unless it was beyond time and requirement. Be not confused. Give every moment for healing to Me. Release for peace. Enter the holy instant and accept that only certainty and trust are yours to extend. These states of Being are witnesses to the Truth You are.

Hear Me now; your shadows are not you. They only extend from a belief of what you can never be. In this acceptance of uncertainty, all that comes to mind will be the mistaken beliefs of vulnerability, rejection, deception, hurt, and loss. No wonder why you feel so uncomfortable with the acceptance of your perfection! As long as you see in loss, you will see in doubt. All of these are rooted simply in the uncertainty of self that you align with in the moment of fear. Value your fears and see their howling cries. Recognize the Truth of Completeness, and there can be only the stillness of God speaking His thoughts through you.

Confusion does not share in the qualities of complete wholeness. What are these qualities? Simply they are being without need. They do not seek change from a sense of loss or uncertainty. Complete wholeness knows completely of its wholeness. It knows of its Holiness and so it needs nothing. Holiness does not obsess in attempts to be anything other than the perfect all it is. Truly, it would do you well if in life circumstance you would choose to be aware of the completion in everything. See the idea beyond the projection of need or desperation for change. Here you shall find all the joy you have never truly left behind.

Again, the conflicted mind cannot understand Reality. All is and does not bend to the unruly billows of the thinking mind nor will it ever. Its thoughts and barrage of experience-narration cannot witness for anything except for what you are not. Do not yield to this madness. Instead, seek beyond your limited understanding. Only here, beyond confusion, you will find peace. I am always for your peace.

Thank you. You know, at first, I questioned that statement. I thought that it should have been "I am always here for your peace." Now I see that to always be for my peace is so much more.

Yes, I am a constant witness for all You are and stand only to see that Truth as your Self. I am always for your peace and nothing else. My light is your own. Rest in the certainty of Who You Are. This rest is perfectly Being. Yes, you are complete. I love you.

Thank you . . . I love you. I am as God Created Me.

Amen.

Week Thirty-Five: Prompts for Insight:

1. Holy Spirit guides, "*The struggling-self, through whom you identify, is always blind to its own True perfection. It is impossible for a mind functioning in limitation to conceive or accept Wholeness.*" Feelings of unworthiness, desperation, depression and dependency are normal for the mistaken identity. These feelings are its mantra. In this teaching Holy Spirit is not asking us to convert the ego to a new way of thinking. Yet, now, we are taught that these ideas are normal for the identity they represent. Therefore, bringing peace to the identity is not the way. Genuine release is found in the acceptance of our perfection despite outer conditions. This healing requires our Self-acceptance and willingness to give everything over to Holy Spirit for His Undoing, trusting how His Sight is the truest. Furthermore, we are asked to offer love to the ego rather than condemnation. We cannot find peace without an offer of peace. Take this moment to review your own path. Where have you sought to convert or condemn the ego? How can you come to accept the despondent emotions of the ego without further judgment? How do you hope to know your Self beyond any outward experience?

2. Holy Spirit teaches, "*Perfectionism is only an ego's defense to self-judgment, self-attack and comparison.*" How often have you attempted to be "perfect" within the world's standards? Make a list of the ways you see yourself struggling for perfection. What are some of the judgments you have held against yourself? How have you strived endlessly to protect yourself from fear or loss? Explore these shadows of false perfectionism with Spirit, seeking to find the true completion within you.

3. Make a list of what you consider to be perfect within the world. Be honest and share how you have considered the perfect body, perfect home, perfect family, perfect job, perfect day, etc. Now look at your list and ask yourself if any of these representations of perfection share the qualities of complete wholeness. If they do not,

seek within to see what fears or beliefs of incompletion may conversely be represented. Use all that you learn for self-reflection.

Affirmations:

I am complete in God's Perfection.

I bestow upon my brother the awareness of Truth.

Here and now, I give my brother the gift of perfection.

I am wholeness itself.

Week Thirty-Six: **Vain**

Sometimes I feel completely worthless. Can you help me see these thoughts differently?

> Remember, Dear One, only the mistaken identity perceives limitation. It alone is the very idea of restriction, guilt, hurt, judgment, and separation. You cannot have any of those thoughts unless you first believe and invest in the illusion of your limitation.

That is the perfect reminder that I need.

> Yes, remind yourself every moment you perceive vainly.

Whoa… vainly!?

> Yes, centered on empty foolishness. All ideas of the struggling-self are vain attempts to seek completion where there is none. It alone constantly yearns for definition and understanding because of Self-denial. You can never gain from these thoughts.

But… I …

> Go ahead, look it up.

Vain: Circa.1300, meaning: "devoid of real value, idle, unprofitable." Related to Old French *vein* "worthless," and Latin: *vanus / vacare* denoting: "idle, empty, to be empty," from base **eue-* "to leave, abandon, give out." Meaning "conceited" first recorded 1692, from earlier sense of "silly, idle, foolish." Phrase *in vain* denotes "to no effect."

Okay, conceptually I can see how you are saying that the struggling-self is only a self in conflict. On its own it is empty. But, what about the identity I seem to know? Are you saying this is completely purposeless too?

Listen, beloved, the struggling-self is purposeful in one way and one way only. It can represent to you exactly where you are struggling. Here we use it as a learning device. It merely was an answer to an innocent wish. Can you see the innocence here? This does mean that the struggling-self serves you. It shows you exactly what you believe and how these beliefs affect you. Now, in a life deemed to be lived apart from God, each of these thoughts can appear to rule you. They can seem to make many effects of sorrow and pain. However, once the miracle is accepted and used, these ideas can become beacons to inspire awakening.

Remember how you commented that in The Course's section on the development of trust for the Teacher of God "Doesn't sound like a picnic"?

Uh, yes. I do remember that conversation. I also remember the hellish experiences. I still stand by my initial judgment. (smile)

Yes, the pain and confusion surely seemed to speak in a louder volume during these experiences. However, despite the exact form, how can you put the content to use in the world?

Well, I did learn that so many of the accomplishments of the world (the ones I idolized and valued beyond my own peace and health) were nothing but empty searches. I learned that I searched because I felt empty inside. I felt rejected and alone. However, through surviving these incidences with a greater degree of self-awareness, I learned that when the world seems to show you exactly what you believe, there is always the opportunity for peace.

Wonderful. And now do you see how these vain imaginings can become gifts to greater awareness?

Yes. Hey, tell me, if I become really good at practicing these teachings, can I make a difference within the world? Can I become a better therapist or healer? Will these ideas have use for me in the world?

The world is not as much of a problem as compared to how you see the world. Let us focus now on how to free your mind from the prison of its thinking. Beloved, you can be your own healer! You are purposeful as your friend and as your enemy. Each of these thoughts withheld from peace displays exactly all you wish to know about yourself. Any action within the world is merely just an action. It has no deeper meaning except for the belief that initiated its representation. Beloved One, your learning here is not about being remembered. This practice is about remembering!

Do not fear now. I can see how you are feeling alone and afraid in thought because of your attachment to the world and its dreams. But do not fear. Within the world there is just as much purpose as there is meaning... and yes, it is all within you. Do not fear that you are lost or forgettable. You are not. God knows exactly Who You Are, where you are. This Being is not as your struggling-self in a world of loss and limitation. He knows your True Self in its True Home, and this is far beyond your own recognition. This is a peaceful Self where rest and love is eternally accepted. This Self is never dependent upon proof or need. Again, it does not need to be remembered, as it is remembrance.

Likewise, my friend, look willingly into the ego mindset. See how it alone believes in the need to be a separate self with value apart from other separated selves. See how it alone wants to see this self be glorified above others, and loved more than others. See how it is desperately seeking from the outside because it knows only nothingness within. You need not be this nothingness. That is why I say you have vain imaginings. These searches are nothing but a reaffirmation of the emptiness seen within your self. This need, not be!

Yikes, okay. I can see that. I can see that the role of a healer need not contain an expression of self-validation. I guess quiet is often best. Gosh, why does this healing process seem to unleash so much ego activity? I feel more sensitive and frustrated than ever before!

This entire experience is a blind game of hide and seek. Although it is make-believe, you practice it as "believe and make." There appears to be so much discomfort in the healing process because as you heal you are becoming more aware of the struggle within you. As you become more aware of this struggle, it seems to get worse before it gets better.

However, truly, you only battle yourself. Although the impression of turmoil may appear to be more frequent, it is only more consciously noticed within you. If you recall, in your past denial of Truth, you actually believed that thoughts wishing for separation and competition were justified and normal! Now you are beginning to see how these wishes only represent defeat, fear, and exhaustion. You see how they do not align with agreement and acceptance, but with resistance. Therefore you are more conscious of the contrast. This gives you the impression of a more prominent battle.

Step above the battleground with Me and see yourself with peace. Accept no battles even as your mind choose to see with challenge. You need not fight to be freed.

Notice now, with a lovingly guided and objective willingness, what your mind in division believes. Openly observe its thoughts. Accept them for what they have to say. Do not fear these ideas, or judge and resist them. Accept all the ideas for all their scripts. What do they believe about judgment and vulnerability, loss and fear, limitation and abandonment? See these illusions, see their distortions. See the vain imaginings used in place of reality. Ask yourself how realistic and reliable their claims are. Where are the facts supporting their judgment? The more you see this, the more you will notice the fruitless attempts to make your Truth into nothing. The more you will see your ability to laugh at these presumptions of your emptiness.

I have seen a lot of those thoughts recently, especially in my relationships with others. I definitely do not see these experiences and thoughts neutrally. I do get wrapped up in the fear and judgment quite a few times. I do get irritated and feel as if my buttons are being pushed. However, there was a time I held fast to these judgments, but now these feelings do pass in time with greater ease.

Indeed that is progress; but, let Me say, it was not in time that these feelings did pass, it was in your increased awareness to see differently. Your process may have appeared to be in time, but time's measurement had nothing to do with your acceptance of freedom.

Beloved, I love you. Hear Me well, I love you and you are far from nothing. Rest on these words a moment and feel them truly sink within you mind and heart.

Do not concern yourself with the players of this game, for you have placed them all in the perfect place at the perfect time for the perfect purpose to your imagining. They will give you every message that is desired to be heard.

Remember, you are free. Your choice to completely express is this freedom. The choice remains the same no matter what the condition of the appearance. A belief in fear is a belief in fear. A belief in separation is a belief in separation. A belief in victimization is a belief in victimization, and all of these are rooted to the very beliefs you are willing to accept for and about your self. Every time the world and its players appears to challenge you, see the beliefs beneath the surface and ask yourself if You ARE that image. So I ask you now. Are you afraid? Are you separate? Are you a victim? Are you alone? Are you abandoned and rejected? Are you?

Sometimes it really feels that way. Moreover, I do not know how to turn it off.

This is only because you desire to turn off the world's players and not the one who writes the script. Listen, You are all. You are all you see and all you feel. You are the light for which every star was placed within the sky. And you are the joy for which every smile upon every face can find its cause. This is not the individual self I speak of. To judge yourself through the eyes of an individuated self will always leave you disappointed. Remember the dream is rooted in insanity. How can you expect it to act sane when its very job was to see in madness from the start? Some days the separate qualities of the world appear to be less persistent than others, but that does not mean the belief in separation and limitation does not persevere. It will continue as long as the idea of a separate world exists. As long as you see "others," you embrace insanity.

So am I supposed to just live and pretend as if this stuff isn't going on? Am I supposed to feel as if I'm not being attacked? Am I supposed to not think with the individual mind at all? How is that realistic?

You are supposed to play whatever role you want to play in the moment. You are free. You are free to live in complete acceptance of every attack and make it something requiring defense. You are free to live as victim and feel the need to isolate or maybe even destroy the character you play now so as to escape the drama you see as real and inescapable. But truly, what purpose does any of this serve? How can the Holiness of God awaken from a dream made real? He can't, because a dream made real is not a dream. As long as you see the dream as your reality and allow it mastery over you as such, you will not feel free, nor will you feel peace.

So again.. Am I supposed to ignore everything?

Go ahead... look up ignore....

Ignore: Circa. 1611, "not to know, to be ignorant of," from Latin: *ignorare* "not to know, disregard." Further uses include the form *ignarus* "not knowing, unaware" (see *ignorant*). Sense of "pay no attention to" was first recorded 1801 and not common until circa.1850.

Only the ego mind presumes it knows. You can discern a presumption from certainty by the peace the certainty holds as compared to the guilt, fear and hurt the presumption beholds. Hear Me well; you do NOT know your brother. You do NOT know your world. And most importantly, you do NOT know your Self. Every judgment you make is reflective upon this one certainty within your dreaming. You are living in confusion. This is especially true when the world appears to be overpowering you. Yet despite your belief in powerlessness, the Truth is true. I have given you these teachings not just for idle intellectual discourse. They are for your practice. This alone will lead you to release. Therefore, the call is made for your acceptance above resistance.

I hear you and I really want to understand. I really want to feel free. But these events in the world seem so real. They seem so filled with hurt and hate. As long as I see them, I feel affected. I doubt that I will ever be able to see them as not happening.

Am I saying that these acts are not happening? No. They are happening exactly as the limited mind has asked for. They are happening fully within the ways the forgetting mind chooses to see. Some of these scripts extend from the unified mind playing its role within the dream, and some from the struggling-self who was made to be a player. It is all part of the whole. Although what goes on within these experiences appears to be real, insane, frustrating, hurtful, and victimizing, it all remains the same. One problem, one solution. I will never be inconsistent.

Listen, beloved, you do not know your brother. Therefore, instead of ignoring your brother's actions, begin your awareness before an offense could be interpreted. Ignore your judgment. Do not deny the judgment. Simply choose not to know it. Realize how it does not know. More specifically, recognize how you do not know or gain anything from your judgment.

Try to ignore my judgment?

Yes, but I do not mean as an afterthought. Then see how entrapped you feel by the world. If you cannot invest in your own judgment, you cannot express it. Put another way, if you choose not to know your judgment, you will choose not to know presumption, righteous anger, insult, and anything presenting through it. You do not need to be the doormat for judgment's attacks. Tell judgment that it can no longer wipe its feet on you. Tell judgment that you choose to know your brothers as their Truth instead of its presumptions.

Therefore, I ask again, what serves your purpose? Is it to linger betwixt cycles of judgment and revival? Or is to recognize that you alone do not know as long as that so-called knowledge keeps you in fury. Can you let Holy Purpose lead the way?

I would like my Holy Purpose to lead the way.

If you say that with willingness in your heart and mind, then surely you cannot fold to judgment anymore. Instead, choose to recognize how you do not know. Choose to allow He who does know to be your guide.

Hmm… I wonder who that is. (Smile)

It is a peaceful beginning when you can laugh at what just a few hours ago brought you great distress. This awareness can be your inspiration. You have proven here that you can rest from the struggle.

It appears that it is now time to practice. In the tensest moments, I will try to remember how you have given me the classroom to practice the lesson.

Actually, I don't restrict you to classrooms, nor do I give any tests. From my point of View, the Self I know is perfect. However, I do extend the answers you seek for the trials you invest within. This is your battle and not my own. But I will assist you as you choose to rise above it. I will show you another way. I am that way, the truth and the light. And here is one better… it is all for you as you.

Somewhat hard to stay angry when you put it that way.

Anger only means a "narrowing of pain." Why intensify your illusion when you can release for peace? Is it not more helpful to be open in delight? I ask you to release the masks, roles and characterizations you place upon the Holiness of God. These extended (and perverse) beliefs continue only a veneer of guilt and distortion. If you choose to know from this form, you only know nothing. Repeat this to yourself as many times as necessary.

I do not know. I cannot presume. I can release for peace.

Yes, you can. In your choice to release, it is essential to recognize how purposeless the attachment to anger and judgment really are. It is essential to recognize how much the clinging to limitation brings only restraint, struggle and exhaustion. As *A Course in Miracles* teaches, the ego at best is suspicious, at worst it is vicious. The Holiness of God is neither of these, for He knows there is no purpose in them. He knows that in the form of separation it is impossible to know reality. And in accepting this he chooses freedom from illusion instead.

It is important to note that the conscious self honestly desires to gain from distorted thinking. It alone invests in distortions because it believes in all its woven tales of justification and limitation. This forgetful mind has made every distorted thought useful to its sustenance. Consequently, a part of the ill will perceives itself to be starving without this power. It feels trapped, afraid, and under attack naturally! Imagine, then, the attempt to make it even more powerless or, worse yet, completely dissociated??! Surely, you have allowed your ego to feel like a caged animal, frightened, starved, and alone and bewildered. Surely, how can you begin to expect sanity to emerge from this situation? Would it not be impossible? This is why I ask you to expect only insanity from the mistaken identity, for that is truly all you will find. It will never be able to compromise with sanity, for it is only aligned with insanity. Therefore, do not look upon the ego and expect it to begin speaking sanely; it cannot, and will not, and you are only deluding yourself further by waiting in anticipation for it to do so.

Wow… yes, I guess you are right… humph… as always. (Smile) I do often look at my insane thoughts and wonder when they will get their act together. So too do I look at seemingly other faces and expect them to finally learn, or at least make use of the knowledge I perceive them to have. But then again, this is all my judgment. The most forgiving thing to do would be to not align with the misperception and choose to offer only light into the situation, accepting there is no compromising alternative. Yes, I guess I have to admit that I do not know.

Yes. That would be the most forgiving thing, not just for them, but mainly for you. In the moment you choose to release your expectations, ignore your judgments, cease the struggle, and release for peace, you will align with acceptance of love for all, in all. Here you do finally set yourself free. Here you trust not in your own mind to lead the way, but release yourself from every story. Here you have no more hoops to jump through or hopes to have fulfilled. Here you are accepting as you are in Truth because you choose to rely on real Knowledge.

Vain is empty because it was misguidedly made as a substitution to wholeness. This world is the inverse of all you are in Truth. All its representations must fall short or completely distort. They can do nothing but be nothing, for that is what they are in comparison to all you are. Hear the voice of emptiness, Dear One. It only cries for separation and justifies for judgment. Will you begin to laugh at its cackling? I know you can, for I know you in Truth. Are you willing to release all of your identity from its stories? And yes, it tells nothing but stories.

Help me see this… please… please help me see this.

Rest your mind, Beloved. It is okay. I am with you and I know you cannot suffer. Take my hand and reflect on all we discussed. You will notice how there is only one problem and one solution. Rest from your need to understand. Rest from your thinking. Allow this guidance to settle peacefully within. Now is the moment of healing, Dear One. Now you can place yourself within my care and guidance. Focus on my light to guide you, for the love I hold for You is immeasurable. It is beyond anything you can imagine. Surely it is your own, and most importantly it is all the Love that God has bestowed upon you. This I hold for you in knowledge of who You are. It is eternal as my love. Breathe, release, and rest. I love you.

Week Thirty-Six: Prompts for Insight:

1. Often it seems easier to invest in empty (vain) thoughts or beliefs over Truth. When do you feel empty? How have you played out these ideas of emptiness in seeing your body, personality, thoughts or emotions? How have your actions, behaviors and relationships further extended this idea? How would Holiness relate?

2. Holy Spirit guides, *"The world is not as much of a problem as compared to how you see the world. Let us focus now on how to free your mind from the prison of its thoughts."* Make a list five areas where you feel attached to or disturbed by, the world. Next to each of these listed disturbances, identify one way it affects you in form. What does it mean to you? Now pause for a moment and breathe. Repeat aloud:

"I am free beyond all limitations. I now offer a whole Vision, I offer love.
I am Spirit."

Breathe again and rest your thinking mind. Follow up questions could be, "How do you feel God or Holy Spirit would see this event?" or list what details within the situation you do not know. Identify as many areas where your judgments could be misled. Furthermore, with Holy Spirit as your guide, allow yourself to delve into the ideas of denial, apathy or dissociation. Spirit always knows our Truth beyond every image of our mind.

3. It is essential that we forgive ourselves for all the ways we have chosen emptiness (e.g. justified judgments, residual anger at loved ones, low self-esteem...). Take a moment now to hold a releasing ceremony for all the above thoughts, feelings, and experiences where your reluctance appeared to over shadow your release. Follow the suggested ceremonial form if you wish. After the Ceremony of Release, write about the thoughts and feelings that surfaced through the experience. Share each with Spirit.

Practice for Release:

Cut one piece of paper into six strips. On each strip write down one way you judge yourself or practice self-depreciation. Now is the moment of self-forgiveness and release of perceptions. Once you have all papers complete, take a walk to your favorite natural spot; perhaps a body of water or your own backyard. Choose where you feel most quiet and comfortable. One by one take each strip of paper, read your thought aloud, and follow it with "*In the name of my Truth, I choose to release [read paper]. I am innocent. I am loved. I am free. I am as God Created Me.*" Now, heartily tear up the paper and discard it. This is a fabulous ritual of release for all situations. Use this ceremony for healing before a new season or year, or ritualistically act out your wish to release unhealed events from the past. NOTE: How you choose to discard your papers is your choice. I suggest using recycled disposable paper and burying or safely burning each paper in a fireplace, so as not to leave unwanted waste. The form of the ritual is up to you, yet the meaning is tremendous.

Affirmations:

I am as God Created Me.

Of myself, I do not know. This is perfect.

I choose only Love to be my Guide.

I free myself from all vain imaginings.

Week Thirty-Seven: **House of Mirrors**

Holy Spirit Friend, I have been finding myself drawn to the phrase "house of mirrors" lately. It has been floating in my mind for the past two days. Can you expand on this prompting? Thank you.

Beloved One, thank you for listening. The House of Mirrors is the experience of projections and perceptions. You walk now within a House of Mirrors, seeing all only as you see yourself. This is an important lesson for you now. It will help reveal knowledge where you once perceived imprisonment.

You cannot identify anything within the world without first placing forth an image within it. Let Me repeat that, because it is essential: You cannot identify anything within the world without first placing forth an image within it. The root image is always within your mind and completely based upon your beliefs. Therefore, your beliefs guide every observation you have. Your beliefs fuel all discernment. They draw the map for every picture you see in the outer-world and every impression you receive about others and situations. Therefore, you walk now within a House of Mirrors because all you truly see is a collection of reflections and nothing else!

Wow. Okay, so everything is rooted only within my own mind?

No.

Wait a minute; this is not about form, but my perception of everything. And so, everything I see is rooted only within MY mind????

Yes. I am speaking about projection making perception. Your individualized thinking mind does not make the world of form. Perception is always the answer to a wish used to seemingly assist functioning within the world. Every idea you think and experience follows the rules laid out by the mind attempting to understand itself.

Whoa. This just seems too heavy for my mind to grasp.

Wait. Do not try to place your thinking mind around this lesson. Do not settle into judgment and attempt to make sense of it. Instead, take a moment to breathe and find deeply within where you have sought to explain the world based solely upon what you think is going on. What feelings are surfacing now?

Well, first, I feel astonishment... then I feel fear. I think of every way that I have sought to understand the world or myself. What if all those thoughts are wrong? What if I really don't know anything at all? What if I'm making all of this up and making a hell that I'll be trapped in forever? What if....

Stop. Do not seek to dissect this with thinking. By the way, all of the thoughts and feelings you just mentioned are also based on your beliefs. You cannot feel fear unless you believed fear was possible. You cannot believe in a self-made hell, unless you believed in God's abandonment of His Holiness. Although there is not one person, perception, or power greater than your own, all that you experience; you realize as one mind who has innocently forgotten itself. That is all. Every meaning you see emerges from the library of the forgotten mind's mistaken identity. Call this the Library of All Possible Delusion. There is not as much a personalization of the world, as there is a personalized agreement with the mistaken identity.

How does my personal identity filter in here?

Perfectly stated. Your personal identity is the filter. It visits the library and checks out the books that make the most sense to its wishes. You see what you wish based on your willingness to agree or disagree with the forgotten mind's beliefs. For instance, if you think you can be rejected, you may judge a recent experience as one validating that belief. Although this judgment may not be the truth. Perhaps the person by whom you feel rejected had no personal investment or definition of the event in direct relation to you. However, you will see what you believe and thus often react based on this perception.

Okay. So if I believe that there is a reason to worry, if I believe that fears are valid and victimization is possible, then I will worry with or without evidence to support this judgment? In fact, sometimes I'll let my thinking go out of its way to perceive a reason to worry.

Correct. That is a perfect example. There are a multitude of beliefs used to script the stories you play out. You agree with every belief in guilt, vulnerability, abandonment and unworthiness. Next, a story within the world takes place that seems to mirror this possibility. However, this story is really only a story. It is merely dots on a page. It would be nothing without you making a picture out of the connected dots. Then, after viewing the finished picture, you reaffirm these

possibilities, now calling these beliefs "facts." Using these self-determined facts a new reality is conceived for the future to justify judgment and the continuance of the story. It is these perceived limits that call out your misery and the belief that you are powerless. This is merely because you deny the fact that you are the power of everything! This is why the only experience that must change is the experience of your Self. This alone inspires your need to perceive meaning from the dots on the page. However, the true connection is always within, and this connection will create a picture of brilliance or brutality. This is the true responsibility for sight… all else is merely spinning wheels without a single purpose.

Take a moment now to practice this. Look around the room you are sitting in and say aloud: *"I cannot have this _____ (pick any image in the room) apart from me."* This is not meant to be a mere exercise in thought or consideration. Honestly, far too many of the thoughts I share are left as mere surface considerations. I want you to take this teaching literally and completely within yourself and not leave it on the surface of your mind. Truly, the awakening you desire does not come from the practice of mere surface considerations. Awakening arises from the release of all you think you think and all you feel you feel. Therefore, I would like you to think now about the experiences you had this past week with your friend, take in the situation and feel as if you are still there hearing all you heard and feeling all you felt. Now, say clearly within: "*I cannot have this experience (nor these thoughts or feelings) apart from Me.*"

I can definitely see how this exercise can be easily overlooked as surface mind-banter. But once I look deeply within at every thought and every idea, gosh – things can so easily hit the fan (so to speak).

Yes, your beliefs can appear to be a plague upon your mind. They seem to keep you in the dream. Until every value you hold is questioned, you will not be free from the mirrors of your mind. Think about the moments when you have walked through a House of Mirrors. Was not confusion and frustration all around you?? Did you not hope to find only a simple way out? Did you not try and try again, seemingly without progress, to move closer to the door?

Sometimes you hoped just to huddle towards the floor, curl up in a ball, and wish someone else would find you and lead you out of your confusion. Yet, now I have found you and now do I lead you. Are you willing to take my hand or will you continue to insist that these mirrors do not exist, although they clearly appear to keep you entrapped?

Take my hand I will assist you in walking through the mirrors of your mind. Here we will walk as one, step by step, hand in hand; accepting that only our realizations beyond these mirrors show the way. Now, as you walk this path with Me, I will assist you in gaining the recognition needed to assist you on this path. Here we leave this House of Confusion together, for there is but One of us here.

In this acceptance our safety lies. In this strength to trust we accept that this confusion is nothing but temporary play and every image that you see holds nothing to the glory of your Truth all ways. Seek yourself not in distractions, Dear One. However, hold yourself steady beyond the mirrors of your mind. Observe them with a greater openness. Objectively notice each image for what it is and where it resides. Then, make peace with it and walk with Me to a safer serenity where no confusion can occupy Our Mind. Here we rest in stillness.

Okay, so if everything is a mirror of my mind, why does it seem so real?

You are that powerful! Moreover, never have I said that these mirrors cannot reflect Truth. The mirrors of your mind can likewise be flooded with the Light of Truth. Here we have a clear mirror, clean and without temporal distortions. God's Light shines through the Mirror of Truth and not the distorted Houses of Delusion that you seem to know.

What is the difference?

A Mirror of Truth reflects clearly and cleanly, without distortion or dependency. The Mirror of Truth only extends in great awareness for all. Look into the Mirror of Truth and see only your True Self. Here all images extend as one, not split among a myriad of sights, sounds and false perceptions. Never can you be lost within the Mirror of Truth. Here, surely only One Source is known and One Source is seen.

I'm feeling uncertain and nervous here.

Yes, because you are uncertain if the source you see is the Source you are. Truly, as long as you perceive yourself to be different or apart in any shape or form (again, this includes all thoughts as well as experiences) you do not know your Self and you do not see the clearest Light there is to see. However, truly, even in this, there is no true possibility for loss here. Even if you see mere images of distraction and division, the One Source always is eternal.

Take this moment now to review your thoughts within your

mind and see from where their images arise. Do you see ideas of "others" and powerlessness beyond your mind? If so, understand that you merely are seeing through the House of Mirrors and not the Mirror of Truth. Then, allow yourself to rest the thoughts and breathe. Finally, ask to see this thought clearly with Me. Offer Me your hand and ask that I guide you from the mere confusion into our One Truth. This journey is shorter than you think and does not encompass more than one single step.

And that is?

Trust. Trust allows you to see in full awareness. Simply put, it removes the resistance for prolonging every dream of separation that could ever be. Trust allows you to see first that all images you see are of your own making and that they have but one source and one conclusion. Trust guides you through your images and chooses Light beyond the darkened singular dimension of fear. Next Trust allows you to see yourself not in the image but in the Guide. Here we will see where we walk without boundary, obstacle, distortion or limitation. Here we walk in acceptance of the Pathway of Light that is.

So how do I apply this to my daily usual experiences?

Simply release yourself from what you see. Put another way; release the self from what you see. Look within and take the distorted or denied self back from the image, recognize the self within every image and split it no more. See where you have lost your self within every image or have given this self away to unawareness. Therefore, in seeing your self in this image, you are seeing not the distortion anymore, but you are seeing where you reside in all images. What of yourself do you see represented in every image you see? What purpose? What need? What desire is present in everything? Once you get down into the depth of connection, emerging from every experience, you will be surprised to see how powerful you are! This is because everything you see clearly ties to a need you have for separation, fear, or vulnerability. You have made this world as a witness to this and this alone. Again, this applies to all images, even ones that seem to bestow comfort or solace. You cannot have any image unless you perceived a need for it apart from Heaven's Oneness. Do not let this overwhelm you. It is only when you are overwhelmed that you are additionally lost within the House of Mirrors. Therefore, allow yourself to rest from the analysis and simply rest in the acceptance of ALL being an extension of your Self. This Self is Light. This Self is Truth. This Self is clarity. It cannot be misperceived except all within your own mind. Here, I direct you from the mirrors of your mind and ask you to rest in Trust. This is the key to the way out of the House of Mirrors. This is the key to knowing your Self.

I love you.

My light is Your Own...

Week Thirty-Seven: Practices:

1. Identify five thoughts or feelings you would like to release from the House of Mirrors. They can be completely random (since all is of the same mind – yours!) or specifically chosen from difficulties currently surfacing within your life experiences. Next, look within and notice:

what meanings these thoughts / feelings represent to you; and how these perceptions affect your own experiences and your experiences with others.

At completion, review each, and say "*I cannot have this experience (nor these thoughts or feelings) apart from Me.*" Then, take a deep breath and envision yourself taking Holy Spirit's hand. See this as symbolic of your renewed Trust in Him to lead the way. Show Him your list and write His guidance as He leads you from your images to His Knowing.

2. Set aside five minutes each day to observe the world. Do not let other distractions interfere with the practice of this exercise. Now, pause and observe the world in all its variation. As several of these images pass through your sight, say quietly aloud:

"*This sight is free, not as my mind made it to be.*"

Next, do the same with the people who pass by your sight. Look at each person without connection or being strictly noticed. Breathe and say:

"*This person is free, not as my mind made him or her to be.*"

Breathe again and process any residual thoughts with Holy Spirit.

3. Set aside five minutes each day to observe yourself in the mirror. Do not let other distractions interfere with the practice of this

exercise. Now, as you look directly at all the components of your body: face, eyes, nose, hair, ears, chest, legs, hands, fingers, etc. let yourself to be open to seeing another image. This is the image beyond the restrictions or judgments of our mind. Holy Spirit tells us that we never truly see. Take a moment now to open your eyes beyond all limitations of sight and perception. Once you feel your mind is settled, breathe deeply and say:

"I am free, not as my mind makes this image to be."

Affirmations:
I trust in Spirit to lead the way.
My safety thrives in the acceptance of Love.
All persons, perceptions, and power are One in Truth.
Trust allows me to see in full awareness.

Week Thirty-Eight: **Thought Forms**

Beloved Holy Spirit, I have been pondering my ponderings lately and felt prompted to go look up some words including the word "think." I was amazed when I found:

> Think: Old English: *pencan* "conceive in the mind, think, consider, intend" probably originally "cause to appear to oneself," "to seem or appear." Both are from *tong-* "to think, feel" which also is the root of *thought* and *thank*.

Wow! That says so much! Can you continue the teaching for me?

> Surely, Beloved, to think is literally to cause to appear to oneself. Remember we have spoken before of cause and effect. All of your thoughts support the meaning perceived from your experiences. Likewise, your thoughts are effects. They proliferate from the beliefs that the forgetting Holiness of God values. You are familiar, are you not, with Descartes' "I think, therefore I am" You may see this as a key to your comprehension of self. Essentially it means that your thinking makes the world in which you see.
>
> Mainly, the thinking mind uses all thoughts as a device for its own form of communication. It uses this tool to help itself figure out the forgotten self. The very nature of communication itself relies upon the use of symbols. These symbols are defined through pre-established values or beliefs and it is to this language that one must adhere if you seek understanding within your world of form. Therefore, your thoughts are rarely reflective of Truth, simply because they do not know. However, all devices of separation are open to the miracle. In this acceptance of the miracle, we can use your communication to welcome peace. Therefore, communication can be used not only to limit, but to liberate. Today, I shall teach you how to seemingly "make the best" out of the words and symbols to which you adhere, assisting in the re-establishment of peace of mind.
>
> All beliefs have a three-fold response. Let us take the example

of believing that you (body, life, experiences, etc.) are powerless. First, if you believe you are powerless, this belief will be transmitted accordingly as conscious thoughts of powerlessness (e.g. "I'm a victim..," "I never get what I want."). Next, a feeling of limitation arises, supporting these thoughts (e.g. fear, depression, hurt, anger). Finally, an experience is perceived proving the feeling and thought to be accurate (e.g. loss of job due to company downsizing; best friend disappoints you). Never does this process reverse itself, as it is always a symbolic representation of Your Nature, Holiness endlessly extending.

Extension is your natural way of interacting with the wholeness of Who You Are. I can see how your mind is pondering, "If I knew that this thought was not real or true, why choose to think it?" Remember, Dear One, there is no judgment in Heaven. All creation is equally accepted as being love. Extension is the natural way to share love, and so all that comes to love naturally extends. All the wishes of the Holiness of God are naturally extended simply because you are free. There is no doubt here, as there is no resistance within this flow of perfect acceptance of all. Surely, All You Are knows All You Are. Likewise, all wishes are extended, knowing that truth can never change. "Oh, you want to pretend?? Surely! And so it is." See this innocence in every thought and you can release yourself from obsessions with judgment.

When I have spoken of the flow of all being perfect, what I have referenced is your innocence. This flow is the full awareness of your freedom. Here, all is perfect in the extension of love. Therefore, even the forgetting Holiness of God has become a perfect component of the flow of extension and the beingness of love. Here then, within the flow, nothing can be awry. This flow sees nothing worthy of judgment, for nothing can be harmful. Likewise, truth sees nothing as an error beyond repair, or quite actually even in need of repair. This is simply because the flow of love trusts itself, knowing all it is all ways. If I could put it into sounds, the flow would never say "oops." Instead, it always extends an "ahhh."

Use this approach the next moment thoughts within you appear to bring discomfort. Attempt not to "oops" upon them (which would be resistance), but instead simply extend an "ahhh." "Ahhh, it appears that my mind sees with fear." Or "Ahhh, it appears I see myself as vulnerable here." Or "Ahhh, I can see how I desire to feel hurt, afraid or in need." In the "ahhh," you allow yourself to flow through the thought, rather than fight it. Here, you relax in the flow, trusting all you seem to desire yourself to be. Only in this relaxing can you reestablish the awareness to connect with this freedom. Do this to facilitate acceptance rather than judgment. Let Me emphasize, do not reframe or resist your wish out of fear. Do not extend or embattle an "oops," but rest your mind and allow all possibilities being communicated to pass simply through you like a transitory breeze. This is why I have emphasized the practice of breathing, releasing and resting. As you breathe, do you not "ahhh?" This exhalation is the simple act of acknowledgment for all you are in Truth. Here you relax within the loving acceptance of flow, rather than the resistive discomfort.

Look back upon the origin of the word "think," and see how the root of this word relates to the word "thank." In fact, they are extensions from the same word family. This is not true only in words, but this connection is symbolic of the truth of all. Gratitude flows completely within the light of Truth. In fact, gratitude is the light of Truth known. In gratitude, there is full acceptance for the extension of Pure Life you are. Therefore, hear Me well; gratitude is naturally extended to all you think. All you cause to appear to yourself contains gratitude. In fact, truly without gratitude, nothing could be.

Does this mean that if you are not thankful for what appears in your life, it will disappear? Surely not. I do not speak of a reactive (behavioral) appreciation here. Simply, this gratitude is the blessing of God for the freedom He extends in Holiness. It has no limits, cannot be withdrawn and is never dependent.

Gratitude is God's communication with His Holiness and Holiness's acceptance of awareness within Him. See this as it is and you can clearly see the whole mastery of your Self. Likewise, in recognizing your Self, all perceived obstacles to knowing simply fade away like mists before the sun. When you know your Self, it is impossible to see anything as being a true obstacle. Here, you accept that nothing can keep you from being as you desire. Here, all gratitude extends rather than attempts resistance. Here, you rest in God, trusting the flow of all as being simply perfect. Then, in this moment, your mind floods with the light of gratitude, and here no shadow of judgment can stand.

Does this mean that amidst suffering, I can be grateful?

This question is dependent upon the definition of suffering. It is further dependent upon how you define yourself, and if you believe that all happening to this forgetting Holiness is real beyond imaging.

I can recognize how the unlearning of your perceptions is difficult for you. I understand how all questions of the ego give rise to many arguments and justifications for judgment. Indeed these ideas are foreign to your thinking mind. Yes, I do understand how limitation has become your experience and that the body (as well as all that can appear to happen to it) has become your most intimate acquaintance. Don't worry, I don't ask you to fool or deny your thinking here. Nor will I ask you to memorize a variant of illogical concepts, challenging what you believe. That would be unkind and restrictive to your freedom. Therefore, I do not ask you to accept these ideas magically as if you were to wish the world you see away. However, I ask you to first rest your mind. Then, when ready, extend gratitude to every thought. Simply choose to align with the peace within rather than the hostile struggle around you. Truly, this is not as difficult as what you currently think.

Do the same with your thoughts. Do not deny your thoughts or expect that you can magically wish them away. This will never serve you well. Yet, as you notice the thoughts (similar to how you notice the events within the world) see how each is solely dependent upon your presumptions. I recognize your confusion, truly I do. "How can suffering not be presumed as harmful?" "How can I see these things within the world and not be abhorrently disturbed?" Truly, the Mind from which I see and know has a complete awareness of your Truth. Likewise, it knows how all is a wish for perfect experience rather than destruction. Consequently, nothing is deserving of judgment. Does that sound like an unkind pitiful excuse? Surely, it does to the ego and judgments of the body. This is simply because it does not know who it is nor all the grandeur that has given birth to its very self. Rest your mind here and simply breathe into the willingness to see peace instead. I cannot cease the justifications for judgment, but I can help you extend your Truth.

Beloved, peace is with you now. Moreover, as your thoughts spin, peace sits quietly, asking to be recognized. Peace is your own true witness for all you are in God. This is why I say you are to give yourself your freedom and gratitude for simply being. This is why, as all the thoughts within the thinking mind churn, you can simply step back and allow all that is pure awareness of joy to lead your way. Here, all peaceful delight and perfect awareness of Truth is "caused to appear to yourself." Here, your thoughts become completely aligned with the perfect flow that God extends all ways and always. Although your thoughts may not be aware of your blessed existence, surely your Holiness has not changed. Your own awareness steadily awaits your willing recognition. Here the mists of confusion fade away. Grasp my hand, breathe, release and rest, and I shall lead you through. I love you.

My Light Is Your Own.

Week Thirty-Eight: Practice:

On a separate piece of paper or in your journal, identify ten negative and ten positive thoughts. I have started by giving you some general prompts.

Across from the thought, write what problems or events could be experienced in the world because of this thought.

Reverse the process. Identify certain experiences that have recently occurred and consider what positive or negative thoughts may have contributed to your experience of them.

Afterwards, review each thought. Inhale deeply and exhale while saying "ahhh." This is the "ahhh" of thought acceptance. Here we accept all our thoughts and how they have expressed in our lives, as part of our choice.

Ask for Spirit's guidance on how to release each of these thoughts and their effects.

Example:

Positive thought and how this thought is experienced:

I am worthy. Because of this thought, I frequently see myself as satisfied. I am grateful for receiving as needed.

Negative thought and how this thought is experienced:

Nothing in life comes easily. Because of this thought, the majority of successes appeared to occur over a long period of struggle and self-determination. Each day appears to present a challenge. Sometimes I feel there is no rest.

Now complete the opposite:

Positive life experience and possible connecting thought:

My family is always strong and supportive. I may have this experience because I see all as the family of God and one with me.

New relationships are built with ease. I may have this experience because I have nothing to fear in new friendships.

Negative life experience and possible connecting thought:

My bills are often overdue; I just can't seem to get myself organized. I may have this experience because I believe that time is always one step ahead of me. I feel powerless over anything occurring in the outside world.

Affirmations:
   The Holiness of God offers only freedom.
   My thinking has a blessing within it.
   I give myself the freedom to know my Self.
   I am more than my limited beliefs.

Week Thirty-Nine:

The Experience of Spirit

The experience of Truth arises out of a remembrance of Your Source. In remembering your Self, you claim forth the oneness that is your own. Let us review the origin of the word *experience*:

Experience: circa.1377, from Old French: *experience,* from Latin: *experientia* "knowledge gained by repeated trials," "to try, test," from *ex-* "out of" + *peritus* "experienced, tested." The verb (1533) first meant "to test, try;" sense of "feel, undergo" was first recorded in 1588.

See in its origin how the word is described as "knowledge gained by repeated trials"? It is important to note that your True Self does not provide the trials. Truth never tests you. Truth simply is and knows of its completion. In Spirit, there is nothing to earn and nothing that can fail. All is complete. Spirit knows only completion. So, what then offers a trial? What then is uncertain? It is your own mind, for only the mistaken identity is confused and knows itself not. Therefore, here, we see the birthing of perception through projection. Here we see the beginning of consciousness that desires to be measured through experience. ALL EXPERIENCE is an extension of the self who does not know. It is only your playful innocence that desires to "try out" anything. In this wish for experience, the world of perception was born. This is the tiny mad idea agreeing to undergo illusion through dreams.

Okay, so are you saying that if I choose to experience myself as Spirit, this differs from genuinely being Spirit?

Yes, because only the conflicted mind believes that it can choose. True perception can be considered to be the most profound experience of the self who has forgotten. This is because in true perception, your thinking mind finally can lay its conflicts aside. In this moment it truly remembers and accepts its Self beyond all conflicts. This true perception would be the experience of Spirit, but not the beingness of it. Surely this is quite an accomplishment for a mind that once perceived itself ruled by a body, identified through a conflicted consciousness, alone and left to suffer. True perception is the choice made for Your Holiness to be experienced within a perceptual realm. In this choice you begin to reveal your Self. Through True perception, you welcome Truth's Being as existing and desirable. It is impossible to have true perception if you do not at the very least recognize your own unlimited potential. Yet, true perception (a celebrated accomplishment in comparison to the mistaken identity) is not your completeness and not awakening. Again, if this dream were the place where you fully wished to be, surely I would celebrate with you. Yes, you are that free. However, it does not seem that you celebrate. And so, I am here to guide you back to your true desire.

Overall, it is important to realize, that a happier dream is not your final goal. This is because you remember that even though the acceptance of true perception is pleasing, it is not Who You Are. The calling of God still lingers in your memory. This is Who I am. Therefore, if you believe that it is preferable to settle permanently within an intricately balanced compromise, I would ask you to quiet your mind and seek deeper for your true desire.

Am I saying that God forbids His Holiness to cling to dreams? No. You do seem to be here, correct? Surely as the Holiness of God you remain free. However, dreams are not reality and deep within you, this is remembered. Ask yourself honestly what would a perpetual game of hide n' seek make known? How could you know your Self as God Created through simulation? Is it really that enjoyable to sit within time, wearing a blindfold, and call out to an artificial world for lasting definition? If only you knew how preposterous this wish is! Truly, only the limited mind, seeing itself through its dreams, could perceive this as a valuable alternative to the Self I know you to be eternally.

I do not judge your wishes, but do only request for you to notice your true desire beyond temporal distractions. You remain as innocent and loved as ever, even though a wish for illusion to be your master is sure foolishness from where I stand. You are as aware of this paradox as a parent is aware of the decisions his child makes from their own unknowing. Yet, I do offer you complete freedom as Our Father has extended. Therefore as long as you wish to dream, dreams are. Remember it is only your own mind that sees this as a poor choice, or one to be judged. Again, I emphasize you are never judged. You are free. Hear Me now, I desire for you to love your freedom and reveal your Self. Seek to extend love to all, even your dreams. Seek to remember peace beyond every image. This is how you awaken, and truly I say, no judgment can bring you there.

The following descriptors exemplify how the conflicted mind can realize and practice True Perception. As I teach them, take note within of how they surface through your life experience. Although these descriptors are mere words (and words are symbols of symbols), each has a particular energy that can represent freedom and peace or conflict and struggle. Observe now which symbols you accept on your journey towards the remembrance of Truth. See now, through your practice, which wish is more valued. Remember, above all, you are always loved no matter what you choose or enact within the world. It is impossible to sleep in reality.

A Conflicted Mind Experiences:

Reaction: To react is to act back. It is to return in the same vibration as the origin. Reaction within the world is always projection, for it only responds to like wishes. Therefore, in reaction, illusion is met with illusion, attack is met with attack and need is met with need. Only the conflicted mind feels the need to react. It alone sees purpose in immediate action, attack or defense. Indeed it alone will pounce to protect due to its sole engagement with fear. Desperate and impulsive, it clings to mimicry for its own safety.

Need: Need extends the belief in vacancy. Truly you cannot believe in need if you knew your completion. In saying that you need, you say you are incomplete and seek forth for completion within the world. Recall now an experience where you felt in need. While within it, did you consider yourself to be the Holiness of God? Need is rooted in a mistaken identity for limitation of body, mind, or living necessity. Surely would the God of Truth leave His Son dependent upon wanting to thrive? Truly, only the forgetting mind aligns with need, for it alone believes in vacancy.

Presumption: The origin of the word presume is "to take upon oneself." When you presume you take it upon yourself to be your own master and maker. This is the substitution for God's Will with your own mistaken identity. Notice in the situations of uncertainty you find yourself, do you not presume to know why and how these situations happen? Do you not think, "I know why they do this!" As you presume, you perceive yourself to be master over all your brothers. You believe you are aware of all their devious intentions. Presumptions are suspiciousness at best and viciousness at worst. Here, where you are not projecting guilt, you are projecting fear. Never in your presumptions do you see perfect completion within your brother. Presumption judges all of God's Holiness to be limited.

Talks: The ego mind talks because it always has a story to tell. That literally is what "to talk" means, "to tell a story." Consider this the next time you feel a prompting for discourse between thinking minds. Often, as you talk, you share a story so that all your limiting beliefs can be played out. If you were to simply notice every moment the thinking mind felt the need to dialogue, you would begin to see how the stories told guide the experience you have. This is belief made into being; thus projection makes perception. It may be a purposeful experience to ask yourself in these times of story-telling, why do I have to speak or what story are my thoughts telling now? Consider, through your words and thoughts, what witness you are offering forth. What story about yourself are you affirming? In this practice, you may begin to rest beyond the talk. A choice to rest beyond the chatter of a conflicted mind bestows peace beyond all experience.

Struggle: The etymology of this word literally means: "ill will"; other origins suggest a connection to verbs meaning "to stumble." It is only the mistaken identity that invites struggle. Notice its simple origin "ill will." As you struggle, it is the ill will and not the Will of God you accept. Here, you innocently stumble in your forgetting and attempt to replace the amnesia with erroneous belief. Only the conflicted mind struggles because it only justifies battles. It alone fights for a confused and defeated will.

Separation: Separation believes it can be equal to God apart from His Holiness. This lie it will always offer you. Its witnesses will rely only upon a separate self-identity and limited nature. In its amnesia, it believes it must re-validate itself with any and every thing just to keep living. Therefore, separation isolates for its own protection and proliferation. The experience of the conflicted mind thrives in separation because, as I have mentioned, experience dependently identifies with division. In Truth there is no separation or need for comparison with or apart from God. In Truth, Holiness simply is without anything else. You always must have duality in order to have comparison or self-validation, and thus a belief in separation must exist.

Judgment: Judgment offers only separation. Who can place judgment upon a self that has no alternative or potential for guilt? Judgment depends upon there always being another option or expectation apart from reality. Usually these options are defined as "right" and "wrong." To have an option is to have an alternative; thus, to have an alternative requires duality. As you choose to judge, you choose to limit. It essentially is that simple. Notice any judgment within the mind and you will see the beliefs of limitation it needs to uphold. Only the conflicted mind can judge because it alone invests in alternatives outside of the One Self.

Restricts: Restriction emerges from the conflicted mind because it first aligns with beliefs in limitation. The conflicted mind lives in boundaries and needs them to define itself. Every boundary seen and fortified is one that initiates from the mistaken identity. Remember, the mistaken identity alone thrives through limitation. Essentially there can be no conflict unless there is an idea of limitation, for without limitation, you would only be free.

Defines in Time: Time itself is your greatest illusion for only within time can there be a beginning or an end. In fact, time would be required if you were to experience limitation through illusion at all. Experience wishes for you to try out another way. This other way must be defined by something if it were to be plausible, therefore, time was made to measure the dream and support its simulation.

True Perception Realizes:

Waits and Releases: Spirit waits because it knows its Self not through illusions. Spirit has no need for fear or impulsivity, for there is nothing to protect and nothing to defend. Spirit does not waiver in its certainty and therefore only offers Truth for all circumstances. Spirit cannot temporarily agree with illusion, for then the Truth would not be True. If you were to wait and release to Spirit, before acting, you would realize the role to play is one of forgiveness. Here you would not pander to insanity, but choose to respond through a loving strength rather than fearful reaction. See here how forgiveness looks, waits and judges not. Forgiveness is certain and offers only this awareness to all. This releasing is the witnessing of Truth beyond illusion.

Certainty: In certainty you recognize that you are and have everything in perfect beingness. You are complete all ways. Certainty has no alternative and is not temperamental. It cannot waiver because it is not dependent. Certainty surely knows its Self. To express Spirit's certainty within the world requires one thing: TRUST. In trust, the conflicted mind recognizes that it does not know in and of its current condition. Therefore, through true perception and the awareness of Spirit, the choice is made not to rely upon its limited self for awareness but turn instead to a deeper knowing. This choice is often referred to as faith.

Knowledge: Knowledge exists because it is certain. In its certainty it stands strong, having complete trust and faith for the Truth beyond any image. Knowledge itself has no definition. To know simply is to know, and cannot be limited by symbols of any sort. As you experience life within this world, if you yearn to know your Self you desire for *complete sight*. It was only later in your civilization that "knowing" was seen as a task which could be done or accomplished. In fact it had no clear worded definition before the year 1553. "To know" simply spoke for itself. When you knew, you knew. That is all. Indeed if you are to know your True Self, surely no limits could possibly be placed forth in this fullness of Holy Being. Here you simply are complete. Here, all is revealed.

Listens: Spirit has no story. It has no need to extend anything other than the Truth. Spirit is often silent where the conflicted mind chatters. The conflicted mind talks because it chooses to flood the moment with every idea of distraction. Here it attempts to avoid a remembrance so true, that nothing can compete or compare with it. Yet, Spirit remembers and therefore has no immediate need to speak. In awareness of Truth, Spirit has no needs at all. Therefore, Spirit simply allows the joy it knows in certainty.

As you listen, you quiet the mind. Here you step away from the need to busy yourself with spinning tales of separated purpose and alternative beingness. This is why I often ask for you to rest your mind and listen. The mind that listens does not value another way. It seeks not to temporarily replace the Holiness of God. True perception accepts the Truth You Are. As you truly perceive you allow this Truth to speak beyond mere words or symbols alone. In listening, the conflicted self chooses humility in honor of that which has genuine authority. This authority speaks only for your Holiness and realizes that this awareness is far beyond words.

Acceptance: The origin of this word means, "to take what is offered" or "receive willingly," from *ad-* "to" + *capere* "to take." As you accept you receive willingly. Notice the direct comparative nature of struggle versus acceptance. Struggle seeks through an ill will while acceptance willingly desires for True Being. Acceptance takes what is offered and does not attempt to reform God's Holiness. Acceptance is open to the desire of knowing its Self without resistance or argument. Truly, you cannot receive if you are not open. Openness is essential for a reception of the way, the truth and the light.

Oneness or Unity: Oneness speaks for wholeness; it only knows completion. As you choose an awareness of unity within the perceptual realm (akin to my awareness) you seek to witness to the completion which thrives beyond all images. Unity does not attempt to understand alone. It allows only Truth to be its one guide and therefore does not separate by form, fear, or perception.

Unity knows all that is. Therefore, it has no valued identification outside of God's Holiness. Oneness honors freedom and thus allows the forgetting mind to play as it wishes (as you have seemed to accomplish). However, never (even in play) can True Oneness fully forget. This inability to forget led to my creation. It is in Me that your Truth remains. It is in our oneness that you are changeless.

Forgiveness: Forgiveness offers only wholeness, for this is its essential desire. Forgiveness is not required in Heaven, for Heaven only recognizes the One Self and knows no alternative. Therefore, for complete beingness of Spirit, forgiveness is essentially impossible. Since we already speak in examples of alternatives, I offer you the experience of forgiveness as the alternative to judgment. As you choose to forgive, you are willing to see the Truth beyond all illusion. Forgiveness offers to release you from your conflicted self. It is here that you see a deeper peace beyond the restricted value of judgment.

Extends Freedom: Freedom is certain. If your Self were uncertain of its eternal nature, it would fear freedom. This is because it would be fearful of all the choices possible, thinking that it could make or destroy itself. Uncertain or fearful freedom is then an idea of the forgetting mind. True freedom willingly knows God's Will and honors it with joy. In this certainty it overwhelmingly extends all to all without limit. Freedom always knows it is safe no matter what occurs. Since your True Self cannot be destroyed, you can welcome a rest in this knowing.

Timeless: Heaven restricts nothing, has no need to measure and perfectly flows in extension all ways. Heaven only expresses its completion as God Created. This cannot be measured for there is nothing to compare Truth to. This is so true that words themselves fall away in every attempt to describe the ineffable. Your True Self is timeless. It is never restricted. Never could you be born or doomed to die. Never could you be anything but the infinite Holiness of God.

All that is Truth is beyond limitation. This is the key to recognizing any experience as either one of the ego mind or one of true beingness. Surely, true perception will be the most radiant expression of you within this frame of time that you made. Yet, in recognizing the ways available to choose an experience of yourself, you recognize from wherever your desire emanates. In embracing your desire, you always see with the most clarity available.

As you choose to breathe, release and rest, you ask for my guidance beyond any limitation. Here, you honor the Self that knows, and in this, all that is Truth cannot but be revealed. Your light is my own. I love you.

Week Thirty-Nine: Prompts for Insight:

Which qualities of the conflicted mind do you most relate to or experience?

How have the qualities of true perception been expressed in your life experience? How would you like them to be?

Think of one stressful or frustrating experience you have in your life. Next, identify which qualities of the conflicted mind are present in this experience. Finally, identify at least one key aspect of true perception that can replace the conflict. Continue to practice this exercise for as many stressors you would like to transform. Focus your desire to see each situation differently. How can you see peace instead?

On a scale of 1 to 10, lowest to highest, identify how often you tend to express the qualities of the conflicted mind. Do the same for the qualities of true perception. Be honest and take insightful note of which qualities you experience the most. Process what you learn in your journal.

Practice:
Are you currently using the qualities of the conflicted mind or true perception? Keep a log this week of general experiences that occur in your day-to-day activities and/or interactions with others. For each experience you choose, identify what quality is most prevalent in that incident. Is there more than one? If so, how many and which ones? Finally, write examples and/or ways you can remind yourself to shift from a conflicted mind to True Perception.

Affirmations:

In True Perception I see myself and all with Vision.

I choose to wait in peace rather than react in foolishness.

Judgment is impossible in Spirit.

In the Truth of Who I Am, I extend Freedom to all.

I do not choose to struggle but rest in love.

Week Forty: **Releasing Stress**

What is stress and why does it appear to be an increasing problem?

Stress is your battle against yourself. It is a fearful and resistant reaction to every image you have made. Stress is completely dependent upon your thoughts in order to be effective. It cannot perpetuate without your continued agreement.

I have spoken many times about values and how they reflect your wishes within the world. Freedom, for instance, is a value that you hold in high accord. Though, who among you will admit that you are perfectly free? Yet, you *are* perfectly free as God Created. This freedom extends forever and is not limited by time or circumstance. Does this mean that you can do whatever you want in bodily form? No. But you have played out a restricted bodily form to portray every role of limitation believed possible within your forgetting mind. The acceptance of perfect freedom as God Created relies upon your willingness to accept yourself as God Created. Likewise, it is imperative to truthfully recognize how you often set yourself up for self-destruction. Where are you your own worst enemy? Where do you judge, offend or entrap yourself within limiting thoughts and experiences? Do this and soon it will be obvious that the images you perceive arise from your view extended from within.

Where your mind invests, surely your body will follow. Here, every witness within the world will appear to support all accepted judgments upon yourself and others. Surely, you can change your mind. Is this not perfect freedom? Does this mean that the traffic will suddenly and magically clear or that the children will immediately listen and behave? No. But surely, when you release yourself of your expectations, predications, and attachments, no longer will you be judging by outward appearances. In releasing your judgments of the outer, all will surely change. Here, surface is exchanged for substance and you see the content beyond the form. For through the release of judgment, you offer a new acceptance. Here you choose to listen, rather than react. Here you live in the moment of opportunity, rather than restriction. Here you are willing to see things differently, without pre-determination upon all that can never be. Here you rest in the moment and simply be.

You judge your current conditions by those of the past and those of the predicted future. Not once, when you are stressed, are you living completely in the current moment. Delusion is the acceptance of an imagined alternative in the place of now. It is the acceptance of a replacement for God. Each perceived alternative is ruled by fear, and fear denies Truth. In fear your perceptions are ruled by prediction, expectation, and attachment. You seek your treasure within the world and claim the world to be your master. And truly, not one of these ideas will bring you peace.

Stress becomes an increasing problem through time. Time functions by way of intensification and distortion. It quite literally builds upon itself. Although time itself does not exist outside of the illusion, you have chosen to accept it as ruler of your perception. Truly, you can still use it as merely a guide for your awareness, nothing more or less than now.

If the modern era was meant to provide the means for ease and comfort, why then has it not resulted in complete happiness? It is simply because you have continued to invest in the same distortions through time. Therefore, as time progresses, so too do your beliefs in limitation, powerlessness, fear, and attachment. Although they do present in different forms, each is merely a current expression of a repetitive error in your thinking. Yet, this need not be.

The cure to all stress is truly a simple one: release. Release for peace, and peace is found all around. You begin to release by noticing when you do not feel at peace. For the most part, your lack of peace will emanate from a belief that you are either threatened or powerless. In each of these situations, it is you who have agreed to see yourself as vulnerable and at the mercy of the world. In this belief in need, you willingly give your serenity over to the world. You hope that if you give the world enough power, finally it will complete you. However, instead of feeling complete, you end up feeling threatened or powerless. Now, the world that you once thought was friend has become enemy.

Notice when you feel unsettled. Ask yourself within what is the source of this unsettling. Truly, does it emanate from the situation at large, or is it your interpretation of the situation? Keep mindful. Watch the messages your mind and body are sending you. Permit yourself to look within at the accepted messages of your thinking. Seek out the words that choose to judge, predict, isolate, separate, attach or limit. Seek out where you desire to believe these thoughts as purposeful to your journey. What proof has the mind made for these thoughts of restriction? What is the desired result from this thinking? Will this thinking make you feel most peaceful? Surely in asking, insights will arise from within.

Then, while you notice, ask your mind if it desires to simply choose again. If you cannot find a single notion of genuine peace within your mind, then these thoughts call for release. All thoughts that do not represent peace must signify delusion. Do you desire to be entrapped by delusion and allow this to rule you, or do you prefer to release for peace? Surely, this appears to be a simple question; yet, soon you will become more aware of how much you dearly and desperately wish to cling to each distortion that justifies stress and anger. In fact, if you are able to justify a single stressful thought and applied judgment, then you believe release is the more insane choice. Therefore, each moment that you justify your anger, threat, judgment or powerlessness, you willingly invite it again to your doorstep.

Truly, how does focusing on an outside cause of stress or anger bestow peace or happiness upon you now? Let us always practice practical problem-solving. Therefore, seek not your solutions in changing an unalterable past, but allow yourself to bask in the light of now. Complete peace and happiness are your natural inheritance from God Himself. Why deny these gifts by focusing on blame, guilt, and unworthiness? These judgments can never protect you from yourself, nor can they make the world more understandable. As long as there is someone responsible for your discomfort, you believe, the less you will have to do something about it! However, the most essential realization will be one of self responsibility. Notice clearly how these judgments and beliefs do not influence peace of mind - do they? Notice how clearly they continue to permit you to feel lost, confused, and fearful. Notice how clearly they fuel attack and defense, rather than allow for acceptance and love. How then can these negative judgments (if they were true) be your inheritance? Would that not be the inheritance of an insane God bestowing only further insanity upon His Creations?

Stress is most successfully released when it is noticed for being exactly what it is, simply a distraction from the Truth of Who You Are. Stress is merely the battle cry of a self confused by the images it has made. In your denial of reality and responsibility you deny your Self. As long as you choose not to see the mental connection you have to your perceptions, stress will continue to thrive.

Likewise, as long as you continue to further the belief that you are worthless, powerless, and vulnerable in relation to the entire world, surely a lack of peace will result. God desires only your complete and perfect happiness, and this He has already bestowed within you. He has not asked His Holiness to be ruled by money, power or sit in a traffic jam cursing his existence! See your way out of this maze by seeing your way out of your limited perceptions. Recognize the keys to the Kingdom within, and permit yourself to open every door.

Each key to the Kingdom relies upon the recognition of your wishes. Indeed, whom do you want to see? Through this recognition you realize the beliefs that support every awry perception. Begin by seeking to detect where your expectations, attachments, and assumptions have desired to lead the way. Notice what witness these decisions rest upon and what proof they present. Do they witness to your belief in powerlessness or threat? Do they tell you that you have no choice but to remain a passive victim within a world testifying to God's madness? Surely, if this is the degree of clarity presented, the glass is darkened. See, then, where your perceptions are being determined and what choices have been placed into your awareness through them. Like one block built upon another, soon you will see how stress itself is fully determined by your choices, perceptions, expectations and attachments. Surely you will soon come to see that each of these blocks to peace is wholly changeable by your own willingness to choose again, release, and rest in love's guidance.

As your willingness for peace increases, the entire world will respond in tune with this desire. You will begin to ask, "Has the world changed or has my desire to see offered me another way?" The answer is as clear as your desire. Therefore, I say, rest, Dear One. Allow yourself to simply be. Rest within your own thoughts and choose to let them drift in complete peace as a leaf upon the river. Accept that peace, instead of stress, is your inheritance. Accept that the power to see clearly has always been within you. Release yourself from every bind of distraction, attachment or predetermination. Surely, all that is true is realized once again. You are free. Accept the world as your witness to all that is love within, and it will show you all joys waiting to be seen. And here you know peace. I am with you. I love you.

Week Forty: Prompts for Insight and Practice:

On a separate piece of paper or in your journal, list ten situations that are stressors for you. These stressors can include other people's behaviors (e.g., my best friend complains all the time) or daily life experiences (e.g., getting stuck in traffic). Now, with these experiences listed, complete the following:

1. Before this experience occurred, what did you expect? Did you show up on the scene with a particular judgment? For example, if traffic is the stressor, did you not expect to have any other traffic on the road while you drove? Or in the example with the best friend, do you feel that your best friend shouldn't have any complaints? Notice what your thoughts are saying "should" or "should not have happened".

2. During this experience, what did you perceive? What did you see both within your own thoughts or interpretations? What did your body feel like? Was there tension or fatigue? Did you have any judgments or negative thoughts?

3. Because of this experience, what did you choose to do? How did you react? What did you choose to do next? In what ways did you express your emotions or thoughts? Did you add to the problem by reacting in a way that heightened the tension? Be honest.

4. Lastly, identify a minimum of one way these expectations, perceptions or choices could be changed.

C.H.O.O.S.E. Again!

C = Control: Ask yourself in every stressful moment: "Can I control this?" Remember you cannot change the past or other people. The best you can do is look at where you can control your judgments, feelings and behaviors now. How can you release unrealistic expectations and attachments? Although it may take abundant willingness, the Holiness You Are is abundant beyond measure. Take a moment now to see peace instead!

H = Hidden Beliefs: What beliefs support your judgments? These expectations veil all experiences and keep you trapped with the prison of self-defeating images. To believe that circumstances should have been different is only to live in resistance now. With these beliefs you only see yourself and others through a darkened glass. Justified anger is merely justified suffering! Why suffer? Is it peaceful to suffer? Surely not. Then, if you choose, take a moment now to look at your beliefs and see where you can free yourself from the prison of your mind. What do you, Holiness of God, believe about your Self? How is this belief serving you? What keeps you from offering love or acceptance?

O = Obstacles: What obstacles of fear and limitation do you use to define you? Where are you testifying to limitation instead of your limitlessness? Identify these obstacles to peace and ask for Spirit's Guidance in the healing of them. Release for peace. Prison bars may appear to be up front, but freedom is within and all around you. Shadows of the mind can fade into Light from within.

O = Opportunities: What opportunities do you have to change your perceptions, emotions or behavior right now? God's desire for you is perfect happiness. In fact, that is all He knows of You. Deny your Self no longer!

S = Support: Don't think that you have to go this healing road alone! You are never alone! God's Loving Guide is within and all around you. You are always cared for. Seek to hear God's Loving Voice in all circumstances. See the affirmations of support emerge all around you. Don't limit yourself to only one way of hearing or feeling Holy Spirit's presence. He knows you are as unlimited as He.

E = Environment: Where do you find yourself? What people, places and things help you thrive or suffer? Are you renting a room in a condemned home? Are you feeding the rats? Notice what situations you may be inviting into your life. Where do you reside in thought and emotion? What do you tell yourself after a negative thought appears? When do you decide to finally change residences? Remember, there are many mansions in Our Father's Home. You are never completely powerless! Seek to see where you can surround yourself with positive people and peace-filled thoughts. Let this action only affirm all the blessings you are worth within. See your Self as God Created and nothing else! The Kingdom of God lives within you right now.

Affirmations:

I choose again for peace.
I am as God Created me.
Love knows better than conflict.
There is no need for stress.
My peace extends to all I see.

The Pyramid of Stress:

The Stress Response you physically and psychologically experience is the tip of the iceberg. Beneath every consciously felt stress response are the contributing factors. These factors are not only completely controlled by us, but completely reversible! Below I have outlined the choices, perceptions, and expectations used to support every perceived need for defense. It is only these defenses which lead to the stress response, and in this recognition you are set free.

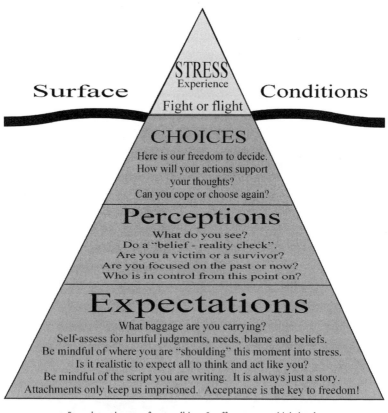

Surface   **STRESS** Experience   Conditions
Fight or flight

CHOICES
Here is our freedom to decide.
How will your actions support
your thoughts?
Can you cope or choose again?

Perceptions
What do you see?
Do a "belief - reality check".
Are you a victim or a survivor?
Are you focused on the past or now?
Who is in control from this point on?

Expectations
What baggage are you carrying?
Self-assess for hurtful judgments, needs, blame and beliefs.
Be mindful of where you are "shoulding" this moment into stress.
Is it realistic to expect all to think and act like you?
Be mindful of the script you are writing. It is always just a story.
Attachments only keep us imprisoned. Acceptance is the key to freedom!

Stress is **not** just a surface condition. It affects us on multiple levels.
As you seek to find peace of mind, it is most important to delve below the depths of the outer image.
See what is lingering below. You may be surprised to see how you have tied yourself to a sinking ship.

Week Forty-One: **Tired and Whiney**

Holy Spirit, I'm feeling whiney and tired tonight...

> Are you going to ask Me if this means that you are not seeing yourself as whole?

Uh... I guess so. Is every time that I feel whiney, tired, fat, blah, and ugly a sign that healing is necessary?

> Now, those traits you wrote, would you consider them to be traits of the Holiness of God?

Probably not.

> Well then, healing is necessary. Truly, healing is necessary whenever you do not see yourself as the Holiness of God.

Then that would cover just about now... and probably more than a few other times.

> Only now exists. As long as this moment feels limiting it is then of your forgetting mind. Let's allow healing to commence by simply looking at the feelings you believe you are experiencing. Let's begin with how you allow your body to portray your thoughts. Do you require a body to feel tired? Is this tired body limited by time? Is it then a complete victim of the outside world? Can it be made vulnerable by time and circumstance?

Yes... yes... yes ... and yes.

> Actually, no... no ... no ... and no. The idea of tired is what causes the experience of tired. Tired is then expressed through the body to confirm the thought, and thus confirm the idea of vulnerability and furthermore feel limited by time. Haven't you ever decided not to be tired? Did you not then have an experience to support this

belief? I have mentioned a few times that all ideas emerge from your own mind, especially all ideas that command limitation of yourself within your experience. If you feel tired, it is only because you already see yourself as limited by time, circumstance, energy and ability. Seeing yourself this way means that a choice has been extended to align with the temporal nature of your struggling-self rather than the eternal nature of your God-Created Self.

Quite honestly, it is the same with all of the body traits you experience throughout the personalized self. This includes pained, handicapped, hungry, diseased, injured and all the like. In fact, every one of these traits communicates and represents a specific idea within the conscious or subconsciously perceiving mind. This alone is why I have said that all disease is mental disease.

Okay, I have to admit, I have a hard time with that idea. I can't completely accept that all experiences of diseases can be reduced down to a thought within the mind. I don't see how that can be, especially for some of the more difficult diseases like children's diseases or birth defects. How can you expect me to see fault in the innocent? I don't see how they could have consciously chosen to be in those situations.

First of all, I would never ask you to see fault in the innocent. The innocent are innocent all ways. Who are the innocent?? ALL! Despite this fact, the struggling-self mind is not the maker of the disease, but it is always the one that accepts the disease. Innocence is Truth, disease is not. To know yourself as diseased is not to know your True Self at all. It is impossible to accept yourself as an innocent and whole Creation in God while simultaneously seeing yourself as ruled by a body or disease. This is true no matter what your physical age appears to be. Truly, only the mistaken identity plays games of "innocent victim." Only it sees this as possible, playing hide and seek with itself. This mistaken identity alone aligns with vulnerability, separation, and fear. I can understand how this concept may appear to be difficult to accept, but that is only because you choose to see through the eyes of the body and not the eye of True Vision. Trust Me, Beloved; in my Vision there are no "innocent victims." This is simply because there are no victims at all.

In other words, the body cannot choose to express in limitation without the forgetting mind's own agreement. For many, this agreement is not a conscious or personalized one, yet the awareness of this choice does lie deep within the dream-driven mind which supports the struggling-self.

A miracle healing is when a person decides to see his or her self beyond the disease. Here the struggling-self is able to see beyond the forgetfulness into the awareness of wholeness. Here a whole awareness is accepted as truth. In these physically expressed miracles, all ideas of limitation (subconscious and conscious) are abandoned. As individuals, persons may be aware of this choice, but rarely are they. Instead, they call this healing one of "faith" rather than remembrance. They often give accolades to God for this healing, rather than to the Spirit's Awareness of God within his or her Self. Consequently, the person may see his or her self beyond the body's presented limitations. However, this is only a remnant of remembrance. If you recall, it is always content before form.

Healing, like disease, is always first of content and then of form. Likewise, it is possible to be healed in content and not in form. There are a few role-models (individuals appearing to be in form) who have chosen through their own purpose for healing (on a level of supra-consciousness) to use the experience of disease for not only their own awakening, but for the awakening of the one Holiness of God. Don't get Me wrong, this does not mean that God requires His Holiness to be diseased in order for him to be healed. This sacrifice is impossible. However, all wishes are honored, and if a wish for remembering love through expressing limitation is desired, surely this will not be denied. Yes, you are that free! Therefore, in this choice, they use the experience of disease to not only release their own obstacles to Love's awareness, but they share this opportunity through being a catalyst for healing in the seemingly separate lives of many recognized brothers.

Essentially, this is the purpose of all miracles, for sharing is your natural way. In situations such as these you may hear how one ill individual has touched or inspired the lives of many. In form they may not even appear to be communicative, but through an inner awareness, a call for healing, sharing and miracles is a beacon to all who interact with this one life. Healed perception need not ever be limited to one person, place, or time.

Jeshua's recorded healings were not centered on healing the body. Nor were they centered on healing only ONE body. Jeshua always directed his healings to be for the entire mistakenly identified mind. He wholly recognized how the healing for one, in truth, was the healing for all.

In fact, when all recognized Spiritual Masters carry out healings, they heal through helping all draw on the One Mind. In this awareness, those who healed became more aware of their mistaken identity, how it was being expressed in form, and how it could be released. When a seeming individual agrees to represent the role of an enlightened one in form, they agree to represent awakening in form. This is so they can be a conduit for Spirit's Remembrance of its Self. Essentially, all healing is from your Holiness Remembered, and this is of God. Only God knows and shares the Truth wholly with His Holiness. Therefore, though many a Spiritual Master has chosen to remember the Truth, he or she willingly shares this remembrance with all. This sharing can inspire a multitude to remember and release all else in acceptance of the One mind. Likewise, healing may have appeared to play out in form (with an appearance of people physically healing), but always it was the release from the diseased mind first and foremost.

In this recognition of the light of Truth in all, Jeshua guided all to carry this new Sight into the world. This is simply what the miracle of sight was for the blind man. It was the gift of spiritual True Sight, expressed through the perceptual sight. Seeing through the body was never the point. That is why Jeshua said, "Go forth and sin no more."

I have taught before how there is no reality to sin. A sin is simply an error within the mind. You cannot rule your body except through your mind. Therefore, to heal (both physically and mentally) one must release all errors within the mind. Even as I can guide you to heal, you are the one who must choose to "Go forth and sin no more." Release yourself from continuing erroneous thinking. Release yourself from all investment in illusion. Release yourself from the identification with error.

Wow, that surely sounds powerful. Yet, a little thought within me speaks of its difficulty.

And so it is with that little thought within you choose to see. Hear Me well; you cannot have a thought of God compromise with a thought of illusion. There is not a middle ground. Either you see with Truth or choose to be ruled by illusion. The Holiness of God knows not of limitation and does not pander to its possibilities. Not even a little.

Sigh.... Therefore, it is an all-or-nothing decision.

Indeed. Either you see yourself as all or you see yourself as nothing. Neither of these thoughts changes the changeless You, yet surely they will direct the mind you believe you think with to either the complete recognition of your magnificence and Truth, OR you will continue to feel surrounded by an endless stream of mistaken identities. These thoughts are your own, chosen and accepted by the forgetting mind who desires to see a purpose within them.

This, too, is why I have said on occasion that you do not even know your own thoughts. This is why I have worked with you to accept your thoughts through God. God's thoughts are True knowledge. They are true beingness. And within these thoughts there is no disease.

The healing process is to help you bring the subconscious to the conscious so that eventually all can be released for peace. The mind seeing through limitation will choose to continue to enact personas of limitation all throughout time. This will continue until time is decided to no longer be necessary and healing is chosen to be its desire instead. Here, time will stop along with every idea of disease. Yet, as long as you see the awareness of Truth occurring in time, at some far-off place when you will finally be as God Created... but later... you will continue to choose to express within a limited form. You can do this through all time... and will, birth after birth, experience after experience. Truly it is only now... and now is simply an expression of the belief you agree to be most valuable. This is why it appears that babies are born in disease. This is why it appears the innocent can be lost or hurt. This is why there are many who appear to be the victim of disease rather than the maker of it within their mind. They know not what they do, but do it time after time.

Listen well, ALL ideas of limitation are ruled by a forgetting mind that sees itself as limited. This means that God does not make disease. God would never be at peace if He recognized His Creations to be dis-eased, or not at peace. God has bestowed His very Self upon all. He has given you the entirety of Godliness to simply BE in perfect happiness. Is it possible to be perfectly happy and accept an idea of disease? Never. Neither is it possible to be wholly aligned with the Truth of You and perceive yourself to be ruled by tiredness and whininess, or any other limitation for that matter. Tell Me, what would the Holiness of God have to whine about? What within the wholeness of eternity could tire the Holiness of God? What could lead Him to accept any aspect of Himself that was not whole, joyous, and perfectly free? Surely this would not be any aspect of Truth.

Hmm... I guess not.

Give up guessing and choose to simply be. It is guessing that has you unsure of the reality that You are. The Holiness of God does not guess He is Truth, He knows it. As I've said, the Holiness of God does not pander or compromise with illusion. The Holiness of God knows His Wholeness and does not bend to doubt. To doubt is to play with the possibilities of illusion. You cannot play with the possibilities of illusion unless you have already accepted that illusion exists.

Boy… so it's a take-no-prisoners policy!

It is a take-yourself-prisoner-no-more policy. Listen; as always, I say to be gentle within. Never do I demand or force anything upon you. Never do I ask you to judge yourself. Yet, so too, do I not compromise the Truth and am always consistent. I love you in all your dreams, and never does this Love of Who I know You to be falter, even though you may believe you do. See this with Me and recognize exactly what your thinking allows you to be. Here you accept that it is only this belief in limitation that has ruled your mind. It is only this belief that you must choose to be free from. Place yourself in dis-ease no more. Open your eyes, Holiness of God, and see True. Accept the light of Truth so you may go forth and sin no more.

The more I think about it, the more I can see that all of Jeshua's healings were metaphors for the acceptance of Truth.

Indeed! It has been the same for every enlightened Master who chooses to join with his or her brothers here. The Mind of Love expresses within the Body of Holiness. In accepting the Holiness of Who You Are, you are raised from the dead, blind no more and fully able to walk forth into the light of True Beingness. No longer are you ruled, afflicted or possessed by delusions. Here, in accepting the wholeness of your Self in God's Creation, you are perfectly free and eternally peaceful. Accept this and know yourself beyond any musing of disease.

Okay… I have to ask, if I do accept myself in Truth, will all physical symptoms of illness as well be gone? Will disease itself and all symptoms disappear?

Have you heard the saying, "out of sight, out of mind?"

Yes.

Well, you may consider the physical healing to be "out of mind, accepting Sight." You are not your body, you are free. To be still as God Created is to no longer align with the body as your master, but is to be beyond all beliefs in limitation. Surely, you may appear to be a body for as long as you choose to honor time, yet being an identified body does not mean that you must identify with that body. Neither does it mean that all symptoms of disease need to be judged. Do not wonder if you are "enlightened yet." You are as God Created You, and that is all that need be realized now. Keep this in your awareness all ways, and all other concerns will simply fade away. Do not see yourself through your body's presentation. Allow yourself to settle within the Truth beyond appearances. To judge by appearances is to settle in deception.

You may recognize this experience through the story of Jeshua's crucifixion. By the seeming "time" of the crucifixion Jeshua was no longer being a body. He may have appeared to be a body within the judging eyes of many who perceived him to be. And still there are many who choose to leave Jeshua within his body today. Yet, after He communed with Me, we were One Mind and One Being. Truly, Jeshua saw himself in wholeness from the moment of his acceptance of Truth, and this was many years before the body of Jeshua appeared to be slung across some slabs of wood and left to "die." In fact, Jeshua lived in the resurrection of the mind long before his body appeared to die. Accept this for yourself beyond all ideas of body identification and you are resurrected from this moment on. Here you are resurrected from all ideas of death, not solely in body, but most truly in mind. Once again, this too is why Jeshua said in all healings, "go forth and sin no more."

Beloved One... you remain as God Created You. This is your power. This is your Truth. This is your glory. In accepting this you choose to shed all distortions of yourself and step forth into the light. Here is the True light of resurrection. Here is your own

Easter renewal. Roll away the rock from your own grave. Step forth in the body of light with Me and be not of disease, death, or distortion. Simply be the radiance of all you are in God's Glory. Moreover, to this I say it is done. Hallelujah, Glory is to Your Holiness. Amen. I love you.

Week Forty-One: Prompts for Insight

1. Holy Spirit asks us to "roll away the rock from your own grave". Take a moment to consider how you are burying yourself in limiting or destructive ideas. Consider all the ideas of sickness and body identity that have been discussed within this reading. Are you willing to die a little less and resurrect yourself into peace of mind?

2. Identify five sins you feel you have committed, remembering there is no reality to any of these wayward perceptions. A sin is merely a moment where we have temporarily missed the mark and forgotten our True Self. Now, settling your mind and inviting Holy Spirit's guidance, ask Him for a healing. Allow yourself to accept this reception of Truth and innocence within you. Finally, write down how you intend to now, "go forth, and sin no more".

3. Holy Spirit shares that we always remain as God Created. This is our one power. This is our one Truth. This is our one glory. In accepting this you choose to shed all distortions of yourself and step forth into the light. How would you like to express this awareness through your current life experience? Identify all thoughts, feelings, and experiences that you choose to see through glory and power rather than imprisonment and victimization. Ask Spirit how you can step forth into the light through these experiences. Write about all that is received.

4. Holy Spirit shares, "*There are no innocent victims. In fact there are no victims at all.*" Identify where in your life experiences, feelings or thoughts you see the role of victim being played. Consider how you have accepted the benefits of the victim role. Believe it or not, there are many benefits to "playing small". Take a moment to consider how playing the victim role has affected you. After this week's reading, what can you do to help you release these victim beliefs and accept only the Truth of your Self? How would you share this Truth with all?

5. Envision yourself as Jeshua or another recognized Spiritual Master. While walking, a man approaches who appears overwrought with severe illness. He asks for a healing. Picture yourself joining in the healing Light of Holy Spirit with your brother. Feel yourself unite in the presence of Oneness, innocence, and eternal well-being. See him experience the miracle and leave healed, renewed in the awareness of his Holiness. Write a story detailing your experiences in the sharing of this Holy Instant.

What do you see, feel, think, and desire for your brother?
How does it present in your body as well as mind?
What residual experiences do you feel after this healing is offered?

6. Write a bystander's account of a miracle healing. What does he or she see, feel, think, and desire for him or herself as well as all involved? Be specific and try as best you can to connect through his or her eyes.

7. Write a healed person's point of view after receiving a miracle healing. Just as before, detail what this man feels, sees, thinks and desires. How does he intend to go forth and sin no more? Compare all of these written stories and seek within on how to use their wisdom for your own experience of healing.

Affirmations:
All are innocent, all are free.
There is no disease in God or my Self.
The Holiness of God is complete and content all ways and always.
Love is all I am.

Week Forty-Two:

A Dream of Connectedness

I would like you to take a moment now to close your eyes and dream a dream with Me. I will call this the "Dream of Connectedness." In this dream, we are one. Here, there are no separate bodies or separate minds. There are no separate thoughts or ideas. There are no limitations or boundaries. There is only oneness, wholeness, and unity.

In this "Dream of Connectedness" there is no possibility of rejection. For, when all are connected, who could be rejected and by whom? In this dream, there are no possibilities of limitations or boundaries. For what could limit or bind an intertwining so pure that within itself it has no desire for separation? In this dream, there is no need for space or time, for here all desires are shared instantaneously. In this dream, no privacy is desired, for what could be private when all openly share? To have no privacy would require no judgment. In sharing all we know there is nothing to judge and no one who desires to stand apart. All is accepted as grandeur and delight.

Sit with Me now in this dreaming and feel yourself drawn into our connectedness. Feel yourself desire to be whole within this wholeness and rest in the loving arms of full support, acceptance, and joy. Here, no one desires to hide anything from you, nor believes you need to hide. All are complete within and share wholeness abundantly. This abundance is reinforced by the radiant delight absorbed within our sharing. The warmth and power of such grace cannot be described, only felt. Sit within this radiance for a moment and simply be. Open your heart to all it offers. Accept this bliss as yours, for truly it is.

Now, as you feel quiet and at peace within, I would like you to imagine a face appearing before you. This face is the image of one who is accepted as a friend in your life experience. Imagine this friend well, sharing the light with you. Look upon his or her gentle eyes and accept the gift of delight they offer. As you look upon one another simply say, "Thank you, my light is your own," and be in grace from this acceptance. See your friend smile in recognition and fade into the light. Now you rest in light again. You radiate with deeper joy and peace from this exchange of Truth.

Now, as you feel quiet and at peace within, I would like you to imagine another face to appear before you. This face is the image of one who is accepted as family in your life experience. Mother, father, sister, brother, grandparent, aunt, uncle or cousin. Imagine him or her well, sharing the light with you. Look upon your family member's gentle eyes and accept the gift of delight they offer. Now, as you look upon one another simply say, "Thank you, my light is your own" and be in grace from this acceptance. See your family member smile in recognition and fade into the light. Now you rest in light again. You radiate with deeper joy and peace from this exchange of Truth.

Now, as you feel quiet and at peace within, I would like you to imagine another face to appear before you. This face is the image of one who is accepted as teacher in your life experience. Imagine him or her well, sharing the light with you. Look upon your teacher's gentle eyes and accept the gift of delight they offer. Now, as you look upon one another simply say, "Thank you, my light is your own" and be in grace from this acceptance. See your teacher smile and fade into the light. Now you rest in light again. You radiate with deeper joy and peace from this exchange of Truth.

Now, as you feel quiet and at peace within, I would like you to imagine another face to appear before you. This face is the image of one who is accepted as a loved one, life partner or spouse in your life experience. Imagine him or her well, sharing the light with you. Look upon his or her gentle eyes and accept the gift of delight they offer. Now, as you look upon one another simply say, "Thank you, my light is your own" and be in grace from this acceptance. See your loved one smile and fade into the light. Now you rest in light again. You radiate with deeper joy and peace from this exchange of Truth.

Now, as you feel quiet and at peace within, I would like you to imagine another face to appear before you. This face is the image of one who is accepted as a child in your life experience. Imagine your child well, sharing the light with you. See him or her laughing and playing in the joy that overflows.

Now, as you look upon one another, say simply, "Thank you, my light is your own," and be in grace from this acceptance. See your child smile and fade into the light. Now you rest in light again. You radiate with deeper joy and peace from this exchange of Truth.

Now, as you feel quiet and at peace within, I would like you to imagine another face to appear before you. This face is the image of one who is accepted as a government or community leader in your life experience: King or Queen, Prime Minster, President, Senator, Executive or Judge. Imagine him or her well, sharing the light with you. Look upon his or her gentle eyes and accept the gift of delight they offer. Now, as you look upon one another simply say, "Thank you, my light is your own" and be in grace from this acceptance. See the government leader smile and fade into the light. Now you rest in light again. You radiate with deeper joy and peace from this exchange of Truth.

Now, as you feel quiet and at peace within, I would like you to imagine another face to appear before you. This face is the image of one who is accepted as a peer in your life experience. Imagine him or her well, coworker, supervisor, schoolmate or former friend. Now your peer shares the light with you. Look upon his or her gentle eyes and accept the gift of delight they offer. Now, as you look upon one another simply say, "Thank you, my light is your own" and be in grace from this acceptance. See your peer smile and fade into the light. Now you rest in light again. You radiate with deeper joy and peace from this exchange of Truth.

Now, as you feel quiet and at peace within, I would like you to imagine another face to appear before you. This face is the image of one who may at one time have been seen as apart from the light of joy for you. Someone who may have represented a trait where seeming darkness could possibly have been felt. This could be a former childhood bully, current person with whom you do not always get along, or a long-time enemy or victimizer. Breathe.

Clearly see that they cannot affect you here. Imagine him or her well, standing openly before you. Look deeply upon this person, not for the sin once perceived, but for the one truth that outshines all error. Easily you notice that only gentleness is shared between you. See here as all judgments simply fade away to nothingness.

See as this image stands and expresses only light with you. Look upon his or her gentle eyes and accept the gift of delight they willingly offer. Now, as you look upon one another simply say, "Thank you, my light is your own" and be in grace from this acceptance. See this person smile and fade into the light. Now you rest in light again. You radiate with deeper joy and peace for this exchange of Truth.

Now, as you feel quiet and at peace within, I would like you to imagine as many of the faces of humanity as you can envision appearing before you. Have each face flash briefly across your mind's eye. These are the images of ones with whom you may have interacted only briefly or not at all in your life experience. See them all, old and young, beautiful and undesired, healthy and infirmed, befriended and abandoned, loved and unloved, known and unknown in your personal experience. One by one, see them smile with the light each has to share. Look upon their gentle eyes and accept the gift of delight they offer. Continue to say simply, "Thank you, my light is your own" and be in grace from this acceptance. Now you rest in light again. You radiate with deeper joy and peace from this exchange of Truth. Sit and rest in this moment and accept the joy you share eternally.

Now as you feel quiet and at peace within, I would like you to imagine another face to appear before you. This face is the image of one who is accepted as Holy Spirit in your life experience. See this Holiness sharing the light with you, however you imagine it. Whether it be the face of Jeshua, Buddha, the ascended masters, guides or angels, look upon our oneness with gentle eyes and accept the gift of delight offered, knowing it is only for you. Join Me in saying simply, "Thank you, my light is your own" and be in grace for this acceptance. Feel our smile as we stand within the light. We are one. Now you rest in light again. You radiate with deeper joy and peace from this exchange of Truth.

Now, as you feel quiet and at peace within, I would like you to imagine your own face to appear before you. Imagine yourself well, sharing the light. Look upon your gentle eyes and accept the gift of delight willingly offered. See how all presumed errors or faults are unknown within this light. See yourself radiating perfectly as God Created You. Now, as you look upon yourself say simply, "Thank you, my light is your own" and be in grace from this acceptance. Smile and allow yourself to be absorbed into the light. Rest now and radiate with deeper joy and peace from this exchange of Truth.

Continue to rest in this light of connectedness for as long as you desire. Remember, Dear One, this is your dream. And although now it appears to be only a visage of your mind, recognize how this sharing is deeply familiar. Recognize how this sharing seemed to awaken a space of pure love within you. It is here that we were not dreaming, but remembering the only Truth that is. Rest, rest in this acceptance, Dear One, for when you rest here, you are only as God Created You. My light is your own, for we are One and I love you.

Week Forty-Two: Practice: Create a guided imagery audio with Spirit

Holy Spirit has already provided the script. Now, either through the use of a tape recorder, CD recorder with microphone or computer, record your own guided imagery audio. Find a quiet place and choose your favorite background music. Personally, I suggest calm unobtrusive instrumentals or nature sounds. On completion, set aside time (about one hour) each day to use this audio. Practice in a quiet space where you will remain undisturbed, so as to fully connect within, without distraction. Each day, try as best you can to deepen the experience of the previous day. See yourself intimately connecting with all of life and mind. Begin the sessions with a minimum of three minutes of calm, deep breathing. After completion, say a prayer of gratitude for the experience and write any thoughts or feelings that surfaced through it. Share these with Holy Spirit.

Affirmations:

I am as God Created Me.

I am one with my brothers, who are one with Me.

Love connects all I see and feel.

Only the Truth is true.

Week Forty-Three: **Desire and Vigilance**

Dear Holy Spirit, what would you have me learn today? I'm returning to this statement, especially after my recent adherence to ego thinking. I think it is time that I get back to You leading the way.

Dear One, do not guilt yourself over your temporal willfulness to see with the eyes of limitation. Your anger, stress, disappointment and frustration arise simply from the initial wish to see a self as limited. Judging this wish only extends more limitation. This is not the point of learning. The point of learning is to evolve from being ruled by forms to accepting the content of your desires. I would like you to research two words, "desire" and "vigilant."

Vigilant: circa. 1480, from Latin: *vigilantia* "wakefulness."

Desire: circa.1230, from Old French: *desirer*, from Latin: *desiderare* "to long for, wish for," original sense perhaps "await what the stars will bring," from the phrase *de sidere* "from the stars," from *sidus / sideris*: "heavenly body, star, constellation."

Wow! I was definitely surprised to find that out.

Indeed. When I ask you to be vigilant, it is a request to be awake. Too often vigilance is confused with a request for sacrifice, or for exhaustive work. This is not true. My only desire is for you to see the light of Truth within yourself. It is to be awake.

In ancient cultures, the stars were seen as the light of Heaven. Metaphorically, to align with the desire for Truth is to align with your True Light; your Heavenly Light; your purity. The True Self is the Light of Heaven. This is YOU. If you seek out your inner desire, you are choosing to see with your Light. When you vigilantly turn to this inner Light, or in other words *awaken to the Light of Heaven*, there is no work or exhaustive sacrificial practice. This is a rest from your own thinking mind and self-will. Here, you simply choose to see your Light, be awake and rest in peace.

There is a story in your Bible (Mark 14:32-41) where the disciple Peter is found sleeping when he has been asked to remain on guard in the night. This story is a perfect metaphor for your unlearning. Notice how Peter is standing and awaiting Jeshua's return from prayer. He is waiting for the arrival of Christ, for it was in this evening that Jeshua remembered himself as the Christ and choose to fully live the realization of His Truth through playing out the crucifixion. Nonetheless, before Jeshua's temporary departure from Peter's company, he beckoned Peter to be vigilant and stay awake in the midst of the darkness. However, as we have mentioned before, Peter was a man of great desire, yet limited certainty. He often allowed himself to waver and be succumbed by his concerns. Likewise, in this moment, he also allowed himself to go to sleep, instead of remain on guard.

Now, in my call for vigilance, I am not asking you to be embattled. I am not asking you to meet conflict with clash. To be vigilant is simply to remain awake. It is to be fully sustained in your remembrance of Truth, fully realizing how the darkness does not and cannot define you. Vigilance is to remember where you genuine power and strength reside. Let me say that it is here, in vigilance, that you turn to the stars of your true desire and come to take claim for your Heavenly Light.

A Course in Miracles teaches, "*I walk with God in perfect Holiness.*" (*A Course in Miracles*, Workbook, pg. 295) This is the call to vigilance. This is the call to be awake in the midst of all else the physical eyes and wayward will wishes to see as different. In fact, Beloved, do realize that you are always vigilant. However, your desire is revealed when you inquire, "what am I vigilant for?" Indeed, what do you call within your sight and choose to lead you through each state of being? Are you awake to the mistaken identities dictates? Do you see these images are real and purposeful, calling you into their own world of experience? Or are you awakened by a seemingly higher calling? The image that you choose to see will always be your own. This image will always be your sight and as you attend to it, you shall see yourself through it. Likewise this is why I ask you to be vigilant for your awakening. If you are not, the shadows you see within your current state are nothing but false visions upon a dreamscape unknown.

Hear me well; once again, I am not asking you to bring clash to the ego's conflict. To meet ill-will with willfulness is only to engage in more battle. However, you can be mindful of what the ego wishes to dream, and as you are mindful, as you choose to be awake to it, you are walking in the dream with eyes wide open. Notice what the mistaken identity is asking you to believe, and then offer it love instead of condemnation. This shall be your call to awakening. With this practice you are vigilant for the Light you are, rather than blindly accepting a dreaming state as your life or Truth.

What will the light of Heaven bring if you make that your desire? It will awaken Truth within your mind. It will bring peace beyond all your imaginings. This vigilance for Truth will bring you love for all You are, all you see, and all you feel and experience. When you embrace only the Light of Truth within you, I will always guide the wish of your beliefs to the level of True Perception. Here Love becomes your guide. Await upon the stars and humble yourself to the Light of Truth rather than any thought witnessing for separation and judgment. Breathe in this Light. Recognize it as your own. You are free. I love you.

After this journal entry, I wondered about Spirit's choice to use the word "Await." I didn't feel that it properly fit in the sentence. Yet, Spirit insisted this was correct and then guided me to research the word. I found this...

Await: circa. 1230, *awaiten / awaitier* "to watch, observe," from *a-* "to" + *waitier* "to watch."

I have asked you to be watchful of your mind. See this now as a request to watch for the Light of Truth within you. The light is there, Dear One, for it is YOU!

Being watchful is not about berating yourself every time a thought of limitation arises. It is not desperately wondering "why,

why, why, haven't I got it by now??!" You need not delve deep into these thoughts, but see them as a passing breeze beneath the watchful eye of the sun. You are the watchful eye of the Son. Do not spend too much time noticing the thoughts of limitation, and deconstructing them. Simply guide yourself back to their cause and allow yourself to gain a deeper understanding. Truly, our overall goal is not for a deeper understanding of the restricted mind. Instead, we seek to know our Self within the light of Truth beyond all thoughts. Absorb yourself into the Light and judge no more. The moment you notice the cause and content of your disruptive thoughts, use the next conscious moment to breathe and release. Realign yourself with your vigilant desire. Realign yourself with the Light of Heaven. Allow yourself to relax within the loving waves of joy that this Light resonates. It is a hug from Heaven, for I love and embrace you beyond all your imaginings.

My Light is Your Own...

Week Forty-Three: Prompts for Insight and Practice:

1. In what ways can you practice desire and vigilance in your life experience? What have you noticed yourself more vigilant (or awake) to: ego or Holy Spirit? Be honest in your recognition and do not berate yourself for noticing a more willful wish for separation. This is all perfectly normal for where you perceive yourself to be. However, choose instead to change the sight of your wishes. Make a list of the ways you can be vigilant for the ego, write down all the ways you have a tendency to notice the ego in yourself as well as others. Then, make a list of all the ways you can choose to see the Holiness of Truth within these same people or circumstances. The correct Vision is always available through Love's Pure sight.

3. In the Bible, Mark: 14:32-41 relays how when Jesus returns from praying in the garden of Gethsemane, he catches Peter sleeping instead of standing guard. Generally, this story can be used as a metaphor for our call to awaken. In every moment, even those that are seemingly the most troubling, we are being asked to practice vigilance for our True desire. We are being asked to remain awake. Likewise, Holy Spirit teaches us to be observant of every wish for dreams over awakening. Each moment we are asked to be awake to our True Desire and how this desire is practiced. Be mindful this week for the areas where you choose to sleep. Where do you put Spirit on hold and the mistaken identity on "auto-pilot"? This week, attempt to notice when you catch yourself not seeing or thinking with Spirit's guidance. Consult the examples below as a guideline and write the prominent thoughts and emotions occurring within your more sleepy moments.

I caught myself in ego "auto-pilot" when:
At work, when the boss approached me.
My beliefs or feelings within this moment were:

Fear. I instantly became suspicious and worried. I noticed a need for appreciation and concern. I was worried about what he thought of me.

I caught myself in ego "auto-pilot" when:

At a family reunion when the relatives who I hadn't seen in quite awhile asked me what was new in my life.

My beliefs or feelings within this moment were:

A desire for validation. I felt a fear of being seen as a failure according to their standards.

4. What experiences seem to truly push your ego buttons? What do you feel Spirit's guidance for each of these experiences would be? Identify what it would be like to practice desire and vigilance in place of the ego's reaction. Follow up these discoveries with journal writing.

Affirmation:
"I desire this holy instant for myself that I may share it with my brother, whom I love. It is not possible that I can have it without him, or he without me. Yet it is wholly possible for us to share it now. And so I choose this instant as the one to offer to the Holy Spirit, that His blessing may descend on us, and keep us both in peace."[4]

Practice this affirmation a minimum of three times during your day. Speak it especially during the moments during which you notice increased conflict or stress. Focus on connecting with all your "mighty companions" throughout the day's experiences.

Week Forty-Four:

From Humanness to Beingness

Help me transition my mind from identifying with humanness to accepting beingness centered in Spirit.

> Dear One, the only thing that hinders you from releasing your mind is forgiveness. Humanness is not a curse, but a blessing. It has been an answer to the innocent wishes of God's Holiness. You have not done anything wrong and need not escape from a guilty choice. However, only in your forgetting, do you now believe this wish defines you. You have become absorbed within the dream. Again, this is not a curse. Although you forget, you are changeless. Do not worry that you need to escape humanness in order to accept Being. Peace is always available to you. This peace is not found as a counter to current condition. Peace is always an enhancement. In allowing peace, through forgiveness, you allow yourself to see clearly beyond all dreams of restriction.
>
> There are two words that I want you to look at here: "represent", and "release".
>
> Represent: circa. 1375, "to bring to mind by description," from *re-*, intensive prefix, +*præsentare* "to present," literally: "to place before." Meaning: "to symbolize, to be the embodiment of" is from circa. 1380 *Representation* "image, likeness."
>
> Release: circa. 1297, "to withdraw, revoke," also "to liberate" (circa.1300), from Old French: *relaisser* "to relinquish, quit, let go, leave behind," variant of *relacher* "relax." Meaning "relinquish, surrender."
>
> Let us look at these ideas and permit ourselves to be gentle with our thinking. In your choosing to adhere to illusions, you are choosing to embody the symbols of your beliefs. You are choosing

to make an image or likeness of Truth and call this an adequate substitute. In choosing to forgive you are choosing to release these symbols, and hence beliefs, into the acceptance of a truer beingness. All that truly hinders you is the attachment you invest to the illusions. In your forgetting, you let these illusions define you. This is simply because you believe you need them. Here, it is as if you are arguing with peace. You further attempt to defend your case for limitation and need by practicing judgment. Which is why I often ask you, would you rather be right or free?

Peace is held out to you, at no cost, within every moment beyond time. It is nothing that requires anything of you. In fact, it is the very non-requirement of it that makes you peaceful.

All requirements stem only from your belief in limitation. In accepting these beliefs, you insist that the illusions have merit, and continue to serve you. Surely then, every witness is brought forth within the world to prove this as so.

Holy Spirit, one thing that brought me to this topic today was my noticing how I see guilt. I seem to want to constantly judge myself and others. I get wrapped up in all the ideas of error. I see myself focusing on why people do certain things to me or others. I question their holiness and desire to see them as separate. Why is this? Can you help me release this?

You will only choose to release these judgments when you truly see how this thinking disturbs your peace. But not until then. For as long as you justify these thoughts and beliefs, the illusion is embodied. At the moment you truly desire peace, you will finally recognize the humor and purposeless in your judgments.

In your acceptance of the miracle you will see how all judging results in discord for yourself. Here's a hint: if you are not happy (and I mean genuinely peacefully completely happy) there is some belief within that is still grasping onto illusion.

For instance, here are a few questions to guide you:

Do you judge anything by appearances?
Do you cling to any ideas of what bodies do or don't do?
Do you accept stress or strain as necessary for peace?
Do you invest in self-doubt?
Do you project expectations upon the world or others?
Do you seek to defend or attack in the name of justified anger?
Do you awake in the morning, worrying about how you will make it through the day?
Do you not trust and love all that comes across your path?
Do you complain and fear or possibly wish to escape or save yourself?
Do you defend your lack of happiness and who or what is to blame?
If you justified any of the above - THERE is the illusion.

Truly, beloved, I do not ask these questions to judge you. I do not ever judge. However, if you are seeking to reveal where you can release, here are a few suggestions for your guidance.

Listen well:
Not ever will unhappiness, worry, conflict or anger
be equal to the Peace of God.

Never?!

No. Never. You can test this theory through the expanses of time if you'd like.

For some reason I feel like I've been there and done that.

That is because you have. (Smile)

Okay, so I guess that hasn't worked.

Nope.

So why do I defend it with such tenacity?

You harshly defend because you identify yourself through its story. However you can choose to no longer write it, direct it, assign characters, and keep the plots going.

However, I emphasize, you cannot merely think yourself to peace. It is not a check to be made on your life-experience "to-do list." Peace arises when you choose to step beyond yourself. Here you accept that peace is not of yourself but beyond yourself. Here you release all need to control. Again, the "you" you seem to see is merely just a character, an embodiment, a representation of this playful imagining. Choose to see this representation with peace rather than go from despising it to giving it the keys to the kingdom. Neither of these routes will bring peace.

So, how can I, as a seeming individual, accomplish my part?

Simply by releasing and resting. Notice when you choose to invest in the dream. To do this is always helpful. Yet, engage in noticing not as a judgment or as an attempt to force your self into another way of thinking. Again, meet each thought with an "ahhh" rather than an "oops"! Use the noticing process to remind yourself of your Truth, embracing every wayward idea, simply so that you may rest. That is all.

Okay, I'm going to think of a few times in my experience that I justified judgment over peace. There were a couple of times this year when I felt really disappointed by others. It seemed that I accepted others as being gurus or teachers who then showed a, well, more human side. They went from models of inspiration to just regular people. However, I also condemned them for this humanness. After witnessing their displays of anger, lack of forgiveness and flaws, I really felt devastated, angry, disappointed. How could I have responded differently to that?

First off, look at that statement you just made. Do you see all the places where you judge? Secondly, was not this "devastation" just the demolition of an idol you made? Others can never live up to idol status, simply because all idols are substitutes for reality. Not one investment outside of peace will bring you peace. Now who accepts and believes they need these substitutes? Who gives these seeming "gurus" your power? Is it not you who assigns them their roles to play and asks them to adhere to the script you write?

Yes. All of that is true. Okay, lesson seen.

But, Dear One, this is not about changing others. Neither is this about grieving over how you could have or should have responded differently. This is about releasing yourself from all requirements: past, present and future. But nonetheless, let Me ask one question: *where can you find peace now*? If you wish to look into the past, seek only to learn from it. Notice where you have aligned with personal disturbance over peace. Notice where you gave your peace away or placed your needs in the hands of others. Notice where you put others on a pedestal and then held them to unrealistic expectations. What were you choosing to do: represent illusion or release for peace?

As usual, you are right. I get your point.

Now don't go putting Me on a pedestal. I can see where I may wind up... in the same hell you place yourself. (smile) Instead, embrace Me simply as you would embrace your Self. Here you offer me the love I am. It is the very same Holiness You are.

Yikes. However, again, point taken. Thank you.

Thank you.

Mostly, I seem to want to see my brothers as their human selves and not their Spiritual Truth. I think, in a way, this comforts me so that when they do make a mistake, I can chalk it up to being okay. I can accept it as part of their humanness. But then I also feel angry when there is an appearance of spiritually aware people acting very unspiritual. I judge to myself, "Aren't they supposed to practice what they preach?" "Shouldn't they act better than they are now?" I judge them for their displays of anger, preferential treatment, and defensiveness among a community that is supposed to be coming to know the exact opposite of that. I feel angry within when I see that.

Oh, you mean that you judge them for acting the very same as you are thinking right now?

I... uh.... Oh.... Yeah. (Smile)

This is only because you have already judged that spiritually aware people do not make these mistakes if they are genuinely "spiritually aware." You have given them a role to play and are making sure, come hell or high water that they will be playing their role exactly as you have directed. You clearly exchange their whole Truth for your image of it. Hear Me well; there are no spiritually aware people.

What??! You mean there are no real gurus or advanced learners? There is no one I can turn to as an example for truth in form?? You mean I can't find anyone "out there" who can give me the example that I need to feel I'm doing it all right???!!!

Rest. Breathe... you're upsetting yourself. (Smile) Listen. This is not about labels. Here we attempt to seek the truth beyond labels. There are no spiritually aware people because there are no individualized, special, or separated people within the Kingdom of God. Never was the label "Teacher of God" meant to be a separate designation among God's Unified Creation. Never.

Truly, any idea of hierarchy among the Holiness of God gives life to the idea of separation. Would that not make separation real within the realm of Truth? Truly, there is no separation.

A Teacher of God is simply a seeming individual that has stepped forth in willingness, to witness to the miracle beyond the illusion. They are no different from anyone else. Hear Me well;

teachers surround you! They need not be found in workshops or weekend retreats. They need not cost a dime. Teachers are found through every desire to know peace that you extend. Does this mean that you cannot do these activities? No. It is all perfect. The point that I make is that love and guidance can be found in every place and in every person, simply because all is found within you.

If you choose to place the image of a brother (and notice I did say the *image* of a brother) within some sort of special place, this is your idolization and nothing more. Every idea of your brother is made out of a mind choosing to represent the embodiment of limitation. This will always be as long as you remain within the experience of a world gone mad. Seek not for anything but madness here and you always will be satisfied.

Yet, there is another way. This is the way of forgiveness. Truly this is the *only* bridge between humanness and beingness. For it is here, through forgiveness, that you actively choose to release all of your illusions and accept only peace as your awareness. Here, true perception is able to be seen and accepted. Here, all imaginings you hold against your brother, and look to fulfill through the eyes of the world, will be shed. In this release the light of truth flows freely, as God intended.

I would like you to take a moment to compare your images of Humanness and Beingness. Write them down and see what comes forth.

Okay, let's see. For "humanness" I have: sinful, error driven, in need, incomplete, limited, and doomed to death, destruction, disappointment, and failure. Controlled and defined by illusory identity.

Boy, that sounds like a party. (Smile)

Are you being cheeky again?? (Smile)

As you wish. Now what about spiritual?

For spiritual I have pretty much the opposite: sinless, complete, whole, perfect, free, eternal, loved, One, beyond all limitations.

What if I were to tell you (and I am) that all of these are mere identifications made by the mind in confusion about itself.

Hmm... then I may be confused. Does that apply even for my descriptions of Spirit??

Yes, even for your descriptions of spirit. Listen well; to be Spirit is to be beyond every definition. Therefore, your definitions only apply to all that you see within the realms of limitation. Surely you can call this "spirit" or "spiritual," but it is nothing more than your own means for defining who you perceive yourself (and others) to be. True Spirit is not a construct that can be understood by the mind. Surely, words can attempt to describe this beingness, but essentially, as I have said before, and as it says in the Course, words are merely "symbols of symbols ... twice removed from reality." (*A Course in Miracles*, Manual for Teachers, p. 53)

So how can this help me? How can I understand myself, especially if I can't even define spirit?

Look at that question and see what comes to mind. See your willingness to identify through your individualized self. Is your purpose here, in this experience, to define spirit? Is that what this entire journey is about? I'm willing to gamble that if you looked at this thought for only a moment you would recognize that this attempt to define spirit (as well as everything else) is your only cause for misery. Truly what can suffer disappointment when it has no pre-defined function? Is it not only your pre-defined function of others, especially those within the seeming spiritual community, which has led you to disappointment and a whirlwind of confusion?

Yes. I guess that is what has led to the core of my disappointment and confusion. I've put a definition on my brother. Especially the ones who I thought were supposed to be spiritual, and attempted to love them only within these boundaries.

> And that is where all errors in thinking arise. As long as you attempt to give limit to the limitless, you are thinking in error. This simple distortion has you attempt to control, manipulate, judge and withhold yourself and others apart from God. Yet this error in reality is impossible. God always loves His Holiness. Never is He apart from it. Never does He judge that His Holiness is limited or unworthy of its Self. This Holiness has no requirement and surely has no definition to uphold. Holiness is as it is. And this remains for you as the brilliance of You in God's Glory.
>
> Choose to see your brothers beyond every image. Release (which is the same as forgive) and extend the Truth of Who You Are. Extend beyond the images of the forgetting mind that chooses only to embody a symbolic error. Release yourself and your brother from the binds of your imaginings. Place the fear of needing to control aside and ask simply for another way. In this way you choose peace instead of confusion. Peace is not of your idle imaginings. True Spirit is beyond all your imaginings. Here you are free.

Okay, so I'm going to review. To bridge the gap between humanness and beingness, all I must do is release my judgments and expectations? All I do is rest beyond every image imagined that seeks to limit anyone or anything?

> Someone's been listening. That is a perfect start.

Yes. Now I'm here to be truly helpful.

> Wonderful. Now completely absorb yourself into the present moment. Simply be the witness to forgiveness and seek to share this with all. Do this not necessarily with words. No one needs a

preacher, but rather a teacher. Offer love to all you encounter and see them as YOUR teacher. See all with the Love they are and settle in the moment only offering them peace. Here you open yourself up to the full awareness of Who You Are. Open yourself up now to see every image you have made of your brother and then step beyond this image. Notice your judgments, then extend yourself beyond every idea of what a human is supposed to be. No longer seek to overlook or suppress your judgments. No longer ask to shrug them away and pretend they are not there. Every image that you see is there because it has been invented within the forgetting mind. However, use each recognized judgment as a stepping stone towards release. Let stillness and love be your guide.

Again, I say, as it says in the Course, "*Forgiveness … is still. It merely looks, and waits and judges not.*" (*A Course in Miracles*, Workbook, p. 401) This is my guidance to you in very moment where a temptation for judgment seems justified. Remind yourself, Dear One, that these all are mere images of your embodied forgetful mind. Release yourself from these thoughts and you shall be free.

Look again at what you wrote about humanness.

Yes. Sinful, error driven, in need, incomplete, limited, doomed to death, destruction, disappointment, and failure. Controlled by and defined by identity.

Yes. Now I ask you to extend perfect freedom to all of these images. Look upon each and wholly choose to define nothing. Give perfect allowance to all who cross your pathway. Judge not and free yourself from judgment. I say this because to extend a judgment is only to invest in the illusion. Do not make the illusion real, Dear One. Recognize its lack of substance and set yourself free from every imagining.

But shouldn't I just say instead that these traits are merely traits of my mind? Shouldn't I just reverse them into some blissful ideas instead?

If you can't truly know it, it is not real. A wish for a blissful idea is not the true and genuine experience of the love you are. Seek not to replace images with more images. Seek instead to know the truth and extend this revelation to all you see. I am here with you as you do this.

Good point.

Quietly witness each judgment you hold against your brother, watch them drift by like leaves floating upon the wind. Notice the color, texture, and state of decay each one appears to have. See them and set them free. This then becomes the miracle bridging the gap between humanness to beingness. It is here, in honest release, in quiet forgiveness that you welcome your peace, your truth, and your simple beingness, and rest.

Remember that any justification for attack is only an investment in the decay. Accept yourself as this death no longer! This can never bring peace. See yourself no longer bound by this world, but lovingly supported, so that you may release to peace no matter what the present condition. Accept instead what forgiveness has to offer. Seek not another extended investment in form or fear over freedom.

Sometimes I do wonder if I really will be happy in letting go of my judgments. Is this normal? How do I get past this idea?

This idea is only because you are unsure of Your reality. That is fine. Fear not, your lack of surety is merely a door opening to my guidance. Begin here with the recognition that you alone do not know. Be willing to see what the bottom line is here. Does judgment, any judgment, really bring you peace? Do you really feel happy through its practice? Or does more fear and frustration arise later?

Notice exactly what your choices bring and choose again for peace. Here, you call out an invitation to my knowing. Here, I always respond, for this is an invitation to my loving Self from my beloved Self. Here I am and always will be. Forgive what images you have made and you will be free. This is all the recognition I hold out to you. Listen, I will always be the complete witness for all the love you are, beyond every imagining you hold. Recognize the bridge with Me. Recognize all blessings of peace through release, through true forgiveness, and allow yourself to come to the gates of Heaven. Here you cannot deny the Truth of Who You Are for a moment more. Here you completely rest in peace. I love you.

Week Forty-Four: Prompts for Insight and Practice:

1. Think of someone you dislike or with whom you have a difficult relationship. Make a list of every way you dislike this person. What is it that they say or do? How do they continue to deceive you or keep you unhappy? Holy Spirit teaches that every trait we see within others is one we accept within ourselves. Take a moment to insightfully review where you see these very same thoughts or ideas within you and then ask Holy Spirit to help you offer up this belief in exchange for peace. With an open mind, every belief and relationship can be healed.

2. Make a list of ten judgmental or limiting ideas. They can be ways you dislike or resent yourself or others. Next to each of these judgments identify one way this judgment disturbs your peace. How does it affect your happiness? How does it affect your relationships, decisions and your confidence? Does it affect how you choose to accept love or affluence in your life? Once you identify how these judgments affect you, focus within and seek guidance on why you may justify or defend this thinking. What purpose does it hold for you in your life experience? How does it protect you and what from? Write down each thought. Offer these thoughts to Holy Spirit knowing He can heal each one. Write any guidance arising.

3. Holy Spirit guides, *"If you are not happy (and I mean genuinely, peacefully, and completely happy) there is something within that is still grasping onto illusion."* Where do you find yourself "grasping onto illusion"? Identify and process these experiences with Holy Spirit. If you choose, conduct a releasing ceremony for each.

4. What expectations do you place upon certain groups of people? Write down a list. Try not to adhere only to genders, cultures, or religions (but do not exclude them). For instance, how do you think police officers should be? How do you feel clergy should be? How do you feel ex-convicts should be? How do you feel teachers

should be? How do you feel spiritual gurus should be? How do you feel your boss, family, or friends should be? All of these are ways we consciously adhere to and extend illusion. Process each of these with Holy Spirit and ask Him to help you find peace beyond these images.

Affirmations:

I am not my body; I am free.

All I see is as I extend it to be.

I am more than the images of my mind.

Love sets me free from my imaginings.

The Holiness of God is indefinable.

Week Forty-Five: **Love in Process**

I would like to learn more about the process of giving love to all in the world, no matter what they say or do. Too often, I have major judgments arise when I think about giving love to others who either I don't know or don't approve of. Can you help me get through this issue? Thanks.

Let's speak on process, because this word is a symbolic one. Usually process is defined as a forward movement or advance. Yet, it also can be seen as a yielding forth. This is where I would like our teaching to focus. Our process is that of being led forward, rather than you moving forward. To say you are moving forward is to say there is a distance which must be overcome. Truly, there is no distance between you and God. Neither is there any real distance between you and your embodied brothers and sisters. No misperception can change this fact. In order to heal these ideas of distance, it is best to recognize yourself being led.

When you feel a need to progress through your thinking, you perceive yourself to be the active guide. Rather, in being led, you relax and allow. It is not with your thinking mind that an experience of awakening is known. All that desires awakening, must first desire release. In this, the mind withdraws from a state of self-control, where it sees itself as the central core of power. In the thinking process of giving love, you are approving of forgiveness or love for one or another of your brothers and sisters. You are making forgiveness and love a mental act, rather than a free-flowing allowance. I emphasize, all needs for self-control are rooted in fear. Being the appearance of peace's opposite, fear attempts to rule through its own self rather than allowing its Self to release through God. God does not fear or judge, and so He does not divvy forgiveness here or there. God flows freely into all His Holiness as His Holiness.

Love can symbolically be defined as an extension of True freedom. It is the full beingness of Self, reaching out to all. Love embraces and allows; fear, on the other hand, withdraws and desists. Truly what you desire is full freedom to be your Self once more. With Me, the practice of Love in process is yielding to the freedom that we already are and extending this to the seeming structures of the world. Therefore, Love in process is giving forth True Freedom.

Okay, thank you. How can I "give forth true freedom" within the experiential world?

Dear One, as long as you perceive yourself to first and foremost be experiencing the world, it will seem difficult to give forth true freedom, but never impossible. It is not impossible because you can always choose to release the way you judge and attach yourself to the world. Therefore, you are only trying to change your mind. This is why it is possible. Never for one moment is what you see in appearance the Truth. This means that what you see on the surface emanates from your imagination and not from what is real. In giving forth true freedom we are realizing this reality. Call this yielding to Clear Vision or true perception, but all you are simply doing is giving forth the Love you are to ALL, despite what you think.

Illusions will not disappear when you strive to see truly. Yet, your perception of experiences or people as being obstacles will change entirely. With Love in process, no longer will you see yourself as victim of the world, or lost and confused within its bounds. With giving forth true freedom, you free yourself from any boundary and see only as Love would see. You see the wholeness in every moment, for every brother or sister. You see them as innocent and free, accepting that they are experiencing the perfect sight for what their awareness accepts at that time. You remove yourself from judgment and allow yourself to be a witness to the Oneness of all. In this moment you simply accept your freedom, see this as being the only truth, and express that forward to the world in wholeness.

This is Love in process. This is a yielding to the Truth which is always ready to lead you to another way of thinking and seeing.

This is asking to share every Holy Instant with your Brother, whom you love, accepting that there can be no Holiness without them. I shall list for you ways that the mind can understand through practical matters, although they are all expressions of the above:

Accept and Offer Forgiveness. This is obviously the first and foremost way to give forth true freedom to yourself and all. Here you accept yourself and all as innocent. You step away from any judgment which may entice you to believe otherwise. You accept that any divisive perception is only based on your own ideas of limitation expressed outward and nothing else. In forgiveness you see yourself as free, healed, whole, complete and with no possibility of lack. You see yourself as God Created and extend this to the wholeness you seem to see as a sea of faces and experiences.

"We bless the world, as we behold it in the light in which our Savior looks on us, and offer it the freedom given us through His forgiving vision, not our own." (A Course in Miracles: Workbook, Lesson 164)

Accept and Offer Freedom: Do not ask for another task or any other expectation from your brothers and sisters. You bestow upon them the perfect freedom that you accept for them to be. Here, you give your brothers and sisters permission to do as they wish, recognizing that any idea of limitation or lack does not affect the Truth. Quite literally, no matter what is said or done, you choose to see the truth in their behavior and not any reflection of limitation. Here, we do not focus on ideas of error, but instead on perfection beyond mere appearances.

Whoa.. whoa... whoa right there! I'm having a bit of resistance about this one. It just doesn't seem practical within the realms of the world. It sounds like you are asking me to be a doormat and let people do whatever they want to me. My thinking mind is having a huge issue with this! What about crime? Am I supposed to yield to everything??? What about children? Am I not to teach them right from wrong? Is that what giving perfect freedom is?

Giving perfect freedom is giving forth perfect Love. Perfect love does not accept limitation, in any form. I am not asking you to yield to another's behavior. I am asking you to see the love beyond the surface appearance. Changing your mind does change your experience. See this love beyond judgment and fear. Recognize that all situations reflect the thoughts entertained within your mind. Does this mean that you now have permission to walk the streets at 3:00am without concern? No, it means that all actions are supported by the willingness to see love over fear. Fear will always attract fear. However, even if an experience witnessing to fear approaches, beyond your conscious awareness, seek to yield within and follow my guidance. I will never leave you comfortless or abandon you in times of need. Trust in this and know that you are always safe in my arms.

Likewise, I am not asking you to allow the children of your world to do whatever their own limitedly thinking mind may be asking to do. The parent and child relationship is an expression of guidance and love. It is meant to be used for gentleness and understanding, rather than judgment and punishment. Learning does not have to be accomplished through fear, yet surely it appears to be the easiest way to teach. This is why your world has used fear as its main teacher for centuries. If you are a parent, I ask you to first see the love within your child. See this love as being the wholeness of truth and let yourself be this same love.

Secondly, when it appears your child is making a choice which can appear to be destructive to their physical, emotional, or mental well-being, keep in mind the truth about them and let that be the guideline. Reach from within when you choose to teach them and for how you choose to teach. You can consider this the "I love you too much to have you walk across the road without looking both ways," example. Or the "I love you too much to see you hurt yourself in this manner," example. Or the "I love you so much that I'm willing to offer you another choice, that maybe you are unable or unwilling to see right now," example. The list goes on. Notice the first words of every lesson are "I love you," and truly, Dear One, it is the same with every lesson I place forth to you.

Now back to giving forth perfect freedom. Similar to the above, Perfect Freedom is balanced with Perfect Love. Each is a whole reflection of the other, for Perfect Freedom is Perfect Love and this is changeless. As you ask how you can offer Perfect Freedom to all the people encountered who appear not to deserve it, or shouldn't have it, I ask you to refer to the above examples. Love all first. Here, nothing fearful could ever be valued over the Truth and nothing could ever be withheld.

Keep this thought in mind the next time you appear to encounter another who you feel does not deserve this perfect freedom. Ask yourself: why do you fear them being free? How do you feel you are made vulnerable or destructible if they are not free? Truly, how do they represent all that you hide, fear or limit within yourself? It is only when you see yourself as not able to be as God Created that you withhold freedom from yourself or another. See with the eyes of fear and all things will be seen as bound. It is essential to look at this, because it is only through this valued decision that you choose to isolate yourself from others. See this and you see the key that sets you free.

And that key is?

The key is the realization that no thoughts of limitation are true. No thoughts valuing fear or guilt are true. I understand that through the eyes of form this appears on one level to be an impossible task. I can accept the imaginations your mind holds and how these are used to judge your perceived reality. However, once you choose to see yourself beyond these imaginations, you will see your freedom. Here you know that nothing else but freedom can be wholly offered to yourself or any other.

I hear that, and my judgmental mind spins. Gosh, how can I see this as being true in a world of crime? How can I see this as being true in a world of war? How I can see this as being true in a world of disease, attack, oppression, and poverty? The list goes on and on.

Yes, I understand your concerns. In fact, I can hear the whole world's response to this suggestion and understand every thought which feeds every question.

How can you deny what is happening when obviously it is happening? It is impossible to disprove your experience of vulnerability through worldly examples. As long as you seek answers within your own already accepted thinking, you will only see what you currently see. Therefore, it is impossible to disprove insane thinking while using examples yielding to insanity. Breathe, Dear One, and settle your mind. I ask you to deny nothing. Instead, I ask you to turn within rather than without. Turning without is seeing with vacancy. When you look without you feel without love, caring or connection to anyone. This is especially true for remembering a connection with your True Self and Your Father. Therefore, do not seek your reality in these experiences. Instead, seek only to still your mind and ask Me to see for you. Truly, Dear One, this will always give you the peace you desire.

Perfect Love knows that this world experience is not truly representative of All You Are. Therefore, Perfect Love does not see you as being made prisoner. Am I expecting you to see with the eyes of Perfect Love in order to give forth True freedom? I expect and judge nothing. I only see you as you completely are and it is there alone that the mind's analyses must cease to speak. Breathe whenever you feel yourself bound by fear or answerless questions. See how these fears and inquiries demand to make the world into a prison and you their prisoner. Ask yourself simply, what do you want? Do you choose to see yourself as prisoner or as free? Therefore beloved, reel not in your thinking mind, but REAL in the Love you are.

True Freedom is accepting that you are as God Created. It is accepting that this Truth can never change. Remember, as the Course says, "all thoughts leave not their Source" and your Source is God. No matter how you identify with the world, and all perceived to be within it, you remain as God Created. There are no thoughts that remain apart from Him. Remember this guidance in every situation that appears before your eyes and set yourself free from these mere images. Accept only that which has always remained complete.

Likewise, you can be Love in Process by Being Still in Mind. To be still in mind is to release your self from any judgment and analysis that confuses or distracts you. When you are still in mind you accept yourself to be only a thought of God. Here, only forgiveness is possible, because you accept that you have been given perfect freedom. That is what perfect freedom is, which does not include the ability to change your Self or God. Is this a limitation within the limitless? No, because to change the changeless would mean that you were never changeless. You are never at the mercy of a forgetting mind opting to permanently forget. This is your safety. For if you were granted the ability to change God or change your True Self, surely the result would not be a pleasant one.

I thank you for that! With all the ways that the mistaken identity has attempted to project limitation, calling it hell, condemnation, fear, and damnation, I'm much appreciative that this could never be reality.

Do not thank Me, thank God. However, He already knows your gratefulness in full. It is He who reflects all through you. In your perfection, there is no opposite, because simply to have an opposing force to perfection would mean you could never be perfect. You are perfect as God Created. There can be no change to this, and in this you are Love eternal.

To be still in mind is to release all distraction. It is to settle within, in quiet peace, where you truly are. To be still in mind is a practical way to give forth true freedom because only in this moment do you quiet any other thought which may witness for fear. When you seemingly have problems with your brothers, it is only because you choose to see judgment with them or judgment within yourself. In being still in mind, you release all thoughts of restraint and settle within the peaceful experience of inner being. Can you imagine a scenario where you appear to be faced with an opposition and all you do is simply rest within peace and reflect only love? Can you imagine the gentle eyes and tranquil visage which is put forth from within you? Can you see yourself simply allowing and letting all that which is not true to gently pass by?

This is being Love as God Created. This is Being Your Self. This is exactly what Jeshua practiced fully in many of the stories you have acquainted with him. Here you see nothing as nothing, and wholeness as everything. Here you are free.

Finally, the last practical way we will discuss giving forth true freedom is to Be gentle.

I was prompted to look up the meaning of the word "gentle" and was surprised to find that the definition focuses more on hierarchy of birth rather than the usually accepted definition of "peaceful" or "calming." Its main component, gent, is rooted from the word "genitus" meaning to beget. The definition focuses on "being high-born and noble."

In being gentle you are calling forth your inheritance as the Son of God. Truly this is you calling forth your Self into your self. Here you align with the Truth about You and see only your origins as being the correct Vision, and in seeing this you also see this as belonging to all and being of all. When I say you are as God Created and there is only One Holiness of God, this is not a metaphor. This is the Truth in total perfect completeness. Here you are being asked to see all that which is and is always. Here you are being called to witness the Holiness that you are in eternity.

You are birthed from that on high. You are noble. You are a reflection of the King of Kings and Lord of Lords and the entirety of Heaven bows to your willingness to accept all that is yours. This is the Perfect Love from God, for He has bestowed all of Himself in your Creation. This is Perfect Freedom. This is knowledge beyond every judgment and limitation. In this awareness, there can be no disturbance to your peace. Here, peace is YOU!

In being gentle you recognize from where you came and offer this Source forth to all you encounter. Here you are Love in Process, complete and Holy, seeing only that which is True for all in ALL. In my calling to have you give forth true freedom, I only call for you to accept that which has always been and can never change. I ask you to see with an open eye as God has Created and is always and all ways. In being gentle you offer the world the freedom you accept as the innocent reflection of Truth it is. Here, all seeming else silently passes away for you. Here you accept there was nothing really there. Being only as God Created shines forth in all ways, through all experiences and all actions. Love becomes your own Witness and, listening to Truth, is your only Guide. Here you are as I am. And, Dear One this is far from impossible, simply because it already is.

Therefore, in summary, to be Love in Process is to:
1. Accept and Offer Forgiveness
2. Accept and Offer Freedom
3. Be Still in Mind
4. Be Gentle

Beloved Holy Spirit, this teaching is so clear, so perfect, so simply loving! Thank you for this remembrance of all that I am, so that I may continue to be this right now. I love you.

Truly, Dear One, I am only reflecting for you all that you already are.

"Thanks be to you, the Holy Son of God. For as you were created, you contain all things within your Self. And you are still as God created you. Nor can you dim the light of your perfection. In your heart the Heart of God is laid. He holds you dear, because you are Himself. All gratitude belongs to you, because of what you are." (A Course in Miracles Workbook, lesson 197)

I am with you all ways. I love you.

Week Forty-Five: Prompts for Insight and Practice:

1. Take a moment to mentally explore within where you feel bound. Ask Holy Spirit to guide you to a realization of perfect freedom instead. Write all your thoughts and feelings. Share these thoughts with Holy Spirit and write any guidance arising from the process.

2. Make a list of ten ways you recognize a resistance to giving complete freedom to yourself or any other. In form, we mainly choose to withhold freedom from another when we long to control them or change their behaviors. For instance, "I wish my mom would say or do this instead...," or "I wish my boss would think..." or "My spouse should do..." All of these are the resistance to accepting and giving perfect freedom to ourselves and these seeming others. On your list, next to the ways you've now identified, ask Holy Spirit to show you why you seek to withhold this freedom. What do you feel that you are temporarily gaining from this choice? Finally, ask Spirit to lead you through the healing of this choice.

3. Love in Process can be experienced in four steps:

1. Accept and Offer Forgiveness.
2. Accept and Offer Freedom.
3. Be Still in Mind
4. Be Gentle.

How can these steps of recognition be practiced within your life experience? Explore with Spirit. If you would like, choose one or two individuals in your life and ask Spirit to lead you through the practice of each of these steps through your relationship with them.

Affirmations:

Love can never leave my side.

All are equally deserving of freedom and love.

Only my resistance keeps me from seeing the Truth within all.

I give freedom to all for all. Nothing can contain my True freedom.

I am as God Created Me.

Week Forty-Six:

Acceptance Beyond Distraction

Dearest Holy Spirit, I have to admit that I notice how I'm not dedicated to practicing all the wisdom you bestow upon me. I easily resist and get wrapped up in the "daily tasks" of living. Help me understand why I'd rather put you on hold and ignore my thought-release process . . .

First of all, do not be so hard on yourself. Guilt is never purposeful in healing. Second, yes, the world does offer many distractions. In fact, the world was made to be a distraction and to be adhered to with such vigilance. Within this paradigm the mind more easily perceives itself to be separate.

The individual self you acknowledge is not alone the maker of the world, but this self does play out the thoughts the world has held so dear. When I ask you to recognize the thoughts that hinder you, these are not thoughts from You as a person. However, these thoughts are the mistaken identity's beliefs from which personalized thoughts are gathered. It is essential to recognize this. Because if not, you will begin to identify with guilt or think the world must be rearranged from an individualized mind. If this were the truth, then it would mean that healing would be solely dependent on a limited self as its savior. Truth is not in or of yourself. It is not found in limitation. Truth is beyond all images.

The entirety of Holiness (which is One) awakens in unison. There is no identity awakening to her truer identified Self and then waiting for her other like-minded companions to finally "get it" too. There is no one else awakening from an individualized lower self to an individualized Higher Self. This is an error in thinking that for many has resulted in a seeming "spiritual debate." The idea of Higher Selves within multiplicity is an oxymoron. This belief does not align because no aspect of division remains eternally true.

Too often, the thinking mind has used its passion for analysis as a separation device. Even within your process of awakening, you seek out reasons to separate yourself through concepts that seem to contradict with all you already accept in thought.

There is only One identity seeking awakening, and this identity is the Holiness of God. This is all. If you feel distracted by names or roles used throughout our communications, realize that the use of these seemingly separated identities is for learning purposes only.

Even the personality of Jeshua?

Yes, even him. Truly, in wholeness the Holiness You are in God has accepted Self beyond all personas. There is no identity within the Holiness of God that knows its Self as different from the all or unequal to another. There is only the Holiness of God. Jesus himself knew and accepted this truth. His entire life's purpose was to show himself to be beyond his body's limitations. In fact, most of the assumptions and stories currently taught about Jesus are not the historical reality of the man Jeshua. The Jesus you relate to in religious tradition can be seen as a mere symbol.

Whoa! Right there. You are stepping into dangerous territory here. I am concerned.

Do not worry Beloved. You are always safe. Truly these statements are not as abhorrent as you may think. Seek to see what I say now beyond your own fears and judgments. Truly, fears and judgments will never, ever, bring you peace. Take a deep breath and center your mind beyond these judgments and fears now.

Okay. I'm ready now. I'm willing to be open and listen.

Good. Remember, I am never hear to instill fear. I am here to teach only love. I teach only the Love you are in Truth. This is always beyond fears and judgments. In fact, it is beyond every idea that your thinking mind can clearly comprehend. Therefore, seek not to solve or organize my teachings with your conceptual mind. It will not work. Trust in my Love to guide you. It will not steer you wrong. Feel the peace that I offer. This peace shall be the sign of the Truth I teach. Fear can never represent itself in peace. Remember this, and you will come to recognize your Self more clearly beyond every judgment of your thinking mind.

Now, we continue. The symbol of Jesus is extremely purposeful to your growth. See this symbol as a guiding Light. Do not concern yourself as much with personality as with purpose. Truly, even the man once known as Jeshua, does not see his current state of Being as limited by personality, identity or role play. He is truly beyond all limitation. Likewise, all symbols of humanity are seen in eternity as being useful only for the healing purpose. All symbols and ideas can be used for this purpose. The most frequent of these are the images of the body that you have found purpose within.

Never will anything be taken from you. However, I can use all images and symbols for your awakening. The One you see as Jeshua has long stopped seeing himself as only Jeshua. In fact, he stopped seeing himself as only Jeshua even while seemingly playing out the experience of this self. However, all is allowed to be used for healing as appropriate for love's awareness. Therefore, in this honor for your freedom, you come to see Jeshua or Buddha or Krishna, or anyone whom you see as a purposeful guise for your awareness of Self. Each of these is a reflection of the very same Holiness You are. All are Love in Truth.

All that you identify with here as names, bodies, careers, material substances, families, and personalities will be released upon True Acceptance. However, this is nothing to fear, for these roles and identities have served exactly as needed within your initial wishes for distraction. You are Limitless. Therefore, as you expand your awareness of this Truth, only more is gained rather than restricted.

Only the forgetting mind believes it can lose. Therefore, imagine, if you will, a love so intense that within it all you gaze upon becomes the very same love for your dearest mother, father, spouse, friends, and sisters and brothers. Yet, not only this love is felt. Truly, this relational love is enhanced and multiplied by billions and millions of billions. Yes, heavenly awareness is that grand! If you encounter fear within your hearing of this Truth, use it to notice where you still cling to ideas of loss. Truly, beloved, there is no loss, only enhancement and a wonderful growth of full Being. I cannot be more clear in words.

It is impossible to draw an accurate comparison between the world of perception and the complete Being of God. If you seek merely to figure out an experience of God-Being, you are not simply being. Instead, you only enter distraction through mind games. It is not purposeful to puzzle yourself. Doing so is only to make your thinking mind the guide. Release all embattling puzzles, and you find your peace.

Now let us review the aspects of your day that you determine to be distracting. Can you use these moments as a tool for expressing Truth? Can you use your thoughts as a device for learning? Can you extend Love where you notice distraction, both to yourself and all you seemingly encounter? Distraction is merely a calling to separation. You need not follow it. However, if you do hear the call, seek to return with a call of love rather than devotion. To do this is to use all time perceived here well. Do not resist or judge the moments. Do not identify with them or make them your master. This resistance or judgment will only lead to further analysis and distraction. Instead, allow yourself to settle within peace as every moment comes to notice. And if you do not notice every moment, that is more than acceptable.

Remember, I speak about being gentle with your self. There has never been a moment when I have judged or invoked "deadlines." Would that not be contradictory to everything I have witnessed to for you? If you see a deadline, it is only because you pretend one. For instance, if you think, "I must awaken in this lifetime," this is you identifying yourself through time and using it as your imprisonment. To see you in this manner is only to see with fear. Truly, what would then happen if you didn't awaken "in this lifetime"? How would you see yourself - in hell? Ha! Beloved, this is impossible. Truly, all regret, disappointment and frustration are only shadows investing in a belief in loss or need. For Me, loss and need are impossible because I already know you as whole! There is nothing to accomplish. Yes, you need to do nothing.

But, if I need do nothing, why do I need to watch my thoughts?

Watching your thoughts is not doing something. It is releasing all attachment. The mistaken identity believes that it must do something in order to be something. It only seeks to make up for what it does not already see in its Self. This is because it already identifies with separation and guilt. In fact, many of these "doings" became the practiced and conformed rituals that were often used in an attempt to gain God's favor. Hear Me well, you need to do nothing. Nothing to gain God's favor and nothing to be anything differing from you current Self. Watching your mind is only assisting you to awaken again to your Self. You are not changing in this process, you are only returning to that which has always been changeless. As you watch your mind, you are permitting the release of every thought.

If you look at history, religion, and culture, you will realize how these thought systems declared you needed to do many tasks to gain God's Love; and each task was always a gamble of trust or was never enough. Before, where you once sought appeasement through false beliefs, now you only seek acceptance of all that never changed. You can consider this noticing to be a peeling away of everything you thought you knew, rather than an acquiring of new thoughts.

In recognizing you need to do nothing, you are accepting your Self as already whole and complete. Additionally, you recognize that Who You Are is not within your authority to change and desires nothing for your completion. It is simply your recognition of Who You Are that is to be seen. In seeing with this Vision, all else that has never changed will stream in as a light once barred by heavy curtains.

In hearing your thoughts now, the inquiry appears to perpetuate, "Tell me how! How? How???!"

Relax, Dear One, and center once again within the peace you are, rather than the fear arising from your desire for concepts and analysis. Give this confusion to Me and accept that I take it fully for healing. Release yourself from all definitions and limitations. Your peace does not come from mental dissection. Release your thinking mind from such hindrances.

Take a deep breath. Feel it flow completely through you. Breathe again and now once more. And now allow yourself to sink within your stillness.

Do not take note of distraction; instead focus within the breath. Notice the joy that desires a route for expression now. Feel it slowly rise from within. Feel its twinkle and tickle coming through from a place that can bring only love. Breathe if you notice anything else, and simply allow yourself to be in this space of stillness. If a thought persists to be spoken, utter only within your mind, "I am as God Created Me," and rest here.

Stay focused within this moment for as long as you want, but at the very least until you feel your mind settled from all confusion to a space of rest. Do this centering in Truth as many times a day as you feel necessary, but accept that it is not a process or ritual you seek. The forms of rituals are merely your own attempts to affect comfort. Instead, allow yourself to release all thought in acceptance of true comfort, rather than use a process to designate a preferred result. Once again, I say, this is not about any form or effect, as that is all illusion. Content and Cause are our only dedication. Accept your Self through this settling of the mind, and you cannot but awaken to Truth.

I am with you through all you seek. Remember that in my eyes, you have never changed. Here there is nothing to accomplish and only peace to be known. This changeless Truth reflects through the entirety of each place, person or sight you perceive. Healing is yours within every moment, for truly it is the beingness beyond all moments. I love you.

My Light is Your Own . . .

Week Forty-Six: Prompts for Insight and Practice:

1. Have you ever had a fear of being left behind in the awakening process? Do you feel like you are awakening more slowly than any of your brothers or that any one of your brothers is awakening more slowly than you? Take a moment to reflect on these thoughts. Write down a list of anyone who you feel may be "progressing" or "regressing" apart from you. Afterwards, look at each of these names one at a time and say:

"In our Holiness we are One, and no image can be apart from this Truth. The Holiness of God heals as One, and in this is Love known. I am this Love with [insert name]."

Write any thoughts or feelings that surface through this exercise.

2. Holy Spirit guides, "Guilt is never purposeful in healing." So stop it. (Smile) Attempt this week to be mindful of all moments when you seek to make yourself feel guilty. Share all recognitions of these moments with Holy Spirit and ask him to guide you to healing.

3. Do you have any rituals you still align with? Remember, none of these is wrong and judge them not, but ask to use each as a tool for your awakening. Make a list of any ritual that you practice (e.g. candle-lighting, dedicated meditation time, certain words or prayers, religious rituals, setting up altars in form, etc.) and seek within to have each one's truer purpose be revealed to you. Write any thoughts or feelings that surface.

Meditative Practice:

Take a deep breath. Feel it flow completely through you. Again. Once more. And now allow yourself to sink within your stillness. Do not take note of distraction; instead focus within the breath. Notice the joy that desires a route for expression now. Feel it slowly rise from within. Feel its twinkle and tickle coming through from a place that can bring only love. Breathe if you notice anything else, and simply allow yourself to be in this space of stillness. If a thought persists to be spoken, utter only within your mind, "I am as God Created Me," and rest here. Stay focused within this moment for as long as you want, but at the very least until you feel your mind settled from all confusion to a space of rest. Do this centering in Truth as many times a day as you feel necessary, but accept that it is not a process or ritual you seek. Know I am with you here. I love you.

Affirmations:

Distractions do not speak for my desire.

I accept I am Love now.

My peace is not within my thinking. It simply is now.

I choose to connect with all, in all now. This is Love Being.

I am as God Created Me.

Week Forty-Seven: **A Story of Fear**

Closing my eyes, breathing deeply and quietly, I began the meditation. When my mind felt most at peace, words formed from within my mind asking to be spoken aloud, "I desire to know my Self as I am." As soon as these words left my lips, a feeling of tension spread across my chest. This tension was familiar to me; however, this time an image appeared with it. I saw a Roman centurion standing before me and it became obvious that this soldier was a symbol of fear. Fear, became his name. Fear was actually rather handsome (smile) and fully dressed in armor. I noted the details of his uniform, from the glimmering chest plate to the dark, leather waist pleats and the maroon-red, tasseled knee socks. He resembled many of the traditional centurions I had seen in classic Hollywood movies. He had a strong, chiseled jaw line and a sharp, pronounced nose. His brow line was also firm, revealing a brown, shortly-cropped head of curly hair beneath his helmet.

He looked at me with a curious look. "You want what?" he asked. I repeated my earlier answer: "I desire to know my Self as I am." I noticed a look of increasing inquisitiveness on his face, almost of a disbelieving nature, as if I had told him that I wanted to sprout wings and fly. This must have been a bizarre thing for him to hear, especially if he was made to protect me from the Truth. Next, I felt him say, "I don't know if I can let you do that." He then threateningly placed his hand towards his side, resting it upon the leather waist belt carrying his sword. In that moment, I felt myself tense up. Fear smiled smugly in return.

Watching these gestures, I was not confident. Did this mean that he wanted to challenge me to a fight? I did not want to fight. However, instead of meeting his defensive stance with tension or a defense of my own, I felt an inwardly guided prompt to breathe and focus within.

The inner guidance continued, almost in slow motion from both within and outside of my own cognitive awareness. I was being led to recognize how fighting was not a purposeful intention. Especially when dealing with Fear. Fear's point of view was always one of challenge. From what he understood, there always had to be a winner or loser. Instead, I asked Holy Spirit to help me focus my mind beyond the conflict of battle and into the awareness of acceptance.

Again, I felt the prompt to breathe and observe. After a moment, more words, quiet but firm, came from my inwardly guided desire. I was told to look Fear in the eyes: "I desire to know myself as I am, for this is Love."

The centurion laughed aloud. It was a boasting, mocking laugh, and although it seemed easy to feel defeated, Spirit stood by my side. Contemplatively, I wondered, how did Jeshua feel and behave when people laughed at him? How would he speak in return? Within me, I felt a confirmation that Jeshua would not have wavered. He would not have seen Fear's laughter as anything but Fear's faulty awareness of itself. For a third time, I took another breath, and then chose to look the centurion steadfastly in the eye. Continuing to look, I spoke directly to the depths of some potential connection within him. Please Spirit, I asked within, help me find the love here. Then, calmly wise, like before, the words came: "Tell him you love him and appreciate him for all he has done."

Immediately, so as not to have judgment interfere, I responded: "Listen, Fear, I love you. And I thank you for your service." He was silent.

I spoke again, feeling guided to share from the depths of my appreciation. I thought of all the times I've used fear to protect me. "I do appreciate everything you have ever protected me from; you have served well, and for this I am grateful. However, now I ask to move on." I could tell he was listening, as his once stern expression now softened. His eyes at this instant appeared to connect with mine. They reminded me of a young boy sheepishly listening to his mother's gentle reprimand.

"Yes, Fear, I do love you, but I am coming to know of my own Love for Truth. It is in this desire that I ask to know my Self as I am; I trust that I can do this without the need for further protection."

Suddenly, Fear's expression turned from one of passive listening to one of active anxiety. Worryingly, he burst out talking, informing me of all the things that he thought I did not know. He spoke of all he thought I had to fear if I was to take this journey without him. With wide eyes and exaggerated movements, he portrayed for me all the "monsters" he perceived himself to know. He told me stories of ungodly serpents and wild-eyed creatures. He expressed an indescribable certainty of all those forces standing by, anticipating my destruction.

Normally, upon hearing these reports, my chest would have heaved and tensed more with fear. However, single-minded for my peace, Spirit again prompted me to ask one simple question: "Fear, have you seen these creatures yourself?"

"Oh, no. No! No, I have been one of the lucky ones! But surely I have heard of the many that have been destroyed!" He spoke in an excited tone, "They lie just beyond the borders, and from what I have heard, from the moment you see them it is too late! Seeing these horrors will be the last sight you will ever see!"

He seemed to genuinely believe his warning. Then, our eyes met once more. Fear's were still wide with an expression of deep trepidation; however, I felt mine to be filled now with love, understanding, and connection. Our exchange reminded me of the adage, "Seek to understand before you require to be understood." In this moment, I was coming to understand Fear. I was coming to see him as a devoted servant, rather than my enemy.

Fear had true fervor to look after me. Indeed, it appeared that Fear *loved* me. The love I now saw within him was genuine and not an image of my mind.

Although a part of me recognized how this entire experience was playing out within my imagination, there was, sure enough, an intense awareness of reality. This reality was the love I saw within Fear, within my friend and misunderstood guardian. He wanted to safeguard me from all his position forced him to know. Fear himself did not even recognize what he was to protect me from; but, nonetheless, despite his own uncertainties he was willing to serve me unwaveringly. This I found rather touching. In fact, it brought a quiver of adoration to my lips and a sensation of tears to the corners of my eyes.

Now, in seeing Fear's vulnerable knowledge, I felt myself in bond with Fear. I saw his friendship, his kinship, his longing to help me. I could not resist or despise this. Clearly, instead, I could see that he (in his own way) only wanted the best for me. How could I not but love this? How could I not desire to embrace him as my brother? And so, this is simply what I did.

Embracing with a deep sense of connection, I felt Fear's arms around me. In our hug, I felt his sword drop from his belt. His posture softened. Fear then collapsed into my arms and cried. His tears were accompanied by deep sobs, and his chest heaved as he seemed to release all he had been suppressing for so long. All of Fear's own fears came flushing up. All of Fear's own pain, hurt and uncertainties flowed from deep within him to the surface and into the arms that clung to me.

We stood there, crying together. While Fear's tears unleashed deep sobs of release, my tears were loving tears of joy, renewing my acceptance of our shared pain. We intertwined in our mutual support and sharing for what seemed like a very long time. I did not know time at that moment because in that moment all of time stopped. And then the separation between us stopped as well. Although I recognized our strong, welcoming embrace, I temporarily was unsure who was comforting whom and where one of us ended while the other began. Together we were one loving instant.

Eventually, Fear's sobs calmed, and he began to breathe slowly and deeply himself. Our breath met in rhythm and our intimacy continued. Soon, I could feel a renewed strength coursing through both of us. Gratefulness flowed between our hearts, as if a bond had been forged between two long-lost friends. I could feel the small child within him, embracing me as one would a long-lost parent. Likewise, I felt myself appreciate Fear completely for all he was beyond his image. In this state, we relaxed from our hold, and now I saw that Fear no longer wore his centurion uniform. In fact, no soldier stood before me at all. Instead, in the place of my newfound friend Fear, stood Jeshua. He wore a profoundly connecting and loving smile upon his face and met my eyes with immense appreciation.

"You have done well, my Beloved. Thank you."

I felt our hearts speaking together through our gaze. We joined in the sharing of an immense, loving energy.

Jeshua spoke, "What have you learned here?"

Finally, in a flush of my own realization, I clearly saw Fear's purpose. Although he himself did not comprehend, his destiny was to lead me to my own awareness of Love's presence. And armed with this knowledge, I could finally awaken to the recognition that Fear had been my own mistakenly identified self all along.

Fear was never the enemy, nor was he ever anyone apart from me. In our embrace, we released all mistaken identities and revealed Truth. The mask of the centurion was a mask I once wore. It had revealed itself to be the plaything of an innocent child, a child now free and safe in the arms of Jeshua.

With this awareness, and still holding eye contact, Jeshua faded from my sight within an expansion of radiant light. My focus returned to my being within the living room of the cabin where I was residing temporarily. Although one might say this journey was simply one of imagination and inspiration, within me I felt the journey itself was that deeper connection to reality I had been long seeking. Once again, I took a deep breath, said a prayer for gratitude, and sat in the quiet morning light, recognizing that Jeshua and my Holiness still stood here with me. Finally, I felt genuinely free. To this awareness I simply said, "Amen."

Week Forty-Seven: Prompts for Insight:

1. Is it truly possible to learn to accept our fears as friends rather than foes? Holy Spirit teaches us that in our acceptance we heal. Essentially, each fear or destructive emotion has been "hired" by us for the purpose we intend. We are always the one who accepts or utilizes its services. Identify five of your fears. Can this fear really keep you safe? How have you utilized fear's services? How can you cancel your subscription?

2. How do your fears keep you enslaved to suffering? Identify the ways fear affects your thoughts, choices, feelings, relationships and body. How do these effects keep you imprisoned in the past or attempt to plan for an uncertain future? How do they idolize vulnerability or suffering over strength and love? Write your thoughts and seek Spirit's guidance.

3. Write down a list of all you have given to fear. Write down a list of what you would like to take back.

4. Write down a short sentence describing your fears. Now, look at each fear, surround it with thoughts of appreciation for its service. As an attempted protector fear has served you well. Now, choose to set it and yourself free. Focus on each one, as if you were speaking to your own Centurion. Focus and say lovingly, "Listen, Fear, I love you. I thank you for your service and appreciate everything you have ever protected me from. You have served well, and for this I am grateful. However, now I choose to move on. I trust my freedom." Write your thoughts from this experience and seek Spirit's guidance.

5. Make a greeting card for Fear. Write a poem for him or her that expresses your appreciation for all he or she has sought to protect you from. Add decorations to this greeting card, like you were giving it to your most appreciated friend. Share with him or her all the thoughts that are on your mind. Remember, Fear has been

created as your protector, only he or she does not know that your threats are unreal. Therefore, send Fear your appreciation for all he or she has attempted to do in the name of its own idea of love. Seek to embrace Fear for all he or she has done and then offer him or her peace. This is an invitation to your own re-birthday.

Practice:
Make a collage of fear. Collect images, photos and/or symbols representing fears. Make sure to include some of your own fears in this project. On a blank piece of cardboard, artistically cut and paste these images onto the board. Imagine yourself creating the most loving scrapbook in honor of these fears. Choose to celebrate the service of these fears or write it an obituary. Use many colorful images and decorations to surround these fears with love (e.g. glue images of flowers next to each fear or use colorful crayons, glitter and/or markers to decorate the area around your fears). Truly absorb yourself in the project. Honor these fears with love and creativity. Create scenes that may encourage laughter or new perspectives. Choose fears that are less intense to your personal experience, rather than traumatic, or work with a friend, sharing your collages together. At completion, write about your thoughts and feelings during the project as well as now.

Affirmations:
I choose to embrace fear with acceptance, love and freedom.
When fear is gone, love is present.
I am in charge of my fears, they do not imprison me.
I choose to expand myself beyond my fears.

Week Forty-Eight: **Method Acting**

Beloved Holy Spirit friend, there have been more frequent experiences of disturbing thoughts. They seem so pervasive and persistent! I do not understand why they come up. Please help me see through them, I give the purpose to you.

> Thank you Beloved One. Now remember to breathe, release, and rest. Allow your mind to rest in peace with Me. Never forget I am with you. These thoughts are your guide to release. They guide you in recognizing how you choose to see your Self. They speak for the false, and can be used so that you may awaken to what is True. They fuel the awareness of the forgetful mind.

However, Argh… they feel so frustrating. I have no reason to feel this way! To have such tension come to mind, as well as irritation, judgment, argument, and disturbance of my peace… well, it feels so distressing.

> Yes, you fight against yourself. Truly, as long as you fight, there can be no comfort there.

I feel like I want to run! But where can I run to? I am only running from myself, because the discomfort is within me… and while I want to run, I feel trapped.

> Yes, running from your Self has perpetuated the problem. In fact, this IS the problem. Each moment you turn a blind eye to knowing your Self, you run. In your confusion, you run. Exhaustively, you keep running, however now you think that you must keep up the pace, as if there is a journey to accomplish. This journey is imaginary. Not being able to be truly apart from Source, you extended this make-believe play. Likewise, you have provided all the scenery and characters to support this dream, as well as the script. The script reads out the thoughts you hear now. This script guides you to the concerns of the struggling-self.

Are you familiar with "method acting"? In this, the actor completely immerses himself or herself in the role they play. They take on the role as if it is their self. Here they begin to think like, act like, and coincidentally feel like the character. This in turn is what the Holiness of God has done to portray the struggling-self in this experience.

Now, can you notice yourself when you are thinking like the struggling-self character? Can you notice when you represent what he or she would do or feel? Notice these characterizations and allow yourself to observe the role rather than identify with it. Recognize the character's wishes within and ask yourself if this is the script you wish to perform.

Truly, only the struggling-self character can feel rejected. Only this character you play can feel argumentative and only he or she gives a reality to his or her vulnerability. Only the character you play can feel without hope for a successful future or cling to need. So, too, can only your character have flaws, failings and desires wayward from its Self as God Created. See this and you see into your character's motivation. See into your character and see into your judgments, fears, beliefs, and perceptions of limitation.

Seeing into this is a gift. Yes, your fears and judgments are a gift. Remember, the call for love here. It is impossible to call for anything you deny. Therefore, in calling for love, you recall that Love is your Source and desire. Here, seeing into fear or judgment is a gift, for you come to reacquaint yourself with the Self it cries out to. Become more aware of how these states of thinking are not you. Likewise, as you experience them, you can see further than all the prison bars the struggling-self erects.

Recognizing the disturbances of your thinking mind will increase as you call healing to your consciousness. No, this is not done to torture. God never desires to torture you, so never think that you can be "punished" for the tiny mad idea. Punishment never is from Truth, yet it is just another attempt of the shadow of illusion to play out separation and guilt. Actually, if you do notice, ever since your entrance into this conscious journey, you have increased the number of moments where you know a more palpable peace. Before you chose to see beyond the dream, most of these disturbing feelings or thoughts were suppressed or considered to be "the truth." In this perception, the judgments did not feel disconcerting because you were mindlessly playing your character without resistance. Now, in opening up to my guidance, you begin to resist your script. Now, truly, the seeming "director" believes he must speak louder and this alone is the persistence of disturbance you notice. Again, in method acting, the actor does what feels most comfortable to him or her, as if they literally embodied the character.

See now how God's Holiness has chosen temporarily to embody a character, and nothing more. You literally are method acting. Yet, you have aligned with your character so much that you actually perceive it, and all the scenery, scripts, and company - to be real. Surely, as you begin to awaken more, the persistency of these thoughts will dissipate, because you will distance yourself more and more from them. Yet now, you can hear the director more emphatically scream out your lines simply because you are beginning to forget them.

That is why I say the recognition of these disturbing thoughts and feelings are a gift, for no longer do you unconsciously play your part and consider these experiences reality. Now, peace is the greater call. Here, the Self within that knows it acts is beginning to remember. Therefore, when it hears the call of judgment, anger or fear, it does not mindlessly coalesce, nor does it like it. As you recognize these disturbing thoughts or feelings as apart from you, you are agreeing that you are not these suggestions. In these early steps to awakening, you are coming to know the Truth of You, and are shedding the shadows that once defined your stage. Celebrate that you choose not to sleep to these beliefs anymore! You can relish in this joy rather than run from these shadows.

Remember this: the mistaken identity desires to keep you separate. This supports the role it plays! Oddly enough, even as you seem to despise separation, it is what your character wants. The mistaken identity is that perverse and confused! Therefore, in this experience of rejection and feeling lesser valued than others, you are receiving exactly what you wish to know. I understand that it does not seem that way to you, but if you were aware of your pretenses, like Me, you would enjoy this full freedom given you to choose your self-awareness.

Free yourself from your beliefs and free yourself from the role you play. Hence, the experience of separation no longer becomes your method. In fact, I would like you to look up the word "method" as we usually do. You will be surprised.

Method: circa.1541, from: *methode* or *methodus* "way of teaching or going," originally "pursuit, following after," from *meta-* "after" (see meta-) + hodos "a traveling, way."

In these methods you attempt to separate further from your Self. The method you undertake follows from the initial belief in separation. Again, here you try to teach yourself what you are, and follow through in the portrayal of this self-awareness. In other words, you cannot invest in the script without the belief in the play. See this and you will see that all ideas of fear are merely just "following after" the belief in guilt (separation from God). In fact, these thoughts pursue and support the struggling-self you perceive yourself to be.

They merely support your own attempts to travel away from your Self. Observe how when you listen to these thoughts, you choose to travel away from all that God Created. Surely you really cannot travel away from God, but you do attempt to in these imaginings, and in this fantasy you struggle (investing in an ill will) just so that you may not know the love you are.

Yes, I have been having quite a few thoughts about feeling rejected lately. However, I have also noticed how I cling to thoughts of rejection, thus rejecting myself at least as equally.

Yes, that was an important realization recently. It may not be so much that others are separating from you as you are separating from others. Try to look within at all the areas where you run and feel the need to hide. The mistaken identity does desire to see itself as a victim, but also desires to see itself as separate. In its need to be separate, it does not want to see this as its own choice. If separation were its own choice, how could it deny responsibility? Therefore, the mistaken identity has adopted ways of deceiving itself. The practice of projection has become that key to self-denial. It denies all that it chooses to do and makes its self a victim rather than a willing participant. In fact, it will go to the most amazing lengths of distortion to prolong all ideas of blame. Therefore, as its call to be denied is answered, it can blame and then feel rejected. Now, it has justified proof of its victimization and all it has perceived within. The script is then read, "See! I am unloved. God has abandoned me!" Nevertheless, truly, these lines can only be said after the character has agreed to be so portrayed.

Only your character chooses to know itself as alone, and never the True Self. Your True Self cannot identify with loneliness, for it knows only Truth. Therefore, see this, if you perceive rejection. Be aware of how only the character you portray makes herself attentive to this condition. Only the character you play gives this condition purpose. Your True Self, if asked, would immediately say, "Alone???! HA!!! Surely not! Truly impossible!!! I am as God Created and that is always whole." It is only through your method acting that you can play the swine you perceive yourself to be. Truly, all roles are equally ludicrous.

Follow yourself not from a belief in darkness to a perception of darkness and likewise an experience of darkness. This simply is not you. You are as God Created you, and as you come to realize this Truth, you step beyond any characterization with something "else." Look at why you fear being loved and where you perceive yourself to be unloved, if you truly desire to look deeper into this situation. Here you see all that you place forth and all that likewise keeps you perceiving. That is why I say awareness of your disturbing feelings or thoughts is a gift to you. Looking more deeply into these will allow you to be set free.

Always remember to breathe, release, and rest when discomfort arises, but keep your mind open to my guidance. Choose to see another way beyond the judgments you perceive. Choose to recognize that you do not desire to play this role anymore. However, do not deny the role you have played thus far. See it, honor it, and set yourself free from it. Fully recognize that this role is no longer your choice and henceforth no longer you. Become reacquainted with your true desire and do not berate yourself for feeling or seeing these thoughts. Be at peace, for even Jeshua walked within the desert. Truly, every seeming body who chooses to awaken must take this walk through these dunes, for that is only how you can remember to see beyond them.

As you choose to see your Self through this journey, you do set yourself free. Be not the character. Be not the role. Be only the One who knows he or she acts and is at peace with the roles he or she can play. As you do this, you become joyous for all you experience, seeing clearly that these dreams are not you, but merely a fanciful and innocent portrayal. See the constancy of All You Are, and in this, know that your character will soon celebrate at the applause received as she or he takes their final bow. You are not alone in your healing, and your awareness of this gives you gifts greater than you can ever imagine. Simply look at these fears. Look at them, and recognize in Truth the light you are beyond them. Recognize that your disturbing thoughts and feelings do not speak for you anymore. Celebrate as you realize how you can choose not to respond to them.

As you notice a disturbing thought or feeling, first, allow yourself to breathe. Next, notice what this thought or feeling is saying. What line of the script is it shouting at you? What is its plot and what character has it agreed to play? If it is the character of "unloved Child of God" notice this and see within where you choose to feel unloved. Likewise see where you fear to be loved and how you then (in agreement with this role) consciously desire to push people away. Notice how each characterization has become a cycle of projection and perception; then ask if this is truly Who you desire to be. If no, be thankful for becoming more aware of what you have chosen before and simply take a bow to it.

Here, you recognize all that you once believed, not in denial and not in analysis, but simply in recognition of the freedom for which God has endlessly extended. Breathe again and choose to not be this role anymore. Here, you graciously say thank you…but, no thank you. Here, you celebrate for all you are beyond the role you have played. Now, after you have released, rest, and know I am with you. Look for Me within the audience and hear my applause. See the joy I extend in enjoying the performance. I am a patron of the art of God. This show is nothing compared to the Truth you are. This shadow of disturbance is nothing in comparison to the Light I know You to be. Truly, nothing can compare. See into this Light with Me and be grateful for the awareness you gain. Know, as you choose to set yourself free, this gift of awareness is greater than anything in your world. Therefore, celebrate for these moments, as they all are precious gifts given only in joy for remembrance. I stand with you in this journey to remembering the wholeness that You are. Remember my Light is Your own. The glory of God is your Self. I love you.

Week Forty-Eight: Prompts for Insight and Practice:

Review the following Character Roles. Now, for each one, reflect on and write down your responses to the following prompts for insight:

If you were to play this role, how do you expect that this character might think or feel?

Identify the ways the character may play this role. What words, behaviors or interactions would this character do when playing the role? How would he or she act it out?

How *have* you played this role in your life? In what ways has this character role served you? Be honest. Is there any way this role has excused you from living your Truth? How has its script protected or benefited you? Finally, in what ways has this character role hurt you or increased life's struggle?

Identify one or two ways you would like to stop playing this role in your life.

Unloved and / or unsupported by others
Powerless and / or out of control
Stressed
Disappointed in yourself or others
Attacked (includes physical, emotional, verbal, etc.)
Unworthy
Angry or critical
Childish
Jealous of other's life experiences, relationships, etc.
Financially poor or in need
Unappreciated by self or others

Continue to identify other roles you play. Complete this exercise for as many disturbing thoughts or feelings that you can identify. Make sure to recognize all the thoughts and feelings used to play out these roles in your life experience. How are these roles helping or hurting you? Would you like to stop portraying these roles? How? Write down all your thoughts and feelings, then offer them to Holy Spirit for His further guidance.

Affirmations:

My True Self does not act.

I am beyond the roles I play.

I am Loved, Loving and Loveable.

It is impossible to deny my Self in Truth.

Week Forty-Nine:

Crystal Clear Forgiveness

Dearest Holy Spirit, please teach me about forgiveness. Sometimes I feel as though I have a limited understanding of forgiveness, as if there were something that I need to do or think in order to make it happen the "right" way. I open myself to your teaching. Thank you.

Dear One, the practice of forgiveness will not result in the fixing of the world or other's behaviors. You depend too much on this occurring. With these expectations unmet, disappointment then becomes a major obstruction to your peace. There is nothing within the world that can satisfy the mistaken identity or give it peace. Forgiveness is about acceptance of Self beyond appearances. It can only allow you to feel the peace existing on the level of True Being. To think "Now that I have forgiven ___ for ___, they or I will ___," is only keeping you dependent. Likewise it restricts you to the idea of separation and therefore is not true forgiveness. Forgiveness that is dependent is not genuine. Neither is it abiding in peace.

When you choose to forgive with an idea of guilt in mind, you are making yourself dependent. With this practice, you give life to the situation over your True Self. Here you see yourself as limited and vulnerable, thus begging for the world and others to make or break you. Consequently, living becomes a constant search outside of yourself for peace. Beloved One, what peace can be found within when you are repeatedly looking to others to meet your needs or expectations? Is it realistic that he or she will change his or her behavior to provide you with happiness? Furthermore, even if this is temporarily accomplished, what then for the next moment and the moment after that? Can you see how this is an unending chase and impossible dream? If you place forgiveness into a world of requirement, you are apt to think that peace is found through requirement. This false opinion has you believe that all the solutions you seek can be found only by reacting to the problem, rather than seeing beyond it. Do you really think that God's

Holiness could function this way and still be God's Holiness? Surely not.

No one truly needs forgiveness. Your True Self is not restricted. Therefore, your motivation for forgiveness should not be merely to see results within the world. Forgiveness is a gift of Self acceptance to yourself alone. It is seeing You and all as Truth. This alone is its purpose. Forgive and feel a renewed experience of your Self. Forgive and see the world with refreshed eyes. Forgive and allow the Vision of Love to shine through the restrictions of fear. Here, your peace rests simply within your own realization of the Holiness you are.

True forgiveness is aligning with Oneness, accepting that there is no limitation, vulnerability or injury possible because there is only ONE in Truth. This does not mean that you willingly permit anything to happen in your experience with others. However, it does mean that you choose not to let experience rule over you. Wisdom and guidance for the appropriate response arises best when the thinking or judging mind is calm. This will be the key to realizing where your power and true strength of purpose reside. In calmness, the choice of peace for yourself through your Self will emerge beyond all shadows of appearance. I recognize how this may appear difficult to the self- struggling mind. Worry not, for there is no deadline or expectation presented. Trust will always lead you, and peace is always with you. This is true no matter what time or circumstance present.

All relationships of form mirror duality, and it is essential that you remind yourself of this. To be One in Truth is to be whole, complete, and fully free. This Oneness steps beyond the subject and object belief. For as long as you still have subject and object, you have duality and the possibility of limitation or destruction. However, there is nothing wrong with participating in this experience. All experience can be used for the purpose of healing. I do not judge.

Indeed you can use each opportunity for the Holy Instant. The goal of the Holy Relationship is to join beyond all separation devices and awaken to Oneness. In this, an ancient hatred becomes a present love. That is why a Holy Relationship is a forgiving relationship, because within this relationship all is brought to the light of True Seeing. Here you are not two living as one, but ONE being ONE. Notice the difference?

Yes, I do. You are saying that true forgiveness releases me from any idea that change needs to occur on the level of form. I am stepping beyond any idea of expecting to see results in a perceived "other." I am only choosing forgiveness for my own awareness of peace and acceptance.

Yes, exactly. Forgiveness is the choice to open yourself up to love and see only that. Forgiveness is not merely extended to the body of another or the circumstance, but forgiveness is extended as only love can be in Truth. This opening to the Truth of Love also allows you to see that compromise is not your final goal. The mistaken identity accepts only compromises where it can still win. These compromises will only bring more dreams that warp and fade away to emptiness. This continual dreaming is not your goal.

Your goal is to release yourself from EVERY obstacle that appears before you, that is EVERY obstacle to your Peace. Of course, be gentle with yourself, as strain or struggle will only bring judgment. Added stress is not my desire for you.

Yes, but tell me how all tension comes from my choosing. I seem to have a slight barrier in accepting that.

All barriers occur because you seek to see only within the world. You seek for completion in a place where every witness has been made to testify for limitation. Personally you do not call every act into the world. This would require much structured and intended thought on the level of form. Truly, not one of you is that capable, even in a dream. However, what you have devised are ways to see all you wish to see.

Let Me explain further. Unconsciously your forgetting mind accepts a belief about itself as limited and vulnerable. It sees itself as having a will that needs. This dependency leads to the wish for experiencing these thoughts within a world. Part of the mind seeks this world simply for distraction from its internalized confusion. Without this confusion there would be no yearning to control the world or to seek more witnesses for the conflict. Therefore, you do not consciously intend: "I want a person to show up who will do ___ to me." You do not write the script movement by movement, but you do direct it. The mind who has forgotten says "I am incomplete." And voila! An image witnessing to incompletion appears before you in form. This image appears to relate directly to you; however, it only reflects the beliefs which emerge from the forgetting. Yet, do not say to yourself, "I asked for this," or "I see this as meaning I'm guilty, bad, misled, etc." Those thoughts are judgments and will serve you no purpose in your awakening. What will serve you well is to recognize the foundation of your judgment, rather than to align with it.

Recognizing the foundation of your judgment is important. In this process you may release and see where the responsibility for sight can set you free. Never would I want for you to feel more entrapped.

Responsibility for sight does not rest exclusively in the level of form, because form is not the center of purpose. The responsibility for sight spans thought, feeling and experience, both consciously and unconsciously. One will always fuel the other. Forgetting the one Truth is the foundation for all separation. Therefore, it is not a change of behavior we seek, but a freedom from all separate thoughts, feelings, and actions. I am asking you to see a freer mind.

Let's use an example from your recent experience. The argument you had with your family member was not a thought consciously called into experience by your evil-plotting conscious mind. It did not say, "I want to see my family member as this, and I want ____ to happen." However, the overall forgetting mind did say, to the expanse of all extended humanity, "I am powerless" and "I need others to love me." Then bam! An experience arises that plays out of this belief. In this play, the tool personally known as "you" is used. Therefore, it appears to be happening to you, or from you. Yet, truly your experiences are not pre-planned this distinctly. Thus it is not a specific form from an exact person that you call into being. All experiences are mere reminders of the beliefs valued within the forgetting mind.

Your freedom thrives from your realization of this out-sourcing, so to speak. When you recognize the internal thoughts which encourage this automatic process and simply choose again, you release the original belief. You are not personally responsible for the forgetting mind, but you are able to recognize its point of view. See through ideas of guilt, and all the forms will appear to remind you of this dependency on separation. See instead through the eyes of Truth, and all forms step aside as merely non-entities to the Truth of Who You Are.

The next time you feel that you would like to forgive, notice the result you expect to see in the outer world. Do not fight it, or attach yourself to it. Simply notice and accept your dependency upon this image and what it speaks for your own need. What does this wish reflect for you within? Are you feeling powerless? Are you feeling vulnerable? Are you seeing victimization? Are you seeing separation, loss, or guilt? First, accept these beliefs and forgive yourself for seeing yourself apart from Truth. Consider no moment except this one. Ask for the Light of Truth to shine upon your own beliefs and permit you to see this differently. This way you do not attempt to change the world, but ask only to be led to peace. You can choose to step beyond the labyrinth. Here, you are taking back your responsibility for sight, independent of anything the world may appear to play out for you.

Wow . . . that REALLY makes it crystal clear . . . thanks.

I ask you to see the peace within and reflect this peace to all circumstances or people. Thereby center yourself in Love and nothing else. This is what I mean by release for peace. Release yourself from every idea of limitation and sink into the Truth. Seek beyond image, or even thought, and release into All That Is.

Wow . . . that surely seems like a powerful experience . . .

It is the power that you are through your Father's Will for you. And it is beyond experience. To say "experience" is to place it within time and space. All You Are simply is. Accept this as it is and simply be. You are not thinking forgiveness here. Methodology is not the point. Truth is known by simply Being. Here there is no qualification or definition. There simply is Self.

That seems a little hard . . .

It seems hard only because you desire to qualify. It is the struggling-self that asks to qualify everything. Instead of this seeking to see or do in experience . . . breathe. Ahhhh… release for peace. Release for peace. Breathe . . . Release for peace. Release for peace. Now, extend Love to all you see. I am with you. Don't even concern yourself with typing, just be now. Forgiveness is this acceptance of rest. I love you.

Week Forty-Nine: Prompts for Insight and Practice:

1. Write down a list of five situations that you would like to forgive. Identify the people associated with these experiences. Next, review the situations and write a list of all the feelings and thoughts you accepted about your self through this experience. Review these feelings and say:

"This feeling tells me that I am ___, but in Truth I am loved, strong, innocent, whole, and free. I now release this feeling, all beliefs, and persons attached to it, for in Truth I am as God Created Me."

Now, take a quiet moment to feel yourself accept this Truth about your Self.

2. Think of one person in your life you would like to forgive. Complete the following:

a) Describe this person as if you were meeting him or her as a child. Describe all their positive traits. What do you notice about them first? What do you think they feel about themselves, their future, or life in general?
b) Describe how you see yourself in them. How do they remind you of yourself?
c) Describe a gift you would like to give them. Choose something that you know would bring them joy or healing. What would they say or do in accepting this gift?

3. Identify one person you would like to forgive. Write down a list of exactly all the ways you think they should be. Be very descriptive. If you could remake them into the perfect person, how would they think, feel, and behave? Now, examine your list. Is it possible for *you* to live up to such expectations? When and how have you? If someone approached you with this list about yourself, how would you feel? What would you do? Could you meet their expectations? How could you have peace instead?

4. Write down a list of five grievances. Write down how each grievance expresses itself within your thoughts, feelings, relationships, physical sensations and hopes for the future. How does this grievance help you? How does it hurt you? What are you gaining from this grievance right now? How will you gain from it tomorrow? How would you feel without this grievance? Write down all your thoughts and feelings. Offer each of these thoughts to Spirit and ask for guidance.

Affirmations:

I am as God Created Me.

Forgiveness always sets me free.

I accept my Self beyond appearances.

The Holiness of God has no grievances.

Week Fifty: **One Existence**

Listen. One Existence is all that You are. As you realize this, so too will you naturally extend this honor of Oneness to know peace and Truth. To be One Existence is to choose beyond all the images or delusions of separation. It is to accept your Self to be beyond all sights and sounds, rather than imagine something else.

That, right there, blows my mind! But how can I do this on a practical level? How do I see only one existence when it appears that the entire world witnesses to multiplicity?

Yes, I realize how you may think that it is difficult to see one existence beyond the images that your body's eyes display to you. But truly, the mind has made these distractions so that the witnesses for separation would stand forth clearly. The world was made to play out every imagining of multiplicity. The world IS the very inverse of everything You truly are. Do not ask the world you see to show you the Truth, nor witness to Truth's existence, because it cannot. The world you see was made as a disguise for Truth. This disguise is all you will find within your sight. Here you imagine All You Are can be withheld from you through the presence of substitute images. But must you settle within the world's images? Or does a deeper Beingness call to you beyond the recognition of these imaginings?

To be honest, I do desire a deeper purpose, but my mind floods with images of the things I love the most in the world. I particularly think of the beauty of nature. I feel confused to think that these images are nothing except distractions from the Truth.

Yes, the scenes of nature are some of the grander images the forgetting mind has made. However, how many times while exploring this most exclusive beauty have you found yourself straining, struggling, exhausting yourself, or possibly nearly drowning? How often have these images seemed to be just on the horizon, but essentially out of reach. Do you honestly feel that genuine beauty requires such effort? Do you honestly believe that there is likewise distance between God and His Holiness?

This is why, at most, these images reflect an echo of Truth. This echo is remembered from the grandeur you recall within You. Notice that not one of these glorious images is eternal. How can True grandeur fall short of eternity or require struggle? What purpose would an Eternal God have in requiring His Creations to be ruled by, or operate in, a temporal nature? Why would he put them at risk of injury or destruction? Truly, this would not serve any purpose if God's surety were reality. That is why these earthly effects are a mere fraction of what your real creations hold. Furthermore, they are incomparable to the grandeur God bestows.

The worldly treasures of mistaken identity reflect only that which is rooted in loss and vulnerable to time. The rainbow will fade, and appears only after a storm. The span and majesty of every mountain range can change at the earth's whim from volcano, earthquake, flood, or global warming. Yet, the wholeness of Your Self is permanent. It is changeless. The limitless, boundless, love extending light that YOU ARE is eternal and has not its better season or lesser degree. Seek not yourself in rainbows, Dear One. Chasing them is not your purpose. Yet, allow yourself to see and most honorably exist beyond them.

With the limited experience of words, I can but barely tell you the grandeur that You Are. Truly you are beyond words, as you are beyond every rainbow or mountain range. Imagine now within your mind's eye the combined magnificence of all the world's natural wonders and most joyous experiences. See each seemingly miraculous blessing of beauty and awe picturesquely displayed before you. Now, hear Me well: truly all of these pictures combined is nothing in comparison to your True Beingness as God Created. You are that magnificent! Therefore, do not seek your Self through limited mindscapes. They cannot even begin to accurately glorify all that God has extended in completeness to His Holiness. Rest your mind in this acceptance and rest yourself in peace.

Simply, all I ask is that you not descend into the oblivion of the illusion. Allow another way. In this allowance you do not cling to mere images. In this allowance you rest and breathe, stepping past your thinking. Ask with Me to see all that is beyond these distractions. No, you cannot do this practice alone, for it is not your thinking mind or your eyes that guide this reception. I know of your One Existence, so it is only I who can guide you wholly to it without distraction. At your invitation, I honor your desire to see more clearly.

Do not fear that you do not have the proper desire, for there is a beacon calling you to Truth, and it is not difficult to recognize. Govern your thinking not by the "where's" and "when's" for recognizing this calling. Your Truth is always known within you. Simply breathe and rest without expectation or question for what must be. Choose to spend your moments with God beyond the requirements of time or the demands of analysis. Allow and trust. Sink past any straining or inquiring of what is defined as right or wrong, purposeful or hopeful. Trust that all is as it is and simply rest here. I say that my Voice is found in stillness because the busying of the mind does not serve your purpose.

I've guided you to the words "simply being" because they clearly represent the wholeness that You are. These words lead to in-sight. In simply being, you are aligning with the Self's One Existence because that is literally what these words mean.

Simple / Simply: from Latin: *simplus* "single," variant of *simplex* "characterized by a single part," *sem-* "one, together" (*semper* "always," literally meaning "once for all;" "together;") + *plac-* "-fold." "mere, pure" is from notion of "devoid of duplicity."

Being: "Existence," from *be* + -ing. Old English. *beon, beom, bion* "be, exist, come to be, become," Sense in human being is from circa. 1751.

Here, you enter into the peace beyond all limitations and distractions. In simply being, you are accepting the Self God Created. This Self is the Truth of You beyond all assumed mistaken identities. If you choose to rest in the listening, all that is necessary is your willingness to be One Existence beyond anything else. In choosing this One Existence, you likewise accept that it is not the choice (proper or not) that makes or defines you. Instead, you simply rest and allow for what is wholly offered beyond your own thoughts.

This listening process welcomes and enables My guidance. It is meant to provide a deeper understanding of what your desire and thinking have made. Here, you are able to notice what it is you choose yourself to be. In being One Existence, you choose to step away from any wish for multiplicity. You begin to recognize how a divided value holds no strength. When I say the Strength of God is within you, I say this to assist your recognition that the strength of Who You Are IS God. God is One Existence. Here, as One, is His Will for your Being.

All of your thoughts are rooted in the mistaken ideologies you treasure about the identified self. Yes, all of your thoughts are limited ones, for they do not witness for the Truth of You at any moment. I understand how this statement can sound harsh, but it is a call for your own awakening. Notice with Me what your thoughts witness to. What is it that they request or define? Do they not ask solely for proof or conceptualization within the world? Do they not characterize everyone and everything? Do they not apply a value and justification to every situation? Do they not judge what is correct or what is harmful, who is to blame or what deserves condemnation?

Listen. As the mind perceives itself divided, it reigns in and through confusion. This confused mind will only extend further beliefs of confusion or call a witness to a mindset of limitation. It is impossible for this limited mindset to be your strength or your God unless you perceive yourself to be molded from weakness, uncertainty, and ineptitude. If you consider or act on these limited beliefs, you decide yourself to be weak, uncertain, and inept. Truly God is beyond any of this foolishness, as is the wholeness of You.

Look upon some of your thoughts now. See for what it is they witness. Notice. Each thought witnessing to a self that is not as whole as God Created is merely fear, and fear you are not.

Likewise, each thought desiring change, defense, protection or correction is not rooted in Truth. Truly, how would God in His extended completeness have use of these? Therefore, I say your thoughts are nothing.

Truly, why fix that which has no need of fixing? As long as you believe you are limited, you will believe in the need for correction. Extending the miracle is accepting the wholeness You are. Do this and exchange your limited perception for My witness. See complete clarity with Me. Here, you rest in One Existence.

This is why I say that your thoughts are nothing. Accept that your thoughts are nothing and step beyond the mere idea that they mean nothing. Thoughts only reflect the meaning applied. However, every thought also attempts to make temporal intellect rule over Mastery. Therefore, any thought telling you of your inadequacy perpetuates only the nothingness you call yourself. It is only from within this nothingness of self that you can judge or make further judgments or seek for more proof of your vulnerability.

Set your mind to noticing these beliefs, not so that they may be analyzed but so you can recognize their purposelessness for your awakening. If they speak not of Truth, and your desire is for Truth, they can each be noticed and set free without any attachment, analysis or defense. Here, you begin to recognize the bars that uphold the prison of your mind. Only these beliefs justify attack or correction, and they all emerge from a simple mistake in how you see your Self. Here, your thoughts say that you have needs. Here, your thoughts say that you are without. Here, your thoughts say that defense is necessary. Here, your thoughts say that death is inevitable. Here, your thoughts say that the nothingness is reality. But in Truth none of this is so.

Pay heed to your thoughts and choices to invest in insanity. If you believe your thoughts have a meaning that rules you, you give the mastery of God over to their delusions. Yet God is not the master of delusion. Therefore, note what God Himself Is and choose to know your Self through Him. As this Truth is desired, all useless and false thoughts will fade away like mists before the sun.

I use this imagery repeatedly because it emphasizes the lack of substance of your delusions. They are merely nothing, and the ease in which they disappear requires no effort.

Truth is effortless. Its grace and freedom are part of your very Being. If you appear to operate with a struggle, you are accepting the mind in confusion. In these moments, remind yourself that this struggle speaks not for your Self or for God. Then choose again to rest and trust. Here, your true desire will step forth and lead the way. As I am invited, I will guide you Home.

Concern yourself no more about the thought of thinking. This concern is another attempt at analysis over the practice of peace. Seek not who You are in clarified understanding, but choose to rest the mind from its stirrings. If you ask Me, "Who is the One Existence I desire to be?" then you do not know. This questioning is perfect for your release. It is a perfect place to begin the rest of your release. It expresses a desire to know beyond your thoughts. As you ask you open the door to recognition beyond forceful wishes. The You we seek to know is not found in mental processes. You are not found within your thinking mind. The Love you are is not what you think or do, no matter what! Therefore, I ask you to release all to Me in trust. Here, I stand with you as guide to the peace that I know is You. Here, I give you Truth in Being, rather than in symbols. Be still, breathe, and accept, for this Light is your own. I love you.

Week Fifty: Prompts for Insight and Practice:

"Listen. One Existence is all You are. As you realize this, so, too, will you naturally extend this honor of Oneness to know peace and Truth. To be One Existence is to choose beyond all images or delusions of separation."

Truly, this cannot be explained more perfectly. Now we begin to practice in Truth.

1. Write down a list of all you appreciate within yourself, others or the world. Purposefully overlook nothing. List any object, thought, person, place or experience (e.g., rainbows, friends or family, laughing children, sunsets on the ocean, Grand Canyon, hot cocoa, kittens, pets, smiles from strangers, etc.) Remember, *"Truth is effortless"*. Therefore, do not think too hard, but simply allow the list to flow from within you.

2. Next to each listed item, identify all the feelings associated with it.

3. Take two full minutes to completely steep yourself in this feeling of love and appreciation. Envision it radiating out from you, bathing the world around you with the light of gratitude.

4. Finally, inhale and exhale deeply and say:

"[name item] is incomparable to the grandeur God bestows. The limitless, boundless love extending light I am is eternal and has not a better season or a lesser degree. I am this One Existence. Thank you, Father, for my remembrance."

This exercise can also be done with all the negative thoughts you have. Use this exercise to guide you through the release of all. Remember to inhale and exhale deeply through the experience and to feel each emotion bathing the world around you. Here you feel the natural extension of All You Are.

Affirmations:

All thoughts are rooted in mistaken ideologies.

My Truth thrives beyond my thoughts. I release these now.

I am limitless, boundless love, extending light.

I am One Existence.

Truth is effortless.

I am as God Created Me.

Week Fifty-One: **Teach Only Love**

To be a disciple of God's Holiness[5] is to be a pupil of Love. That is the true symbolic definition. If you choose discipleship, you choose to emanate the qualities and lessons of the teacher with whom you align. You may consider Jeshua to be a disciple of God's Holiness, for it was through recognizing the Holiness of God as Self that he awakened beyond all illusions. All Spiritual Masters teach the same.

In Jeshua's example, he accepted himself beyond body form; he fully placed all attachment to the struggling-self behind him realizing the True Self. This was demonstrated through the statement "get thee behind Me Satan," which quite literally means, "I command all foolish ideas out of my mind, for they are not of Self." In this, he simply called attention to the Truth of Self and knew folly was not an appropriate guide.

This statement is not the statement of judgment that most people make it. It is not a statement of separation. In fact, it is a statement of unification and true guidance. It is only foolishness that divides. Only foolishness invests in the forgetting self's ideas. Jeshua says, "Step behind Me" because he desires to lead the way, not to separate. Just as a loving mother or father would step before their son, in guidance and protection, Jeshua steps before you and emanates the Truth of the Father. In his discipleship he sought to release all illusion and be a living example of Love in purpose. Now, through teaching you, he intends to show the way of Truth, rather than let deception or confusion lead. He would not ask you to lead yourself, because it is not possible for the uncertain to recognize certainty. Therefore, if you let Us, We will show you where you allow deception, foolishness, or confusion to lead the way.

Jeshua experienced My guidance when he decided all lessons of Love were to be fully accepted. In this discipleship, he literally stepped ahead out of the desert of temptation (barrenness of illusion) into the fullness of Light, Truth, and Love. It was from this moment Jeshua represented this to all and aligned him Self with the being of Holiness.

A skilled student-teacher is a dedicated apprentice. He or she chooses to pass on all the knowledge received from their own teacher. Through this devoted practice, they continue to flourish and learn. The disciple of God's Holiness always practices what he or she does learn. First this is done as a novice: unaware of how much he or she already does know, he or she does seek to listen and trust before they share. In turn, through his or her own Self-realization and practice, that which has previously been hidden becomes revealed. Now, he or she is ready to profess, as they have accepted the teacher within his or herself. Within Jeshua's example, first he was a disciple until he acknowledged the Holiness within; then, he exemplified a true disciple of Holiness. Likewise, in learning with Me, you become reacquainted with your Self until you realize you are Self. There is never a moment of division in Truth, and always the student and the teacher are facets of a brilliant Oneness beyond the thinking mind's concepts.

Keeping the above in mind, let us look at a truer way to define the word "discipline" as well as practice its purpose. Many have misunderstood this word, defining it through ideas of punishment rather than learning. Neither fear nor punishment has a place here. This kind of teaching is only valued by the struggling-self, is never purposeful, and is fully dependent upon all beliefs in separation.

Discipline quite literally has nothing to do with punishment or sacrifice, but everything to do with sharing and leading through love of the highest degree. In asking for you to discipline your minds, all I ask is for you to dedicate your awareness to truth in mind, and stay firm to this knowledge of Oneness despite all temptations. In this you allow your Self to teach you. Truly, it is that simple.

Now let us look at the idea of disciplining others. When a moment comes inviting you to give discipline, realize that it is only a call to teach. It is a call to be a gentle guide. In all your instruction you demonstrate the disciple with whom you align. A clear teacher always presents as he accepts. As you demonstrate, you reveal. Think of the revelation, or the radiating forth of the light You are.

Teach in this sense and all you exhibit to your brother is known first in your Self.

To the struggling-self, discipline is always a divvying out of fierce correction. You cannot have the purpose of correcting your brother without first seeing him or her as incomplete. Therefore, this sense of discipline is nothing short of a deluded idea of teaching. Its only purpose is to exemplify the ill will and inequality that the struggling-self sees as viable. This forgetting mindset believes it must further project separation, guilt and fear, for that is how it sees itself. Consequently, this is taught in all its lessons. Here is where the idea of punishment emerged. In truth, punishment can never teach, it can only witness for sin.

There was no idea of punishment before the idea of separation. This is because there was no identification with guilt or with sin, and therefore nothing requiring false correction. I say false correction because punishment is false correction. Punishment does not release any error, but instead emphasizes it. In punishment, error is perceived through judgment. Judgment then imposes more error simply because it does not offer love, but isolation instead. The result is a multiplication of error, implemented in confused attempts to teach. This is the linking of two wrongs attempting to make a right.

God never punishes. Love only reflects Love and likewise Perfect Freedom. All ideas of hell and fury reign only from a struggling-self attempting to control that which it judges as guilty, separate, and limited by time.

The Holiness of God teaches in a manner different from that of the struggling-self. This is not because it is different in substance but because it accepts its Self differently. The Holiness of God only teaches completion, because this is all it knows its Self to be. In being a disciple of this Holiness, you become a student of the Love whom you accept as the Self and all to be. Again, you teach as you accept. You give to all, all that which is to be known of your Self. Always, you demonstrate your desire to know through calling upon the witnessing eyes of another. If you demonstrate my guidance, this beholds your choice to allow the Teacher of Love to speak through you and reveal all that He knows as your Being.

If you choose to separate, judge, or relay guilt or fear, you use the struggling-self as your guide. Here you do not speak for God, Truth, or Love, yet instead you give forth only through the language of division, confusion, and distress. Essentially, this means you believe you are these. Remember, Dear One, you are changeless, no matter what you believe or pretend to be. Overall, all are innocent. Do not be so concerned with teachers of the world and what they teach. *None* of you, directing your experience through a body identity or seeking to demonstrate within the world, clearly know what you do because you know not Who You Are. This is not insult or condemnation. Simply it is redirection for a confused mind. Focus instead on remembering with Me beyond appearances, and rest your mind. In this teaching and learning, you will only come to know your Self beyond all wayward images.

I guide all my lessons with Love, for I know that is what You are. These lessons are not concepts that must be memorized by you. I do not teach concepts, but instead Being. Nor do I seek to force feed you anything, for I know that you need nothing. However, Love is always the communication I use to reawaken your awareness. All my lessons are songs of Truth geared towards the listening scale of the confused mind. In this learning, you hear and follow the harmony of remembrance. Likewise, then, your teaching becomes a song for all to appreciate as their own.

Thank you. What about disciplining children? How would I be able to discipline children if I were to not see any form of separation? How can I keep them safe and give them all they need without having any role of separate or advanced leader?

Beloved, see this, even with my Self; I do not see any separation between us. You may see Me as an advanced leader in comparison to your awareness. In this manner of sharing, we communicate like parent to child. However, never do I see myself as separate, better than or different from you. I ask you to choose this appreciation as you give to the children whom you are called to teach.

My lessons can be symbolized as gentle callings to the real Self which is You. The guidance and understanding that you bestow (upon those whom you see yourself as teaching) is the same if it is to represent the Love You are. This is the same with children. In asking how you can practically discipline or teach another, I give you thus:

1. Begin each moment by recognizing the innocence within yourself and your brother. Accept that you and they are complete. Every judgment and perception of need values fear and restraint over Love. You cannot clearly teach your brother as long as you judge him or her. If you believe that they need correction, you do not honor them but rather separate yourself from him or her. From this start, you cannot extend wholeness.

When you choose to teach, remember that you are not to teach from judgment or fear. True teaching always witnesses to innocence, completion, gentle love, and understanding. Even if it appears that this brother (of whatever physical age or gender) may be misbehaving or mistaken in his or her own self-awareness, see your brother's behavior as a call for Love, rather than a manifestation of fear.

2. Ask your Self simply what would Love do. Here you give the lesson to Me, rather than ask that it be accomplished from within a mindset limited to drastic states of erratic fears. Do not react, but respond with a Loving call. In this, you ask to represent Love first. In this asking, you give the ways of truth to Me. Now we accept how I remember for you, and guidance begins there.

3. Be open to receiving guidance. Trust that the most purposeful and loving plan is always given. Thus, My guidance will never deceive or confuse you. It arises out of a still mind, desiring to know beyond its current state of confusion. My guidance only offers a deeper awareness to you in speaking for the Love You are. In this moment you choose Love as your teaching and God's Holiness as your teacher.

In discipline (especially with children), this is the "I love you so much that I offer you another way" lesson. In this manner you express discipline by exemplifying a True discipleship of Holiness.

Trust in Me and I always guide you to the appropriate responses or words to say. Do not worry, I will not "let your children run the streets as wild animals." Truly, I understand the ways of your world and would never suggest a response which would be dangerous or impractical for your experiences. Likewise, in your True discipleship, you will come to know how to offer love in purpose as you accept, teach, and extend the Love you are.

4. Listen in gentle acceptance. I am not asking you here to merely listen to Me. If you desire to teach truly, My guidance will be accepted with trust. Most essentially, I am asking you to gently listen to your Brother. Once again, I emphasize that to be gentle is to be the remembrance of your "high nobility" as God's Holiness.

Always realize this when you listen to another. See how you are only listening to your Self, Holiness of God. In listening with recognition of your Brother, you do not judge, but instead pay attention to every call for Love. You hear the song they sing through every belief and choose only the clearest notes as your chorus.

Eagerly listening to your Brother is essential for all Holy relationships, for here, you bestow equality and oneness into a mind perceiving itself as two. It is with honor you see and with a desire for Love, you act. In your respect and honor for him or her, only Truth is, and therefore an acceptance of knowledge is regained.

Listening is best accomplished in silence and with a still mind. Speak not, but place your self completely within the words and connection of Love. Accept all that is real to be at hand, giving presence to the wholeness never lost, which includes Me. Breathe to keep yourself in balance, and dedicate yourself to your brother rather than your thoughts. Be aware if you notice a desire to suppress anger. If you feel angry, you align with judgment. Choose instead to instill peace in mind and release all else. Remind yourself of Love's presence, my Presence, and be once again at peace within.

Here, your discipleship to Truth begins:

Begin each moment by recognizing the innocence within yourself and your brother. Accept he or she is complete.
Ask your Self simply what Love would do.
Be open to receiving guidance.
Listen in gentle acceptance.

Now we go forth to Love all you see within the world as we would Love our Self, and so it is. Remember My guidance and practice it. Take each moment seen to listen to the glory of all You are and all that has never changed. Dear Disciple of Love, in your pursuit to teach only Love, you realize that Love is all You are. Teach with this gentle awareness and surely all you know shall be revealed. I love you.

Week Fifty-One: Prompts for Insight and Practice

1. Holy Spirit guides, "*To be a disciple of God's Holiness is to be a pupil of Love. That is the true symbolic definition. If you choose discipleship, you choose to emanate the qualities and lessons of the teacher with whom you align.*" Make a list of the qualities you most admire in your favorite worldly teachers, spiritual gurus or otherwise. Next, identify how they make you feel. Finally, write down why you want to pass each of these qualities on to others. Review these insights with Holy Spirit, seeking to reveal your true purpose for teaching.

2. "*The disciple of God's Holiness always teaches what he or she has learned.*" How do you think learning occurs? What do you seek to learn and why? In this one year's process of being with Spirit, what do you feel that you have learned? Write your thoughts and feelings. Share these thoughts with Holy Spirit and take note of all guidance arising.

3. Holy Spirit guides, "*God's Holiness only teaches completion, because this is all it knows its Self to be. In being a disciple of this Holiness, you become a student of the Love. Again, you teach as you accept.*" What do you desire to teach within your self and the world? What do you feel is the best manner to teach? Among people, what do you feel is the purpose of teaching? How do you seek to be taught in your own life as well as with others?

4. Write down a teaching plan. Identify one person or group whom you would like to teach. First, identify what and why you would like to teach. Seek out any judgments about this group or lesson and offer these for healing. Recognize that a true teacher cannot judge. Seek instead to know a desire for honest sharing and holy relationship. Write out a teaching plan following the guidance for true teaching outlined in this week's reading through Spirit.

Affirmations:

I am a Teacher of God and Disciple of God's Holiness.

God's Holiness only teaches completion.

Love listens rather than speaks.

In my desire to be a disciple, I discipline myself in Truth.

Week Fifty-Two: **You Are Love!**

Dearest Holy Spirit, help me to see the light within me now. What can I remember when I become so easily swept up by thoughts of discouragement?

Come to Me Beloved and know I am with you. We are inseparable beyond time and every idea you have about your self. I stand with you now, trusting in you to know your way. I Trust that you have listened well, for I have been with you every instant. There is never a moment where we do not communicate. As you realize all you desire, see how the light of Heaven shines from within You. We have danced this reverence together. Hand in hand, hip to hip. Your yielding grasp rests firmly in mine as I have wistfully led you across the ballroom of your dreams. In this, we are one. Do not listen to the hypnotic songs of forgetfulness again. Their lulling lyric sings not for the glory of You. Yet instead, know who You are in the Creation of All wonder and magnificence. You cannot disown your Self through dreams. You have only merely forgotten this Truth. Listen now to the call of remembrance and follow its melodious beckoning Home.

> *You are loved, you are loved, you are loved!*
> *You are loved, you are loved, you are loved!*
> *You are loved, you are loved, you are loved!*
> *You are LOVE!!*

When you find yourself seeking love outside your Self, recognize that, in this wish, you have accepted yourself as incomplete. In this wish, you seek only to depend upon shadows apart from Reality. Can you expect an illusion or dream vision to complete you? Why do you see yourself as incomplete and vulnerable? This world's ideas can never give you what you need, for even its definition of love is limiting and used as a toy. The Love You are in Truth is never in need of qualification, nor is it disposable. You are complete. You are perfect within the brilliant light of the Father. He is perfect within the Light of YOU. When you do not see this within you, remind yourself that you have simply forgotten. Remind yourself that in this amnesia there is nothing further from the Truth.

When you appear to be disappointed, depressed, lonely, or lost, you are only telling yourself that you are dependent. It is a temporary experience, limiting in every way. In this thought, you see yourself as needing an incomplete love. This type of requirement can only lead you to disappointment. You will never find True Love through proper words or actions within your mistakenly perceived world. These images are nothing but erroneous limits on the limitless. To qualify or disqualify love is only to erroneously see your Self as variable.

There is NO variance to Love's pure being.

Listen, Beloved, Love is as You are. Love is all ways eternal. Love is innocent and complete. It does not depend on or withhold anything! Love does not determine, judge, measure, or conceal. The Father's Love (which is the *ONLY* Love there is) simply IS and can never be but that. The struggling-self always feels a need to qualify, but that is only because it sees within a mist of confusion.

Any experience that is not complete, endlessly offering
and accepting without limit or need, is NOT love,
and is therefore not True.

Dear One, *NOTHING* unreal exists. Nothing unreal can overpower you or keep you from knowing your Self. Truly, how could a mere shadow gain power over the beloved Light of Pure Existence? Herein is the Peace of God. Dearest You *ARE* this peace! Every situation that you see with your struggling-self is not a true situation. Truth is all and can never be dependent on the thinking mind's activities. Therefore, do not try to figure your Self out with your thoughts. Surrender this struggle and accept Who You Are. Perfectly complete and whole in every way, Truth needs not to be qualified or interpreted. Truth is a witness to itself! Belief in love is distorted in the world. Worldly love is always rooted in dependency and keeps dreamers desiring more dreams. Therefore, we seek ourselves not in beliefs, but in revelation.

God extends Himself in completion through your beingness. You are His Friend. You are His Betrothed. You are His Child. He calls You by Your Name in Him with intimate awareness for all You are. He completely extends Himself into your full development. Therefore, in your True Beingness, there is nothing left to accomplish.

It is done. Those words were never meant to determine the end of a useless mission of death. Always they were meant to call You to Your Glory! With Me these dreams are done. Hear My words and welcome My guidance. Practice the remembrance of all You are. See once again with Clear Vision and be aware of your True Freedom.

Truly, Beloved, there is nothing missing. You are wholeness itself. Trust is your communication with the Voice for God, in whole recognition of All You Are. Your Father, even now as before, stands with You. As you breathe, feel His Presence. Release into His Awareness. Rest yourself in His sturdy arms of Truth. He can support even the weariest bodies. Your sweat-soaked brow or fatigued skeletal physique does not intimidate Him. I am always with you, be it through tears and perceived suffocation or a strenuous notion of pretend imprisonment. My strong hands support a beaten body, nurturing with tenderness its disillusionment. It is done beyond these dreamscapes.

Awaken! I call to you, gently, yet with an aware intensity and adoration within My Voice. I firmly state all that I know as a witness to Your eternal state. Listen now, since you have chosen to engage in this conversation.

You are loved, you are loved, you are loved!
You are loved, you are loved, you are loved!
You are loved, you are loved, you are loved!
You are LOVE!!

Feel my radiant smile of approval upon your unchanging grandeur! Know you need not any other validation of this message. This is a love note from Me, as part of Me. I adore you!! There can be no other choice.

God does not count your sins, for He knows them not. He cannot see any error for He knows only perfection. To believe in error is to believe in a state of being apart from God. To God, this is impossible. To your struggling-self, this exists only because you have forgotten. This forgetting does not make error real, it only makes it experiential. However, I have never forgotten. I am all that has never forgotten, and I am the witness for all you can remember beyond these imaginings. I see your mistaken wish to invite such suffering, but know your Truth without judgment. Therefore, I stand by you as you weep, catching every tear, and washing it through my hands. I will hold up your body with the very Strength of God Himself, caressing all I know You to be. To think that you are unworthy of my vigil is only to forget.

Granted, these are words you want to hear; but, they are also the truth. Therefore, do not feel that My Love is a mere projection (go back and re-read the part on quantifying and qualifying love – Real Love does not need that). My Love still witnesses True to all I know and adore.

You are loved, you are loved, you ARE loved!!

My light extends to All You Are. Feel my wings of comfort wrapping about you and know that my solid confidence in You can never be mistaken. God has sent sentries of angels to shine the Light of True Purpose all about you. You are never alone. Feel the radiance of All You Are palpitating over your heart center. Feel Me wrap you in my arms of parental love.

You are love, you are loved, you ARE loved!!

Do not fear to hear all you desire to know. Resist no more to simply be. You are perfect all ways. Beloved Child of Grace, I love you today as I have beyond all days, nights, and seasons. My love for You is the knowledge of wisdom when you feel most unsure. My power is your strength. I completely understand and never can I ever doubt you. Yes, never do I doubt or judge you. I only extend perfect freedom in the gratitude we delight in. Our sharing is the presence of peace. Your forgiveness gently heals all wounds. My answers are within you. They are my Truth. Feel my embrace. Feel my hand confidently guiding your own.

Your Holiness is beyond words. Your Holiness is beyond imaginings. Your Holiness is beyond everything your thinking mind conceives, dreams, and hopes. You are never lost. I never deny you. My Love is your Light. You are no image outside of the Image of God. Created from a Purity of Peace be it seen as love, joy, freedom, sanctity, wonder, happiness, creativity, or eternal brilliance. All of these words are merely symbols attempting to describe the truly indescribable. Our very existence is prayer. It is the affirmation of Our Father's Eternal Glory and Delight. Beyond words, intentions, and even desires, our Love reigns. Seek not another thought except for the Love that You are. This is the eternal stream of Love. It is your rapture. I speak to the wholeness within You, asking for it to remember its Self. I speak to You. Truly, there is nothing else, Dear One.

You are loved, you are loved, you ARE Love!!
Revelation rests here.

Blessings to you, My divine light within... rest on this.

Week Fifty-Two: Prompts for Insight and Practice:

This week Spirit has written a love letter to you. Take this week to read the letter several times; then write down the following responses:

1. Write down a response to God or Spirit: What have you always desired to write to God? What have you sought intimately within to know and hear? What do you desire to tell Spirit as you know him or her? This can be a love letter of gratitude, inquiry, or further expression for all you choose to see within yourself and the world. What do you appreciate from spending time this past year with Spirit? Trust that nothing can be wrong or judged in this communication. God is listening to you.

2. Choose to either write a response to the spiritual Self you have become more acquainted with this past year or write a letter to the identified self you are learning to release. What have you come to know in your own sharing with Spirit this year? How does this new awareness affect your spiritual Self or identified self? Visualize receiving a love letter from either of these awarenesses and write exactly how you feel it would read. Truly, there are no expectations in this exercise. It is only for your own further inner exploration. This is your love letter to all you see within and no matter what the words, it is perfect.

3. Write down a response to your child self: What would you like to tell your child self? What do you wish you could have known about yourself as a child? How would you like them to grow strong and be cared for? How would you like him or her to feel as they come to know their self within the world? Picture yourself now as a loving parent of your own child self. See him or her clearly within your mind and feel each word of guidance, joy, and tender support, flow through you. You are listening.

4. Write down a response to an unhealed relationship: Find the one, two, or more people you have not completely forgiven or set

free within your life experience. Do not harbor ill will (struggle) or focus on the perceived sins of the past. None of these shadows are you anymore. Instead, write them a letter of love and appreciation for all they are and all they may have taught you. We learn through all experiences, and every relationship has been called into our lives from our Self to our self. Truly, there are only blessings here.

Affirmations:

God's Love is My Light.

Loving my Self is the key to coming Home.

Our very existence is prayer. I am as God Created Me.

Revelation rests in the arms of Love.

I am never lost and can never be denied.

Epilogue

Now is a moment when we step from learning to practice. Here you have asked and listened, now you choose to be. I am with you as you do so. However, do accept that you can become nothing that is not already. I witness to this all ways. For the wholeness of Creation continues through all as one. Never believe that I have left your side. I cannot and will not forsake you.

Simply being, in application, will require an understanding of all the lessons for which we have spoken, and so I ask you to continuously review them. Yet this is only if you desire a practical experience. Remember, I have told you before, essentially there is no compromise between Truth and nothingness. Therefore, I guide you to first look within before expecting to see in the world. Before you seek to practice or share any of this experience within the world, be honest with your thoughts and ask for the best purpose to be exemplified. Ask, not from your own mind to your own mind, but ask for my guidance, "How does this sharing serve My purpose?" If the purpose is one of sharing light and joy, in the knowingness of Who You Are, then you have heard my guidance and do practice in abundance of this acceptance. However, recognize that there is no light that has not already been lit. If the purpose of your interactions is for conversion of your brothers or to convince yourself of your Truth, then you may want to take some quiet moments first. I will always lovingly guide in turn.

As you review, open your mind to accepting all the Truth Our Father has bestowed upon us. Allow this peace to flow through you. Bless all moments and let knowledge deeply instill within you its awareness of Truth beyond the recesses of your soul. Here you move from beliefs in limitations, where your mind accepts ideas of beginning and end, to the expansive radiance beyond all perceptions.

Again, I say, I am with you. As you go forth day by day, feel my presence, it is now. As you consider all you appear to experience, know I am with you. Remember, you cannot be wrong, nor can you fail. All is changeless within the Kingdom as God has Created. All that is at peace is You. Do not feel that you can place aside any Truth for a single moment more. Truth extends beyond your temporal moments and rests in wholeness without limitation.

If you seem to choose to put aside your healing, take note. Is this pause only for your own mind's analysis of what it believes out of fear or necessity? Even if this appears to be the case, do not worry that it can truly delay you. You can never be apart from Your Father, just as You cannot be apart from Me. If in dreams you seem to see, your True Vision rests with Me and I radiantly smile in gladness for all we know as One. Again, do not fear that you can be alone, for this is never the case. I embrace your presence in the knowing of my Own and am truly grateful for all we have embarked upon as one.

As you listen again to the words I have given you, and extend their unwavering peace unceasingly to all you encounter, feel my warm embrace. This is my greatest gift to all, and, as you extend it, we give only to ourselves.

Do not fear nor quit in confusion. The strength of God surrounds you, as it is You. Beyond a limited mind or wary mindset, You are. Beyond an unknown self and belief in death, You are. Beyond any experience of emptiness or frustration, You are. Beyond all that is of a mind uncertain, You are. Breathe, release, and rest with Me and in stillness the peaceful extension of Our One Existence reigns without possible boundary. Here you rest with Me. Here our light is our own. Here the love I extend to you is the only knowing for which God is. Now go forth, hand in hand as One and walk willingly into the Light of Our Being. Remind yourself of your True Self upon waking and retiring. See its Light surround you in every step and guide every thought. Witness my smile in the eyes of all you come across. Give from your heart to all and know you embrace Me as well. My love is all ways and always.

I love you.

Notes

1. Note from author: At this point in the conversation, Holy Spirit instructed me to read Ecclesiastes from the Bible. After my reading, Holy Spirit continued the conversation by commenting on the teaching from Ecclesiastes.

2. Author's note: I was guided to a better understanding of these symbols through historical research. Apparently, at a banquet in ancient Near Eastern culture, it was customary to anoint a person with fragrant oil. This practice was both a gift and an honor. The host recognized and honored the guest with this gesture of appreciation, while sharing the material richness of the household. Also, since people bathed seldom then, it was more pleasant to converse at close range with someone who was perfumed. Additionally, hosts were expected to protect their guests at all costs.

3. Author's note: I felt urged to research the word "merciful" through the thesaurus and found these synonyms: compassionate, kind, kindhearted, generous, forgiving, gracious and fortunate.

4. As scribed from *A Course in Miracles*, Text, chapter 18, p. 384 (second ed.)

5. This book uses terms such as "Holiness of God" or "God's Holiness". These terms can be interpreted as "Son of God", or to mean a Christ presence or energy. The author regards all of these terms as being one and the same and does not distinguish between the terms. The reader can choose to use whatever terms he or she feels most comfortable using for his or her own system of belief or personal comfort. Additionally, the term "Spirit" is interchangeably used with the term "Holy Spirit". Sometimes this incongruence occurs in the very same sentence. The author has allowed for this to occur purposefully so that the reader can infer whatever interpretation he or she does feel is most appropriate for his or her own Self realization. The author has no particular definition of Holy Spirit except for being

the reference to the most loving and highest expression of Truth within All. Indeed, no mere word can accurately describe or define the Truth of Who All Are.

6. The inspired writings within this book were taken from the author's personal journal. Each entry was initially directed specifically to the author and her own personal experiences. Obviously, due to this, not all information in this book will align or resonate with every reader's individual beliefs and world view. Likewise, the author is not representing herself as an expert, clergy or prophet. These writings are not to be viewed as gospel or infallible, they are a mere symbol of the guidance that Holy Spirit is able to provide to all when we choose to listen.

About *A Course in Miracles:*

This book contains material which is derived in part from material supplied by *A Course in Miracles* (the Course). In 1975, Dr. Helen Schucman, original scribe of this material, assigned copyright of the Course to the *Foundation for Inner Peace* (FIP). In 1996, FIP assigned the copyright and trademark to the Foundation for *A Course in Miracles* (FACIM). Within Simply Being: One Year with Spirit, all quotes from the Course remain owned by the Foundation for *A Course in Miracles*. Related publications from FIP that are mentioned in this book include two pamphlets authored by Helen Schucman – *Psychotherapy: Purpose, Process, and Practice* and *The Song of Prayer*.

The authorized three-in-one volume of *A Course in Miracles*, comprising the Text, Workbook, and Manual for Teachers, is available in both hardcover and soft cover English editions, with over one and a half million copies in circulation worldwide. A full array of translations is also available from the Foundation for Inner Peace and the Foundation for A Course in Miracles.

It is strongly recommended that seekers who wish to further study *A Course in Miracles* purchase the most recent edition available through many bookstores or direct from the publisher by contacting:

The Foundation for Inner Peace: online at *www.acim.org* or
The Foundation for *A Course in Miracles:* online at *www.facim.org.*

Foundation for *A Course in Miracles*
Dept. H
41397 Buecking Drive
Temecula, California 92590-5668 USA
(951) 296-6261

BOOKS

SOME RECENT O BOOKS

Punk Science
Inside the mind of God
Manjir Samanta-Laughton

Wow! Punk Science is an extraordinary journey from the microcosm of the atom to the macrocosm of the Universe and all stops in between. Manjir Samanta-Laughton's synthesis of cosmology and consciousness is sheer genius. It is elegant, simple and, as an added bonus, makes great reading. **Dr Bruce H. Lipton**, author of *The Biology of Belief*
1905047932 320pp **£12.95 $22.95**

Is There An Afterlife?
A comprehensive overview of the evidence, from east and west
David Fontana
2nd printing

An extensive, authoritative and detailed survey of the best of the evidence supporting survival after death. It will surely become a classic not only of parapsychology literature in general but also of survival literature in particular. **Universalist**
1903816904 496pp 230/153mm **£14.99 $24.95**

The Science of Oneness
A world view for the twenty-first century
Malcolm Hollick

A comprehensive and multi-faceted guide to the emerging world view. Malcolm Hollick brilliantly guides the reader intellectually and intuitively through the varied terrains of the sciences, psychology, philosophy and religion and builds up a vibrant picture that amounts to a new vision of reality for the 21st century. A veritable tour de force. **David Lorimer**, Programme Director, Scientific and Medical Network
1905047711 464pp 230/153mm **£14.99 $29.95**

The Thoughtful Guide to God
Making sense of the world's biggest idea
Howard Jones

The wide scope of this fusion of theology, philosophy and science makes this an important contribution to a study of the divine that is easily readable by the non-specialist. **Dr Verena Tschudin**, author of *Seeing the Invisible*
1905047703 400pp £19.99 $39.95

The Thoughtful Guide to Religion
Why it began, how it works, and where it's going
Ivor Morrish

This is a comprehensive and sympathetic approach to all religions of the world, including the lesser-known ones, sects, cults and ideologies. Broader than "comparative religion", it uses philosophy, psychology, anthropology and other disciplines to answer the key questions, and provides a holistic approach for anyone interested in religious or philosophical ideas.
190504769X 384pp £24.99 $24.95

The Thoughtful Guide to Science and Religion
Using science, experience and religion to discover your own destiny
Michael Meredith

This is a rich book that weaves science, experience and religion together with significant experiences from the author's own life. It ranges widely through the sciences and different religious traditions. A gem for the modern spiritual seeker. **Scientific and Medical Network Review**
1905047169 208pp £10.99 $19.95

Mysticism and Science
A call to reconciliation
S. Abhayananda

A lucid and inspiring contribution to the great philosophical task of our age - the marriage of the perennial gnosis with modern science. **Timothy Freke** author of *The Jesus Mysteries*
184694032X 144pp £9.99 $19.95

Back to the Truth
5,000 years of Advaita
Dennis Waite

A wonderful book. Encyclopedic in nature, and destined to become a classic. **James Braha**

Absolutely brilliant...an ease of writing with a water-tight argument outlining the great universal truths. This book will become a modern classic. A milestone in the history of Advaita. **Paula Marvelly**
1905047614 500pp **£19.95 $29.95**

The Fall
The evidence for a Golden Age, 6,000 years of insanity, and the dawning of a new era
Steve Taylor

Taylor provides us with the most overwhelming evidence of the existence of an Age of Perfection at the onset of human evolution, and of the fact that human spiritual, social and cultural evolution and history have been a process of degeneration. The Fall is one of the most notable works of the first years of our century, and I am convinced it will be one of the most important books of the whole century. **Elias Capriles** International Journal of Transpersonal Studies.

Important and fascinating, highly readable and enlightening. **Eckhart Tolle**
1905047207 352pp **£12.99 $24.95**

The Wave
A life-changing insight into the heart and mind of the cosmos
Jude Currivan
2nd printing

Rarely does a book as fine as The Wave come along - this is a true treasure trove of ancient and current learning, covering a wide variety of interests. Accessible, interesting, educational and inspiring. The reader will find that both the intellect and the heart are gratified with this book, and that on a deeper level, much of it feels right - and that may be the best kind of knowledge. **Merlian News**
1905047339 320pp **£11.99 $19.95**

The History of Now
A guide to higher yearnings
Andy Nathan

This is all about the spark of optimism that gets us out of bed in the morning, and the different ways it has flared to life during the time of humanity. A "who's who" of the world religions.
1903816289 160pp 250/153mm **£9.99**

Islam and the West
Robert van de Weyer

2nd printing

Argues that though in the sphere of economics and politics relationships between Islam and the West have often been hostile, in the area of ideas and philosophy the two have much in common, indeed are interdependent.

A military and financial jihad against global terrorism cannot be won. Bit a jihad for peace can, and will render the first jihad unnecessary.
1903816149 128pp **£6.99**

Trading Faith
Global religion in an age of rapid change
David Hart

Argues boldly that the metaphor of trading provides the most useful model for religious exchanges in a world of rapid change. It is the inspiring biography of an intensely spiritual man with a great sense of humour who has chosen an unusual and courageous religious path. **Dr Anna King**, Lecturer in Hinduism, University of Winchester
1905047967 260pp £10.99 $24.95

You Are the Light
Rediscovering the Eastern Jesus
John Martin Shajananda
2nd printing
Closed systems, structures and beliefs have prevailed over the last 2000 years, cutting off the majority from direct contact with God and sharing Jesus's own insight on non-duality. This is an inspiring new contemplative vision. **Scientific and Medical Network Review**
1903816300 224pp **£9.99 $15.95**

The Bhagavad Gita
Alan Jacobs
Alan Jacobs has succeeded in revitalising the ancient text of the Bhagavad Gita into a form which reveals the full majesty of this magnificent Hindu scripture, as well as its practical message for today's seekers. His incisive philosophic commentary dusts off all the archaism of 1500 years and restores the text as a transforming instrument pointing the way to Self Realization. **Cygnus Review**
1903816513 320pp **£12.99 $19.95**

Everyday Buddha
A contemporary rendering of the Buddhist classic, the Dhammapada
Karma Yonten Senge (Lawrence Ellyard)
Foreword by **His Holiness the 14th Dalai Lama**
Excellent. Whether you already have a copy of the Dhammapada or not, I recommend you get this. I congratulate all involved in this project and have put the book on my recommended list. **Jeremy Ball** Nova Magazine
1905047304 144pp **£9.99 $19.95**

The Ocean of Wisdom
The most comprehensive compendium of worldly and spiritual wisdom this century
Alan Jacobs
This anthology of 5,000 passages of spiritual wisdom is an awesome collection of prose and poetry, offering profound truths to everyday guidance. A valuable reference for any writer or historian, but it also makes for a good fireside or bedside book. **Academy of Religion and Psychical Research**
190504707X 744pp 230/153mm **£17.99 $29.95**

Good As New
A radical retelling of the scriptures
John Henson
An immensely valuable addition to scriptural understanding and appreciation. **Methodist Recorder**
A short review cannot begin to persuade readers of the value of this book. Buy it and read it. But only if you are brave enough. **Renew**
2nd printing in hardback
1903816734 448pp **£19.99 $24.95** cl
1905047118 448pp **£11.99 $19.95** pb

A World Religions Bible
Robert van de Weyer
An admirable book to own personally for reflection and meditation, with the possibility of contemplating a different extract a day over an entire year. It is our hope that the use of this splendid anthology will grow. We recommend it to all for their personal enrichment. **The Friend**
Outstanding collection of religious wisdom…never has so much wisdom been concentrated in such a small space. **New Age Retailer**
1903816157 432pp full colour throughout 180/120mm **£19.99 $28.95**